A Global History
of Christians

A Global History of Christians

How Everyday Believers Experienced Their World

By
Paul R. Spickard
and Kevin M. Cragg

with
G. William Carlson,
Michael W. Holmes,
James E. Johnson,
Cornelis H. Lettinga,
Roger Olson

Baker Academic
a division of Baker Publishing Group
Grand Rapids, Michigan

© 1994 by Paul R. Spickard and Kevin M. Cragg

Published by Baker Academic
a division of Baker Publishing Group
P.O. Box 6287, Grand Rapids, Michigan 49516-6287
www.bakeracademic.com

First published in 1994 as *God's Peoples: A Social History of Christians*

Printed in the United States of America

Library of Congress Cataloging-in-Publication Data
Spickard, Paul R., 1950–
    [God's peoples]
    A Global history of Christians : how everyday believers experienced their world / Paul R. Spickard and Kevin M. Cragg; with G. William Carlson . . . [et al.].
        p.   cm.
    Originally published: Grand Rapids, MI : Baker Books, c1994.
    Includes bibliographical references and index.
    ISBN 10: 0-8010-2249-5 (paper)
    ISBN 978-0-8010-2249-4 (paper)
    1. Church history. I. Cragg, Kevin. M. II. Carlson, Gordon William. III. Title.
BR145.2.S73 2001   00-058493

To
Naomi Spickard,
Daniel Spickard,
Luke Cragg,
and Nat Cragg

Contents

Preface

This is a history of Christians. It is not primarily a history of the church as an institution, although it recounts at least the outline development of various movements, denominations, and orders. Neither is this mainly a history of theology nor a chronicle of heroes of the faith, although it treats theology from Origen to Karl Barth and tells the stories of many prominent Christians, from Nestorius to Billy Graham.

Our goal in this book is to provide this generation with a look at how typical Christians of the past experienced their world. Many fine books explain the development of theologies and the formal institutions of the church—what we usually refer to as church history. The reader will find lists of such books in the suggested readings at the end of each chapter. We will emphasize a different reality, the lives of average Christians—often the vulgar and unlearned—rather than the famous, well-documented leaders.

Three sets of questions guided us as we turned to each era and part of the globe: First, how did Christians in this time and place experience God? How did they conceptualize him? How did they worship? How did they experience him in daily life? Second, how did Christians relate to one another? What varieties of Christians existed in this time and place? How did they perceive and act toward each other? Third, how did Christians relate to the society around them? Where did they fit in the social structure? What cultural contexts and power relationships shaped their encounters with non-Christians?

This is a presumptuous undertaking, for in many periods our information about common people is scattered, fragmentary, and often recorded by members of an elite who did not necessarily share the views or attitudes of those whose lives they recorded. It requires us to put ourselves in the shoes of long-dead folk, struggling to understand the emotions and thoughts they might have experienced.

A further aim separates us from other authors of textbook histories of Christianity. Most texts describe Christian history in the Mediterranean world, Europe, and North America but have little to say about the many millions of Christians in Asia, Africa, and Latin America. Christians outside Europe and North America have been important to the Christian story for many centuries. They have been actors in Christian history in their own right, not just passive objects of Western missions.

As we enter an era when most Christians live outside Europe and North America—when more than one-half of God's church is black, brown, or yellow—the time has come to treat the various peoples in equal fashion, as part of a single, integrated, world Christianity. The present volume represents only a beginning toward that end. We challenge historians of the Third World to write the stories of non-Western Christians more comprehensively and in greater detail. But this beginning at least enables the reader to learn something of Christian experiences outside the West.

We proceed with a few assumptions that may surprise some readers, though they are common among historians:

First, Christians were never unified, at least not after the era recorded in the early chapters of Acts. In the first generation there were conflicts between Jewish and Gentile believers, and factions divided among followers of Peter, Paul, and Apollos. Later, even the supposedly monolithic medieval Catholic church was rife with dissenting movements. Differences among Christians help us understand a great deal about how they experienced their faith. Heresies and heretics can tell us almost as much about the nature of Christian experience as do orthodoxy and saints. A corollary to this assumption is the observation that people we know as heretics were not always wrong doctrinally; sometimes they were simply the losers in political or institutional controversies.

Second, theology is a human creation, and not the same thing as divine revelation. This is essentially the Protestant assumption that Scripture is more authoritative than tradition, for humans see only in part and are bound by the senses of their social and cultural contexts.

Third, the ways power and prestige are arranged in society affect the ways people—including Christians—understand and act in their world.

Fourth, despite tremendous social and cultural diversity, there is an essential unity to human nature that makes it possible to recapture something of the worldview of people from a bygone era.

How did we decide which groups or individuals to include in our story? After all, nearly two thousand years of Christian history, covering the whole globe, provides at least a billion possibilities. Our choices are basically present-oriented. We asked: Does this group or person have late twentieth-century descendants, either as followers or teachings? The number of explicit followers of someone like Francis of Assisi may be very small at the end of the twentieth century, but the Franciscan piety continues to affect large numbers of Roman Catholics and Protestants. Even that standard does not eliminate very much, so we asked a second question: What would be most helpful to people beginning their study of Christian traditions? What follows is our response to these questions.

We called the hardcover edition of our book *God's Peoples: A Social History of Christians* to emphasize that the work was about people more than ideas or institutions, and that it dealt with many groups of Christians outside of Europe and its extensions. The new title, *A Global History of Christians: How Everyday Believers Experienced Their World*, re-emphasizes the global nature of the Christians' story. After all, Christian history has always been global, though many books in the past (and a few in the present) treat it as if it were primarily European. The explosive growth of Christian populations in Africa, Asia, and South America makes a global perspective key for understanding our world.

In the years since this book was first released, several new works of church history have come on the market. For further reading, the authors recommend *A World History of Christianity* edited by Adrian Hastings (Grand Rapids: Eerdmans, 1999); *Christianity: A Social and Cultural History*, 2d ed., by Howard Clark Kee et al. (Upper Saddle River, N.J.: Prentice Hall, 1998); and Roger E. Olson's *The Story of Christian Theology: Twenty Centuries of Tradition and Reform* (Downers Grove, Ill.: InterVarsity Press, 1999). In addition, *Christian History* magazine is an excellent source of information about the social history of Christians. Visit their website at *www.christianhistory.net* for a list of past issues.

This book was a project in cooperative writing. The primary authors, Kevin M. Cragg and Paul R. Spickard, are responsible for the book's structure and the chapters as they appear here. Each contributing author prepared the initial draft of one or more chapters, plus paragraphs to other authors' chapters. The various authors' initial contributions are: G. William Carlson, chapter 5; Cragg, chapters 1, 2, 3, 4, and 12; Michael W. Holmes, chapters 2 and 3; James E. Johnson, chapter 11; Cornelis H. Lettinga, chapters 7, 8, 10, and 15; Spickard, chapters 5, 6, 9, 11, 12, 13, 16, and 17; and Roger E. Olson, chapter 14.

We are grateful to the good people at the libraries of Bethel College, the Billy Graham Center, Brigham Young University–Hawaii campus, Capital University, Macalester College, the University of Hawaii, the University of Minnesota, and various other libraries who assisted through interlibrary loan. The Bethel College Alumni Association also provided a grant that helped us cover many of the costs of photocopying, typing, and mailing involved in this project.

1

The World of the First Christians

The earliest Christians came to Christ, not simply as new creatures, but as human beings with personal histories and social environments. Their lives may have been transformed, their sins forgiven, and their eyes opened, but they continued to live their new lives in a social and historical context. While an initial confrontation with Christ melted their hearts, growth in Christ occurred within a community of fellowship and discipline—the local congregation. That congregation most resembled a Jewish synagogue in its organization and pattern of worship. Some Christian groups, in fact, operated simply as cells within an otherwise Jewish assembly. The synagogue in many ways mirrored the social world of the early Christians.

In the first century of the era we now date from the coming of Christ, three cultures supplied the environment for life in the synagogue. Most important, of course, was the Jewish heritage, but Greeks and Romans also made an impact. The world of the earliest Christians was shaped by the interaction of Jewish, Greek, and Roman cultures.

The Jewish context

Synagogue life

It is difficult for well-scrubbed twentieth-century American Protestants to imagine visiting a first-century synagogue or church. The most startling difference would have been the odors. Although ritual bathing occurred at intervals, no deodorants or soaps reduced the general funkiness of Eastern Mediterraneans. The warm climate, a diet rich in onions and garlic, infrequent changes of clothes, and the smoke from oil lamps and cooking

An archaeologist's sketch copies the layout of a fresco featuring the Good Shepherd and Adam and Eve behind the Christian baptistry in the synagogue at Dura-Europas. (The Dura-Europas Collection, Yale University Art Gallery)

fires combined to produce an extraordinarily earthy atmosphere wherever people gathered. Add a little incense and breezes wafting from the dung heap outside town and the aroma would drive modern hygienic Westerners to their knees (not necessarily in prayer).

After recovering from that shock, a modern person stepping into that scene would next have been appalled at the noise and disorder. Even modern synagogues are not characterized by reverent quiet but by greetings and hugs. The community gathers like a weekly family reunion. Imagine the interaction among Jews not conditioned by 500 years of living near the Protestant ideal of decorum nor 200 years of Enlightenment rationalism. Most of us probably would have been offended.

The synagogue building itself varied widely in size and design. Small congregations frequently used a single room for meeting and study. Larger and wealthier ones had more elaborate structures, built in the best local style and decorated with expensive mosaics and paintings. One of the most famous synagogue buildings, at Dura-Europas

13

in what is now Syria, was decorated with frescos depicting such Bible stories as Adam and Eve and the exodus.

Diaspora—"the scattering"

Long before first century A.D. Jews had begun to leave their Palestinian homeland for other parts of the Mediterranean Basin, large colonies of Jews took up residence in the Hellenistic cities, especially Alexandria in Egypt, founded by Alexander the Great (356–323 B.C.) and his generals. Since most of these cities were centers of trade and manufacturing, Jews likely moved there for economic opportunities.

Whatever their reasons, Jews living amid a Gentile majority made significant contributions to Jewish thinking. Alexandrians translated the Scriptures into *koine* Greek, the most widely understood language of the era. Philo of Alexandria attempted to synthesize Jewish and Hellenistic thought, laying a foundation upon which Christians later built. They were distant from Jerusalem and the temple, so synagogue life and the teachings of the Pharisees—who emphasized the moral law over the ceremonial—dominated over the views of the Sadducees. Saul of Tarsus was one such Diaspora Pharisee.

Proselytes

By the first century A.D. many Gentiles had been attracted to Judaism. The repugnance we may feel toward the capricious, immoral Greek gods affected sensitive souls then, too. Many philosophically-inclined persons looked to monotheism for a Creator of the universe behind the images of Zeus or Jupiter. They despised the superstition and idolatry of the credulous masses. The God of righteousness, justice, and love portrayed by the rabbis appealed to them. Many Gentiles studied Scripture at the local synagogues. Fewer kept dietary and behavioral laws, and very few fully converted to Judaism through baptism and circumcision. Scholars speculate that many early Gentile converts to Christianity came from this part of the synagogue population. One estimate is that one-fifth of the Eastern Mediterranean population was Jewish.[1] Such a high figure seems unlikely, but certainly Jewish tradition was well-known, if not well-understood, among Mediterranean inhabitants of the Roman world.

Lifestyle

Although Jewish behavior had not yet evolved into the pattern now known as *kosher*, Jews lived distinctive lives. Rules about clean and unclean foods and ceremonial purity were common among peoples of the Eastern Mediterranean, but the Jewish rejection of idols in worship and their emphasis on righteous conduct were unique. Further, the study of *Torah* and the accompanying stress on literacy set Jewish men apart from their pagan neighbors in the same occupations. Stiff-necked resistance to Roman rule and assimilation particularly distinguished many Jews in Palestine. Others gradually succumbed to the gentle pressure of Romanization. Except among Palestinian Jews, it was deemed more expedient to accommodate than to resist.

Ideas

Ideas, as much as lifestyle, distinguished Jews and made them far more historically significant than the proportion of their numbers. Jewish ideas form a basis for the values that, until recently, characterized all of Western civilization. These concepts significantly shaped Christians' ways of looking at things.

Revelation

One distinctive Jewish religious idea was that God was a God who revealed himself to humans, sometimes in a still, small voice, as to Abraham; sometimes dramatically, as to Moses at the burning bush. Although nature pointed to this God, he was not fully evident, so occasionally, in his own good time, he revealed himself to and through prophets, kings, judges, and poets. Scriptures are the congealed records of that revelation.

Covenant

A core idea in this revelation is that God developed a special personal relationship with the descendants of Abraham. He would be their God, and they would be his people. Though affliction might buffet them, causing the majority to lose hope in the promise, God preserved a remnant faithful to the covenant. For Jews the symbol of the covenant was the Ten Commandments, which summarized love for God and neighbor. This love was exclusive, not to be shared with gods who could be represented in images of wood, stone, or metal.

Justice

In contrast to the gods of surrounding peoples, Yahweh was less interested in animal sacrifices and offerings than in a loving heart obedient to his ethical guidelines. At the core of Judaism was a high view of humanity. Created in God's image, people were to be treated with respect and mercy, whether resident alien, widow, orphan, disadvantaged, or highborn. Abuse of one of God's children brought warnings of reproach and even destruction. The prophetic books of the Old Testament record the Jews' difficulties in learning to share this high value of all human races.

The purpose of history

In contrast to the view of history among most peoples of the time, Jews saw history as moving in a direct line from creation to final judgment. Events and people were unique; they did not repeat unending patterns. The Greeks and Near Eastern civilizations thought history moved in a cycle, that human civilization grew, prospered, decayed, and devolved into chaos, reemerging to repeat its cyclical pattern. Some thought that even

15

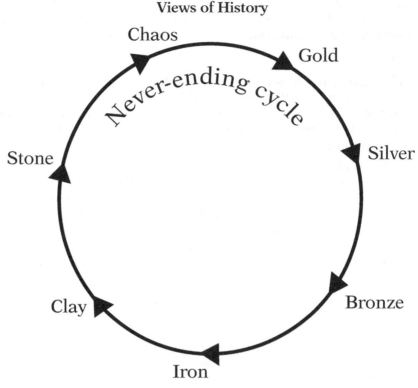

Figure 1.1

the individual would be reborn, live, and act in exactly the same way (albeit millions or billions of years later). So the Hebrew idea that history was going somewhere, that it had purpose and direction, gave greater meaning to events and actions and to the life of the individual (see fig. 1.1).

Sovereignty

Since God was the Maker and Sustainer of the universe he was sovereign in his control of history. Thus, nothing could happen that was not part of his ultimate scheme. Calamities were instruments of chastisement, calling his people back to him. When Jews were displaced to Babylon as captives after 586 B.C., they found that God was still among them. He was not tied to the geographic location of Palestine. When they repented of idolatry and injustice to the poor, sure enough, they were restored to the land as the prophets had promised. Thereafter, whatever difficulties Jews experienced were understood as a call to repentance. They steadfastly hoped for an eventual return of God's blessing. When the wicked Assyrians seemed to prosper, the servant of God could know that "this too shall pass away."

Messianic hope

Especially after the Babylonian captivity, Jews hoped for a restoration of the good old days of the Davidic kingdom through the Messiah. In Hebrew *messiah* means "anointed one," which translates into Greek as *christos*. *Christ* is a title or description, not a name. Jews hoped this Messiah would restore Judah to its rightful, powerful place among the kingdoms of the Middle East. His coming would bring *shalom*, an era of peace and prosperity and an end to troubles. The apparent fulfillment of this hope in the establishment of an independent Jewish kingdom under the Hasmoneans (Maccabbees) in 142 B.C. was dashed both by the disappointing performance of the leaders and by the Roman absorption of the Hebrew kingdom in 63 B.C. At the time into which Jesus came, this hope seemed more intense, even desperate.

Factions

Jews in Palestine in the first century A.D. disagreed among themselves over many issues. While they may have projected an image of unity to their pagan neighbors, several factions found their way into the text of Scripture. These factions, which developed theological, political, and social implications, contributed to the social backdrop for the earliest Christians.

Sadducees

The Sadducees worked around and for the temple, seeing to it that ceremonial laws were properly observed. In the context of first-century Palestine they were conservatives, adhering strictly to the sacrificial system established in the books of Moses and rejecting many innovations wrought by the Pharisees and the oral tradition. For example, they denied the immortality of the soul, the bodily resurrection, and the existence of angelic beings. They constituted a hereditary, politically powerful elite, connected to the family of the high priest, who emphasized temple worship and blood sacrifice as the way to please God. Because the high priest had been the functional ruler of Judah since the early days of Roman rule, the Sadducees faced the difficulties of mediating between the restive masses and the occupiers. They thought their political role was to ensure the survival of the Jewish nation, even if that meant the occasional sacrifice of an inexpedient individual. Because Sadducees sometimes compromised with the Romans, they were regarded by many as collaborators. Other Jews proclaimed the need for their priestly services. Sadducees could adapt to alien (Hellenistic) culture with less difficulty than could other Jews because they based righteousness on proper performance of rituals rather than on lifestyle. Thus, Sadducees conversed amiably in Greek with the Romans, sometimes even mingling socially, able to hold their own in discussions of literature or philosophy. Yet they never forgot that at the heart of Judaism was the worship of Yahweh in the temple.

17

Pharisees

In contrast to the conservative, high-ranking Sadducees, the Pharisees should be seen as the liberals of the day—a marked contrast to the way we usually read the Gospel accounts of this group. Instead of promoting the sacrificial system of atonement for sins revered by the Sadducees, the Pharisees tried to prevent the commission of sins in the first place by designating appropriate lifestyles. In contrast to exclusive reliance on the Pentateuch for authority, Pharisees also accepted the books of history and prophecy and relied heavily on the interpretations of commentators ("the oral tradition") to understand the Scripture. Rather than focusing on temple worship, Pharisees stressed the local synagogue and the hearing, studying, and fulfilling of the law. In a sense, they helped the lower classes by reducing the need for costly sacrifices and trips to Jerusalem. Although the Pharisees themselves may have thought they were trying to produce a nation of priests, they effectively humanized the system and made it less onerous on the poor. Hence they enjoyed greater popularity than the aristocratic Sadducees. Modern Judaism and Christianity derive many understandings of worship and spirituality from the Pharisees.

Zealots

Zealots were not a religious faction in the sense of the Pharisees and Sadducees. Rather, they continued the spirit of resistance to outside influence that had brought about the revolt of the Maccabbees against the Hellenistic Seleucid Empire in the second century B.C. Zealots were anti-Roman terrorists who liked nothing better than to slit the throats of hapless Roman soldiers on patrol. Naturally, Sadducees and other Jews who cooperated with the hated Romans also felt their knife points. The Romans, who understood nothing of the nationalistic spirit that underlay such actions, viewed zealots simply as brigands. Bar Abbas, the "bandit" freed in place of Jesus, was one of these.

Essenes

A group small in number but great in impact, the Essenes withdrew from the wickedness of society into communal desert settlements. They focused on an ascetic life of washings, fasts, and self-denial. A strong leader, called the "teacher of righteousness," guided the group. Repentance, marked by baptism, was a major theme. They are not mentioned specifically in the New Testament, but John the Baptist, Jesus' cousin, parallels their style, whether or not he was personally influenced by them.

Others in Palestine

Greeks and Samaritans also constituted sizable minorities in Palestine. Samaritans supposedly descended from unions of Jews and idol-worshiping Canaanites and were regarded as ceremonially unclean by purer Jews. Samaritans recognized the five books of Moses but differed

A woman teacher and her students, from an early Christian church fresco. (Image Bank for Teaching)

from the Jews in practice. Their own temple had been sacked by the Maccabbees in 128 B.C. Mutual hostility characterized relationships between Jews and Samaritans.

Greeks, especially the Greeks of the cities of the Decapolis (Greek for "ten cities") east of Galilee, also resented the Jews. In the second and first centuries B.C. Galilee had had a very large Greek population. Through political and military actions the Greeks were moved out or "converted" at sword's point so that Jewish settlers could move in. Joseph the Carpenter, Mary's husband, was probably one of these recent settlers since he had to return to his birth town of Bethlehem for the census recorded in Luke. The attitude of the Greeks, as one might expect, resembled that of twentieth-century Palestinians; they felt they had been unjustly displaced from their homes. Greeks related to Jews, especially Galileans, similar to the way the Palestine Liberation Organization related to Jews in the late 1980s. Within most cities in Palestine a small Greek minority remained, full of resentment over perceived Jewish privileges. Jews escaped military service and paid different taxes. Yet outside Palestine, Greek culture formed a pattern common to all parts of the Roman Empire and served as a cultural glue among the elite.

The Greek context

Greek culture contributed significantly to the development of Christianity. While the creative period of Greek art and philosophy occurred in the fifth and fourth centuries B.C., Greek culture spread abroad in what is called the *Hellenistic Period*, after the conquests of Alexander the Great. As Alexander conquered the Near East (334–323 B.C.), he planted colonies of Greek-speaking soldiers throughout his empire. Soon it became clear to any ambitious young man in any of the conquered territories that the way to succeed in the world created by this conquest was to learn Greek and adopt a Greek lifestyle. So the mosaic of cultures coexisting in the Near East was overlaid by a superficial Greek veneer. While this culture was shallow, it was one of the few things the peoples of the area shared. Should a Phoenician wish to trade with a Philistine from Gaza, Greek was frequently the only language understood (roughly) by both.

Through this crude communication and the usual process of trade, certain kinds of ideas and patterns of life became commonly understood throughout the Mediterranean Basin. This Hellenistic ("Greek-like") culture was the framework within which the earliest Christians understood and explained themselves. It, along with the Judaism of the Diaspora, formed the context for the Gospels and the Epistles of the Christian New Testament.

Intellectual values

Modern people often picture the ancient Greeks as great thinkers and philosophers, and certainly Greek thinkers laid the foundation for our formal ways of thinking. Bear in mind, however, that some of this is simply the accident of survival. What was copied and recopied over the centuries represented the *best* of Greek thought. What was mediocre or average or bad simply was not copied. Nonetheless, Greek thought—both what was lost and what survives—had a great impact in its own time. Certain strains of it affected the way the Jews thought about things as well. And Greek ideas formed the intellectual framework that Christians used to develop their own ideas.

Emphasis on reason

Greeks had a long tradition of emphasizing reason over passion. One might suspect that this was at least partly a response to the violence and passion that characterize much of Greek political history. Greek philosophers of the sixth century B.C. (before Socrates) started differentiating natural from supernatural causes of such events as eclipses of the sun— a root of modern scientific thinking. Thereafter, thinkers and debaters in the Greek world always proclaimed that their own ideas comported better with reason than the ideas of their intellectual opponents. Appeal to reason has characterized intellectual argumentation in the West ever since. As recorded in Acts 17, Paul used this appeal to the Greek thinkers on Mars Hill in Athens. Several Greek thought forms contributed significantly to the world of the early Christians.

Platonism

The Athenian Socrates (c. 470–399 B.C.) is sometimes thought of as the founder of Western philosophy. But Socrates's star pupil, Plato (428–347 B.C.), recorded most of what little we know about the famous stonemason-teacher-philosopher, and it is the reasoning process expressed by Plato that has shaped Western thinking. Whether all Western philosophy is but a footnote to Plato—and that was certainly true until the twentieth century—Platonic thinking set the categories through which pagan, Jewish, and Christian thinkers spoke to their world.

Two emphases of Plato especially should be understood. First, Plato asserted that the ultimate nature of reality is not material or physical. The things we sense in this world (dogs, tables, eagles) are mere shadows of reality, like the shadow of someone walking in front of a movie projector. The shadows resemble the real person; they are even recognizable. But the shadow is not the reality. Plato extended this analogy to such concepts as justice, which we can approximate only dimly in this world. Plato taught that ultimate reality dwells in the realm of ideas. Only there could the real "dogness" be found, the real "tableness," the real "justice."

Plato strongly asserted the existence and reality of things not fully perceptible through the senses. The "real you" is not the visible form that others see, with its scars and wrinkles, but the *psyche* (soul)—that unchangeable essence of character and personality that is temporarily clothed in flesh. Plato speculated that souls once also dwelt in the realm of ideas but they had somehow become condemned to live in shadowy, unreal envelopes of flesh. Platonists had a slogan, *"soma sema"*—"the body is a prison." Death, then, is a release from the prison. While still alive one still can be freed from the limitations of the flesh through contemplation and reasoning. This is best accomplished through the study of mathematics.

Very few people actually accepted Platonic thinking wholesale. His best pupil, Aristotle (384–322 B.C.), spent a lifetime revising and rejecting Plato. Yet the ideas of Plato and Aristotle gave a long-term bias to the culture, so that it tended to separate the real, true, ideal, or spiritual from the banal, fake, material, and physical. Greeks tended to look down on the physical as deceitful and base. This did not mean that Greeks were less materialistic in lifestyle than people of other cultures, but rather the intellectuals who wrote and the people who wanted to be thought of as intellectual reflected this Platonic bias.

Hellenistic ethical theories

In contrast with this great period of philosophical development in the classical era of Greece, Hellenistic thinkers concentrated on how to get along in the new world created by Alexander's armies. Plato and Aristotle functioned in the relatively small scale of the Greek city-state (*polis*) where all fellow citizens were supposed to be able to recognize one another on sight. Hellenistic Greeks were often part of large new kingdoms or empires over which they had little personal influence. In a sense theirs was the first "mass culture."

In such an impersonal society the question of how the individual should live was no longer settled by saying "follow the way of the ancestors." Circumstances had changed radically since the ancestors' time. The individual was adrift in the cosmos or (more positively) became "cosmopolitan," a citizen of the world rather than of Athens or Sparta. People living in Alexandria, for instance, existed in a pluralistic society, where a variety of Greek gods were worshiped alongside gods of Syrians, Jews, Arabians, Egyptians, Persians, and ethnic groups whose very names have been lost. This was confusing. The need for moral guidance in a morally confusing environment was as great in that era as in the modern world. Cults and superstitions helped fill the gap for the masses, but those who saw themselves as more thoughtful preferred to find solutions in philosophical theories. Therefore, in the Hellenistic era thinkers spent most of their effort constructing ethical guidelines for living in new circumstances. Again, each of these systems affected Christians as they confronted the same confusions.

Stoics

The *stoic* ethic (named after the porch or *stoa* where stoics gathered in Athens) was the system most respected by both Greeks and Romans. Romans especially appreciated the stoic emphasis on doing one's duty, for it reinforced traditional Roman values. Stoics were no mere impractical eggheads. They lived respectable lives and were active in public affairs.

Stoics believe that the cosmos is ordered by reason (Greek, *Logos*) or providence. Whatever happens is therefore due to necessity or fate and is ultimately good. We have some sense of the stoic ideal when we speak of someone who endures pain dispassionately as "stoic"—accepting the inevitable as part of the natural order of the universe and therefore as good. The behavior of the individual ought to conform to reason, to welcome the inevitable. Human life should be ordered according to the pattern of nature. Stoics regarded the moral order as a discernible part of nature. All people are equal in their essence, although each has individual duties. Stoics believed in the unity of humanity under the rule of providence. They might have approved of the slogan: "The brotherhood of man under the fatherhood of God," used by some twentieth-century liberal Christians, although stoic providence was too impersonal a reality to be called "Father." Paul's phrase "All things work together for good" (Rom. 8:28) would have won stoic approval.

Epicureans

More disreputable in the Hellenistic and Roman worlds were the *epicureans*. Sensual people who like expensive or exotic foods are called "epicures," but this modern term is based on a misunderstanding of the original Epicureans. Epicureans were philosophical materialists who believed that everything, including souls, is composed of atoms. Death occurs when the soul-atoms unhook. Therefore, there is no life or individual consciousness after death. No one should fear dying.

Why be virtuous, then? Epicureans noted that, although virtue may have no reward, vice usually has unpleasant consequences. They advocated seeking pleasures that had few side effects. One should never overeat, for example, because indigestion may follow. Drunkenness produces hangovers and regrettable behavior. Political participation produces enemies and heartbreak. Therefore, Epicureans sought quiet pleasures with few negative consequences: conversation with friends; walks in the garden; contemplation by the fireside.

These materialist and quietist attitudes offended both the antimaterialist bias of the culture and the ardent belief in the virtue of public participation in community life. Epicureans were the "commies" of the ancient world—liable to be caricatured for rhetorical purposes in any argument. Christians and Jews shared in the popular prejudice expressed toward them.

Cynics

"Beatniks" of the Western 1950s and "hippies" of the 1960s had some parallel in the *cynics*. Even their name is unconventional, derived from the Greek *kunos*, "dog." These weirdos challenged conventional behaviors of all sorts because they held that moral virtue is the only good and that traditions of dress and decorum are morally neutral customs. Greeks called them "dogs" because, like dogs, they did everything in public. Cynics preferred a simple lifestyle and avoided the entanglements of possessions and fashion. They liked to tell the story of Diogenes. Alexander the Great supposedly asked what he could do for Diogenes. Diogenes thought for a while and then requested that Alexander move a bit to the left, for he was blocking the sunlight. This illustrates the cynics' indifference to mere power and conventional greatness. Early Christians were occasionally mistaken for cynics because of their moral earnestness and rejection of symbols of status and power.

Hellenistic esthetic values

Esthetic values lay at the root of serious conflicts between the Greeks and the Jews. Greeks liked balance, reason, and order in their art—for example, they often prescribed mathematical proportions to designate the most pleasing human body shapes. Even those Greeks influenced by Plato reveled in the beauty of the human body and shuddered at circumcision, seeing it as an act of mutilation that diminished the body's natural form. They worked hard at athletics to keep themselves in shape. Athletes practiced and performed nude, and statues portrayed both male and female natural beauty.

In contrast, Jews regarded the body as private and intimate, to be shared only with one's mate and with God. Nakedness was a symbol of Adamic innocence, and since humans were no longer innocent they should not appear publicly as if they were. For a man to be exposed was humiliating and denigrating. Noah's son was cursed for viewing his father's nakedness while Noah was drunk (Gen. 9:21–27). For a woman even to expose the hair of her head tempted men to illicit lust. An circumcision signified the covenant, God's intimate relation to Israel.

When some Jews adopted Hellenistic culture they had to reject this view of the body as private, but when they went to the gymnasium to exercise, their circumcision horrified their Greek colleagues and subjected them to ridicule. Some sought painful surgery to undo circumcision to be like the other athletes. Considering the absence of anesthetics and the danger of infection, they must have been strongly motivated.

In addition, the commandment against graven images meant statues, naked or not, offended Jews. Though some Jews used decorative depictions of plants, animals, or geometric forms, they abhorred the portrayal of humans. Several Jewish revolts were provoked (usually ignorantly) by Greeks or Romans who set up statues of great leaders or gods in locations offensive to Jewish sensibilities.

The Roman context

The Roman Empire framed political reality for the earliest Christians. While Hellenistic culture dominated Jews, Romans, and Greeks, political power was a monopoly of the Romans and their surrogates. Geographically the Roman Empire encompassed the Mediterranean Basin (including North Africa), plus what became France and Britain (see chart).

Scholars guess that this realm included about 100 million people, mostly peasant farmers. In area, population, and economic resources the nearest modern equivalent is Indonesia. Romans, therefore, had to rule cheaply. They had limited money and military and bureaucratic personnel, so for the most part they exercised their efforts gingerly and relied on local allies and puppets to maintain the order that the Romans prized. The Romans had other values that shaped their peculiar role in Jewish and Christian history.

From Pentecost to the Birth of Islam
The Spread of Christianity through A.D. 600

A.D. 33
Regions represented in Jerusalem on day of Pentecost

Arabia
Asia Minor
Cyprus
Macedonia/Greece

Italy
Mesopotamia
North Africa
Persia

A.D. 100
The end of the apostolic period

Asia Minor
Coastal North Africa
  (Alexandria, Carthage,
  Cyrene)
Eastern shore, Adriatic Sea
Hispania (Spain)
Macedonia/Greece

Mesopotamia
Palestine
Southern Italy/Rome
Syria
Possibly India, Western
  Persia

A.D. 200
Expansion under persecution

Arabia
Armenia
Asia Minor
Iberian Peninsula (Spain)
Illyricum
Italy/Rome
Macedonia/Greece
Mesopotamia (Edessa)

Palestine
Persia
Rhineland
Roman North Africa
Southern Britain
Southern Gaul
Syria
Some evidence of a church
  presence in India

A.D. 325
The church of the Council of Nicea

Arabian Peninsula
Armenia
Asia Minor
Britain
Ceylon
Gaul
Germanic tribes
Iberian Peninsula (Spain)
Illyricum

India
Italy
Lower Nile Basin
Macedonia/Greece
Mesopotamia
Palestine
Persia/Persian Gulf
Roman North Africa
Syria

A.D. 600

Arabia
Armenia
Asia Minor
Britain
Ceylon
Eastern Africa (Abyssinia)
Gaul
Hesse
Hispania (Spain)
Illyricum
India

Ireland
Italy
Macedonia/Greece
Mesopotamia
Netherlands
North Africa
Palestine
Persia
Saxony
Scandinavia
Syria

Peace

Romans loved peace. The only reason for war was to secure peace. Tacitus's remark that "the Romans make a desert and call it peace" is only a little exaggerated. They would put great effort into restoring order and tranquillity. One of the most frequent reasons for rebellions among subject communities was that the Romans would not allow them to go to war when they wanted. Urban riots, such as those between Christians and Jews recorded in Acts, always brought the ire of the local Roman troops, whose job was to keep the peace. Anything necessary was done to quell disturbance. Only when the police action touched a Roman citizen, such as the apostle Paul, did problems emerge from the Roman perspective. Roman citizens had rights of appeal that had to be respected before a magistrate could punish them. Ultimately, the citizen could appeal to the emperor.

"Older is better"

In contrast to contemporary American values, the Romans generally valued traditional ways of doing things and viewed innovation as inherently dangerous. Rather than choosing a product because it is "new and improved," the Roman mindset would buy something old and proven reliable, something unchanged since great-granddad's time. Jews were given unusual privileges by Romans, primarily because their religion was venerably old—Moses lived 500 years before the founding of the city of Rome. Only after the Romans distinguished Christianity from Judaism (and therefore as new and dangerous) did persecution begin.

Roman religious values

Roman religion, as Greek, stressed the contractual relationship between humans and the gods. The gods liked sacrifices and rituals and rewarded people who did them properly. In turn, worshipers thanked the gods for favors by giving them offerings. The gods had peculiar tastes. They liked the smell of burning fat and bones from animals and chants recited in archaic language that nobody understood.

It is difficult for modern Westerners to understand that the gods of the classical world had almost no ethical content in their characters. Even among most atheists in Western society, the god they reject is deeply interested in morality and lifestyle. In contrast, the ancients saw morality as a secular affair. The Roman gods, in contrast to the righteous God of the Old Testament, were powerful juveniles—adolescents running the universe. They were drunken, capricious, and adulterous liars. Therefore the priests and practitioners of Roman religion need not be particularly moral. Julius Caesar violated nearly every moral law, yet he was perfectly acceptable as *pontifex maximus*, chief priest of the Roman religion. What made a good priest was his ability to memorize and repeat large chunks of esoteric language and to perform ceremonial rituals in exactly the right way to please the gods.

For Romans the purpose of religion was to secure the favor of the gods, especially on behalf of the state. The gods liked the whole populace to witness the ceremonies, so nonparticipation was dangerous—the ceremony might not work. In a sense, religion existed to serve and strengthen the state; therefore, religious practice was preeminently a patriotic or political issue. This perception precipitated conflict with Christians. Any sect whose religion rejected participation in Roman rites endangered the state. To be a Christian was to be a traitor to Rome.

Jesus and the disciples

Jewish, Hellenistic, and Roman elements blended in the cultural world of the first Christians. From the Jews they inherited a basic religious and moral framework. The Greeks supplied the intellectual and cultural orientation. Rome established political and legal realities. Into this cultural mix came Jesus, the focus of Christian worship, love, and hope.

Data of Jesus' life are recounted simply and plainly in the four New Testament books Christians came to adopt as Gospels. While each Gospel appears to speak to a particular audience and modern people have trouble fitting together all the chronological details, the Gospels together form a biography as complete as that for any person of the ancient world.

According to the accounts, Jesus was born to Mary, a virgin betrothed to Joseph, a carpenter of Nazareth—an embarrassing and miraculous event announced supernaturally by angelic messengers. Mary was probably about fourteen and Joseph about eighteen. The date was probably about 6–4 B.C., during the reign of Herod the Great, the Romans' puppet king of Judea from 37 to 4 B.C. Jesus grew up in a skilled craftsman's family with slightly higher status than the average Palestinian peasant and so excelled in his synagogue studies that he confounded the scholars of the temple when he visited them before his *bar mitzvah*, the ceremony that signaled coming of age for a thirteen-year-old Jewish boy. His years from twelve to thirty are blank in the records, though later Christians supplied all kinds of interesting fictions to fill them in.

At about age thirty he was baptized by his unconventional cousin John and began a three-year public ministry. The meaning of this baptism often has been disputed, because Jewish baptism ordinarily symbolized repentance or conversion of a pagan to Judaism. When Jesus underwent it, the witnesses say, the Holy Spirit descended on him in the form of a dove.

At any rate, Jesus spent the next three years wandering around, preaching and teaching and gathering followers. His message had three elements:

The good news: God's prophesied kingdom of righteousness is at hand. Wrongs will be righted. Captives freed. Shalom will reign. The unrighteous will be judged. Many in the audience heard this as an announcement of a political kingdom, but others recognized it as the end of history promised by the prophets. Every devout Jew saw such a kingdom as a good thing.

The bad news: None are righteous enough to receive that kingdom. Keeping pharisaical tradition is not good enough. The Law must be inward as well as external. The danger of the Pharisees lies in thinking they have attained righteousness. The Sermon on the Mount illustrates a standard by which every human being is found wanting. The need is for supernatural intervention and forgiveness. Such a message would also be recognized as part of the message of the prophets and the experience of Jewish history.

The way: God has made a way for the unrighteous to achieve the kingdom through trusting Jesus. This involves both intellectual assent that Jesus is the Messiah and personal commitment to follow him and keep his commandments, trusting him for forgiveness and redemption.

The first two-thirds of this message could be accepted as clearly within the prophetic tradition of Judaism; the last third was extravagant and blasphemous from a Jewish perspective.

Jesus validated his claim by doing miracles, from healing lame people to raising children from death. Our modern consciousness tends to reject miracles out of hand or to assume that ancient people were simpleminded and credulous. It is important to understand that ancient Jewish religious leaders where skeptical of all claims of miracle-working. They exposed illusionists and sleight of hand work. Jesus was never accused by these experts of faking a miracle, although he was accused of performing miracles by the power of Satan. The clincher came after Jesus was crucified, dead, and buried, when he rose from the tomb, surprising (and frightening) even those who thought they had truly believed—the disciples.

The disciples of Jesus are often depicted as a ragtag band of poor ignoramuses. The Gospels do not tell the occupations of all twelve in the inner circle, but what we are told ranks the men relatively high in socioeconomic status for first-century Palestine. Capitalist fishermen and publicans were essentially small businessmen, in contrast to the peasant majority. The reasons Christ called them are not apparent; for the most part they were not a particularly promising lot until after the resurrection.

Jesus' death and resurrection are the central acts of history for Christians. While post-Christian American culture prefers Christmas (partly, no doubt, from memories of childhood gift-getting), Good Friday and Easter are the keys. Death and rising again, despair and hope, bloody sacrifice and expiation—however the days are joined, they changed everything. Nineteenth-century theological liberals, nervous about the historicity of the resurrection accounts, still asserted that "something happened" because of the radical change in the behavior of the disciples. From a sniveling group of quarrelers the disciples were transformed into bold preachers, proclaiming the message of salvation through Jesus throughout the Roman world and perhaps as far as to India. Furthermore, they died for that message.

Additional good news was that Jesus promised that he would come again to end time and bring in his kingdom wherein all the good things prophesied would happen—no more sorrow, lambs and lions lying down together, etc. As we shall see, this hope has been important for Christians ever since and has shaped their every thought.

Suggested readings

Barclay, John M. G. *Jews in the Mediterranean Diaspora: From Alexander to Trajan (323 B.C.E.–117 C.E.)*. Edinburgh: Clark, 1996.

Freyne, Sean. *Galilee, Jesus, and the Gospels: Literary Approaches and Historical Investigations*. Minneapolis: Fortress Augsburg, 1988.

———. *Galilee, from Alexander the Great to Hadrian, 323 B.C.E. to 135 C.E.: A Study of Second Temple Judaism*. Notre Dame, Ind.: University of Notre Dame, 1980.

"The Life and Times of Jesus of Nazareth." *Christian History*, 17.3 (issue 59, 1998).

Meeks, Wayne A. *The First Urban Christians: The Social World of the Apostle Paul*. New Haven, Conn.: Yale University Press, 1983.

Neusner, Jacob. *From Testament to Torah: An Introduction to Judaism in Its Formative Age*. Englewood Cliffs, N.J.: Prentice Hall, 1988.

2

Christians in the Roman World

Jesus' death left his band of followers without a leader and without hope. His resurrection and ascension changed them forever, but these earliest Christians still faced the difficult task of surviving in a hostile world. How would they keep Jesus' message alive? How would they avoid being absorbed by their Jewish or Gentile neighbors? How would they obey Jesus' commandment to spread the gospel of salvation to the ends of the earth? How should they conduct Christian lives amidst so many temptations and foes? How should they think about all they had experienced in walking with the Messiah?

Christians spent the three centuries after the resurrection working out answers to these fundamental questions in the context of Roman civilization.

After the resurrection

The disciples, dispirited by the crucifixion of Jesus, hid out while they tried to understand what would come next. When the women brought news that the tomb was empty and Jesus was alive, the male disciples did not believe it until they saw for themselves (a woman's testimony was not considered reliable in Jewish tradition). The religious authorities asserted that the disciples had perpetrated a hoax and removed Jesus' body; they never asserted that the tomb was not empty. Considering that the disciples' later zeal extended to the point of martyrdom, it is unlikely they would have died to defend something they knew was a hoax, misleading millions of others in the lie.

From their meetings with the resurrected Jesus in the next few weeks the disciples concluded three things:

1. Jesus was, in fact, equal to God as he had asserted, and he had dominion over all creation.
2. His ministry of salvation was not finished in his death; rather it was just beginning.
3. He would continue to communicate to the disciples, not face-to-face, but through the Holy Spirit.

The Spirit came upon the followers most dramatically at the Jewish festival of Pentecost, when tongues of fire appeared over the believers' heads and they proclaimed the gospel in languages they had not known previously. Jews and proselytes from all over the Middle East heard the message in their own languages, and 3000 joined the fellowship of Jesus' followers on this one day.

Immediately the disciples were thrust into leadership roles over a large group of enthusiastic people. In the excitement many new believers stayed in Jerusalem to learn more. Jesus' people pooled their resources to feed and maintain the group, while they met together (in the temple) for prayer. Other converts returned to their homelands, taking the good news of Jesus to people in many parts of the Eastern Mediterranean world.

Yet to most people in Jerusalem, these followers of Jesus would appear to be simply a Jewish subgroup. Other Jewish groups had been enthusiastic about their leaders. Others had shared goods and meals. And these Galileans continued to go to the temple daily, proof of their Jewishness. Beneath the outward appearances was a fundamental tension: Jesus' followers claimed that he was the Messiah, the Promised One of Israel. But Jews expected that the Messiah would be a conqueror—not someone who had been executed as a criminal. According to Deuteronomy 21:23 someone executed on a tree was under God's curse. How could an accursed man fulfil God's covenant of salvation? Jesus' followers also taught that he was the center of God's new covenant, displacing the covenant with Abraham, which had centered in the law and the temple. This seriously challenged the whole Jewish framework of tradition.

The most outspoken advocates of this new covenant immediately attracted big trouble with the religious authorities. The Jewish leaders stoned Stephen to death, partly because he boldly proclaimed that Jesus was the Messiah and partly because he rebuked the highest Jewish religious council for not listening to the words of the prophets. This brought on a general persecution that scattered the Jerusalem community widely. An exception was when apostles miraculously escaped from prison and were spared further persecution. The scattering, in turn, brought two related developments: First, the gospel began to be preached to Samaritans and Gentiles in communities outside Palestine. Second, the introduction of Gentiles into the fellowship raised questions about believers' lifestyle. For example, should all of Jesus' followers keep the Jewish dietary and ceremonial laws?

Some of those fleeing persecution preached at Antioch in Syria. There the followers of Jesus were first called *Christians*. The name is appropriate, for it is derived from *Christos*, a Greek translation of the Hebrew title *Messiah* (literally, "anointed one"). Followers of Jesus who hold the historic Christian beliefs continue to assert that he is indeed the Messiah. This distinguishes them from other worshipers of the God of Abraham (Jews, Muslims, most Unitarians, religious humanists, followers of Baha'i, and civil religionists). *Christ* is technically a title, not a name, even though referring to "the Christ" sounds pretentious in ordinary English. The use of the Greek name *Christian* foreshadowed the time when the majority of Christians would come from Hellenistic, rather than Jewish, backgrounds.

Were Christians also Jews?

Was Christianity a reformed and purified variety of Judaism, or a new religion rising to supplant the faith of Israel? For the early believers this was an extremely difficult question. If Christianity was a new religion, Jewish believers would need to change their assumptions and habits radically in order to accept Gentiles fully. If Christianity were a form of Judaism, on the other hand, Gentile converts would need to learn many new rituals, study Torah, and face the daunting ceremony of circumcision. There was a very practical side to this theological battle. Pagan converts brought their cultural lifestyles with them into the church, and this caused great distress to some of the Jewish Christians. The phrase "Gentile sinners" was, after all, redundant in Jewish thinking. Trained since birth to avoid unclean people, some found it difficult to associate with their non-Jewish fellow believers.

The impact on Jewish evangelism was serious. Imagine that you, a law-observing Jew, are invited by your Jewish Christian neighbor to a congregational service. Somewhat curious, you agree reluctantly to go. Upon entering the meeting room you unexpectedly find yourself with several people who appear to be pagans. Worse, some of those people bump into you as they find their places, rendering you ceremonially unclean. After the service the main course at the potluck fellowship is a mess of juicy barbecued pork ribs. Of course it was difficult to convert Jews in that kind of setting.

A council met at Jerusalem in A.D. 48 or 49 to settle the issue (Acts 15). This set a pattern for the ecumenical councils that would become both traditional and authoritative. These leaders noted that the gift of the Spirit came to Jewish and Gentile believers in the same way— through trust in Jesus, not observance of the Law. Since God treated the two groups equally, Gentiles should not be required to become Jews. Gentile believers should, however, be sexually pure, avoid idolatry, and abstain from nonkosher meats; violations of these practices would grossly offend Jewish believers.

The insights developed in this council unalterably shaped Christianity. It became a transcultural movement, not tied to historic Judaism or any particular human cultural pattern. When trust in Jesus is the criterion and the presence of the Holy Spirit the evidence of faith, the gospel message can appeal to a much wider range of people and cultures.

Praeparatio evangelium: Prepared for the gospel

The coming of Christ is spoken of in the Gospels' Greek as at the *kairos,* the "exactly opportune moment." In many ways the Roman world was at just that point when Christians appeared. Circumstances came together in a way unique in history to allow the Christian message to be spread easily and understood readily.

Language

Throughout the Mediterranean world, the *koine* (common) dialect of Greek served as a second language for a large number of people. In any community, a person who spoke Greek could find someone who could translate into the local language. Most of the time this was done for business purposes, but the dialect was flexible enough to express a wide range of ideas. Greek-speaking apostles could travel from synagogue to synagogue and be heard and understood. It was quite practical that the Gospels and Letters were written in Greek to ensure the broadest dissemination. Such linguistic universality over a side area is only now being approached again, this time by English.

Travel

Travel in the Roman world reached an ease that was not seen again in Europe until the late nineteenth century. Roman roads were built primarily for the rapid movement of troops and supplies, but they worked for the civilian population as well. Travel by sea was preferred for comfort over the buffeting one suffered on the back of a mule or in a carriage without springs, the more so since the Romans had eliminated pirates at sea. As a provincial gentleman, Aelius Aristides, wrote, c. A.D. 150:

> A man simply travels from one country to another as though it were his native land. We are no longer frightened by the Cilician pass or by the narrow sand tracks that lead from Arabia into Egypt. We are not dismayed by the height of the mountains, or by the vast breadth of rivers or by the inhospitable tribes of barbarians. To be a Roman citizen, nay even one of [the emperor's] subjects, is a sufficient guarantee of personal safety.[1]

Peace

For most of the first and second centuries A.D. war occurred only on the Roman frontiers. Dislocations and economic disruption that accompany armed conflict stayed far from the centers of commerce and culture. Missioners could thus travel with minimal concern.

Spiritual hunger of the underclass

Perhaps the major contributor to the *kairos* of the era was the spiritual hunger of the masses. Those who were lowly found little comfort in the formal religions or philosophical systems of the time. Both Roman and Greek religions projected a vague and unpleasant afterlife, a colorless, fog-shrouded, cold existence, not tortuous but boring. Stoicism's noble challenge to accept one's fate in life was cold comfort for a hungry, oppressed slave. In general, the underclass tended to be indifferent to state religion and the philosophical alternatives.

Instead, the oppressed sought spiritual homes in the mystery and Oriental religions (the latter called "Oriental" because they arose in the Eastern Mediterranean). These religions differed in places of origin, gods, rituals, and ideas, but some common features appealed to the masses.

First, all provided some personal contact between individual and deity—often through frenzied dancing or chanting that induced a trance or ecstatic experience. This was not so passive an experience as attended the state rituals. Second, they promised a happy, personal afterlife for the believer—much better than the grim reality of this world. The future life would be marked by warmth, sunshine, plenty of food, orgies (for some), and general well-being in union with the deity.

Third, the worship experience was marked with considerable drama and emotion, often reenacting some important event in the story of the god. An initiate to full status in the cult of Mithras, for example, was baptized in the blood of a bull (a symbol of Mithras). The initiate stood beneath a framework onto which the bull was led. Then the animal was slit open and the blood gushed down upon the candidate. Such a ceremony dramatically impressed the watchers and vividly portrayed doctrine that might otherwise have been obscure to semiliterates. Fourth, the mystery religions often had levels of attainment within them. A person could progress in knowledge and status within the religion, regardless of status in the culture as a whole. This allowed the lowly a place where their lives made a difference.

In contrast to modern ideas about religious conviction (and perhaps similar to New Age religions), ancient religions rarely demanded the total commitment of adherents. Since the existence of many gods was accepted, no single god had a right to demand exclusive loyalty from a worshiper. So inhabitants of the Roman Empire saw no inconsistency in attending the state sacrifices to Jupiter, participating in Bacchic rites, and visiting a Mithraeum—all in the same day! Many would cover their spiritual bets by sacrificing to all the available gods or by moving from one cult to another in search of inner peace.

A parallel might be found in the restless transients of the late twentieth century who wander among personal therapy fads—from transactional analysis to rolfing to primal therapy to est—all of which have vaguely religious overtones. To the first-century malcontents the claims to exclusive truth by Jews and Christians smacked of fanaticism and superstition. The spirit of the age, like that of our own era, instinctively rejected claims of absolute truth. At the same time, this attitude made them more willing to listen to new ideas. Luke in Acts 17:21 notes how the Athenians especially liked to hear about anything new, including the good news of Jesus.

All of these elements allowed the gospel message to spread rapidly and widely. Soon most Christians were from Gentile backgrounds. Accepting Gentile converts and removing the burden of Jewish ceremonial requirements, however, led to another question: To what extent should Christians accommodate the Greco-Roman culture that surrounded them? Which Gentile practices and beliefs were unacceptable? What would happen to the teaching of the apostles when they were reinterpreted through the frame of Greek thinking? To a large extent, Christians wrestled with these questions for the next 400 years.

Patterns of church life

As Christians emerged from widely divergent geographic areas, they experimented with various methods of organization. If Jesus had laid down a particular pattern for church government these early Christians apparently did not know about it. They made *ad hoc* church government decisions to fit local traditions and personalities. Thus, supporters of

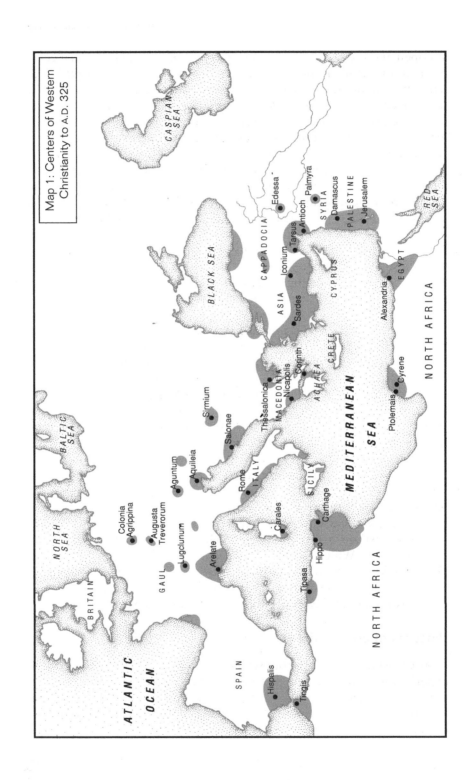

Map 1: Centers of Western
Christianity to A.D. 325

virtually any modern form of church government can legitimately claim precedents for their system in the New Testament church experience. A hierarchy of bishops clearly dominated in some locales, especially where leaders had known Jesus before his departure. In other places a group of elders or presbyters exercised a collective leadership resembling the ordinary synagogue pattern. In still other places grassroots leadership appeared through efforts to build consensus among the congregation.

Congregations enjoyed the benefits (and sometimes the tensions) of being ministered to by both resident pastors and itinerant apostles and prophets. Christians began to meet regularly before dawn on Sunday in celebration of Jesus' resurrection, and the number of Gentiles among them who also observed the Jewish Sabbath dwindled. Added to the traditional synagogue service of Psalms and readings from the Old Testament were Christian hymns and creeds ("Jesus is Lord" was one of the earliest creeds) and readings from the new Christian Scriptures—Gospel accounts and the letters of Paul. Much of the worship liturgy would be memorized oral pieces. Christians who came from non-Jewish backgrounds were likely to be illiterate.

Events surrounding A.D. 70 significantly altered the Christian experience. The great fire that burned much of Rome in 64 brought the first major official persecution of Christians and began two and one-half centuries of difficult relations with the Roman government. In these early persecutions most of the remaining disciples and other eyewitnesses to the acts of Jesus died. A new generation had to decide how to replace the apostolic authority that had been a core structure for leadership. What would hold together a people of such geographic and cultural diversity?

The destruction of the temple at Jerusalem in 70, during the Roman repression of the First Jewish War, completely transformed Judaism into a religion of the synagogue. This new Judaism was dominated by the tradition of the Pharisees, since the Sadducees had no temple to focus on and the zealots had perished in battle. This change in the institution of Judaism also alerted most Romans and Greeks to the separate character of Christianity. If Christians were not Jews they were not entitled to special privileges traditionally granted to Jews by the Roman Empire (reduced taxes and freedom from military service). Rabbinical scholars, who replaced priests as the Jewish leaders, defined the distinctions of Jew and non-Jew more sharply. They introduced curses into the synagogue service that clearly excluded Christians from fellowship.

At the same time Christians were cut off from their Jewish intellectual roots, Greek thought was greatly influencing the development of Christian ideas. There even was a gradual shift of the center of rabbinical scholarship eastward from Palestine to Babylon. The distance between the two traditions grew ever greater.

37

2.1. Women's Ministry in the Early Church

The role of women in the early church has roused much controversy in recent years. Some believe that Paul's injunction that women should keep silent in the churches (1 Cor. 14:34–35) was thoroughly and consistently adhered to by the early church; others argue that Paul's delaration in Galations: 3:28 that there was in Christ no longer "Jew nor Greek, slave nor free, male or female" formed the practical basis for church organization, and therefore women enjoyed full equality with men in their churchly duties. The evidence, however is ambiguous. We need to remember that the experience of the early church happed in thousands of different congregations with distinctive local circumstances, which led to flexibility in the application of these principles.

Certainly, women exercised some sort of leadership role within churches. Paul in Romans 16 refers to Phoebe as deacon and patron of the church. The same passage decribes Junia, a woman "noteworthy among the apostles." Acts 21:9 speaks of the four daughters of Philip as prophets, and the fourth-century historian Eusebius said they belonged to the first stage of apostolic succession. References to orders of deaconesses, virgins, and widows in Scripture and in other early Christian writings represent some kind of recognition of distinctive roles in the churches. In addition, some art from before 300 seems to portray women leading Christian commuion services. The question of whether women were ordained in the period is anachronistic, since there is no evidence of a standard concept of ordination to church ministries until the 250s. Rather we see in the *Didache* that the church could recognize the gift of the Holy Spirit, but not confer it. And clearly women prophets had the Spirit as well as men.

The narrowing of women's roles in the third century seems to reflect pressure to accommodate better to the prevailing culture. Some scholars suggest that this reflects the church moving from an essentially private, house-church format to a more public sphere, where the unusual prominence of women in the fellowship would be likely to offend the Romans' sense of public decency. Nothing like the deacon's role in serving the poor or administering the church occurred for women in either Roman or Jewish cultures.

Recent debates over the ordination of women relect the same tendencies. Churches in less formal or immigrant traditions that ordained many women before the 1940s (including Pentecostals, many Baptists, Holiness, and Evangelical Free churches) have moved toward the more traditional and "respectable" ecclesiastical practice of limiting their roles, while the old mainline denominations, which had traditionally closed most leadership postions to women before 1940 opened them up, as women's status and activism rose in the broader American society. An informal observer might suspect some correlation with the rising social status of Christians, just as occurred in the third century. As Christians get more respectable, they adopt many of the respectable practices of the society around them.

Increasingly, as those able to recall the early days died off, Christian congregations began to rely more on written sources of authority. The Gospels, Acts, and some of the Epistles of Paul were collected and copied among the churches and treated as essentially equal to the Old Testament for public reading. These writings authoritatively told of the same Jesus of whom the old Scriptures prophesied. In short, the apostles and other leaders were replaced by collections of written documents derived from them, though there was as yet no concern to determine the contents or boundaries of these varying collections.

Leadership apparently was further standardized by increasing the authority of the bishops. Ignatius, bishop of Antioch, in about 117 asserted that communion could not be properly celebrated unless a bishop was present.[2] While there was a lot of variation, even at that date, the trend was for the local bishop to acquire importance, almost to the level that had been reserved for apostles. Correspondingly, the influence of spectacular itinerant prophets and "apostles" diminished. References to women in ministry and leadership positions likewise diminished significantly in the era after 70 (see box 2.1).

Church services probably became more standardized and "liturgical" (*liturgy* literally means "the work of the [lay]people"). The *Didache*, a second-century how-to-do-it advice book, contains formulas for baptism, communion, and the Lord's prayer, plus assorted ethical admonitions on applied Christianity. It seems to anticipate memorization (see box 2.2).

Persecution

Government prosecution

After Romans recognized that Christians were not Jews, the governing authorities began to prosecute Christians. Although most Christians martyred before 300 were killed by their neighbors rather than by the

---

2.2. Baptism and Fasting

Now concerning baptism, baptize in this way: After you have said all these things, baptize in running water in the Name of the Father and of the Son and of the Holy Spirit. If you have no running water close by, however, dip in other water. If you cannot do it in cold water, do it in warm water. If you have neither close by, pour water on the head three times, in the name of the Father and of the Son and of the Holy Spirit. Before baptism the baptizer and the one who is to be baptized shall fast, and a few others as well, if they can. Challenge the one who is to be baptized to fast one or two days.

Your fasts shall not take place with those of the hypocrites, for they fast on the second and fifth days after the Sabbath. Fast instead on the fourth and on the day before the Sabbath.

—Didache

Translation from the English edition of Eberhard Arnold, *The Early Christians after the Death of the Apostles*, trans. and ed. by the Society of Brothers (Rifton, N.Y.: Plough, 1970), 185.

Roman government, official opposition by the government gave psychological approval to the lynch mobs who did much of the killing. The reasons for government persecution are confusing. The New Testament, except for the Revelation, pictured the Romans as protectors of Christians against Jewish opposition. Paul and others frequently enjoined Christians to obey the governing authorities and to pray for the emperor (Romans 13; 1 Tim. 2:1–2; 2 Peter 2:10; Jude 8). At least before 65, government officials seem to have considered Christians as members of a Jewish sect, who were occasionally swept up in a general exile of Jews from the city of Rome. When Rome burned in 65, Romans blamed the Christians, apparently recognizing them as distinct from Jews. The historian Tacitus (55–118) proclaimed them innocent of arson, although he thought maybe they should be punished for other evils, especially for "hatred of the human race" (see p. 43). But thereafter, the official position of the Roman law held that being a Christian was a capital offense. We do not know the legal rationale for such persecution.

Roman authorities were not particularly bloodthirsty, but they were conscientious in performing their duties. One of them, Pliny the Younger (62–113), governed the Roman province of Bithynia in what is now north central Turkey around 110. Confused about his duties with regard to Christians, Pliny wrote to the Emperor Trajan, who ruled from 98 to 117. The letter is exhibited in box 2.3 with Trajan's reply.

2.3. Pliny–Trajan Correspondence

Pliny to the Emperor Trajan

It is my custom, Sire, to refer to you everything about which I am in doubt. For who can better guide my uncertainty or instruct my ignorance?

I have never been present at trials of Christians; therefore I do not know what or how much to punish or to investigate. I am also very unsure whether age should make any difference, or whether those who are of tender age should be treated just the same as the more robust; whether those who repent should be pardoned, or whether one who has once been a Christian shall gain nothing by having ceased to be one; finally, whether the name [of Christian] as such should be punished even if there is no crime, or whether only the crimes attributed to this name should be punished.

Meanwhile I have followed this procedure with those who were denounced to me as Christians: I asked them whether they were Christians. If they confessed I repeated the question a second and third time, and, moreover, under threat of the death penalty. If they persisted I had them led away to their death, for I had no doubt that, whatever it was that they confessed, their stubbornness and inflexible obstinacy certainly deserved to be punished.

There were others, Roman citizens, who showed the same madness, and I noted them to be sent to the city [Rome]. As often happens during legal investigations, the crime became more widespread and there were some particular incidents. An anonymous accusation was presented denouncing a large number of persons by name. I felt I should acquit those who denied that they were or had been Christians, if they followed my example and called upon the gods; if they offered before your image incense and wine which I had brought for this purpose with the statues of the gods; and if they reviled Christ besides. It is said that those who really are Christians cannot be compelled to do any of these things in any circumstances. Others, whose names had been given by an informer, first said they were Christians but then soon denied it, saying in fact they had been but had ceased to be, some saying three years ago, others longer, and some as long as twenty years ago. All of these worshiped your image and the statues of the gods and cursed Christ.

They continued to maintain that the sum of their guilt or error lay in this, that it was their custom to meet on a fixed day before daylight and, alternating with one another, to sing a hymn to Christ as to a God. They also bound themselves mutually by an oath, not in order to commit any crime, but to promise not to commit theft, robbery, or adultery; not to break their word, and not to deny entrusted goods when claimed. After doing this, it was their custom to part from one another and then to meet again to share an ordinary and harmless meal. But even this they said they had ceased to do since my edict in which, in compliance with your injunction, I had forbidden closed societies.

I thought it all the more necessary, then, to find out finally what was true by putting to torture two girls who were called serving girls. But I found nothing but a depraved and enormous superstition. Consequently I adjourned the investigation and now turn to you in advice.

The matter seems to me worthy of consultation, especially because of the large number of those imperiled. For many of all ages, of every rank, and of both sexes are already in danger, and many more will come into danger. The contagion of this superstition has spread not only in the cities, but even to the villages and to the country districts. Yet I still feel it is possible to check it and set it right. Of this I am sure, that people are beginning once more to frequent the beautiful temples which have been almost deserted, so that the long-neglected sacred rites are being restored and so that fodder for the animals to be sacrificed, for which there was until now scarcely any demand, is being bought and sold again. From this it is evident that a very great number of people can be brought back to better ways if they are given the opportunity to repent.

Trajan to Pliny

Pliny Secundus, you have followed the correct procedure in examining those who were accused before you as Christians, for in general no hard and fast rule can be laid down. They should not be sought out. Those brought before you and found guilty should be punished, provided that anyone who denies that he is a Christian and actually proves this by worshiping our gods is pardoned on repentance, no matter how suspect his past may have been. Anonymous accusations, however, should not be admitted in any criminal case, for this would give a very bad precedent and would not be worthy of our age.

Translation from the English edition of Eberhard Arnold, *The Early Christians after the Death of the Apostles*, trans. and ed. by the Society of Brothers (Rifton, N.Y.: Plough, 1970), 63–65.

We can infer several things from Pliny's questions. Clearly trials of Christians did not happen often because Pliny had never been present at one; accompanying his father and other male relatives to court was part of the normal education of a Roman aristocrat. Pliny did not know what principle of law to use to justify executing Christians; he resorted to the concept that people should obey the legitimate order of a Roman official to sacrifice before the emperor's statue as a sign of loyalty.

This was an entirely adequate reason from the Roman perspective. To the Roman government, Christians posed a political threat. As we have seen, Roman religion existed to serve the state. Its purpose was to secure the favors and blessings of the gods for the commonwealth. Anything that threatened that relationship was a political danger. The gods liked lots of people to sacrifice to them, but Christians refused. That made the gods angry. Therefore, government needed to force Christians to behave patriotically in ceremony (to keep the favor of the gods). The government did not particularly care whether Christians actually changed their beliefs.

After Pliny we hear little about empire-wide persecution until about 249, although lots of local outbreaks occurred with the collusion of local Roman officials. By 249, however, the Roman world was in bad shape, with inflation, plague, political instability, invasions, and war. Almost anything that could go wrong had gone wrong. The Emperor Decius (249–251) decided to return to the old-time religion. He hoped that if everyone in the empire sacrificed to the Roman gods, the deities would be pleased and bless the empire. So he required everyone to obtain a certificate from the local Roman magistrate certifying that the bearer had sacrificed to the gods. Local committees, not unlike vigilantes, had the responsibility for enforcing the decree. Christian leaders who made a fuss about refusing to sacrifice were executed. Many Christians went into hiding or obtained forged documents that protected their consciences from idolatry and also saved their skins.

The death of Decius ended the official persecution in 251, but it was renewed in 257 under the Emperor Valerian (c. 253–259). His order reveals how Christians were to be treated. Bishops, elders, and deacons often were punished with death immediately. High status laity would lose their social distinctions (honorary titles, for example) and their property. Those who persisted in being Christians would be executed. High status lay women lost their property and were exiled. Christians in the imperial bureaucracy became slaves on the emperor's estates. Valerian's persecution ended swiftly when news came that he had been defeated by the Persians. When he died in captivity he was skinned and stuffed to make a footstool for the Persian throne room. Many, including Valerian's own son and successor, believed the God of the Christians had smitten Valerian, and the official persecution ended almost immediately. For the next forty years Christians operated openly in an atmosphere of toleration, unharassed by the imperial government, though technically still an illegal cult.

Unofficial persecution

While the sporadic persecutions by the government caused Christians great fear and anxiety, the unofficial, informal actions may have been more deadly. Modern Christians can at least understand some of the state's reasons for killing off politically-suspect Christians, but it is more difficult to understand the violent hatred Christians provoked in their neighbors. Pagans knew the virtues of Christians, how they cared for the sick, took in abandoned children, treated each other lovingly. It was well known that their ethic forbade lying, adultery, and theft. But pagans hated them anyway.[3] The Roman historian Tacitus noted that they were "loathed for their vices" and died unjustly after the fire of Rome "in spite of a guilt which had earned the most exemplary punishment." He echoed a common charge hurled at Christians by their neighbors—"hatred of the human race." Why would Romans dislike Christians so much? To modern readers these Christians hardly sound "loathsome." How could anyone feel violent rage against them? Romans charged Christians with several crimes. From the Roman perspective, the Christians were "atheists" because they did not believe in the gods authorized by the state. The charge of atheism appears often in official documents. Pagans knew that Christians ate flesh and drank blood in their secret meetings (a misunderstanding of the eucharistic feast), so they logically assumed Christians to be cannibals. Some Romans thought that was what happened to the abandoned children Christians collected. Roman pagans further suspected that Christians committed incest at their se-

Agnes, a Roman Christian martyr, probably died in the early 300s and was the subject of a mostly fictional writing, *Passio*. (From Edith Simon, *The Saints* [London: Weidenfeld and Nicolson, 1968])

cret "love-feasts," since they called each other "brother" and "sister." From common cultural experience Romans expected any evening banquet to devolve into some sort of orgy.

On top of these specific charges, Christians appeared to their pagan neighbors as spoilsports. They refused to participate in many of the normal duties and activities of civic life and injured their neighbors further by rebuking others for doing so. Christians avoided the arena and condemned others for enjoying the blood-letting. To Romans the arena was the moral equivalent of televised football. Christians refused to join in patriotic festivals when their local government paid homage to its patron god. Christians condemned the popular theater as pornographic (so did some Romans). Most regarded the theater as light entertainment. Christian attacks on the practice of putting unwanted babies on the refuse heaps challenged the traditional right of the Roman father over his children. For such activity they were regarded as anti-family. No doubt many Christians expressed a "holier-than-thou" attitude toward their neighbors, particularly galling when Romans saw them doing what clearly appeared to be immoral things.

Such daily irritation erupted into mob violence whenever some catastrophe occurred. As Tertullian (c. 160–230) said, "If the Tiber reaches the walls, if the Nile does not rise to the fields, if the sky doesn't move or the earth does, if there is famine, if there is plague, the cry is at once 'The Christians to the Lions.'" Roman officials would attempt to prevent a "lynching" by conducting trials of those accused, but mere confession of being a Christian was sufficient for execution. Depending on his or her status within the society, the criminal could die by the sword (usually beheading, an honorable death) or be sent to the arena to be torn by beasts or die in some other way the Romans found amusing (essentially a slave's death). Often, however, vigilantes killed Christians by beating or stabbing before the Roman authorities could stop the rioting. A mob reportedly roasted one martyr on a grill.

Not only did Christians suffer physical persecution; they also were subject to attacks by cultural leaders. Lucian, a second-century satirist, wrote several works in which he mocked Christians as foolish and gullible. His style was akin to that of late night television comedy, though more clever and humorous. A more serious, and therefore less damaging, attack was launched by the intellectual Celsus in about 178. He wrote primarily because he thought Christians were just plain wrong and a threat to the traditional values of Greco-Roman civilization. On that latter point we shall see later that he was correct. Celsus's work provides a good summary of the basic charges against Christians:

1. Intellectually, their doctrine was nothing more than a new perversion and corruption of ancient tradition.

2. Socially, this disagreeably non-conformist organization was characterized by such evil and strange practices as incest and cannibalism. Its hatred of all humanity was legendary.
3. Politically, Christians were atheists who despised the ancient gods, undermining and threatening the structure and stability of society and government.

Tertullian (c. 160–c. 230), an African theologian and Montanist, wrote apologetic writings answering attacks from outside Christianity and polemic arguments in early christological debates. (Billy Graham Center)

Apparently Christians took Celsus seriously, for Christian intellectuals addressed the issues he raised for the next century or so. The *apologists* (their "apology" meaning a defense of their convictions) vindicated Christian beliefs in various ways. Some pointed to the ancient roots of Christianity in Judaism, something Romans could respect. Some noted ideas common to Christianity and Platonism, for example, the concept of an ultimate unseen reality. Some pointed out inconsistencies and corruptions in Greco-Roman religion and philosophy and offered Christian beliefs as more coherent and logical. Some, especially Tertullian, turned the satirist Lucian on his head, observing with devastating sarcasm and mockery the foolish gullibility of pagans.

The apologists answered misunderstandings by explaining what went on in Christian services and the meanings of some Christian vocabulary. Some information about early Christian practices comes from these apologetic explanations, such as the communion service, where the bread and wine were called "flesh" and "blood," respectively. The Christian "hatred of the human race" was harder to refute from a Roman perspective. Some apologists pointed out that it was the Christians who rescued exposed babies from the garbage dump, who welcomed the outcasts of society, who ministered to victims of sickness, even during times of plague, that no one else would touch.

Others stressed the loyalty and ordinariness of believers. As Tertullian put it in about 200, "We pray unceasingly for all emperors . . . a secure empire . . . brave armies . . . a peaceful world." Further, "we too live in the world, sharing with you the forum, the market, the baths, the shops . . . and all other commercial activities. We, no less than you, sail the sea, serve in the army, farm the land, buy and sell." At the same time, however, the church drew some lines between itself and aspects of society antagonistic to the church and its values. This is reflected in some baptismal instructions from Hippolytus of Rome in about 220, including a list of occupations deemed unsuitable for Christians. Actors, pimps, gladiators, prostitutes, and jugglers (among others) must quit those occupations or be rejected for membership. A soldier must agree not to kill or to take the military oath; a military commander with capital authority must resign or be rejected. The latter rules amounted to a functional ban on Christians remaining in the army.

Clearly this approach reflects an effort to fit in with society, to become socially acceptable to some degree. It also demonstrates a clear sense of limits as to how far this might go; for most believers there was an undeniable tension between church and society. Not all were satisfied with this accommodating approach. Some sought to assimilate further, but assimilation usually meant compromising faith at some point, and such people disappeared into the culture. Others sought to increase the tension between church and society, which usually led to the rejection of society. The monastic movement found its roots in this impulse to reject and create some kind of Christian alternative to society.

The Gnostic challenge

The church was changed by its struggle with Greco-Roman culture. Nowhere is this more evident than in the conflict with *Gnosticism,* which was finally cast off but left a permanent imprint.

While Gnostic tendencies may be observed as early as the middle of the first century in Corinth and only a little later in Colossae, Gnosticism as an organized movement was largely a second-century phenomenon. It then claimed the allegiance of many of the church's brightest intellectuals and in some areas, such as Alexandria, may at one time have been the dominant form of Christianity.

Essentially Gnosticism is Christianity as understood from within a dualistic Greek worldview that considered spirit to be good and matter evil. For Gnostics, sin was primarily a matter of yielding to bodily appetites, rather than a spiritual issue of the conflict of human and divine wills. Thus, while professing the same doctrines as orthodox Christians and being often as Christocentric, their understanding of these doctrines differed radically. Resurrection, which for Paul was bodily and physical, was seen by the Gnostics entirely in spiritual terms—the body was something to be escaped. Yahweh, the god of the Jewish Scriptures, could not be the spiritual Father of Jesus, since such a spiritual being could not have created an evil material universe; Yahweh, who did so, must be an inferior divinity. Their Jesus was a docetic

(Greek *dokeo*) one who had only *seemed* to be human. Scripture was a mystical maze of secret teachings to be understood allegorically rather than literally. Plato and Pythagoras were as authoritative as Paul.

Structurally, Gnostics organized cells of spiritually elite initiates; their leaders were teachers rather than pastors. Their lifestyle tended towards either asceticism's denial of bodily needs or libertinism, which said "do whatever you want with your body because it is only temporary and not ultimately important." They felt themselves free from the constraints imposed upon lesser beings by ignorance, fear, or law, and their social perspective was as elitist as their theology.

This is scarcely the religion of the apostles, despite the Gnostics' claims to possess a secret tradition from Jesus that he had concealed from the masses. The main body of Christians rightly perceived it to be a different religion than that preached by Jesus and, therefore, vigorously opposed it. One of the primary issues involved authority and interpretation: Which writings and traditions were authoritative? How were they to be interpreted? The impact of such issues on Christian thinking continues.

Instead of appealing to the Gnostic "secret tradition," mainstream Christians appealed to what they called the "rule of faith" teaching that had been passed down through a chain of elders unbroken from the apostles. These were the beliefs taught in every mainstream congregation throughout the empire. Instead of placing the writings of Gnostic teachers on a par with the Gospels, Epistles, and Hebrew Scriptures, or rejecting the Hebrew Scriptures entirely for their materialism, mainstream Christians recognized the authority of the Old Testament and the bulk of what later became the New Testament. Scriptural authority was based on the principles that these writings were used everywhere for public reading, that they originated with the apostles or those closely associated with them, and that they agreed with the rule of faith. There was immediate and widespread consensus regarding a central core of twenty New Testament books: the Gospels of Matthew, Mark, Luke, and John; Acts; 1 Peter; 1 John; and thirteen letters of Paul. Around this core there existed a variable fringe of about thirteen books: Hebrews; James; 2 Peter; 2 John; 3 John; Jude; and Revelation (all of which eventually were included), and the *Didache*; *1 Clement*; *The Shepherd of Hermas*; *Epistle of Barnabas*; *Apocalypse of Peter*, and *Acts of Paul and Thecla* (all of which were eventually excluded). Debate about the fringe writings continued for centuries. The formal recognition of the list of books authorized for public readings came in 389. Christians now possessed an authoritative Scripture (tradition in written form) and an authoritative rule of faith (tradition in oral form), which established the proper perspective from which to interpret that Scripture—crucial steps in the formation of a normative catholic Christianity.

Responding to the Gnostic challenge stimulated the development of Christian intellectuals and led to the beginning of theology in the formal sense of that word—an effort to carefully and systematically explain the Christian faith in rational terms. Many of the questions raised in the debate continued to be discussed for the next few centuries. And informally, Gnostic tendencies continue to be the most common heresy in folk theology. The desire to separate the spiritual from the material, to accept spiritual healing while doubting physical miracles, to think one way on Sunday and another way the rest of the week, to emphasize Christ who saves our souls more than one who changes our lives is both understandable and comfortable. It reduces the tension Christians feel from being a part of two worlds—visible and invisible. Tension produces anxiety, and humans seek to reduce anxiety whenever possible. That tendency helps to explain the appeal of Gnosticism, both in the second century when it most conveniently matched the intellectual bias of the time, and in our own era.

Sin

Of course, most Christians in the Roman world concerned themselves much less with the ideas of the Gnostics than with recurring issues of Christian living, especially sin, sex, and money.

Christians particularly feared for the eternal destiny of those who had money. The concern was a real one in light of all the Gospels have to say on the subject. The answer, according to the *Shepherd of Hermas*, a popular devotional book written in sections from 90 to 150, struck a pragmatic balance between the imperatives of the Gospel and the constraints of everyday life. It was an option, but not necessary, to sell all one possessed and give the money to the poor. The rich should support the poor, who in turn would pray for the souls of the rich through their more powerful prayer life. Thus, both would benefit.

In an age that was more sexually indulgent than the late twentieth century, if that can be imagined, Christian sexual ethics stood in sharp contrast to those of contemporary society. For one thing, Christians held men to the same standards of sexual exclusivity as women. Their attitudes towards divorce (only for adultery) and remarriage (greatly discouraged, even for the widowed) were unparalleled among the morés and practices of the time. This already made them distinctive, but they went even further. Christians had abolished, at least in theory, social distinctions of rank and degree, but had not thereby killed the competitive desire that lay behind such distinctions. Competitiveness soon found an outlet in sexuality. Certain biblical texts suggested the existence of differing levels of spirituality, and the Gnostic ascetic tendency provided a suitable goal for spiritual overachievers and competitors—virginity.

Thus the stage was set for a great deal of gossip, discussion, and debate about sex. Should married couples have sex for pleasure or only to produce children, or should they have sex at all? *The Shepherd of Hermas* suggests that they should not. Was marriage or virginity better? Should avowed virgins dress normally or in a manner indicative of their condition? What about avowed virgins who lapsed? Many of the apocryphal writings were penned to promote a particular viewpoint. In one story a lion was converted and baptized by Paul and afterward vowed never to so much as sniff a slinky lioness again.[4] Abuse of strict moral codes was common; bishops were openly skeptical of couples who claimed to preserve their chastity while occupying the same bed on a nightly basis. Others never even tried. One bishop wished for a wall inside the church separating women from the men, whose behavior reminded him of stallions in a brothel.

Questions of Christian lifestyle were important, for the general view at this time was that forgiveness for sins committed after baptism was secured only with difficulty. Some thought sinners could be forgiven once more only, and there were some, like the Emperor Constantine, who postponed their baptism until near death. Others, in need of an additional second chance, sought absolution from a believer about to be martyred. These spiritual heroes were thought to possess special spiritual authority in view of their impending fate. This is part of the origin for the medieval custom of praying through the intercession of saints. Whatever the view, repentance often involved some form of public confession, penance, and humiliation in the presence of the congregation.

Toward "catholic" Christianity

After about 200, Christians began to move toward a universal or catholic doctrine. One canon of Scripture and a single rule of faith were generally recognized, and the Christian community had standardized worship and a hierarchical administrative structure.

An increasingly important element of standardized liturgy was the Eucharist. Justin Martyr (box 2.4), written about 150, describes a manner of celebrating the Lord's Supper that would have been familiar to Christians throughout the empire. The requirements for baptism were also becoming more uniform; a *catechumenate*, or initiatory period, involving three years of instruction was typical by Justin Martyr's time. Immediately before baptism (most often at Easter), those presenting themselves had to respond to a series of questions about what they believed. These formal "confessions of faith" contributed in turn to the formation of the first fixed creeds (from the Latin *credo*, "I believe"). The most important of these was the Old Roman Creed, the foundation of nearly all later creeds and especially the Apostle's Creed (see box 2.5).

2.4. The Lord's Supper

At the end of the prayers, we greet one another with a kiss. Then bread and a cup containing water mixed with wine are brought to the overseer of the brethren. He takes both and gives praise and glory to the Father of the Universe, through the name of the Son and of the Holy Ghost. He offers copious thanks that by Him we have been deemed worthy to receive these gifts. At the end of the prayer and thanksgiving all the people assembled give their assent, saying "Amen." . . . When the overseer has given thanks and all the people have assented, those we call table stewards (deacons) give each one present some of the bread and wine with water which was accepted with thanksgiving and take some of it to the homes of those who are absent.

This meal we call "Thanksgiving" (Eucharist). No one is allowed to partake in it except he believes that the things we teach are true, who has received the bath for the forgiveness of sins and for the new birth, and who lives according to the teachings handed down by Christ. For we do not partake of this meal as if it were ordinary food or ordinary drink. Rather, through the Logos of God our Healing Savior Jesus Christ became flesh and accepted flesh and blood for the sake of our salvation. Hence, as we have been taught, the food taken with thanksgiving in the words of prayer He handed down to us is the flesh and blood of that Christ who became flesh. Our flesh and blood are strengthened by this eating and drinking for our transformation.

The apostles in their own memoirs, which are called Gospels, handed down as they were commanded:

Jesus took the bread, gave thanks, and said, "Do this in remembrance of me. This is my body." In the same way he took the cup, gave thanks, and said, "This is my blood." And he gave it to them alone.

—Justin Martyr (c. 150)

Translation from the English edition of Eberhard Arnold, *The Early Christians after the Death of the Apostles*, trans. and ed. by the Society of Brothers (Rifton, N.Y.: Plough, 1970), 223.

It was formulated around the end of the second century. Also, by the mid-second century infants of baptized believers were baptized.

The penance and discipline required of sinners seeking readmission to the church was also being formalized and standardized during this time. Known unrepentant sinners were excluded from the Lord's Supper. Readmission involved repentance, public confession, prayer, fasting, and good works, and during this process the individual stood outside the meetingplace while the congregation celebrated the Eucharist. To be sure, discussions of this topic precipitated some sharp disputes, and there was considerable debate over just how rigorous this process of readmission should be as the church sought to balance mercy and holiness. But the very existence of the disputes testifies to the strength of the concept that there ought to be a binding universal standard for such matters; the existence of this concept characterizes the emerging catholic church.

Administratively, Christians organized themselves in an increasingly centralized and hierarchical manner. A bishop typically served as head of the Christians in a particular city and its surrounding region. Individual congregations still met in homes under the leadership of elders and deacons. New subordinate office bearers, such as readers, doorkeepers, acolytes, and "widows" (whose precise origin, status, and qualifications remain unclear beyond the New Testament references) proliferated, and the distinction between clergy and laypeople was increasingly clear. In about 250 the church at Rome reportedly had more than 1500 people on its payroll.[5] Bishops within a region met periodically to debate and discuss issues of broad concern, such as errors of teaching or the proper date to celebrate Easter. Consensus at these meetings contributed to the standardization of belief and practice codified in creeds and such handbooks as the *Didache*. This helped Christians withstand the pressures of the surrounding society. Whereas the early Christians had generally lived in eager anticipation of the imminent return of the Lord, the church now acted more and more as an institution structured to be around for the long haul.

These developments were not without their critics. Viewed from a different perspective, the centralization of the church can be seen as a power grab on the part of the clergy at the expense of laypeople, women in particular, who were now restricted to a more narrow role within the congregation than in apostolic times. Centralized governance also increased the ease with which administrators could (mis)appropriate the church's ever-increasing wealth, a temptation to which leaders were not immune.

Others were unhappy with changes in doctrine or practice. The impartation of the Holy Spirit, for example, traditionally associated with baptism, became more closely associated with the laying on of

---

2.5. Apostles' Creed (eighth-century "received" form)

I believe in God the Father Almighty, Maker of heaven and earth.

And in Jesus Christ, his only son, our Lord, who was conceived by the Holy Ghost, born of the virgin Mary, suffered under Pontius Pilate, was crucified, dead, and buried; he descended into hell; the third day he rose from the dead; he ascended into heaven; and sitteth at the right hand of God the Father Almighty; from thence he shall come to judge the quick and the dead.

I believe in the Holy Ghost, the holy catholic Church, the communion of saints; the forgiveness of sin, the resurrection of the body and the life everlasting.

Amen

Philip Schaff, *Creeds of Christendom*, vol. 2, *The Greek and Latin Creeds* (New York: Harper and Row, 1931), 45.

hands by the baptizing bishop or his designated representative. To some, this seemed to restrict the Spirit's work under the control of the church hierarchy. Then there was the matter of penance and discipline. Zealous for holiness and purity of life, certain people—spiritual over-achievers perhaps—thought that the church was too lax in its treatment of sinners within the congregation.

These undercurrents of dissatisfaction flowed within the church—most deeply among those who felt they had been disenfranchised by a church that was falling away from apostolic teachings and practice. Within this context the *Montanist* movement should be understood. Usually regarded as a heretical movement within the church, Montanist

2.6. Montanists

The Montanist movement was started by a man named Montanus in rural Phrygia (Asia minor) some-time between 156 and 172. His key associates included two women, who, like the daughters of Philip (Acts 21:9), claimed to be inspired by the Holy Spirit. Phrygia had a reputation for producing crackpots, and because of the group's teaching about the millennium—one prophecy claimed that Jesus would return to establish the New Jerusalem near the backwoods town of Pepuza—many dismissed the Montanists as more of the same Phrygian nonsense.

Despite the ridicule, however, the movement gained a devoted following in regions far more sophisticated than Phrygia. It was especially influential in Rome and North Africa. Its appeal, moreover, was deep and lasting: Groups claiming Montanist roots clung to their beliefs in the face of persecution for centuries.

The key to their appeal lies in their teaching about the Spirit. Apparently basing their claim on John 16:13 ("But when he, the Spirit of Truth, comes, he will guide you into all the truth. . . . he will tell you what is yet to come"), Montanists believed that the Holy Spirit was giving new guidance to the church for new times and answers to some of the important issues of the day.

Much of the guidance in these prophecies was strict: No remarriage was allowed. A second repentance was not to be granted. Fasts were long. Persecution was not to be avoided. Montanist life offered a contrast to the less spontaneous and more lax discipline of the organized church.

To many Christians this was a new and timely breeze stirring the church. To many in leadership it was threatening and dangerous. Beyond the criticism of authority inherent in Montanist teaching, the possibility of establishing doctrine on the basis of individual prophecy threatened to overturn the orthodox consensus achieved in the struggle against Gnosticism.

The Montanist movement and the organized church's reaction offers parallels to the Pentecostal movement and the mainline church response in the twentieth century. Many orthodox leaders, no doubt stung by Montanist criticism, were suspicious of Montanist ecstatic utterances. True prophets, it was argued, spoke in their right minds, not in a trance or ecstasy. The Montanists labeled their opponents "slayers of the prophets" who quenched the Spirit.

At heart the controversy reflected a clash between differing cultural values and visions, not simply the choice between "an organized urban and hierarchical church with set forms of worship and discipline and a set relationship with the outside world, or a church of the Spirit in which men and women participated equally as the vehicles of the Spirit."* At its core the choice was between an emphasis on grace, mercy, and forgiveness and an ascetic, unbending legalism. In expelling the Montanists the orthodox showed little concern for understanding and possibly learning from them, which could have strengthened orthodoxy and offered women more status in the church. For their part the Montanists showed little understanding of, and concern for, believers who failed to maintain a level of discipline that only an elite few achieved.

*W. H. C. Frend, *The Rise of Christianity* (Philadelphia: Fortress, 1984), 255.

piety should also be seen as a protest against a perceived loss of freedom and spontaneity within the church (see box 2.6).

The great persecution

Late in the third century, after a generation of relative indifference and disregard by the government, Christians suddenly found themselves again the subject of official persecution under the strong emperor Diocletian (240–316). Diocletian, who reigned from 284 to 305, sought to restore the greatness of the Roman Empire after a period of near collapse, and he believed this best could be achieved by centralized power and more societal uniformity. Thus, he consolidated his control of the army, coordinated an empire-wide system of taxation, and promoted cultural unity—including uniform religious sacrifices by all subjects.

Christians were identified as a particular threat to the state in this effort. Egged on by his virulently anti-Christian son-in-law and successor, Galerius (250–311), Diocletian began in 298 to remove Christians from the civil service and army. The necessity for their removal shows how far Christians had gone in accommodating to their culture during the years of peace.

In 303 the emperor ordered that Christian churches be destroyed and Christian writings be burned. Christians who refused to comply could be executed for refusing a legal order. This was the same reasoning Pliny the Younger had used in trying Christians of an earlier day. The next step was to order Christian leaders to make Roman religious sacrifices.

When Diocletian retired in 305, Galerius intensified the anti-Christian campaign, and laypeople as well as leaders were martyred. Before the persecution ended in 311, thousands died, especially in Egypt and North Africa. Thousands more were displaced or in hiding. In 311, as Galerius was dying from what is thought to have been stomach cancer, he lifted the persecution in the eastern part of the empire and asked the Christians to pray for him and the government. Although sporadic persecutions continued in some locales, this *de facto* toleration signaled a remarkable change and set the stage for a new era in the Christian experience.

Suggested readings

Benko, Stephen. *Pagan Rome and the Early Christians*. Bloomington, Ind.: Indiana University Press, 1986.

"Converting the Empire."*Christian History*, 17.1 (issue 57, 1998).

Eusebius. *Ecclesiastical History*.

Frend, W. H. C. *The Early Church*. Philadelphia: Fortress, 1982.

———. *The Rise of Christianity*. Philadelphia: Fortress, 1984.

"Heresy in the Early Church." *Christian History*, 15.3 (issue 51, 1996).

"How We Got Our Bible." *Christian History*, 13.3 (issue 43, 1994).

"Paul and His Times." *Christian History*, 14.3 (issue 47, 1995).

"Persecution in the Early Church." *Christian History*, 9.3 (issue 27, 1990).

Stark, Rodney. *The Rise of Christianity: A Sociologist Reconsiders History*. Princeton, N.J.: Princeton University Press, 1996.

Veyne, Paul. *A History of Private Life*. Vol. 1: *From Pagan Rome to Byzantium*. Cambridge, Mass.: Harvard University Press, 1987.

"Women in the Early Church." *Christian History*, 7.1 (issue 17, 1988).

"Worship in the Early Church." *Christian History*, 12.1 (issue 37, 1993).

3

The Fourth-Century Turning Point

The 300s ushered in a bright but strange new world for Christians. Suddenly, instead of being persecuted, Christians found themselves favored by the political establishment. Rather than being socially anathema, Christian faith was an asset on the road to worldly success. In fewer than three generations Christians went from ignominy to power.[1] Throughout the centuries, Christians have interpreted this change in a variety of ways, from "the triumph of the church" (Roman Catholics and Eastern Orthodox) to "the great betrayal" (the Anabaptist tradition) to something in between (most Protestants). What changes occurred and why are they important?

Much of the change came about because a Roman emperor, Constantine (d. 337), became a Christian in response to what he considered a miracle in his own life. According to the bishop Eusebius of Caesarea (c. 260–c. 339), Constantine told him that in 312, while facing an imposing enemy army, Constantine prayed to the sun god for help. In response he (and his army) saw a cross flaming in the sky at midday, emblazoned with the words, "In this sign conquer." That night Christ appeared to him in a dream and instructed him to use the sign as a safeguard against his enemies. Constantine did so and won a surprising victory—his rival, Maxentius, drowned in a river before the battle began. Impressed with the power of the Christians' God, Constantine began moving toward adherence to the formerly-despised religion.

Historians have speculated about Constantine's motives for identifying with the Christians. Nineteenth-century critics assumed that he did it for political advantage. They noted that Christians represented the single largest religious faction (although only about 10 percent of the total population) and that they were particularly strong in the East, the region controlled by Licinius, Constantine's major rival after the drowning of Maxentius. By appealing to a large, frustrated group, Constantine could weaken that control. These historians noted that Constantine made no overt actions that would formally announce his religious allegiance until his deathbed baptism. His personal moral behavior differed little from that of pagan emperors. He murdered his wife, children, and most of his relatives on suspicion of treason, and he maintained many of the pagan rites.

Others have argued that Constantine was genuinely, if naïvely, converted, but that he was pragmatic about revealing his new allegiance. He attempted to make his faith clear to Christians while not offending the pagan majority whose contentment he needed to stay in power. They observe that his alliance with Christians brought him more political trouble than peace, because Christians began to expect the emperor to settle their internal disputes, at times with imperial troops. Constantine managed to be away and unavailable at most of the times when tradition required the emperor's personal participation in pagan rituals. He delegated such tasks to others. He gradually replaced overtly pagan symbols on coins with more ambiguous inscriptions that could be understood as either pagan or Christian. He contributed cash to the building funds of Christians—according to one account, the equivalent of 400 pounds of gold a year to churches in the city of Rome alone. Pagans received less generosity. His mother, presumably using funds from her position as queen mother, gave enormous amounts. Constantine's advisers were drawn increasingly from among Christian leaders, although these leaders often were frustrated by their apparent lack of influence on his actions. Bishops also took the role of judges in civil suits involving Christians. Since Christians were forbidden by Scripture from going to court like unbelievers (Matt. 5:25; 1 Cor. 6:1–8), the church developed a mediation system under the bishops. Constantine officially authorized that system and granted bishops the powers of magistrates.

Constantine's actions

Edict of Milan

The edict of toleration, usually referred to as the *Edict of Milan*, in 313 extended toleration to all religions in the Roman Empire. This effectively decriminalized Christianity and gave it the same sanction as other religions. Galerius had granted such toleration in the eastern region two years earlier. This edict did not give Christianity any special status but made it equal to other religions. Being a Christian was no longer a capital offense. Naturally, the Christians were relieved and grateful.

They could now build churches and meet openly. The church as an institution could inherit lands and legacies. Scriptures could be copied and distributed without restraint.

Nicea

The *Council of Nicea* was the child of this new epoch, and church fathers who gathered in 325 were establishing more precedents than they could have understood. First, Nicea was the first council of the church after it was decriminalized and reflected the freedom of Christians to fight openly with each other. Second, it reinaugurated the pattern of deliberation by world council that had been established in the Jerusalem Council described in Acts 15. This

Constantine (d. 337) moved Christianity from outlawed sect to favored faith in the Roman Empire. (Billy Graham Center)

pattern continued, at least among Roman Catholics, through Vatican Council II in 1964. Third, Nicea began the process of settling questions of orthodox doctrine not clearly addressed in Scripture. Fourth, it linked inextricably the destinies of the institutional church with the temporal authorities—establishing a relationship of tension and creativity that lasted until the Reformation.

Constantine welded this last bond when he called the meeting himself to resolve the conflict between factions of the church in Alexandria over the relationship between Christ and God the Father. An Alexandrian teacher named Arius (c. 260–336) had concluded logically that Jesus was not like any other human being, yet he was unlike God because he came in flesh, whereas all good Greeks knew that God was a spirit. Arius proposed that Jesus was a special created being midway between God and human—a demigod. This reasoning solved logical problems about the Person of Christ, was esthetically satisfying to the Greeks, and comported well with the ideal of superhuman hero revered among the Germanic tribes on the Roman borders.

Best of all, Arius's solution was easy to understand. Athanasius (c. 300–373), the opponent of Arius, asserted the seemingly paradoxical idea that Jesus was both truly human and truly God—a difficult concept to comprehend. The supporters of these two had taken to rioting in the streets of Alexandria, and deaths had resulted. Constantine, as a good Roman, hated disorder and feared disunity among the members of his largest bloc of supporters, so he called the church bishops to Nicea to settle the issue (see box 3.1). Even though Constantine presided at the meetings we have no evidence that he understood or cared about the theological issues involved. He wanted the issue settled so he could go on to other things.

Constantine was pragmatic about reaching the settlement. He supported whatever ideas the majority of bishops favored and pressed dissenters to agree. Eusebius says that Constantine introduced the formula *homoousion* (literally, "of the same substance"). All complied, except for Arius and two bishops, who were exiled. The council damned Arius and his views and affirmed the view that Jesus, God the Father, and the Holy Spirit were three Persons in one; they thought this relationship necessary for salvation to work. The struggle between *Arians* (not to be confused with *Aryans*, the racial term Adolf Hitler used to describe his master people) and Athanasians continued throughout most of the fourth century, complicated by rivalries among Constantine's successors. Eventually, however, the orthodox Athanasian position was upheld by a later council with less political coercion. These ideas are summarized in the *Nicene Creed*. Arian tendencies can be found today among Jehovah's Witnesses and some Unitarians.

3.1. Nicene Creed

The Nicene Creed (325) emphasizes differences between the orthodox and current theologies considered heretical. Proclaiming God as Creator of all things refuted Gnostics, who were still around in small numbers. The christological section answered Arians.

We believe in one God the Father almighty, maker of heaven and earth, and of all things visible and invisible:

And in one Lord Jesus Christ, the only-begotten Son of God, Begotten of the Father before all the ages, Light of Light, true God of true God, begotten not made, of one substance with the Father, through whom all things were made; who for us men and for our salvation came down from the heavens, and was made flesh of the Holy Spirit and the Virgin Mary, and became man, and was crucified under Pontius Pilate, and suffered and was buried and rose again on the third day according to the Scriptures, and ascended into the heavens and sits on the right hand of the Father, and comes again with glory to judge living and dead, of whose kingdom there shall be no end:

And in the Holy Spirit, the Lord and Giver of Life, that proceeds from the Father, who with the Father and Son is worshipped together and glorified together, who spoke through the prophets:

In one holy catholic and apostolic church:

We acknowledge one baptism for the remission of sins. We look for a resurrection of the dead and the life of the age to come.

Later councils were presided over by imperial legates (for example, the Council of Tyre in 335 by Count Dionysius). While this poses difficulties for those unaccustomed to having the state dictate to the church, people of the day thought this arrangement both normal and sensible.

How ordinary believers reacted to these controversies is unclear. Most of what we know was written by church leaders who participated on one side or another and had a definite stake in the outcome. In later centuries Christians in the Greek-speaking parts of the empire were intensely interested in fine points of doctrinal disputes, and Gregory of Nyssa (330?–c. 396) reported, "If you ask anyone in Constantinople for change, he will start discussing with you whether the Son is begotten or unbegotten. If you ask about the quality of bread, you will get the answer: 'The Father is greater, the Son is less.'" We might suspect that such widespread interest and respectability was appreciated by the average churchgoer and that accommodation to Christians by the emperor might make them feel that things were going their way. Certainly spokesmen like Eusebius expressed grateful enthusiasm for the new state of affairs:

> so that now . . . a thing unknown heretofore—the most exalted Emperors of all, conscious of the honour which they have received from Him, spit upon the faces of dead idols, trample upon the unhallowed rites of demons, and laugh at the old deceits they inherited from their fathers: but Him who is the common Benefactor of all and of themselves they recognize as the one and only God and confess that Christ the Son of God is sovereign King of the universe and style Him as Savior on monuments, inscribing in an imperishable record His righteous acts and His victories over the impious ones, in imperial characters in the midst to the city that is Empress among the cities of the world.

The collusion between the Emperor Constantine and the orthodox bishops raises one of the most important issues for students of Christian history: Was this a disaster that wrecked the purity of the early church and led to later compromises with the culture? Or was this the way God chose to secure the church's existence, to "contextualize" the gospel, and to build a base from which to spread to the whole world? Theologically, Protestants usually see the negative view of this relationship, but what about socially? Did the gospel gain wider hearing among half-converted pagans than it might have otherwise? Did more people hear the Word proclaimed? Did relations with the state merely accelerate or augment existing tendencies toward ritualism?

These changes in the external conditions of Christians brought many internal changes as well. Christians no longer needed to worry that imperial power would be wielded against them. They could legally proclaim their ideas in public and expect the government not to abet those who would shut them up. A few respectable positions in the civil service became available. In general, Christians were less preoccupied with the threat of death or torture and could spend their energy on other pursuits—even fighting over doctrine. Christians suddenly moved from a position of weakness to a power alliance with the state that forced them to reconsider traditional assumptions and teachings. In gratitude and relief, the bishops removed the prohibition against army service by Christians at the Council of Arles in 314—after all, Christian soldiers now served a Christian emperor.

Institutionally, the church quickly began to amass wealth from the estates of dying faithful who willed their lands. This posed added questions. How should people focused on the other world manage great wealth in this one? What was good stewardship? Added to the personal and spiritual attractions of converting was the clear favor of the imperial family. Lots of people wanted to join. How should they be brought in? As Christians gained a stake in the society, they began to take more responsibility for its maintenance, including the education of Christian young people. If the culture was no longer all bad, how could Christians discern what was expedient and useful from that culture?

The education of would-be converts posed major problems. Traditionally, someone wanting to become a Christian took three years of training in the faith before being baptized. Catechumens would learn stories from the Old and New Testaments, memorize hymns and praise songs, be discipled in Christian ethical behavior, and be taught elementary doctrine. Elders examined them for both knowledge and character before they were allowed to participate fully in church life. They died to sin and rose to new life as they were baptized, preferably by immersion before the assembly. Now too many interested folk crowded that system for it to function well. Plus, the popular feeling was that baptism was necessary to be saved, so there was some urgency in getting people to that point. There were teeming multitudes who might otherwise go to hell. The church lacked sufficient teachers to train large numbers in the traditional three-year course.

Churches began to reduce the time and content of the course—first to one year, then to three months, and eventually to the period of Lent's forty days before Easter to reach as many as possible. This meant, of course, that large numbers entered the church ill-prepared or half-converted. An uneducated laity would cause enormous problems later. Modern Christians may find it easy to take pot-shots at the fourth-century leaders who acted hastily or thoughtlessly to reduce membership requirements, but how many modern converts would endure a three-year education program before gaining full membership in the church?

Many earnest Christians took offense at the influx of the masses into the church. Previously, the potential for persecution had filtered out most weak or vacillating disciples. But safety and respectability removed that self-selection. Christians who sought a purer or holier fellowship sometimes left the urban churches to seek solitary lives of prayer and contemplation in the deserts. Others engaged in ascetic practices they thought pleasing to the Lord. These factors contributed to the eventual development of monasticism.

The writings of Augustine (354–430), bishop of Hippo, laid an ecclesiastical framework for the medieval church and a doctrinal foundation that still influences both Protestants and Roman Catholics. (Billy Graham Center)

Christian intellectuals

After Constantine, the intellectual leadership of the Roman world shifted from pagans to Christians, and Christian-influenced thought dominated Europe from then until the eighteenth century. Three thinkers particularly loom large in the fourth century: Augustine, Jerome, and Ambrose. Each of these dealt with issues of integrating Christianity with classical Greco-Roman culture.

Augustine (354–430) was the dominant thinker of the early Middle Ages. He permanently shaped the Christian mind by his philosophical studies and warmed the heart of faith by the passion of his personal testimony. Using the terminology and categories of Greek philosophy, Augustine laid a systematic foundation that others have built on ever since. In addition, his *Confessions* recorded his inmost spiritual feelings and struggles toward a final dramatic conversion. This book stands in contrast to the list of deeds that constituted previous autobiographies. His was the first internal, psychological autobiography, a model for writers ever since.

Augustine grew up as a bright underachiever in Roman North Africa. Although his mother was a Christian, Augustine viewed her as simpleminded and spent his adolescence in whoring and petty delinquency. The death of his father provided money for him to study at Carthage, where he continued his wanton ways until he got a nice girl pregnant. Augustine settled down somewhat, although not enough to marry the woman, and began to enjoy his studies. He excelled in rhetoric as a sort of a "communications" major who combined studies in writing and persuasive speaking. Augustine also became dedicated to the pursuit of truth and was drawn into the *Manicheans*. This Gnostic-flavored movement differentiated the God of the Old Testament who created the evil material world from the God of the New Testament who freed our good spirits from the world. Full of unanswered questions about how all this worked, Augustine was assured that when a Manichean leader visited Carthage all his questions would be answered. But Augustine was bitterly disappointed at the superficiality of the answers when he finally met and questioned this leader. Disillusioned, Augustine concentrated on his career, becoming a professor of rhetoric at Carthage, then at Rome, and finally at Milan in northern Italy, the emperor's administrative capital. Here Augustine exercised great influence as a speech writer for members of the emperor's entourage and taught the sons of important people. He moved in the best circles.

Yet Augustine felt empty. He still wanted to grasp truth and found what became for him a beginning point when he adapted the Platonic view of evil as the absence of good. Pagan philosophers helped him resolve the problem of how a good God could create a world filled with evil. If evil is the *absence* of good, not its *opposite*, just as darkness is the negation or absence of light, not its opposite, then neither evil nor darkness exists alone as a substance. Their only claim to reality comes when they are set alongside what truly *is* real. If there is darkness there must be light. If there is within a person the ability to see and experience evil, there must be a corresponding, ultimate good that the human will was created to take delight in.

Such scholarly reasoning might help few seekers, but it filled Augustine with hope. He knew that there was evil in his own heart. He even had experienced a mystical moment of being filled with light. Based on his conception of light and good, this mystical presence could only mean the existence of a real, personal god whose being was wholly good.

But these ideas, even added to his material and professional success, gave him no personal peace, for he reasoned that such a God could never accept him in his heart's dark evilness. Perhaps out of professional curiosity, and his mother's insistence, Augustine began attending the church in Milan where the preacher Ambrose (c. 339–397) had a reputation as an excellent speaker. Much to Augustine's surprise, he found Ambrose's sermons appealing intellectually and emotionally, as well as rhetorically. In these sermons Augustine began to see an answer for his inability to find God. Perhaps God could find him. More than ever before Augustine seriously considered Christianity. It was Romans 13:13–14 that finally broke through in one of the most dramatic conversions to Christ ever recorded. He served the church for the rest of his life.

Although the witness of Augustine's faithful life has shaped Christian consciousness, his greatest impact has been in the ideas that continue to frame the formal thinking of several Christian traditions. In forty years as an active pastor and teacher (391–430), Augustine wrote many letters and books to answer questions raised by Manichaeism, Donatism, Pelagianism, and other conflicting ideas among Christians. He did so by explaining the Bible using structure and vocabulary from Greco-Roman philosophers. The acceptance of most of his ideas by later Christians meant that his formulations strongly influenced Western orthodoxy.

Intuition dominated reason in Augustine's system. "Do not seek to understand so that you might believe, but believe in order to understand," he stated.[2] This reflects his own inability to experience truth in merely human systems before he was confronted by God through Scripture. When Adam and Eve fell, sin entered into the human race in a pervasive way that twentieth-century science might call genetic, though in one writing he associated original sin's transmission with the parents' sexual act that resulted in conception. All humans inherit a divided will that has lost its attraction to God and seeks only self-happiness. The human being has enough freedom to be considered responsible for personal actions, but ultimately the will lacks the ability not to sin. Only God's grace can release the will from this bondage. Augustine fixed infant baptism as the norm for children born to Christian parents, for it was baptismal grace that washed away the inherited stain of sin and made the child redeemable.

Augustine framed much of this understanding in the context of his controversy with the British priest Pelagius, who believed that human nature is not inherently evil, so that a person can choose the right freely, guided by the example of Christ and the martyrs. Rather, Augustine countered, only God's grace frees a person to be able to choose to do right.

The conception of *predestination*, with which Augustine is associated, must be understood within this interpretation of Scripture's teachings concerning humanity's inability and God's sovereign grace. To safeguard human free will, church apologists of the second and third centuries had reasoned thus:

1. God is omniscient and immutable.
2. God knew before the creation who would choose to serve him and who would remain independent.
3. By his sovereign governance God graciously guides their intentions and actions and takes the initiative to make a way of salvation.

3.2. "Maker of All"

Maker of all, eternal King
Who day and night about
dost bring:
Who weary mortals to relieve,
Dost in their times the
seasons give. . . .

Look on us, Jesu, when we
fall,
And with thy look our souls
recall:
If thou but look our sins are
gone,
And with due tears our pardon
won.

Shed through our hearts thy
piercing ray,
Our soul's dull slumber drive
away
Thy name be first on every
tongue,
To thee our earliest praises
sung.

All laud to God the Father be;
All praise, Eternal Son, to
thee;
All glory, as is ever meet,
To God the holy Paraclete.

—Ambrose of Milan
"Aeterne rerum conditor," transla-
tion from *Hymns of the Breviary Missal*
(New York: Glencoe, 1948).

Augustine also proclaimed human responsibility, but he rejected God's foreknowledge as the deciding factor. What God knew by foreknowledge was that absolutely none would come to him without being changed. Therefore, in accordance with his perfect wisdom he *elected* or chose to change the wills of some, without regard for their individual merits. Then he effected their saving faith in Christ. God continually grants the power to his chosen people to fulfil his commands, ensuring their perseverance in saving faith. Augustine avoided saying that God predestined others to damnation. He taught that all are, without grace, deserving of damnation, but God chooses to save some through his free gift of grace, simply leaving the rest to follow their sin-bound wills to destruction.

Augustine also laid a foundation for Western thinking when he developed a philosophy of history in the work, *City of God*. Originally written to refute charges that the sack of Rome in 410 by the Visigoths happened because Romans had abandoned their traditional protecting gods for the new Christian one, the book claimed that the world is a mixed bag. Since Adam and Eve, two "cities" or communities have existed side by side: the city of God (those who serve God), and the city of man (those who serve themselves). Although these communities share some goals (peace, for example), they have different destinies—eternal life for the city of God and eternity without God for the city of man. The two cities are mingled in every earthly institution, including the visible church, and will be separated only at the last judgment. The earthly city is quite capable of doing good things, such as passing just laws, which the godly can share in and appreciate. But ultimately they are on different tracks. Thus, while God had averted destruction from the city of Rome while the Romans spread peace and order over the Mediterranean, the city suffered the natural consequences of pagan idolatry and bloodlust when his protecting hand was removed.

For medieval Christians and later Roman Catholics, Augustine's emphasis on baptismal grace and the church as the dispenser of grace strengthened the role of the church as an essential institution. For reformers both monastic and Protestant, his idea of the invisible church coexisting with the institutional

Ambrose (c. 339–397) pioneered in the development of preaching and influenced the custom of congregational singing in Christian worship. (Billy Graham Center)

church preserved the ideal of a higher standard and brought comfort when human realities fell so far short of the biblical ideal.

The idea that the two cities could, in fact, work on common goals legitimized Christian cooperation and participation in civil government. While a minority have always emphasized enmity between Christians and the powers, the majority of Christians recognize some limited legitimate duties owed to the state. Augustine's views allow the phrase "Christian citizen" to be a logical possibility.

Ambrose (box 3.2) and Jerome, like Augustine, had great influence on the common folk of their own period and of later times. Ambrose

Jerome (c. 345–c. 419), an early monastic leader, is best known as a Greek and Hebrew language scholar who produced the Vulgate translation. (Billy Graham Center)

65

had been governor of Milan and was drafted to become its bishop. He devoted himself to the administrative affairs of the church, defending the Nicene formulation against the occasional pressures of emperors who countenanced Arianism. He was a great preacher, as Augustine found out, but his greatest contribution was the introduction of Latin hymns, which could be learned quickly by the average parishioners. These hymns communicated and popularized Christian teachings with rhyming tunes.

Likewise Jerome, though an ascetic and scholar, ended up having great popular impact by using his scholarship to produce a translation of the whole Bible into the Vulgate, the Latin of the people, so that even those who were illiterate could hear the word of God in their own tongue. Jerome's work was so successful that it became the official translation for the Roman Catholic church, and has influenced its theology and liturgy ever since.

Suggested readings

"Bernard of Clairvaux." *Christian History*, 8.4 (issue 24, 1989).

Eadie, John, ed. *The Conversion of Constantine*. New York: Holt, Rinehart and Winston, 1971.

"Everyday Faith in the Middle Ages."*Christian History*, 15.1 (issue 49, 1996).

Fox, Robin Lane. *Pagans and Christians*. New York: Knopf, 1986.

"Francis of Assisi."*Christian History*, 13.2 (issue 42, 1994).

"John Chrysostom." *Christian History*, 13.4 (issue 44, 1994).

Jones, Arnold H. M. *Constantine and the Conversion of Europe*. New York: Macmillan, 1949.

MacMullen, Ramsay. *Christianizing the Roman Empire: A.D. 100–400*. New Haven, Conn.: Yale University Press, 1984.

———. *Constantine*. New York: Routledge Chapman and Hall, 1987.

"St. Augustine."*Christian History*, 6.3 (issue 15, 1987).

"Women in the Medieval Church." *Christian History*, 10.2 (issue 30, 1991).

4

The Age of Faith

The Middle Ages is one of the most misunderstood periods of Christian history. Some authors, secular and Christian alike, fall into the trap of seeing it as the "dark ages"—characterized by the Crusades, the Inquisition, and general intolerance. Others fall into the error of seeing it as the ideal period when Christendom really existed, everyone was Christian, and the church dominated over secular values. Both views contain some truths and some falsehoods. The Middle Ages, after all, span almost 1000 years (about 500–1500)—half the life of the Christian church. Things changed enormously during that time. The experiences of Christians during the Middle Ages marked the church in ways that continue to show up. This chapter reflects on several aspects of medieval Christian experience that fall outside the more usual discussions of kings, crusaders, and knights, but which shaped Christians' faith in fundamental ways.

Protestant myths

Conservative Protestants often wonder, "Where were all the Christians in the Middle Ages?" Tending to presume that Roman Catholics do not quite qualify as Christians but knowing that Martin Luther did not come around until after 1500, Protestants tend to visualize a sort of underground church. Essentially, however, all Christians in the Middle Ages were in the church. The church in the Middle Ages encompassed virtually all tendencies in Christianity now represented by Protestantism and Roman Catholicism, as well as some emphases no longer approved by either (self-flagellation as a religious act, for example). So it was possible for the individual to find somewhere in the church the expression of any particular personal faith, from glossolalia (speaking in tongues) to adoration of the host (a high church liturgical practice). Real faith and piety were common; most people lived and died believing that they were trying to follow God's will. Most clergy genuinely felt called to the cure of souls and sought to minister faithfully. We hear more about the exceptions—immoral and lazy clergy—because, then as now, bad news was news, but good news was not.

Germans

During the first 500 years of the Middle Ages the major achievement of Christians as a group was the conversion of the northern barbarians. The cultural foundations of Western culture stand on an amalgam of classical, Judeo-Christian, and Germanic roots. The Germanic element stems from this early medieval era. The wandering tribes of Germanic-speaking peoples had bothered the Roman Empire from about 200, but after 400 these migratory farmers simply overwhelmed the numerically diminishing Romans. For the most part they were not the plundering, ravaging hordes portrayed in movies; rather, they moved with wagons, cattle, and farm equipment like American pioneers along the Oregon Trail, seeking good farmland to feed their families. Nonetheless, these peacefully-intentioned farmers still disrupted the Roman world in many ways because of major differences in values. For instance, while the Roman elite possessed an abstract concept of the state that transcended the lifetime and character of any individual emperor, Germans tended to personalize loyalty to a successful war chief. When the old war-leader died, loyalty might transfer to whomever might prove himself an able leader. Loyalty dissolved with the death of the individual leader. Whereas Romans understood the idea of taxes to maintain the state, Germans expected the leader to pay the costs from his own estate and from war-booty. While Catholic Christians dominated the Roman elite by 400, most of the Germans who converted from paganism had been loosely evangelized by Arian missionaries, so Catholic Romans viewed them as heretics as well as barbarians.

But then Clovis, king of the Franks (d. 511), adopted Catholic Christianity. When he and his descendants conquered Gaul, the most agriculturally productive area of northern Europe, and emerged as the most militarily powerful of the "successor" states (those that succeeded or followed the Roman Empire), they did so with the slightly reluctant blessing of Catholic leaders. Wherever Arian Germans settled, the East Goths or Ostrogoths in Italy for example, they remained an occupying minority, separate in language and religion from those they ruled. In

Gaul, on the other hand, Franks and Romans at least met each other at church on Sunday, and after a couple of generations, intermarriage among the Roman and Frankish elites produced a new, amalgamated elite, mostly Frankish in culture, but Roman Catholic in religion.

The process of conversion of these barbarians does not entirely match twentieth-century models. Many conversions were tribal in nature. That is, a king or leader would decide to make Christianity the tribal religion and his loyal followers were expected to follow suit. Motives for conversion varied, from actual personal conviction by a king, to desire to please a Roman wife (King Ethelbert of Kent in 599), to fear of the Lord evinced by demonstrations of spiritual power, to hopes for a military alliance with the Romans against other barbarians. Often a combination of motives prevailed. At any rate, followers were expected to do as the king did. Occasionally a Christian leader forced a tribe he defeated to become Christian as one of the consequences of loss.

We should not be too surprised to learn that the understanding of what it meant to become Christian was not very sophisticated. The earlier trend to ritualize continued. So, for many barbarians, becoming Christian meant that they had gone through the ceremony of baptism, usually conferred in unintelligible Latin. When the great Frankish conqueror Charlemagne (c. 742–814) forced the defeated Saxons to become Christians, for example, he ordered the Saxon army to march between two lines of Frankish warriors through a river as priests pronounced the baptismal formula. A charming story says that the Saxons kept their sword arms above the water so that part of them could continue to do "pagan" work— bloodshed. That this produced any change of heart among the converts is doubtful. But the Saxon story indicates that the warriors expected immersion to make a difference in the immersed parts of their bodies. Further, twentieth-century examples of mass tribal conversions in Irian Jaya (formerly western New Guinea) suggest that the program may work. Decades later a strong, vital Christian community exists where tribal chieftains decided that the group would become Christians.

Through such conversions, as in the earlier mass conversions after the Emperor Constantine, many misconceptions and semi-pagan ideas entered the community with the Germans. Adherence to Catholic Christianity indicated loyalty to a leader or king, so kings treated reverters to overt pagan practices as traitors. This drove paganism underground, from which it occasionally emerged as witchcraft. Some priests adapted pagan practices to Christian uses or permitted them to remain. For example, the Yule log, mistletoe, and Christmas trees all were originally part of druidic worship.

In addition, the general decay of public services like roads and police that accompanied the German migrations made life insecure and unpredictable. Education generally retreated and weakened throughout Europe as individuals sought more direct control over their survival by becoming farmers. Without a certain food supply from outside his own resources, the rational person spent time farming rather than studying. Fewer students chose careers in the church. Combined with the pressures of assimilating large numbers of pagan Germans, this caused a dilution in the preaching and teaching of the gospel. Around 600 an observer might have despaired about the future of Christians in Europe.

Rescue came from unlikely sources. Away off in the northwest corner of Europe the Irish and the Anglo-Saxons, who had never been under the control of the Roman Empire, had become vibrant and scholarly Christians (some through tribal conversions). Centered around monasteries, their stronger educational tradition continued, focusing on the study of Scripture in Greek. An evangelistic zeal was exercised first on the pagan Picts and Scots who shared their islands but after 590 turned toward the European continent to Christianize the Christians. The Irish and Anglo-Saxons understood the low level of Christian knowledge and vitality on the continent and felt called to do something about it.

The evangelistic method they chose may seem odd: They founded monasteries—frequently in out-of-the-way places. How could monks, whose chief duty was prayer, and ritual prayer at that, be evangelists? A group of Irish or Anglo-Saxon monks selected an area to settle. They needed to be self-sufficient economically and so produced their own food, clothing, and necessities. In addition to the feelings of awe with which local people normally regarded monks (they regarded celibacy as unnatural, if not supernatural), farmers noticed that the monks usually produced better crops than they. Conversations with the monk-farmers led to the willingness of locals to listen to their ideas and visit their chapel. This often annoyed the local priest, whose lifestyle rarely matched the gospel austerity of the monks. Monks also taught local boys who showed promise for literacy and potential for church service as priests or monks. Monks might actually also preach at local crossroads and gathering places. Gradually the influence of these monks moved out from the monastery to the countryside, and slowed and eventually reversed the repaganization of Europe. After 750 or so these monastic evangelists began to move into parts of Europe that had never been part of the Roman world—Germany, Poland, Czechoslovakia, and Scandinavia—to introduce the gospel to areas where it had rarely been preached. The northern pagans resisted and many Christians were martyred, but by about 1100 a Christian veneer covered all of Western Europe.

Theology

The development of theology in the Middle Ages was dynamic. It changed and grew over the course of a thousand years. What finally came to be thought of as typical Roman Catholic thinking was established by 1215. Most often, theology arose out of a crisis or challenge that forced Christians to confront new questions or to clarify old ones. The challenges were dealt with on at least two levels: formal (usually written) and informal or folk theology. First, we will highlight the framework of formal theology. In other sections we will look at the meaning of these ideas for ordinary people.

Salvation

At the heart of Christian experience is concern about personal salvation. "Where will you spend eternity?" is not a twentieth-century slogan written to be painted on barns, but rather the heartfelt quest of the ages. Christians teach that without Christ eternity will be spent apart from God, a condition of lonely torment. Salvation through Christ, then, means eternal fellowship with God, fulfilling the purpose for which humans were created. Medieval theologians maintained that salvation was by grace through the death and resurrection of Christ. Christ made salvation possible. But the individual had to cooperate in salvation by doing good works (working out salvation, Phil. 2:12) and acts of piety (alms-giving and prayer vigils, for example). Baptism was required to wash away original sin, so no unbaptized person would go to heaven. Once cleansed, the individual was responsible to balance his sins with good works. The Holy Spirit made this possible.

Nonetheless, few were able to reach death without unconfessed or unrepented sin in their lives. God, being completely holy and righteous, could not look upon sin, so logically the sinning Christian could not enter heaven until free from the taint of sin. Thus, there was a need to be purged of the least taint of sin. That need was met in the idea of *purgatory*, where believers underwent further training until they were able to love God with a perfect love and thus attain the *beatific vision*—they could look God full in the face in purity. Purgatory was not punishment, then, but character formation or basic training for heaven. And like basic training for military service, it was rigorous and something one would rather avoid or reduce.

The way to avoid or reduce time spent in purgatory was to be righteous. There were two paths to righteousness: One could live the gospel life—doing good works, ministering to the poor, serving others, and praying without ceasing. Or one could depend on the grace of Christ distributed through the sacraments administered by the institutional church. The paths were not exclusive, but complementary; Christians ought to follow both.

71

In general this became a sort of two-tiered system: The *religious* in full-time ministry attained more of their salvation by good and pious works; laypeople relied more on the sacraments and the church. Among the religious, the really first-class Christians were the monks, who could live according to the gospel in poverty and prayer. The *secular* clergy had to worry about administering parishes and ministering to a flock; they could not be quite so pure. Laypeople had to worry about feeding their children and other exigencies of life and were taught to be obedient to God's will as revealed through the church. For them, being faithful meant doing what the village priest taught them to do—reducing the amount of sin in their lives, doing penance, and participating in the sacraments.

Sacraments

In medieval Christian thinking the seven sacraments kept the believer in tune spiritually. They were the means of grace or the way God chose to bless the earthly faithful. They both signified and conveyed grace as spiritual food. Sacraments roughly corresponded to chronological periods of human life.

1. *Baptism* occurred at birth.
2. *Confirmation* came at the age of reason or when the child could be held morally accountable for personal behavior and decisions.
3. *Penance* and
4. *communion* provided the means for the accountable individual to deal with falling from a state of grace into sin.
5. *Marriage* or
6. *ordination* marked the point for young adults to decide how to serve God with the remainder of their earthly lives.
7. *Extreme unction* or *last rites* portrayed the church's ministry of grace to mortally ill persons as they lay at the brink of death.

From womb to tomb the faithful Christian was nurtured on the grace of God channeled through the church. What did these sacraments mean to people?

Baptism

The development of the idea of baptism follows a twisted path. Early Christians seem to have used the ceremony primarily as a public statement of the believer's identification with Christ and the church. Baptism in the Jewish tradition symbolized repentance and entry into the community by Gentile converts. Probably in the early Jewish Christian congregations this understanding was most common.

As Christians came more and more from the Gentile population, something of the ritualistic emphasis of Roman religion affected the believers as well. At least it becomes clear that some Christians viewed the ritual as efficacious in itself for salvation. The Emperor Constantine himself put off being baptized until his deathbed because he believed it washed away all sins, so he wanted to wait until he was unable to commit many more to get the whole lot taken care of at once.

By the Middle Ages infant baptism, usually by immersion, was the norm for children born to Christian parents. Both the formal and the folk views held that the ceremony represented God's grace washing away original or inherited sin and hell. Christ's grace entered the infant at that point and enabled a person truly to choose between right and wrong. Thereafter, the individual was responsible for his or her own particular sins. Fortunately, the church provided a system to take care of those sins—the sacramental system.

Confirmation

Confirmation became more important as baptism of infants became more common. Before 400 the adult convert entered into full membership in the Christian community upon a public declaration of faith through the act of baptism, which followed three years of instruction; medieval Christians, baptized as infants, were confirmed sometime after the age of seven, following a period of instruction in the faith. The Western church marked the ceremony by the bishop anointing the confirmand with oil, followed by first communion. Often the trip to the bishop's cathedral church, which could be up to 20 or 30 miles away—more than a day's walk—was the only time a peasant might leave the village of his or her birth. Roman Catholic theology now stresses that confirmation marks the coming of the Holy Spirit through the laying on of hands by the apostle Peter's spiritual descendants, the bishops, but that idea was less clear in the Middle Ages. Many people would have understood it then as a rite of passage, a Christian *bar mitzvah* that marked the initiation of the confirmand to full adult participation and responsibility in the church. So the rite was accompanied by as much celebration as the relatives could muster—new clothes for the confirmand, special foods, and a general party.

Penance

The gift of the Holy Spirit did not automatically turn believers into perfect beings. Medieval theology assumed that the Christian would continue to sin while on this side of glory. But the system of penance was developed to deal with that reality and to provide the faithful with continuing infusions of grace. Based on injunctions from the New Testament, penance consists of four steps. The sinner first must repent of sinful acts or thoughts; this was an inner change of heart and mind, sincere and uncoerced, without excuses or self-justification. Second, the believer must confess sins orally, revealing fully the real person. This honest humility allowed bearing one another's burdens (James 5:16). Whereas in the early centuries confession could be made to any fellow Christian, and in some areas took place in front of the whole congregation, Irish missionaries popularized private confession to a priest after 500. Eventually private confession became the norm. Third, following repentance and confession, there must be restitution, somehow making things right. For temporal sins the penitent made temporal restitution, returning stolen property, for example. For spiritual sins, such as blasphemy, the penance was designed to promote reflection and soul-searching. Medieval church leaders believed that living on bread and water, for example, was not punishment for sin, but rather an aid to reflection and spiritual discernment. Fourth, the individual is reconciled to God and the church through the Eucharist which renders one pure, holy, and acceptable.

In the early days, this pattern of penance was reserved for gross sins, such as reversion to pagan practices or obstinate quarreling with other Christians. But as private confession to a priest became standard, the practice of penance became more widespread. Instead of happening once or twice in a lifetime, more frequent confessions became common. Eventually, in 1215, the church required all Christians in good standing to confess to a priest at least once a year. More scrupulous or guilt-ridden believers might go weekly. When Martin Luther was a monk he frequently spent six hours a day in confession.

Eucharist

The central sacramental focus for the church of the Middle Ages was the Eucharist, also called Holy Communion, the Lord's Supper, or the Mass (from the Latin phrase *ita missa est*, "so go forth," with which the priest ended the service). Although it took a long time to define what was going on in the Mass (from the simple potlucks of the New Testament to the ringing bells and incense smells of a medieval high Mass), the element of mystery was clear from the beginning. Especially as the Latin of the ceremony came to bear less resemblance to the everyday language of the faithful, the atmosphere must have gotten spookier for the average swineherd or dung-hauler. Indeed, the doctrine of the Eucharist that the church eventually adopted had "magical" elements to it—the bread and wine turned into Jesus' flesh and blood when the priest said the right words, even though it still looked like bread and wine on the outside. And the peasant knew it was good spiritually to eat the bread, though eventually, to avoid spilling, only the priest took the wine. Somehow the Mass brought eternal life and the continuing power to live a Christian life.

The official teaching adopted at the Fourth Lateran Council in 1215, called transubstantiation, taught that in the Mass the *substance* or *real essence* (philosophically hearkening back to Platonic categories) of the bread and wine, was transformed into the real body and blood of Christ, even though the *accidents*, the appearance, remained the same. Thus the believer consumed the body of Christ. Jesus, after all, said, "This is my body. . . . This is my blood," and medieval Christians took those words literally. The Eucharist commemorated the sacrifice of Christ on the cross, obeyed his command to the disciples to continue the practice, and symbolized the idea that the church functioned as the body of Christ until his return. The celebration of the Lord's Supper reconciled believers to God and to one another.

Ordination

Marriage and ordination were complementary sacraments. Both were God's means to confer grace on the faithful, but rarely would an individual experience both. Ordination set one apart for special service within the church; in some ways it represented marriage as a bride to Christ. It was exclusive and could not be dissolved. Control over the sacraments accompanied the conferral of the symbol of priestly office, a chalice and the laying on of hands. Henceforth, the ordained person had divine authority to conduct the miracle of the Mass, not because of his personal righteousness or closeness to God, but because of the office itself.

Marriage

Marriage happened when two baptized individuals covenanted with each other to wed for life. In the early Middle Ages this created problems when couples exchanged vows just before intercourse, then had second thoughts about the commitment the next day. So practical safeguards were developed to reduce the likelihood of hasty decisions made in the heat of passion. It became customary for the couple to exchange their covenants publicly, at least before a priest and two other witnesses. Further, an attempt was made at what might be called premarital counseling, to make sure the couple understood the lifetime nature of their mutual commitment and marriage's sacramental nature as a type or living symbol of the union of Christ and his church. Properly covenanted marriages were indissoluble until the death of one of the partners, but there were many reasons to declare marriages null— duress, impotence of the male, or kinship closer than the fifth degree (sharing even a single ancestor as far as five generations back, a practical problem in small villages). Church ideas often conflicted with the traditions of patriarchy in European cultures, because the church insisted that young lovers of age could make a valid marriage without securing the consent of their fathers. This enraged fathers who hoped to unite lands or fortunes by judicious matings of their children. Thus the role of the go-between priest in Shakespeare's *Romeo and Juliet* reflects realistically how values taught by the church undermined traditional patriarchal values held by the common people.

Last Rites

Extreme unction as a sacrament stemmed from the teaching in James 5:14–15 that sick believers should be anointed with oil for healing and forgiveness of sin. In English it came to be called the *last* rites because it tended to be reserved for those in danger of death who had some expectation that healing might yet happen. Yet it was efficacious for removing the remains of sin, a concept not very well defined. It strengthened the sick in body to fight a spiritual fight against despair and to repent. An average medieval person likely perceived it as a forgiveness pill, administered at death to reduce time spent in purgatory.

Church year

Christians did not hesitate to develop their own celebrations and holidays to counter pagan festivities that they refused to attend in Roman times, or that they hoped to eliminate among the half-converted in the Middle Ages. Easter, the celebration of Jesus' Sunday resurrection and the foremost feast of the Christian year, followed the Jewish Passover according to the Scriptures. In northern Europe, however, its timing coincided with the coming of spring, so Easter absorbed some fertility customs featuring eggs and rabbits, the latter association because of rabbits' reputation for breeding prodigiously. The English name itself probably comes from Eostre, the Anglo-Saxon goddess of spring. In fixing the celebration of Christ's birth at December 25 Western Christians, sometime before 326, consciously chose the birthday festival of the sun-god, with its general merriment, gift-giving, and use of candles. The Roman mid-winter festival thus was gradually transferred to a Christian celebration. Pentecost fell at the Jewish harvest festival of the weeks or firstfruits, but the Christian version commemorated the extraordinary manifestation of the Holy Spirit in Acts 2—often called the birthday of the church.

Eventually, a whole series of seasons and days developed. Lent, the forty days preceding Easter, started as a period for candidates for baptism to reflect on what they were about to do and to repent of their past lives. Sometime before 600, all Christians began to keep Lent as a fast in preparation for Easter. Fasting meant they abstained from worldly luxuries, like meat, wine, or bathing, to focus on spiritual themes. Lent began with Ash Wednesday, when Christians were marked with ashes as penitents. Later in the Middle Ages, after 1050 or so, when the church was able to enforce the Lenten fast almost universally, Ash Wednesday was preceded by Carnival (Shrove Tuesday in England, Mardi Gras or Fat Tuesday in France). Apparently, Christians were advised to use up all the meat and fat in their households in preparation for the Lenten fast; in many places it became a veritable orgy of self-indulgence. Advent developed as a parallel to Lent to remind believers of the coming and the second coming of Christ.

Folk theology

Saints

Saints as special Christians originated as a group of heroes for ordinary Christians to model. Those martyred for the faith often excited great admiration. Only a small percentage of Christians died because of the persecutions during the Roman era, but their witness cheered their survivors. The lives and sufferings of these martyrs became examples of spiritual heroism. Official Roman Catholic teaching still emphasizes this modeling for average Christians.

Protestants born before 1955 have more likely heard of miracle stories and devotional practices that seemed to abuse the idea of sainthood. Praying to the saints, lighting candles before their images, the use of St. Christopher medallions as good-luck charms—all looked superstitious and far removed from what Protestants regarded as faith in a living Lord who was sole mediator between God and human beings. Certainly some of the abuse of the saints was due to a conflation of Christian and pagan ideas. Partially converted pagans were used to the ideas of spirits inhabiting springs,

Among a plethora of patron saints recognized in medieval churches were, from left, Apollinia (dentists) and Zita (domestic servants). (From Edith Simon, *The Saints* [London: Weidenfeld and Nicolson, 1987])

odd rock formations, and the like. It took little imagination to transfer characteristics of these local spirits to some of the dead Christian heroes extolled in legends and stories. And these saints always seemed a bit more approachable than the Great Judge of the Universe, as Christ was perceived.

Trial by ordeal

In contrast to the Romans, medieval Christians were skeptical about the ability of humans to really discern truth. So in judicial situations, rather than hoping that the reason and common sense of a judge could ferret out the truth among conflicting testimonies, the medieval pattern was to ask God to determine the truth. This took several forms. In *compurgation*, an accused person who could get some number of his neighbors to swear that he or she was not the kind of person to commit such an offense could be acquitted. Since they assumed that anyone swearing an oath falsely would be struck dead, perhaps even on the spot, this was not an empty exercise.

Trials by ordeal were based on the assumption that God would not allow the innocent to suffer. One example required the accused to pluck an object out of boiling water and carry it so many paces. His arm would be bound up and examined a few days later. If it was healing properly or unharmed, the accused was considered innocent; God had vindicated him. If not, clearly he was guilty. Another option was trial by water. First a pond was blessed to make it holy water. Then the accused was trussed up and tossed into the water. If he floated to the surface, he was guilty, for holy water would not receive an unconfessed perjurer. The innocent person who was received by the holy water and sank was dragged out soon, hopefully before drowning. After 1215, when there was a renewed understanding of Roman law, the church forbade these practices.

Structure of the church

As it became a fully developed and organized institution, particularly by the second half of the eleventh century, the structure of the church reflected the administrative style of the Roman Empire. It rose hierarchically from the lowly parish priest through bishops and archbishops to the singular earthly head of the church, the pope, with many intermediate gradations. The parish served by a priest usually encompassed one village with some outlying hamlets. Revenue from church land and the tithe (roughly 10 percent of the harvest) supported the priest and such parish works as charity. The local lord often appointed the priest in consultation with the bishop. Priests knew enough to read and often to write, but they were rarely highly educated. For a bright peasant boy with a gentle disposition a career in the church offered a way out of a life of agricultural toil and hearty coarseness.

A group of parishes constituted a diocese administered by a bishop. Traditionally, bishops had their headquarters in the old Roman cities at a cathedral church (one with a *cathedra*, a bishop's chair). The bishop had a great deal of power and authority. He supervised the lower clergy of the diocese. He administered the revenues and lands of the church in his diocese, a major responsibility. He presided over the ecclesiastical court for the diocese. Before 1050, bishops were the most powerful men in the church; after that date the growth of papal power and the reform of the church slightly reduced their powers. Originally the priests and people of the diocese elected the bishop. The dislocations and disruptions that contributed to the growth of feudalism eventually led to their virtual appointment by powerful local lords or kings. After the papal reforms of the eleventh century the priests attached to the cathedral church did the electing as representatives of the diocese. Sometimes the king nominated a candidate.

In theory, the archbishop stood over the bishops of his province or a cluster of dioceses called the archdiocese. In practice, the power of the archbishop depended primarily on his character and political skill. Bishops resisted any attempts by the archbishops to interfere in the internal workings of the diocese. The only formal privileges that distinguished the archbishop from the bishop were his right to call a provincial synod or meeting of bishops and his right to hear appeals from the bishops' courts. Archbishops also were more likely to have been to Rome to visit the pope, and sometimes they delivered messages for him.

Growth of the power of the pope

At the pinnacle of the church hierarchy sat the pope. Over the centuries church councils had adopted many of the ideas advocated by the bishop of Rome. This high theological batting average added to the prestige of the office and supplemented the claim of the Roman church leader to primacy among bishops. As early as 95, heads of the local congregation at Rome had asserted a special position among otherwise equal bishops. They based this primarily on Scripture, citing the special authority given Peter in Matthew 16:18–19 and the tradition that Peter was the first bishop of Rome. Therefore his authority passed down to the succeeding bishops of Rome through the laying on of hands.

In addition, of course, the central political role of Rome in the first three centuries and the later removal of the capital to Constantinople left the Roman bishop as the most important general leader in the West. When, in the seventh century, Muslims conquered three of the five major centers for Christians (Antioch, Alexandria, and Jerusalem), the bishops of Rome and Constantinople faced off as potential rivals. But the Eastern leader was frequently overshadowed by the emperor or had his actions constrained by political considerations. So, more often it was the Byzantine emperor who rivaled the bishop of Rome for ecclesiastical leadership. The Byzantines simply retained the Constantinian tradition that the emperor was the head of the church (the bishop of Constantinople functioned as a minister for religious affairs, to carry out policy and administer the church).

The reemergence of strong secular leaders in the West led to a similar rivalry. These rulers wanted to control the bishops—and the lands and knights assigned to the bishops—in their realms. Out of that conflict the bishop of Rome emerged as the clearly recognized spokesman and leader of the Western church. The removal of the emperors from the West after 476 left a vacuum of authority that bishops of Rome filled with varying success. The alliance of the Frankish kings with the Roman bishops in 751 added practical military and political clout. But the collapse of the Frankish Empire and the Norse invasions undercut this support, and the office lost much of its luster.

·The low point came in the early tenth century, when selection of the bishop became a political football disputed among leading Roman families. A Roman woman, Marozia, at various times secured the election as bishop of (1) her lover (Sergius III, 904–11), (2) her mother's reputed lover (John X, 914–28), and (3) her illegitimate son by Sergius III (John XI, 931–35). Eventually, her grandson, John XII (955–64), was deposed by the German leader Otto I on charges of bribery, incest, and keeping a brothel in the papal residence.

Otto's intervention marked the beginning of a century of attempts by German monarchs to exert an influence on the selection of the Roman bishop. Much of their interest was baldly political, but some of it was due to the impact of the Cluniac monastic reforms on the bishops in the German principalities. The Cluniacs hoped to reform the church, first through monks who lived up to the rule of Benedict, then through imposing high (even monastic) standards on the secular clergy. The Cluniacs began their reform of monasteries by claiming to be under the authority of the pope, rather than the local bishop. At a time of weakness in the papacy this allowed them to function essentially without supervision. Therefore, it was logical for them to hope to begin the reform of the secular clergy at the theoretical top, the bishop of Rome.

Eventually, Pope Leo IX (1049–54) personally transmitted the reform ideals to the church by traveling to various parts of Europe and confronting clergy over abuses, including the buying and selling of church offices. Other efforts followed. In 1057, a church council transferred the election of the pope from the Roman people to a council of the "cardinal" bishops (originally, those from dioceses near Rome). Removing the papal election from the direct influence of Roman political factions and German monarchs enhanced the prestige of the papacy. Such prestige became the major weapon in the struggle that ensued between the church and the secular authorities.

At issue was the appointment of bishops. This is called the *investiture controversy* because appointment was symbolized by investing the new bishop with the ring and shepherd's crook of his office. The church wanted bishops who were spiritually called to ministry. Kings and princes were accustomed to using bishops as secular administrators of their interests in an area in return for revenues from the land. Rulers did not necessarily object to bishops with a spiritual calling; they just wanted to be sure that none of their rivals' relatives got the office.

The church's weapons in the conflict were moral. First, excommunication excluded a recalcitrant ruler from all Christian fellowship and freed from their vows those who had promised him loyalty. Second, placing a city or area under interdict halted all church activities, threatening the eternal well-being of all citizens. This brought mass pressure on an unbelieving ruler. Third, bishops occasionally anointed a rival ruler as legitimate, suggesting that good Christian warriors should support the rival. Against this the secular rulers had mere military prowess and force. By 1200 the popes had won, though not without struggle.

Crafty rulers could occasionally seize the moral high ground. During a conflict between Pope Gregory VII (1073–85) and the German Emperor Henry IV (1056–1106), Gregory excommunicated Henry. Threatened by a revolt of his subordinate princes, Henry appeared as a penitent, barefoot in sackcloth before the gate of a mountain castle where Gregory was staying. As a priest Gregory was obliged to grant forgiveness to a repentant sinner and to restore him to the church. He did, however, make Henry wait three days in the snow before granting absolution. Later, when his situation was less precarious, Henry ignored papal decrees and took Gregory captive. But the rest of Henry's reign was rife with rebellions, so he never fully enjoyed his victory.

For the average medieval Christian, most of this hierarchy of the church was so distant that it was not even an abstraction. For most, the church meant the parish priest, who was around the village daily. The Christian might not even see the bishop more than five or ten times, and contacts would be rare with the various specialists who served the bishop—summoners who brought people to the bishop's court, pardoners, and an occasional friar.

Reformers

The greatest challenge that the institutional church faced in the Middle Ages came from its interconnection with the feudal system, the intricate societal pattern that mixed landholding with political and military power. Following the barbarian migrations, the decaying Roman economy abandoned any system of coinage. Farmland, which could produce usable wealth (food and fiber), became the dominant economic resource for medieval Europe. Whoever controlled land thus controlled wealth. Pious believers often willed lands to the church, so eventually the church became the major landowner in Europe. Church leaders needed to administer these legacies as careful stewards and to deal with the income in goods that was produced. Their economic interests were similar to those of other landholders.

At the same time, political and military leaders wanted to control lands for themselves. The disappearance of money meant that a king who wanted to field an army had to find other ways to pay his soldiers. Income from lands became the obvious resource. Therefore, someone aspiring to be a military leader needed lots of land.

Technological changes made landholding even more important in the eighth century. Armored cavalry, what later became the knights, emerged as the decisive element in military tactics. But this required full-time warriors constantly in training, who could not actually do the farm work. In addition, the armor and horses were expensive to purchase and maintain, requiring additional productive land. The Frankish leader Charles Martel (689–741) solved his land needs by confiscating land from the church, but later lords simply required the church to supply a certain number of knights from its lands. Thus, the institutional church found itself enmeshed in the complex and bloody world of feudalism.

Many medieval Christians did not think that was right. The most common reform theme in the Middle Ages was the hope to diminish connections with the world that were inconsistent with the teachings of Christ. Initially, these reformers worked to purify the monasteries of their connection to the feudal system (see box 4.1). Later they turned to the church in general, focusing on the leadership of the pope. Change took a long time and was never entirely successful, but reform became a major theme within the church.

Doctrinal definitions

Many, but not all, doctrines or teachings that distinguish Roman Catholics from other Christians stem from the Middle Ages. Not until

1870 were Catholics required to believe that the pope could speak infallibly in certain circumstances. The particular position ascribed to the Virgin Mary has developed mostly after the Protestant Reformation of the sixteenth century. Patterns of piety, such as refraining from red meat on Fridays to honor the Lord's death, have varied from country to country and over time. But the core of Roman Catholic doctrine developed in the crucible of the thousand-year Middle Ages.

As in other ages, medieval Christians formulated doctrine in response to challenge. After the initial centuries of sorting out the differences between Christian and pagan thinking, most of the challenges were internal, attempts to clarify which views held among Christians were most correct. Internal challenges came from two sources: (1) the gradual change in perspective between the Greek-speaking Eastern Mediterranean and the West, where Latin became the dominant language of the church, and (2) the series of broad reform movements designed to purge the church of worldly laxity and pagan leftovers. Coloring these changes was the taint of politics and economic necessity.

Differences between the East and the West stemmed from a variety of contrasts. Greek is a more subtle and complex language than Latin; it can express nuances of meaning impossible in Latin. After 400, the Eastern church was more closely tied to the emperor in Constantinople, whereas the bishops, especially of Rome, functioned more independently in the West. For complex cultural reasons, Eastern Christians preferred a more spiritual or mystical religion, a residue, some argue, of Gnosticism. The Latin church was more pragmatic and administrative.

4.1. Cluniacs

The monks of Cluny should serve as an enduring inspiration to those who would see reformation in the church.

In 909 a group of seven men, who wanted to lead a righteous life in the midst of a world given over to debauchery and chaos, left a lax monastery to found a new abbey in France. The founders especially wanted to avoid entanglement with the worldly system in which monasteries achieved wealth through land holdings within the feudal system. Those at Cluny Abbey determined to lead the life of poverty and purity embodied in the Benedictine rule. Within 150 years the Cluniac movement had grown to a network of communities (almost 1100 at its height) spread over France, Italy, England, Germany, and Spain. Their example single-handedly changed the nature of Western Christianity.

Their example was followed by other monasteries and became the standard by which even parish clergy were judged.

The impact of these cultural differences was seen primarily in three areas:

1. The use of images as devotional aids.
2. The role of the bishop of Rome in relation to the emperor at Constantinople.
3. An obscure issue about the relation of Christ and God the Father. Was Christ "of like substance" (Greek, *homoiousis*), the understanding Easterners preferred? Or was Christ "of the same substance" (*homoousis*) with the father, the conception adopted in Western theology?

The spiritualizing flavor of Eastern Christianity coincided with the need of the emperors to weaken the power of large monastic estates in what was becoming the Byzantine Empire (*Byzantine* from *Byzantion*, the Greek village that had existed near the site of Constantine's city). Monastic workshops produced a steady flow of *icons* (Greek, *eikōn*, "image") of important figures in Christian history, especially the madonna and Child, John the Baptist, and the crucified Christ. Christians used these as devotional aids on which to focus their prayers and meditations. Opponents of the practice known as *iconoclasts* ("image-breakers") charged that the practice verged on idolatry—that devotion to the image itself or the person it represented replaced the pure worship of God as spirit. A series of emperors supported the iconoclastic view and ordered images removed from all places of public worship. Riots ensued throughout the Empire and the bishops of Rome rebuked the emperors. Doctrinally, the Western position asserted that if Christ could not be represented as fully human in a three-dimensional statue, the Nicene assertion that he was equally God and man was cast into doubt. That, they argued, carried Gnostic implications. The Eastern church eventually accepted two-dimensional figures that focused on the moral and spiritual qualities of the person portrayed to avoid idolatry. This compromise vindicated the views of the bishop of Rome. The tendency of some believers to attribute miracles to the images, however, continued to make some leaders in both branches nervous, at least officially.

Such tendencies toward superficial worship frequently prompted reform movements to promote clearer definitions of doctrine, especially during the central centuries of the Middle Ages (900–1200).

Architecture

Almost equal in importance with worship to the medieval Christian was the building where worship was carried out. To understand why the setting of worship was so significant we should consider the difficulty

An early Portuguese church is an example of the massive, fortress-like Romanesque architectural style. (Chester E.V. Brummel, in Carlos de Azevedo, *Churches of Portegal* [New York: Scala, 1985])

One of the most ornate of Europe's Gothic cathedrals is Notre Dame in Paris.

of conveying gospel truths to illiterate people where actual Bible study is impossible or impractical. A modern parallel might be the education of preliterate children. While medieval folk had the maturity and intelligence of adults, their reading skills were less than those of a preschooler. They rarely even saw written material, whereas four-year-olds in industrial cultures are bombarded daily with text in advertising, cartoons, and the like. How do educators teach four-year-olds? They use audio-visual materials—filmstrips, posters, videotapes, and even old-fashioned flannelgraphs—to portray visually the truths of Scripture. In exactly the same way, medieval designers used visual stimuli to remind and teach Scripture, primarily in the church building itself. Their audio-visuals were statues and carvings, paintings, and stained glass. In fact, the great cathedrals of the later Middle Ages have been characterized as "Bibles in stone" because they portray the most important stories of Scripture on various parts of the edifice. Local parish churches would mimic those features as much as possible—usually at least in a statue of Jesus, the Virgin Mary, or the saint after whom the parish was named.

Two styles, Romanesque and Gothic, dominated ecclesiastical architecture in the Middle Ages. Romanesque or "Roman-like" buildings were characterized by rounded arches and heavy walls. Romanesque churches looked and felt solid and secure, God's fortresses against the surrounding world. Given the violence and disorder of the early Middle Ages, that solidity may have comforted Christians. God and Christ could be portrayed as a strong King or Emperor, protecting his subjects against earthly and demonic enemies. Worshipers in such buildings experienced a sense of God's power and their weakness before him. Such impressions, however, did not lend themselves to feelings of intimacy with Christ. More often, the fear of the Lord resembled terror. Jesus was often seen triumphant on his throne, condemning the world as a stern and mighty Judge. Even the righteous cowered before his eternal judgment; the most courageous believer would find it difficult to get close to such a majestic figure.

Sometime after 1150 changes in construction technology, in economic prosperity, and in Christian piety combined to produce a new architectural style that gradually supplanted the Romanesque in church buildings. While the name *Gothic* implied barbarian in contrast to the "civilized" Romanesque, this style soared high into the air with pointed arches and swaths of light-capturing windows. In contrast to the squat, fortress-like Romanesque churches, Gothic churches echoed the form of praying hands or the flight of the soul heavenward. Even today, the eyes of anyone entering these cathedrals are drawn up, away from the grubby earth. The worshiper feels awe, not so much at power or might, but at the beauty of it all. Stained glass artists began to represent Christ less often as the Judge, but more often as the Good Shepherd, the Suffering Servant or,

Christ the judge sits at the apex of "The Last Judge" tympanum at Rheims. Beneath him the dead rise from their graves. At the next level the blessed sit on thrones. At the bottom saved souls are being brought to Abraham's bosom, and the condemned are dragged by devils to the cauldron of hell. Seated angels look on from the arch of the doorway.

especially, Mary's Baby. Jesus became easier to identify with, less fearsome, more loving, not so distant, someone who had a mother. Jesus became someone to love, not just to fear or respect.

This feeling went beyond the stone of the building to the passionate preaching of Bernard of Clairvaux and the Cistercian order of monks. Their message wooed Christians to a new, more emotional piety in the eleventh century (see box 4.2).

Bernard of Clairvaux (1090–1153), a French reformer and mystic, founded the Cistercian monastic order. (Billy Graham Center)

Monks

Monks and monasteries mightily shaped the medieval West. If the Catholic Church was the dominant institution of the European Middle Ages, monasticism was the dynamic force shaping the church from within. Ironically, at its roots monasticism sought to escape the restraints and bonds of institutional Christianity, to protest the bureaucratic structure and stability that began to characterize Christianity as early as the third century. The earliest monks took their cue from John the Baptist and Jesus and went to the desert to pray and to "pommel the body" (1 Cor. 9:27, RSV). Often, they practiced fasting, sleep deprivation, and other actions designed to discipline their bodies away from worldly comforts. Ascetic Essenes and some Pharisees demonstrated that impulse within Judaism and made an impression on self-gratifying pagans. Men and women sought desert solitude, partly to protest moral laxity in the church during periods of toleration and partly to escape the temptations (especially sexual) produced by that laxity. Of course, many found that the temptation continued from within and turned to more direct conflict with evil. Even today monks vow to "do battle with the devil."

Most desert monks lived in solitude, but some drawn to asceticism began to wonder how such a lifestyle could fulfil commands to "forsake not the assembling of yourselves together" or to share communion fellowship. Eventually (in about 320) a converted army officer, Pachomius (c. 290–346), organized a communal monastic venture in Egypt. There monks were subject to the discipline of the community to avoid extremes of bodily abuse. Periodic fellowship was required. Later, Basil (330–379)

4.2. Bernard of Clairvaux

Bernard, abbot of the Cistercian Abbey of Clairvaux (1090–1153), was the most important preacher of the Middle Ages.

As a twenty-two-year-old in 1113, he joined the recently formed Cistercian order, which sought to live by a strict interpretation of the Benedictine rule. They avoided all meat, built plain and simple chapels, and required all monks to do manual agricultural work. Bernard thrived under the harsh asceticism, and his faith was heartfelt and mystical. He viewed philosophy as vain and foolish and had little use for a rationalistic approach to God.

Bernard believed that humans best understood God by loving him passionately. His preaching sought to produce that emotional response in his listeners. He was popular with all classes, although he felt more at home with peasants and shepherds than with kings. Realizing that many medieval folk feared Christ as the righteous Judge, Bernard sought to soften their hearts by picturing Christ as a babe in Mary's arms and causing them to recall the tender feelings of their own mothers. He popularized the role of Mary in personal devotions until eventually her veneration rivaled that of Jesus.

Bernard exhibited in his own character the compassion he preached about in God, particularly toward the poor. He wrote, "The church is resplendent in its walls and wholly lacking in its poor. It gilds its stones and leaves its children naked. With the silver of the wretched it charms the eyes of the rich."

Bernard was a gifted writer, as shown in translations of his well-loved hymns, "Jesus, Thou Joy of Loving Hearts," and "O Sacred Head, Now Wounded":

Jesus, thou joy of loving hearts,
Thou Fount of life, thou Light of men,
From the best bliss that earth imparts
*We turn unfilled to thee again.**

O sacred Head, now wounded
With grief and shame weighed down;
Now scornfully surrounded
With thorns, thine only crown;
O sacred Head, what glory,
What bliss till now was thine!
Yet, though despised and gory,
*I joy to call thee mine.***

Bernard wrote voluminously in letters and sermons. He attacked vigorously any movement or idea that he thought threatened the faith of the simple. He advised kings and rulers. His intervention determined the outcome of a disputed papal election in 1130. His spiritual vigor and love changed the face of European Christianity by reviving the personal and passionate side of faith. His preaching attracted hordes of young men to the Cistercian order and it soon became a powerful agency of reform and revival throughout Europe.

*From a translation by Ray Palmer, 1858.

**From a translation by Paul Gerhardt, 1656, and James Waddell Alexander, 1830.

added an emphasis on serving others and tied monasteries administratively to the broader church, under the supervision of the local bishop. The Eastern (Orthodox) churches adopted Basil's pattern, whereas the Western (Catholic) church modified it.

The monastic *rule* developed by Benedict of Nursia (c. 480–c. 547) became the standard for the West. Benedict, like Basil, intended to reduce abuses and provide a way of life that could be endured. He advocated a moderate lifestyle, one that resembled that of the average Italian peasant of his day. The simple food and clothing suggested were quite sufficient for a modest lifestyle. Only later did those of more affluent eras regard the rule as particularly harsh or sacrificial. Adequate food and rest, combined with the requirement that monks work as well as pray, produced a stable, self-sustaining community. The monk's day was structured around prayer and work. In accord with Psalm 119:164 ("Seven times a day I praise you"), monks gathered for corporate prayer, usually intoning a liturgical prayer or a psalm, on the assumption that God gave perfect prayers in the Psalms. They arose for prayer in the middle of the night (*nocturns*), went back to sleep until first light (*lauds*), meditated privately till sun up (*prime*), breakfasted and worked until about 9 A.M. (*terce*), worked until noon (*sext*), ate and sometimes napped until mid-afternoon (*none*), worked until sundown (*vespers*), supped and went to *complines* before bed. The routine varied from monastery to monastery and season to season, and some monks would miss one service or another to do their work. But the system allowed a balanced life of work, prayer, and rest, with little chance to engage in extreme asceticism.

The *abbot* ("father") governed the monastery absolutely, but he was elected by the monks. The rule specified that he should be chosen for his kindness and compassion toward the others and for his humility. An individual wishing to join the community tried it out for a while before he was allowed to make a lifetime commitment. On taking his vows he gave up control of his personal property to the group, so that all his needs were met by the community. Monks stayed under the control of the monastery they joined for life. The work performed by monks varied. The monastery needed to be self-supporting, so much of the work involved farming and tending animals. Some monks would specialize in cooking and food handling (everyone took turns serving the food). Copying books and manuscripts also counted as manual labor; in fact, it was considered arduous because of the concentration required. But copying required literacy, so monks also engaged in education. Monks conducted what little education occurred in Europe between 600 and 1150.

Most monks were not priests. Priesthood required ordination, and each monastery had only a few ordained priests to celebrate Mass.

Neither were they laypeople, for in the Middle Ages anyone under the authority and protection of the church was considered clergy. The church referred to monks as *regular clergy* because they lived according to a rule (Latin, *regula*). Parish priests were *secular clergy*, since they lived in the world. Informally, at least, medieval people regarded monks as heroic models for other Christians to emulate. Monks often felt that theirs was the only way to live the gospel life and to fully follow Jesus' commands. As celibates, monks were free from the need to support a family. Without the baggage of family ties they could more easily defend themselves against the random violence of the age. They could follow the precepts of the Sermon on the Mount. Men of scholarly or gentle temperament found in the monastery a refuge from the more brutal aspects of medieval life.

Monasteries attracted serious Christians who believed the monastic way of life fit God's will for humankind more closely than did other patterns. In the course of the Middle Ages monastic reformers encouraged other parts of the church to follow their patterns. Monks eventually persuaded the church to make celibacy mandatory for all clergy. They urged the disentanglement of church officials from secular political and economic affairs. Anglo-Saxon and Irish monastic missionaries probably introduced the practice of private confession that eventually became standard.

Most monks seem to have come from noble families. Rarely would a peasant's son be recognized as having the temperament or desire to enter a monastery, though bright ones might become parish priests. Perhaps because of this family connection to the military class, people thought of monks as "prayer warriors," fighting for the spiritual welfare of Christians just as the knights fought to protect Christians physically.

Establishments for women paralleled those of the monks. Nuns would need a male priest to do the Mass, but otherwise strove toward self-sufficiency. Their routine of prayer, work, and rest was similar, although the work they did often excluded copying and emphasized more feminine tasks, such as sewing and caring for the sick and dying. To some extent, nunneries served as dumping grounds for unmarried noblewomen.

Friars

A late medieval variation of the monastic life were the friars, who kept monastic vows but traveled about. The characteristic groups for this movement were the *Franciscans* and the *Dominicans*. Although initially the church hierarchy was suspicious of these groups, they eventually proved useful in combating heresy and in missionary activity.

4.3. Francis of Assisi

Giovanni de Bernardone (1182–1226) further developed the piety advocated by Bernard of Clairvaux. Better known as Francis ("Frenchie") of Assisi, he spread the message of passionate devotion to Christ beyond the cloistered Cistercian monks to laypeople and a new kind of order—the friars.

Francis contributed to changes in Christian emphasis for the monastic orders and the parish system. Previously both had been conducted within a totally rural pattern of life. Now they had to take into account the newly developing urban centers that were establishing a new way of life for Europeans.

Raised in an upper-middle-class family, Francis embarked on a career as a soldier. He served a year as a prisoner of war, suffered severe illness, and then returned to the fight. A series of visions, however, convinced him that God had a special call on his life. Once, when Francis was praying in a dilapidated church, Christ addressed him from the crucifix and told him to rebuild the church. Taking this message quite literally, Francis sold some of the cloth from his father's warehouse to raise funds to rebuild the chapel where he had been praying.

Called before the local bishop to answer for the theft of his father's goods, Francis asserted that God was his father and renounced all family ties and material possessions. He worked on repairing church buildings for awhile but then heard the version of the Great Commission found in Matthew 10:9–11 that commands the disciples not to take money or extra goods with them and to stay with whomever welcomes them. Francis believed that this was his call to the gospel life and began to preach to laypeople in the towns.

When a number of men joined Francis they went to get the pope's approval for their new order, the Brothers Minor or Lesser Brothers. Similar groups that emphasized preaching and poverty had been declared heretical, but the *friars* (from the Latin *fratres*, "brothers") asserted their compliance with church authority and were approved in 1210.

Essentially, the Franciscans were lay street preachers who were supposed to work each day for their daily bread but to own nothing either as individuals or as an order. Only if they could find no work were they allowed to beg for the day's need. The goal was to imitate Christ as literally as possible.

Modern writers have often portrayed Francis as a simpleton and nature freak. While he may have preached to the birds and is alleged to have convinced a wolf to repent of sheep-killing, he had more in mind than a romantic appreciation of nature. Francis stressed the created order to refute a current reappearance of the Gnostic heresy that rejected the material world. In his preaching and action Francis taught that the material world—including animals, sun, and moon—were part of God's good creation.

His intense identification with Christ culminated in the appearance of *stigmata* (wounds like those of Christ in the hands, feet, side, and sometimes the brow) after a period of prayer. Since that time stigmata have appeared more frequently, usually among Italian Catholics, but even

Francis of Assisi (1182–1226) organized Franciscan monastic orders for men and women, stressing preaching and caring for the poor. (Billy Graham Center)

among Texas Baptists. In the case of Francis the wounds never healed and constantly oozed blood; this probably weakened him and contributed to his death.

A second contribution to his death was the dissension that broke out among his followers. Francis was a dramatic, charismatic leader, but he lacked organizational skills. When the Brothers Minor grew beyond a handful and spread geographically, problems developed. Franciscans were supposed to be obedient, but to whom? They were supposed to preach the true gospel against heretics, but where were they to learn the details of Catholic ortho-

doxy? How could they study if they had no books or dormitories?

Eventually, a majority of the brothers elected to bring more structure and hierarchy. They could own property as a group (not as individuals) and, later, brothers began to study at the newly emerging universities. Francis was disgusted and heartbroken at these events and withdrew from active participation about three years before his death. A minority of Franciscans, known as the "spirituals," maintained the peculiarities of the early days and vigorously resisted attempts to make them conform until they were declared heretics and exterminated in the fourteenth century.

Parish discipline

The average medieval person felt the impact of the church on his or her life through worship and church discipline. The institutional church throughout the Middle Ages faced the continual challenge to encourage Christian behavior. Not only did the church try to inculcate a Christian worldview, but it also sought to cultivate the theological virtues of faith, hope, and love. For many people, that translated into rules of behavior, taught positively by examples from Scripture and the lives of the saints, and negatively through the prescription of penance for disapproved behaviors. To assist parish priests, suggestions for appropriate penances were collected in lists called *penitentials*. From these we can deduce the kinds of behaviors that most concerned church people, although we cannot be so sure what the laity thought. Not surprisingly, sins of the flesh figure prominently in the penitentials. Sexual sins—adultery, fornication (homosexual and heterosexual acts treated essentially equally), rape, abortion, contraception, and bigamous marriage—appear frequently, but the penance for them was less severe than for some other crimes. For example, the English penitential attributed to Theodore, first Archbishop of Canterbury, prescribed seven years' penance for adultery. Murderers did penance for seven to ten years; those who shed blood in warfare at least forty days. Apparently shedding blood in war was not justified or excused; it was still regarded as sin. Thievery entailed penances of three to seven years, depending on the circumstances of the theft. It was a more serious crime to steal from a church.

Some canonical or liturgical penances indicate the reverence medieval theologians held toward the Eucharist. Anything that hinted at disrespect needed to be curtailed immediately. A priest who mislaid the host, so that rodents ate it, was supposed to do penance for three weeks. Someone who ate an animal killed by a predator did forty days' penance (based on levitical laws). Fasting on Sunday (a feast day) required a fast for the rest of the week.

Doing penance could involve a variety of spiritually beneficial acts. Fasting usually meant living on bread and water, not as punishment but for spiritual purification. Extensive prayer vigils or sacrificial alms-giving might also help to correct the crookedness of soul that required repentance. Penitents usually were restricted from full participation in the life of the church. For example, they might have to stand apart from other communicants at the Mass. Some might even be denied entry to the church building for a time. Eucharist for them might be restricted to major feasts, such as Easter or Christmas. The ultimate goal of acts of penance, however, was to restore the sinner to full fellowship with other Christians through repentance, confession, and restitution.

The worship experience of medieval Christians varied widely from parish to parish. The central drama was the communion liturgy, which was based on the Roman Mass. There were some regional variations, especially in Frankish areas. Gradually the service developed into a form that would be recognizable to modern Roman Catholics, except that most of it was in Latin. As vernacular languages changed and bore less and less resemblance to their Latin roots, the service must have become more mysterious to laypeople. Even some priests learned the service by rote, not really knowing what they were doing or what the phrases they chanted meant. If a person attended Mass at a cathedral church, however, the bare-bones service was replaced by one rich in sumptuous textures of fabrics, smells of incense, and music by well-trained musicians and choirs. Combined with the ambiance created by Gothic architecture, this must truly have been an emotionally uplifting experience.

Heresy

Heresy provoked major concern throughout the medieval era. The kinds of heresies that arose varied. Some involved ceremonial and liturgical issues; the church in England in the 600s spent much energy deciding between the Roman and the Irish technique for determining the date of Easter. The Roman system eventually won at the Synod of Whitby in 664. Many heresies were administrative. The twelfth-century Waldensians, for example, initially became heretics for refusing to accept the authority of the pope to regulate their preaching. As with several other movements, the Waldensians' initial rejection of the institutional church's administrative authority eventually led them to challenge its doctrinal authority. This sent them in the direction of another type of heresy—theological teaching that contradicted the consensus of the church. Contemporary Christians usually think of this latter type of heresy, but medieval church people rarely distinguished among the meanings.

The *inquisition* became a tool for rooting out heresy after about 1200. In general, treatment of heretics grew increasingly harsh. To people in the Middle Ages heresy was as feared as a deadly infectious disease. One reason modern people tend to tolerate a wide variety of views is that they rarely care deeply about the consequences of such views. But if a virulent, highly contagious disease arose to threaten them they would react with far more emotion to carriers, especially those who refused to quit spreading the disease. Quarantine, protective custody, treatment with medications, therapeutic surgery—all the techniques of a modern public health system would be mustered to combat the outbreak. Rights to individual freedom and self-determination might be set aside on behalf of the public good.

Actually, medieval church leaders viewed heresy as worse than an infectious disease. A plague threatened the temporal body, but heresy infected the immortal soul of the heretic and the heretic's deluded followers. The heretic needed to repent, confess, and be restored to fellowship. Persuasion was the only method to secure reversion to true faith. Torture was allowed once in an interrogation, but a confession secured under torture had to be confirmed voluntarily later without duress. Unre-

"We're working on a promising new treatment for heresy." (New Yorker)

pentant heretics had to be removed from the community. Usually this meant long-term confinement in a monastic cell, a "penitentiary."

Since heresy was a crime as well as a sin, sometimes the state intervened to execute the unrepentant heretic for treason. A second lapse into heresy after repentance led to immediate execution because of the danger of spreading the infection. Certainly not everyone accused of heresy ended up being burned at the stake. In fact, evidence suggests that many were acquitted absolutely, and others were assigned relatively mild penance, although they were watched carefully for any evidence of a relapse. Inquisitors bore culpability if they caused someone to bear false witness; they had a vested interest in securing honest testimony. The worst abuses of the inquisition happened, not in the Middle Ages but in Renaissance Spain, where the monarchs Ferdinand and Isabella used the inquisition for political purposes to enforce unity on the formerly independent Iberian kingdoms.

More heretics died in straightforward military campaigns conducted by the secular leaders under the authorization of church. One of the most famous was the series of Albigensian Crusades (1204–29). Forces from northern France commissioned by a representative of the pope fought against heretics and the political authorities who protected them in southern France. The northerners had other motives beside pure piety; the pope offered them title to any lands they could seize from heretics. When the population of the town of Béziers, both Catholics and heretics, sought sanctuary in the cathedral, the military leaders of the crusade asked the papal legate how they should distinguish the Catholics from the heretics. He replied, "Kill them all, for God will know his own."

Mysticism

The Franciscan spirituals were tied into a broad movement in the thirteenth century that is often called mysticism. In general, people who participated in this movement focused on the aspects of God and Christian life which were beyond (not counter to) reason. Some participants experienced visions and revelations; some prophesied against a corrupt and wealthy church. All emphasized the experience of God's love over its intellectual and doctrinal definition and description. One mystic, Joachim of Fiore (c. 1135–1202), wrote of a series of revelations he experienced and by which he believed he could interpret Scripture. The Joachimites believed that a new age of the Holy Spirit would begin in the year 1260, when Christians would no longer need the mediations of church and sacraments to live in God's love. Needless to say, his ideas were condemned by church leaders and philosophers alike.

More moderate mystics took to living in household communities where they shared lives of prayer and hymn singing, while maintaining their occupations in the town. Usually celibate, these groups sought to enhance personal spiritual development. Groups of male Beghards, female Beguines, and such others as the Brethren of the Common Life emphasized poverty, personal piety, and love of the group over liturgical or sacramental piety. These groups continued into the Reformation period and most frequently developed along the Rhine River.

Economic changes

During the later Middle Ages, many changes transformed the pattern of European life. From a rural society dominated by the feudal aristocracy, Europe became a culture dominated increasingly by urban merchants. Most people continued to live by farming; the triumph of urban mercantilism was not complete until the twentieth century. The cultural dominance of cities became more obvious during the Renaissance, but the groundwork was laid during the medieval period, especially with the invention of capitalism.

While the earliest written records appear to be inventory lists, and the idea of private enterprise is as old as civilization itself, the specific pattern called *capitalism* is relatively recent. Capitalism is the idea that one should invest profits to make more profits, usually investing in machines or other means of producing more to sell. Before the thirteenth century, profits were normally consumed—either at banquets where the merchant feted the whole town, or as a gold or silver plate that could be displayed on the fireplace mantle, or in buying a country estate so the merchant could look like a respectable gentleman farmer. Rich people were expected to display generosity; if they did not, their excess could be confiscated by the church and distributed to the needy. Thus, social expectations dragged significantly on the merchants' ability to reinvest profits.

Further, church law forbade Christians to charge other Christians interest on loans (based on Jesus' commands in Luke 6). This discouraged the pooling of money for investment and slowed economic development. Those caught charging interest could suffer the same penalty as a heretic, so subterfuge was often used. Jews were allowed to charge interest on loans (but not to other Jews) and had few other occupations open to them because Christian oaths were involved in land holding and most crafts. Jews also were not subject to church discipline. So the medieval image of the Jewish moneylender was not entirely false, nor was it entirely voluntary on the part of the Jews.

On the other hand, medieval Christians believed that merchants were entitled to a fair profit and theologians spent centuries trying to define a just price. If someone charged a price that exceeded the cost of the materials and the labor to make it, was that stealing from the purchaser in some way? Eventually the theologians decided that the market price was ordinarily the just price, assuming there was no manipulation of the market such as hoarding to create artificial scarcity.

Most medieval peasants saw the merchants as greedy and sneaky. The feudal nobles viewed them as stingy, ill-born, and a threat to their monopoly of economic power. It took centuries for businessmen to become respectable, and even then it occurred primarily in urban areas. Even Martin Luther in the sixteenth century still despised merchants and capitalism and seriously doubted that God's grace could encompass them. Not until John Calvin preached that all callings are holy did a sizable portion of Europe's population accept the idea that businesspeople were not sleazy and fundamentally anti-Christian.

Universities

Medieval Christians invented the modern system of higher education. While individual Romans had sought tutors for advanced studies, Europeans in the Middle Ages brought students together in groups to follow a prescribed course of study leading to a recognized degree or certificate—

A medieval woodcut indicates the honor that has been accorded to Thomas Aquinas (1224–1274) as the foremost medieval scholar. (Harvard University)

the pattern currently in use. While only a tiny fraction, even of the elite, actually attended universities, these institutions were both a symptom and a cause of many changes in the lives of medieval Christians.

Universities arose to meet specific needs in a changing medieval world. They were created to develop a corps of literate and analytical men to primarily help administer the more sophisticated and bureaucratic church that developed from the reforms and the growth of the power of the pope. Secular lords, especially kings, also needed administrators to help them make best use of their resources. In addition, the recovery of some of the works of the ancient Greek philosopher Aristotle and interaction with philosophers in the Muslim world posed new intellectual challenges to Christians that required carefully trained thinkers to respond. Modernization of production provided enough surplus to allow a few people the time to engage in speculative thought. The result was that strange blend of vocational training and purely intellectual work that still characterizes the university.

Students came to universities primarily to assure themselves of better jobs in the future. Rarely would a peasant attend; most students would be from the ranks of the minor nobility, like the higher clergy. Students were considered clergy and therefore under the authority and jurisdiction of the church. Students needed either wealthy parents or a well-placed ecclesiastical patron to foot the bills while they studied. Most would come seeking a career in teaching; the initial degree, the *bachelor of arts*, effectively certified the bearer to teach in one of the many cathedral schools (secondary schools) that had developed all over Europe for the training of the parish clergy. A few scholars might proceed on to other degrees, but the B.A. was basic to almost all programs. The university could grant the Master of Arts degree to graduates after they had gained a few years' experience. This certified that the holder could teach apprentice teachers. Other degrees available after more years of study included:

medicine, learned entirely from textbooks and primarily a theoretical discipline;

civil or *Roman law*, useful primarily in Italy;

canon or *church law*, the most important discipline to master for advancement in the church's bureaucracy;

philosophy, advanced studies in the liberal arts, the root of our Ph.D. degree;

theology, the most prestigious degree, requiring about thirteen years of work beyond the B.A.

The universities had varied influences on European Christians. Increasingly, the skills associated with theology gained the power of prestige within the church hierarchy. The seductive charms of theological speculation at times outweighed other concerns, such as administrative efficiency and pastoral care, in powerful church leaders. Needs of the average, illiterate church-goer could be neglected. On the other hand, university-trained teachers eventually increased the number of readers in the European population, especially among the nobility and the great merchants, which in turn spawned a group of people who read the Bible outside of the normal context of the church. Many of the lay piety groups that emerged in the fourteenth and fifteenth centuries depended on the reading of Scripture as a source of their inspiration. Likewise, some of the assumptions of the later Protestant reformers required a fairly widespread literacy.

Another contribution of the university was to nurture Thomas Aquinas's philosophy. Thomas Aquinas single-handedly put together a systematic exposition of all the knowledge available in Europe at his time, from art to zoology, and showed how it fit in with Christians' faith. His effort was a microcosm of the effort made by medieval society to put all of life within the context of Christian faith. Although the synthesis of Aquinas satisfied Europeans for only a generation or so, it admirably demonstrated the medieval penchant for unity of thought, word, and deed in the context of Christian faith.

This unity did not survive. It fell a victim to changes that emerged in the fourteenth century.

Suggested readings

Bede. *The Ecclesiastical History of the English People*, repr. ed. Harmondsworth, England: Penguin, 1990.

"Bernard of Clairvaux." *Christian History* [a special issue], 7 (1989).

Brooke, Rosalind B. and Christopher N. L. Brooke. *Popular Religion in the Middle Ages: Western Europe, 1000–1300*. London: Thames and Hudson, 1984.

Bynum, Caroline Walker. *Holy Feast and Holy Fast: The Religious Significance of Food to Medieval Women*. Berkeley, Calif.: University of California Press, 1987.

"The Crusades." *Christian History*, 12.4 (issue 40 , 1993).

Herlihy, David. *Cities and Society in Medieval Italy*. London: Variorum Reprints, 1980.

———. *Medieval Households*. Cambridge, Mass.: Harvard University Press, 1985.

"How the Irish Were Saved." *Christian History*, 17.4 (issue 60, 1998).

Knowles, David. *Christian Monasticism*. New York: McGraw-Hill, 1990.

Ladurie, Emmanuel Le Roy. *Montaillou, the Promised Land of Error.* New York: Random House, 1979.

Lopez, Robert. *Birth of Europe*. Philadelphia: Lippincott, 1966.

"A Severe Salvation [Vikings]." *Christian History*, 18.3 (issue 63, 1999).

Southern, R. W. *Church and Society in the Middle Ages*. New Haven, Conn.: Yale University Press, 1992.

"The Waldensians."*Christian History*, 8.2 (issue 22, 1989).

5

Eastern Orthodoxy: Christians Who Never Changed?

As light fades from the avenues of San Francisco's Richmond district, a slight young man of apparent Central Asian origin, with high cheekbones and a wispy black beard, slips up polished steps and through a high, carved, wooden door. Above the door, the building's onion domes sweep upward, dominating the neighborhood. Once inside, the man puts on an elaborate, embroidered robe over his black gown and dons a high hat. He then enters the sanctuary and waits as it begins to fill with worshipers. While he waits he pauses to draw inspiration once again from the ornate grandeur of the sanctuary and to take comfort in the company of the saints whose lives are depicted on the walls. Finally, in Church Slavonic, the centuries-old language of Macedonian Slavs, he leads the congregation through the chanted prayers and readings of the evening service. He is a priest of the Holy Virgin Church of the Russian Nation in Exile—what some people would call an Eastern Orthodox Christian.

Begin with the patriarchs

Orthodoxy is the term by which the older churches of Greece, Russia, the Middle East, and much of Southeastern Europe are commonly known. It comes from the Greek for "correct teaching." Like most Christians, the Orthodox think of themselves as people whose understanding of the gospel is more accurate and more complete than the understandings of other sorts of Christians. But Eastern Christians mean more than that by the term *orthodox*. They mean that theirs is the faith of the founders of Christianity, that their religion is unchanged from the first generations after Christ. Therefore, to understand the Eastern Orthodox, one must turn to the patriarchs, the spiritual giants of the first centuries.

Orthodox hold a particular view of the time of the patriarchs, of course. They see the early church as characterized by certain themes that have been present more richly and consistently throughout the ages among Eastern Christians than in other branches of Christianity. They believe the early Christians all believed approximately the same things and that doctrinal disputes were settled early, and for all time, in a series of councils held by church leaders in the first few centuries. They believe that the early church was a local church, with all the believers in a community taking part and without central control by a single, international church bureaucracy. Within that local church, however, government was hierarchical, with a bishop at the head.

Orthodox believe that the international unity of doctrine and harmony of spirit were achieved through the coming together of bishops in all-church councils at several critical junctures in early church history, starting with the council at Jerusalem in Acts 15. That precedent makes Orthodox Christians look to church councils for major decisions, and it makes them defer to the decisions of past councils. It makes them backward-looking, very conscious of the importance of precedents in deciding questions for the present and the future.

The sacraments were tremendously important among the early Christians, Orthodox insist, and they should remain so today. The life of the spirit flowed out of the practice of ritual. Christ's whole body was present in the Eucharist, and the Holy Spirit was especially God-with-us as people performed the sacraments. Eastern Christians are also mindful that the early Christians faced persecution and martyrdom, and they see their own history and present reality as echoing the chords of the martyr theme. Monks and monasteries were early, important features of Christian experience, and Orthodox Christians are especially aware of the persons and actions of monks.

The persons of the patriarchs are important, too. More than any major group of Christians in the West, Eastern Orthodox believers surround themselves with the early fathers of Christianity. They know the stories of the lives of the early saints, from Clement of Alexandria to Gregory of Nyssa. If they are intellectually inclined they have read the writings of these two, Origen, Tertullian, and others. How many Western Christians can say the same? Orthodox Christians keep pictures of the patriarchs in their homes and churches, and if they do not worship them, they certainly do appreciate the present company of the fathers as they go about their lives in the world.

For Eastern Christians, the greatest of the patriarchs are:

Basil the Great (c. 330–379), a bishop, ascetic, and theologian who drew up the code followed by Eastern Orthodox monks to this day, infusing the monastic life with a vibrant sense of love and community;

Gregory of Nazianzus (c. 329–390), a friend of Basil and a fierce verbal warrior on behalf of the church's accepted theological interpretations; and

John Chrysostom, the greatest of all preachers (see box 5.1).

5.1. John Chrysostom

John, who was dubbed *Chrysostom* ("golden-mouthed") by later admirers, was the most celebrated preacher of the fourth century.

Born around 347, he grew up and served most of his life in Antioch, the ancient Syrian city in what is now Turkey. Raised in a Christian family and baptized, as was the custom, in his early twenties, he attended religious school and became a monk. John withdrew into a cave where he followed such a severe ascetic regimen of fasting, prayer, and writing that he became ill and was forced to return to Antioch after two years. There he became a deacon and then a priest and ministered to sick and poor people.

John devoted much of his time to preaching—every Sunday throughout the year and daily during Lent. He abandoned the altar, where other preachers of his day stood, and came down among the people to speak directly.

Even today John's homilies ring with surprising power and immediacy for one who wrote sixteen centuries ago. Vivid word pictures and practical advice were expressed with elegant language that lasted beyond its time. He wrote "All the world is a stage" twelve centuries before Shakespeare.

In the following passage, which begins his second homily on John 1:1, the reader can hear the swirling cadences of a master preacher:

"In the beginning was the Word" [John 1:1].

If John were about to address us and to tell us about his own affairs, it would be necessary to speak of his family, his native land, and his education. However, since not he, but God through his agency, is speaking to humanity, it seems to me to be superfluous and beside the point to inquire into these details.

Yet it really is not superfluous, but very necessary, to do so. When you learn who he was, and whence, and his parentage, and what sort of man, and after this you listen to his voice and all his teaching, then you will know truly that these utterances were not his, but belonged to the divine Power moving his soul. . . .*

St. John possessed gifts for leadership as well as preaching, and in 397 he was called to be bishop of Constantinople. There he ran afoul of Byzantine imperial politics. In 404, he was banished to Armenia and then to an even more remote spot near the Caucasus Mountains where he died in 407.

*Roy Joseph Deferrari, et al., eds., *The Fathers of the Church: A New Translation*, vol. 33, *Saint John Chrysostom: Homilies 1–47*, trans. by T. A. Goggin, S.C.H. (New York: Fathers of the Church, 1957), 12.

But there are countless others regarded and venerated as heroes of the faith and cofounders of the true way of the Christian. There is no authoritative list, and not all the fathers lived in the first few centuries. To take a few examples, John of Damascus (c. 675–749) and Gregory Palamas (1296–1359) date from an era that Western Europeans would call medieval, and Maximus the Greek (c. 1470–1556) was nearly modern. To say there cannot be any more Christians added to the list of spiritual fathers would be to deny the ongoing power and activity of the Holy Spirit.

John Chrysostom (c. 344/354–407), bishop of Constantinople, was influential in both his writings and his lively preaching. (Billy Graham Center)

In part because of the enormous spiritual prestige of these patriarchs, there was a special authority invested in those individual church leaders who during their office also bore the title *patriarch*: the bishops of Rome, Constantinople, Alexandria, Antioch, and Jerusalem. Each patriarch was the unquestioned leader of the church in his geographical region. It was among these regional patriarchs that most Orthodox church politics took place over the centuries. Patriarchs were typically appointed by political leaders, and their spiritual offices often became entangled in the politics of their regions (see pp. 110–18).

Byzantium

Eastern Orthodox Christians, like Christians from other traditions, looked to their roots in the Middle East in the time of Jesus and the disciples. But it was in Byzantium in the fourth and fifth centuries that the Orthodox began to take on a distinct identity. Up until that point, Christians throughout the Roman Empire had seen themselves as members of a common communion of faith, a "catholic," or universal, church. Between the founding of the city of Constantinople in 324 and the division of Eastern and Western churches in 1054, the main trunk of Christianity gradually divided into two large branches, one centered around Rome in the West and the other around Constantinople in the East.

When the Roman Emperor Constantine had unified his empire and became a Christian, he decided to build a new capital in the eastern part of the empire. His motives were mainly to reinforce the political and economic unity of the empire, but he also wanted to build a *new* Rome, unstained by the pagan associations of the old capital. He chose the town of Byzantium, located between Greece and Anatolia on the Bosporus, the narrow waterway linking the Black Sea with the Mediterranean; he named the capital New Rome. Others called it the City of Constantine or Constantinople. When the Roman Empire fell in the West, the Byzantine Empire continued the imperial glory in the East for another thousand years.

Constantinople was one of the world's greatest cities in its heyday in the tenth and eleventh centuries. It contained more than 1 million people from all over the Mediterranean region who spoke a dozen tongues on its streets every day. It was the center of a network of trade that extended thousands of miles. The Byzantine Empire was headed by an emperor who held his position through constant artful intrigue, playing off factions of the court, the military, and an elaborate bureaucracy against one another. The empire sometimes achieved peace over a large part of its domain. At other times it was wracked by internal rebellion and assaulted from without by Franks, Goths, Persians, Arabs, Mongols, and Turks.

The organized faith of Orthodox Christians was inextricably bound up with the fate of the Empire. The separation between church and state that means so much to modern Americans knew no place among the Byzantines. As one emperor put it, "I recognize two authorities, priesthood and empire; the Creator of the world entrusted to the first the care of souls and to the second the control of men's bodies. Let neither authority be attacked, that the world may enjoy prosperity."[1]

Hagia Sophia ("Holy Wisdom") was constructed in Constantinople by the Emperor Justinian between 532 and 537 and is regarded as the foremost example of Byzantine ecclesiastical architecture. Its dome rises 180 feet and is 107 feet across. Minarets were added years after the Turkish capture of Constantinople in 1453. (Zernov)

In practice, church and state were tightly intertwined. Emperors appointed and deposed patriarchs of the church at Constantinople, and Christian leaders frequently got caught up in court intrigue. Sometimes, they found themselves used as little more than instruments of the imperial will of their emperors.

The church of the seven councils

Orthodox Christians refer to their church as the "church of the seven councils." By this they signal their emphasis on orthodox belief, on the understanding of Christian faith and practice that became codified at ecumenical councils—international meetings of bishops—in the third through the eighth centuries. The first two of these councils—at Nicea in 325 and Constantinople in 381—formulated the doctrine of the Trinity and expelled Arians as heretics (see pp. 57–60). The next four—at Ephesus in 431, Chalcedon in 451, and Constantinople in 553 and 681—dealt with the nature of Christ as both God and human and tossed Nestorians and monophysites out of the increasingly European-dominated church (see pp. 137–38). These six councils are the common heritage of both Western and Eastern Christians, but Easterners pay more attention to them. By looking back to these very early councils, which came at a time when essentially all Christians except a few Nestorian and Ethiopian outliers were members of a single international communion, Eastern Christians stake their claim to being the true heirs of the faith of the first Christian generations.

The seventh council took place at Nicea in 787, but it was part of a much longer-running controversy that began to separate Eastern Orthodox Christians from the West. The question addressed by the council was how Christians ought to relate to religious images. The situation is similar to that in modern churches that have a picture of Jesus. A worshiper going by that painting is reminded that it represents the living God, who came to earth to die in a person's place to pay for his or her sins. What a debt of gratitude is owed to Jesus! If the person gazing at that picture thinks these thoughts, emotionally it has enormous impact. The very thought of what Christ did might reasonably cause the person to sink to his or her knees and express gratitude in prayer. Such is the emotional response among many to a picture of Mary, the innocent young girl whom God chose out of all the women of the world to bear God's son into the world. An emotionally sensitive person who is committed to Christ spiritually might have a similarly strong response to a picture of the apostle Peter, Saint Francis, or some other ancient exemplar of the faith.

107

At what point do such worshipful responses to religious images become idolatry—worshiping the object instead of the God who stands behind it? A radical Christian (or Muslim or Gnostic) might argue that any intense emotional response to a representation of a figure in Christian history amounts to idolatry and ought to be forbidden. But most Christians recognize there is a certain legitimacy to spiritual emotions that are triggered by images.

Orthodox Christians in the eighth and ninth centuries argued about this question. Those who attacked the religious use of icons, or images, were called *iconoclasts*. Since most of them came from the Eastern provinces of the empire, some historians have seen in their iconoclasm an Asian protest against Greek domination. Those who defended the images were called *iconodules*. Many of them were Greeks, and they carried with them the Platonic idea that behind mere earthly objects there stood ideal forms. For St. John of Damascus, images were essential testimony to the fact that God became flesh in Jesus. He defended icons with these words:

> Of old God the incorporeal and uncircumscribed was not depicted at all. But now that God has appeared in the flesh and lived among men, I make an image of the God who can be seen. I do not worship matter, but I worship the Creator of matter, who for my sake became material and deigned to dwell in matter, who through matter effected my salvation. I will not cease from worshipping the matter through which my salvation has been effected.[2]

Some iconodules went further. A twentieth-century observer of the Russian Orthodox Church explained the reaching after spiritually ideal forms that lay at the base of icon-making:

> [Icons] were for the Russian not merely paintings. They were dynamic manifestations of man's spiritual power to redeem creation through beauty and art. The colours and lines of the [icons] were not meant to imitate nature; the artists aimed at demonstrating that men, animals, and plants, and the whole cosmos, could be rescued from their present state of degradation and restored to their proper "Image." The [icons] were pledges of the coming victory of a redeemed creation over the fallen one. . . . The artistic perfection of an icon was not only a reflection of the celestial glory—it was a concrete example of matter restored to its original harmony and beauty, and serving as a vehicle of the Spirit.[3]

In the end, the Eastern Orthodox Church hierarchy at the second Council of Nicea came down on the side of the iconodules. The heavy emphasis on the patriarchs in Eastern Orthodoxy naturally lent itself to an expression of faith where icons assumed a large importance. It was one religious item that emphasized the growing cultural separation of the Eastern and Western bodies of Christians.

5.2. Bogomils

The Bogomils flourished as an underground sect in the Bulgarian provinces of the Byzantine Empire (and for a time in Bulgaria when it was an independent state), starting in the tenth century. Influenced by ideas of the Manicheans (see p. 62) and a lesser-known heretical Christian sect called the Paulicians, the Bogomils perceived the cosmos to be the battleground for a war between the forces of God's two sons: Satanael, the first-born, author of all that was material and evil, and Logos, the second-born, who came to earth as Jesus to save humankind from his older brother.

The movement was organized in the middle 900s by a priest named Bogomil (whose name means "beloved of God"). His followers, who may have numbered in the tens of thousands, generally stayed in the Orthodox Church and were closet dissenters. They saw a radical disjunction between the body, which was evil, and the spirit, which was good. Bogomils rejected the basic structures of the church, including the priesthood and the saints. They insisted that church buildings were not special places but mere "common houses." They venerated neither icons nor sacraments. Baptism was just water and communion was just bread and wine. Both were material ceremonies that honored Satanael. The Bogomils rejected the institution of marriage and urged married couples to separate. Every Bogomil believer was capable of being inhabited by the Holy Spirit, and the Bogomils practiced mutual confession.

The Orthodox Church, a highly structured, hierarchical institution, obviously could not accommodate such a radically anti-authoritarian group. Leaders initiated several purges when Bulgaria was part of the Byzantine Empire, although they could do less when Bulgaria became an independent kingdom. These purges weakened the Bogomils but did not stamp them out completely. They were finally crushed at the end of the fourteenth century, not by the church hierarchy but by the invasion of the Turks.

The break with the West

The attitude of the Eastern Orthodox toward Western Christians—Protestant or Roman Catholic—is summed up in the words of the modern Russian theologian Alexis Khomiakov: "We are unchanged; we are still the same as we were in the eighth century. . . . Oh that you could only consent to be again what you were once, when we were both united in faith and communion!"[4] As we shall see, the variety of faith practiced by Eastern Christians in fact changed a great deal, as every living faith must, under the impact of ever-changing social and cultural circumstances. But the attitude of looking to the past and carefully preserving that which was handed down from the ancients is central to Orthodoxy. It was one of the issues that divided the Eastern and Western bodies of Christians.

As Byzantium and the smaller states to the west grew apart from each other in politics and culture during the Middle Ages, and as their experiences as peoples became quite different from each other, two distinct civilizations emerged. The West was a collection of warring principalities; the East was a unitary and bureaucratic state, headed by a single emperor. Each culture zone encompassed a variety of peoples and languages, but in the West the language of leadership and religion was Latin, while in the East it was Greek. The West's church was headed by the bishop of Rome, whom Western Christians increasingly regarded as the monarch of the church. The East recognized the primacy of the pope, but to Easterners he was merely the first among equals—a colleague, not a commander, of the other patriarchs in Constantinople, Antioch, Alexandria, and Jerusalem.

The Eastern and Western churches split apart formally in 1054. The issues of the moment were a dispute over the authority of the pope and a theological argument about the *filioque* clause. Nicetas, a twelfth-century archbishop of Nicomedia, described the controversy over the pope from the Eastern perspective: "We do not deny to the Roman Church the primacy amongst the five sister patriarchates; and we recognize her right to the most honourable seat at an ecumenical council. But she has separated herself from us by her own deeds, when through pride she assumed a monarchy which does not belong to her office."[5]

The *filioque* debate was a more subtle controversy, which surrounded the original and proper wording of the Nicene Creed. Eastern Christians accused their Roman counterparts of changing the creed to fit political expediency; Western Christians denied the charge. For nearly two hundred years, from 858 to 1054, controversy on the subject waxed and waned. It became entwined with competition for the souls of Bulgars between Byzantine evangelists and German missionaries loyal to Rome. Religious differences also got mixed up with other sources of friction between West and East—Norman military activity in Byzantine possessions in Italy, and Italian merchants taking control of trade in the Eastern Mediterranean.

The matter came to a head in 1054. Normans in Italy made Greek Christians conform to the Latin Mass, and Michael Cerularius (d. 1059), the patriarch of Constantinople, told Latin Christians in Constantinople to adopt the Greek order of service. When the latter refused, Michael closed their churches. Pope Leo XI sent an emissary, Cardinal Humbert, to Constantinople to investigate. Humbert and his colleagues excommunicated Michael; Michael responded by doing the same to Humbert, and fellowship between Rome and Constantinople was broken.

5.3. Hesychasts

In the West in the Middle Ages the faith of the first generations was replaced by the scholasticism of Thomas Aquinas in the twelfth and thirteenth centuries. In the East, the major change from the faith of the patriarchs came in the tenth through thirteenth centuries at the hands of Hesychasts (from the Greek word for "quiet").

These mystics drew on the meditative traditions of desert monks. Like Pure Land Buddhist mystics chanting the name of the Amida,* the Hesychasts would endlessly repeat the "Jesus Prayer": "Lord Jesus Christ, Son of God, have mercy on me." They adopted postures and performed physical exercises to help them concentrate their spiritual energies to get in touch with that which lay beyond ordinary human sight. In particular, they wished to touch the "divine and uncreated light" that surrounded Jesus at his transfiguration. Through that light they sought communion with God himself.

The Hesychasts were attacked by people who thought God to be completely transcendent—wholly other and unknowable. Some considered Hesychasts hopeless materialists in their view of God. But Gregory Palamas (1296–1359) defended them, and their emphasis on mystical union with a knowable God became a major thread of Eastern Christianity. The Hesychasts became identified with the vast monastery on Mount Athos in Greece, the most vibrant center of Orthodox spirituality for most of the current millennium.

The Hesychasts had a deep influence on Orthodox spirituality ever after. A set of "Brief Directives for Prayer of the Heart," popular with the twentieth-century group, reads like this:

1. Sit or stand in a dimly lit and quiet place.
2. Recollect yourself.
3. With the help of your imagination find the place of the heart and stay there with attention.
4. Lead the mind from the head into the heart and say, "Lord Jesus Christ, have mercy on me," quietly with the lips or mentally, whichever is more convenient; say the prayer slowly and reverently.
5. As much as possible guard the attention of your mind and do not allow any thoughts to enter in.
6. Be patient and peaceful.
7. Be moderate in food, drink, and sleep.
8. Learn to love silence.
9. Read the Scriptures and the writings of the Fathers about prayer.
10. As much as possible avoid distracting occupations.

Helen Bacovcin, *The Way of a Pilgrim* (Garden City, N.Y.: Doubleday, 1978), 194.

*Pure Land sects of Mahayana Buddhism are particularly influential in Japan and Korea. They are so-called for their goal of attaining enlightenment and being reborn in the "pure land," which was established for them by a man who through enlightenment became Amida Buddha. Their distinctive meditational practice is to recite the Nembutsu: *"namu-amida-butsu"*— in English, "I place my faith in Amida Buddha." The faithful may say this phrase many thousands of times each day.

The split between Eastern and Western Christians was sealed by the Crusades. Ostensibly, the two wings of Christendom were cooperating to free the Holy Land from Muslim control, and sometimes they did get along. But friction was frequent. The last straw from the Eastern point of view came in 1204, during the Fourth Crusade. European crusaders stopped on their way to Egypt to intervene in Byzantine politics and ended up attacking Constantinople. They spent three terrible days pillaging the city. After that atrocity, no Byzantine could imagine re-establishing fellowship with the West.

Under Turkish rule

By comparison to the crusaders, the foreigners who took over the Byzantine Empire in the fifteenth century seemed friendly. A new group of Muslims—Turks whose ancestors had come from Central Asia not many generations before—were expanding their political and military power over much of the Eastern Mediterranean. The Byzantines tried to patch up their religious differences with European Christians in time to confront the Turks, but they were not able to obtain the military help they needed. In 1453, Turkish armies took Constantinople and brought an end to a thousand years of close connection between the Byzantine Empire and Eastern Christianity.

Nonetheless, Christians thrived under Muslim rule. The Turks, like other Muslims, saw Christianity as an incomplete religion, but not one wholly wrong. Like Jews and Christians, Muslims looked to Abraham as the progenitor of their faith. God had revealed himself successively to Jews, Christians, and Muslims. Jews and Christians were "people of the book"—the Bible—who could be accorded a measure of toleration so long as they did not seek to overthrow the Islamic state.

There were some limitations placed on Christians in the Turkish empire, however. They were not persecuted, but they were given, in effect, second-class citizenship and encouraged to convert to Islam. Christians paid extra taxes, had to wear special clothing, and were not allowed to serve in the military unless they converted. Christian missionary work was forbidden, and to convert a Muslim drew the death penalty.

Yet Christians enjoyed a degree of communal autonomy. The Turkish Empire was a collection of many peoples. The Turks governed those peoples through ethnarchs—one leader for each ethnic or religious community. The leader of the Christians was the patriarch of Constantinople. Bishops became de facto members of the civil government as well as religious leaders. Christian institutions and politics once again became hopelessly intertwined. The patriarch was appointed by the Turkish sultan and replaced frequently. This kept the Christian leader beholden to the Sultan and prevented Christians from forming a stable, separate center of power. The principle of ethnic divisibility also meant that the Eastern church lost some of its institutional cohesion. Since the Turks governed their empire as a collection of ethnic units, in time Christians in Bulgaria, Serbia, and Romania acquired their own patriarchs and national churches. Where the Byzantine era had experienced a universal church in the East, the Turkish era saw the rise of several branches of Orthodox Christianity as expressions of various nationalities.

5.4. Devshirme

Islamic law forbade Turks to enslave other Muslims, but it was all right to make slaves of Christians. Some slaves they captured in wars, but others they recruited through a unique tax called the *devshirme*. Sometimes the young Christians were coerced, but sometimes they volunteered, for the *devshirme* was the one way a Christian could ascend to the highest ranks of Turkish society. In 1585 a Venetian ambassador described the *devshirme*:

There are two types of Turks. One is composed of people native-born of Turkish parents, while the other is made up of renegades who are sons of Christians. The latter group were taken by force in the raids . . . on Christian lands, or else harshly levied in their villages from the sultan's non-Muslim subjects and taxpayers. They are taken while still boys, and either persuaded or forced to be circumcised and made Muslims. It is the custom . . . to send men throughout the country every fourth or fifth year to levy one-tenth of the boys, just as if they were so many sheep, and after they have made Turks of these boys they train each one according to his abilities. . . .

Not only is the Turkish army made up of these renegades, but at one time they used to win all the chief positions in the government . . . and the highest commands in the armed forces, because ancient custom forbids that the sons of Turks should hold these jobs. . . .

After they have been taken away as young boys the renegades are sent to different places to be trained according to the jobs they will be given. The handsomest, most wide-awake ones are placed in the seraglio [palace] of the Grand Signor, or in one of two others . . . and there they are all prepared to rise to the highest government offices. . . .

The other boys . . . [are] in a kind of seminary for the janissary corps [the Sultan's elite guard]. [*]

The *devshirme* was just one instance of pressure on a Christian to convert to Islam. If a person should decide to return to Christianity after embracing Islam he or she was subject to the death penalty.

[*]J. C. Davis, *Pursuit of Power: Venetian Ambassadors' Reports on Spain, Turkey, and France in the Age of Philip II, 1560–1600* (New York: Harper and Row, 1970), 135–36.

Not just a Greek church

Conversion of the Slavs

After the founding of Constantinople, the second most formative event in the history of the Orthodox Church is the conversion of the Slavs. In 1988 the Orthodox Church in Russia celebrated the millennium of Russian Christianity, commemorating the conversion of Prince Vladimir in 988. In fact, however, the first penetration of the Slavic peoples by Orthodox Christianity occurred more than a century earlier.

There is some speculation about possible evangelical efforts by the apostle Andrew and others aimed at the Slavic peoples in the Ukraine in the first century, but major mission efforts among Slavs really began with the work of Cyril and Methodius in the mid-ninth century. In 860, these two brothers received instructions to spread Christianity to the Khazars, a Central Asian people who lived north of the Caucasus Mountains. The Khazars, however, opted for Judaism instead.

Then the brothers directed their attention to Moravia, in what is now the Czech Republic. They wanted to be able to communicate the gospel in the language of the people, so they developed a Slavic alphabet, which they used to translate selective passages from the Gospels and to develop a liturgy. They used the variety of Slavonic they had spoken as children in Macedonia around Thessalonica. Thus, the Macedonian dialect became Church Slavonic. This use of a vernacular language was very different from the mission efforts and style of worship one found in the Latin West. It is parallel to modern efforts to indigenize Christianity in native cultures, and it aided the development of national orthodoxies in a number of Slavic areas. Cyril and Methodius were eventually beaten in the contest for Moravian hearts by German missionaries loyal to Rome, but their contribution lived on. They had translated the Greek religion into the idiom of a Slavic people. In time, Bulgars, Serbs, and other Slavic peoples came to adopt the Eastern variety of Christianity. The most numerous of these were the Russians.

Russia

The major event in the christianization of Russia was the conversion of Prince Vladimir of Kiev and his baptism by Byzantine missionaries around the year 988. The establishment of Christianity in Russia had two characteristics that may strike late twentieth-century Christians as unusual: the method by which the political leader chose Christianity for his people and the act of conversion of a whole people at once. Kievan Russia was establishing itself as a kingdom of some significance, and Prince Vladimir thought it needed a national religion. He inquired about the major religious faiths: Islam, Judaism, Roman Catholicism, and

Vladimir (956–1015), after a civil war against his two brothers for control of Russia, adopted Christianity as the national religion. (Andre Ruzhnikov)

Orthodoxy. He listened to emissaries from each religion as they explained their faith and debated the merits of their competitors' beliefs. Then he sent delegations to each community to examine both the practice of their faith and their style of worship. His investigators reported the following:

> When we journeyed among the Bulgars, we beheld how they worship in their temple, called a mosque, while they stand ungirt. The Bulgar bows, sits down, looks hither and thither like one possessed, and there is no happiness among them. . . . Their religion is not good.
>
> Then we went among the Germans, and saw them performing many ceremonies in their temples; but we beheld no glory there. Then we went to Greece, and the Greeks led us to the edifices where they worship their God, and we know not whether we were in heaven or on earth. For on earth there is no such splendor or such beauty, and we are at a loss how to describe it. We only know that God dwells there among men, and their service is fairer than the ceremonies of other nations. For we cannot forget that beauty. Every man, after tasting something sweet, is afterward unwilling to accept that which is bitter, and therefore we cannot dwell longer here.

> Then the boyars spoke and said, "If the Greek faith were evil, it would not have been adopted by your grandmother Olga who was wiser than all other men." Vladmir then inquired where they should all accept baptism, and they replied that the decision rested with him.[6]

In shopping around for an appropriate religion, Vladimir was doing nothing more than other political leaders had done at a similar stage of national development (the Khazars, for example). Byzantine Christianity was Vladimir's choice, not only because it seemed spiritually superior to him, but also because of the close political, commercial, and military ties that Kiev was developing with its powerful neighbor Constantinople.

It is not unusual for the religion of the political leader to be the main religious belief of the people of the realm—that is the case in England and Japan, for example. But it may seem unusual for a people to convert so quickly, and apparently so completely, based simply on the conversion of a political leader, as they did in Russia. Yet such it was. Of course, it took some generations for vestiges of pre-Christian religions to become extinct in remote parts of the countryside. Vladimir and his successors went to great pains to remove remnants of past "idolatry" and spread the message of the miraculous powers of the Christian faith. They were quite successful in bringing the bulk of the Russian people into the embrace of Christianity. A chronicler of the events describes a baptismal scene:

> Thereafter Vladimir sent heralds throughout the whole city to proclaim that if any inhabitant, rich or poor, did not betake himself to the river, he would risk the prince's displeasure. When the people heard these words, they wept for joy, and exclaimed in their enthusiasm "If this were not good, the prince and his boyars would not have accepted it." On the morrow, the prince went forth to the Dnieper with the priests of the princess and those from Kherson, and a countless multitude assembled. They all went into the water; some stood up to their necks, others to their breasts, and the younger near the bank, some of them holding children in their arms, while the adults waded farther out. The priests stood by and offered prayers. There was joy in heaven and upon earth to behold so many souls saved. But the devil lamented, "Woe is me! How am I driven out hence! . . . I am vanquished . . . and my reign in these regions is at an end."[7]

For twentieth-century Western individualists, this account presents significant problems. Can one be meaningfully converted on the threat of the prince's displeasure? Are there social and political dangers for Christianity once it has become the official religion of the realm? Do mass baptisms lead to an adulterated Christian commitment? Individualists might say yes to such questions, but the case of the Russian conversion argues the contrary. In the case of Vladimir and Russia, the conversion of a political leader resulted in a genuine embrace of Christianity by his people.

The first Russian Christians practiced their faith as a frontier outpost of Constantinople. But from the middle of the fifteenth century on, the Russian church functioned independently, as what Orthodox scholar Timothy Ware calls "the Third and last Rome, the centre of Orthodox Christendom."[8] As Russia grew in territorial extent and rose to world power, and as Greece receded to become a mere province of the Turkish domains, the Orthodox center of gravity shifted north-

St. Basil's Cathedral near the Kremlin in Moscow reflects the towers, turrets, and twisted domes of Russian Byzantine architecture. The cathedral was built between 1554 and 1679. (Zernov)

ward. In 1589, the patriarch of Constantinople and his peers recognized the Russian ascendancy by raising the Russian Metropolitan bishop to the level of patriarch.

Tension still existed between Orthodox Christianity as defined by the Greek Christians and the Russian religion. One example of this tension was the schism of the Old Believers (*raskolniki*). Throughout much of the seventeenth century, a group of reformers led by Archpriest Avvakum (1620–1682) and others attempted to revitalize the spirit of Russian Christians. In the 1650s these reformers, who were also proud Russians, ran afoul of the new patriarch of Moscow, Nicon (1605–1681). Nicon was fond of saying that "I am a Russian and the son of a Russian, but my faith and my religion are Greek."

The schism occurred over a seemingly trivial matter of hand signals. Nicon tried to get Russian Christians, who had been enthusiastic supporters of Avvakum's reforms, to abandon their practice of making the sign of the cross with two fingers, and substitute instead the Greek use of three fingers. Many Russian Christians followed their patriarch, but just as many saw this as an unnecessary Greek infringement on

117

Russian ritual autonomy, and refused. Disputes over many other rituals and certain theological matters soon followed. Avvakum and his followers defied the official Church prescription. They broke off to form a separate, conservative church that would practice ritual the way Russians had practiced it in the past. They became the Old Believers (*raskolniki*), and they exist in Russia to this day.

A greater change came to the Russian church during the reign of Peter the Great (1682–1725). Peter was the great modernizer and westernizer of Russian social and political institutions. He asserted his authority over the centers of power in Russian society, from the nobility to the church. In 1721 he abolished the office of patriarch and set up a spiritual college or holy synod, an official bureaucracy of religion, modeled on Protestant synods in Germany. Like Henry VIII in England, Peter confiscated the church lands, sold them, and used the money to support his own projects. He declared himself chief of the church and defender of the faith, even as he strove to bend the church to his will. He issued the *Spiritual Regulation*, which was a bureaucratic charter laying out the duties of the administrators of the church, a fifty-page list of regulations and procedures that bound Christians.

Like many West European monarchs of his time, Peter the Great claimed to govern by the "divine right of kings," and he saw himself as a benevolent despot. The flavor of Peter's view of the church comes through in the following selection from the writings of Feofan Prokopovich. Prokopovich actually penned Peter's *Spiritual Regulation*. He was also the author of these words in a *Primer* for believers.

Question: What is ordained by God in the fifth commandment?

Answer: To honor all those who are as fathers and mothers to us. But it is not only parents who are referred to here, but others who exercise paternal authority over us.

Question: Who are such persons?

Answer: The first order of such persons are the supreme author-ities instituted by God to rule the people, of whom the highest authority is the Tsar. It is the duty of kings to protect their subjects and to seek what is best for them, whether in religious matters or in the things of this world; and therefore they must watch over all the ecclesiastical, military, and civil authorities subject to them and conscientiously see that they discharge their respective duties. This is, under God, the highest paternal dignity; and subjects, like good sons, must honor the Tsar.

Despite Peter's attempt to curb the power of the church by putting it in bureaucratic harness, popular piety swelled in the eighteenth and nineteenth centuries. Young monks and theologians continued to pour forth from Mount Athos and other centers, burning with zeal to renew the spirituality of the Russian masses. Although Peter and his successors took control in the formal offices of the church, the Christians of Russia continued to practice the presence of Christ, as they had learned mystical Christianity from the monks in a much earlier time (see box 5.5).

5.5. The Way of a Pilgrim

The great classic of Russian spirituality is *The Way of a Pilgrim*. Written by an anonymous nineteenth-century peasant, it is the gradual unfolding of the spiritual consciousness of a person deeply in love with God. It tells of the Pilgrim's search for a teacher who could tell him how to pray without ceasing. Along the way, both the Pilgrim and his reader discover countless small gems of spiritual insight. *The Way of a Pilgrim* has been widely read and meditated upon by Orthodox Christians for over a century, and has in recent decades come to Western Christians as well. Some excerpts:

By the grace of God I am a Christian, by my deeds a great sinner, and by my calling a homeless wanderer of humblest origin, roaming from place to place. My possessions consist of a knapsack with dry crusts of bread on my back and in my bosom the Holy Bible. This is all!

On the twenty-fourth Sunday after Pentecost I came to church to attend the Liturgy and entered just as the epistle was being read. The reading was from Paul's First Letter to the Thessalonians, which says in part, "Pray constantly." These words made a deep impression on me and I started thinking of how it could be possible for a man to pray without ceasing when the practical necessities of life demand so much attention. . . .

What shall I do? I thought. Where can I find a person who will explain this mystery to me? I will go to the various churches where there are good preachers and perhaps I will obtain an explanation from them. And so I went. I heard many very good homilies on Prayer, but they were all instructions about Prayer in general: what is Prayer, the necessity of Prayer, the fruits of Prayer, but no one spoke of the way to succeed in Prayer. . . .

I traveled through various places. I read the Bible and asked for the whereabouts of a spiritual teacher . . . On a long and wide road, . . . an old man caught up with me who looked like a member of some religious community. . . . The elder blessed himself and began to speak. . . .

119

St. Paul clearly states that Prayer should precede all actions: 'First of all, there should be Prayers offered' (I Tim. 2:1). The Apostle's directive indicates that the act of Prayer is fundamental because without Prayer it is not possible to do good. Without frequent Prayer it is not possible to find one's way to God, to understand truth, and to crucify the lusts of the flesh. Only fidelity to Prayer will lead a person to enlightenment and union with Christ.

I say frequent Prayer because purity and perfection in Prayer is not within our reach, as St. Paul the Apostle indicates. The Spirit comes to help us in our weakness when we do not know how to pray (Rom. 8:26). Consequently, our only contribution toward perfection in Prayer, the mother of all spiritual good, is regularity and constancy. 'If you win the mother, you will have the children also,' says St. Isaac of Syria. Acquire the habit of Prayer and it will be easy for you to do good. This basic truth regarding Prayer is not clearly understood or presented by those who are lacking practical experience and who are not acquainted with the mystical teachings of the holy Fathers. . . .

The ceaseless Jesus Prayer is a continuous, uninterrupted call on the holy name of Jesus Christ with the lips, mind, and heart; and in the awareness of His abiding presence it is a plea for His blessing in all undertakings, in all places, at all times, even in sleep. The words of the Prayer are: 'Lord Jesus Christ, have mercy on me!' Anyone who becomes accustomed to this Prayer will experience great comfort as well as the need to say it continuously. He will become accustomed to it to such a degree that he will not be able to do without it and eventually the Prayer will of itself flow in him. . . .

The elder opened the Philokalia *to the account of St. Simeon the New Theologian and began reading: "Sit alone and in silence; bow your head and close your eyes; relax your breathing and with your imagination look into your heart; direct your thoughts from your head into your heart. And while inhaling say, "Lord Jesus Christ, have mercy on me," either softly with your lips or in your mind. Endeavor to fight distractions but be patient and peaceful and repeat this process frequently. . . .'"*

Then I began to say the Jesus Prayer interiorly to the rhythm of my breathing according to the directions of St. Gregory of Sinai and of Callistus and Ignatius: That is, while looking into the heart and inhaling I said, "Lord Jesus Christ," and while exhaling, "have mercy on me." At first I did this for an hour or two, and then I increased it so that in the end I spent practically the entire day in this exercise. When doubts or heaviness or slothfulness would come upon me, I would promptly read the section of the Philokalia *which speaks of the activity of the heart and in this way I would renew my desire and zeal for Prayer. After three weeks I began to feel pain in the heart, then a very pleasant warmth, delight, and peace. This encouraged me to even* more earnest practice of the Prayer, so that my thoughts were now directed to this and I experienced great joy. From this time, periodically, I began to experience various feelings and perceptions in my heart and mind. Sometimes I felt a sweet burning in my heart and such ease, freedom, and consolation that I seemed to be transformed and caught up in ecstasy. Sometimes I experienced a burning love toward Jesus Christ and all of God's creation. Sometimes I shed joyful tears in thanksgiving to God for His mercy to me, a great sinner. Sometimes difficult concepts became crystal clear and new ideas came to me which of myself I could not have imagined. Sometimes the warmth of the heart overflowed throughout my being and with tenderness I experienced God's presence within me. Sometimes I felt great joy in calling on the name of Jesus Christ and I realized the meaning of the words, "The kingdom of God is within you" (Luke 17:21).**

And on the Pilgrim went.

*See The Philokalia, trans. by G. E. H. Palmer, et al. (London: Faber and Faber, 1979). The Philokalia is a collection of meditations written by Eastern Orthodox masters between the fourth and fifteenth centuries and collected in 1782 by monks from Mount Athos. It had an enormous impact on Russian spirituality and was much beloved by Fyodor Dostoyevsky.

**The Way of a Pilgrim, trans. by Helen Bacovcin (Garden City, N.Y.: Doubleday, 1978), 13–19, 40–41.

Russian Christians exhibited all the enthusiasm for icons that the most ardent iconodule could imagine. Henri Troyat described the uses to which Russian believers put icons in the late nineteenth century:

In war, the Russians always carried a few holy ikons into the field and any success was attributed to them. The Virgin of Smolensk was dear to the whole Orthodox West after the victory of Poltava. Our Lady of Kazan owed her fame to the capture of Kazan under Ivan the Terrible, but it was also thanks to her than Minin and Pozharsky had driven the Poles from Moscow and that Alexander I had halted the French invasion of 1812. On the eve of the battle of Borodino, Marshal Kutuzov went in person to beg the help of the miraculous Virgin. Reproductions of the most famous ikons kept watch over all Russian homes, and there had to be at least one in every dining-room and every bedroom. In certain, particularly pious, households there was a real oratory in miniature. The holy pictures by their infinite multiplication, were integrated into domestic life. No important action was taken without their intervention. They were taken down from their corners to watch over the sick and the dying, to follow the dead to the cemetery, to keep an eye on a birth, and to serve as witnesses to big business affairs and small oathes. When a young man asked for the hand of a young girl, the parents blessed the betrothal with the house ikon. This same ikon, held by a boy, accompanied the girl when she went by carriage to church on her wedding day. When some member of the family was about to leave on a long journey, everyone gathered before the ikon, sat down together in silence, then rose, crossed themselves and kissed the traveler to wish him *bon voyage*.[9]

Monks were special targets of Russian popular reverence. They came in several ranks, from lay brother to deacon to priest-monk to archimandrite to bishop. Russian people saw monks as spiritual giants—as one put it, "learned, remote and mysterious . . . ascetic and contemplative." People thought monks could perform miracles, and in time of uncertainty they went to the monasteries to seek their advice.

Perhaps the most notable characteristic of Russian popular spirituality was an intense and lugubrious piety. Henri Troyat spoke of this quality when he recalled:

> Without doubt, the Orthodox Russian people were unstintingly pious, as in the early days of Christianity. The forms of worship, sacraments, benedictions, relics, candles, chants, signs of the cross, and the genuflexions all played a great role in their expression of faith. They were sensitive to the beauty of the ceremonies, but their instincts forced them to find a very deep and very simple evangelical truth behind these ceremonies. Its religion drew its inspiration chiefly from the Sermon on the Mount: "Blessed are the poor in spirit, for theirs is the Kingdom of Heaven. Blessed are the meek, for they shall inherit the earth. . . . Blessed are those who weep, for they shall be comforted. . . . Blessed are the merciful, for they shall obtain mercy . . . " Touched by the Galilean's predictions, the most humble moujik had infinite compassion for his brothers in distress. But, lavish with mercy for others, he ardently hoped that he would receive it himself. [10]

Alexander Vassilievitch described the same quality:

> Russia is haunted by the idea of sin and punishment. In Christ it sees the One who came on earth to save souls in peril and to promise the repentant sinners a better heavenly future than the righteous who thought themselves at peace with their consciences. Is there a criminal that cannot be redeemed by a sincere impulse of the whole being towards the All-Highest? We do not think so. We do not hate the thief, the depraved or the murderer; we are sorry for him, we call him *neschastnyi*, the unfortunate. Always in our minds is the memory of Christ granting the Kingdom of God to the thief who was crucified beside him on Calvary. This is a very pure, very ancient Christianity, stripped of all metaphysics, a reverie on

Russian Orthodox Church Patriarch Timotheus. (Zernov)

suffering, death and future justice, a vague and childish love of everything that breathes, a confused desire for brotherhood, a step towards indefinable felicities.[11]

Such was the soulful beauty of the Russian faith.

Conclusion

Eastern Christians present theirs as the faith that did not change, and in many ways they are correct. For two millenia, they maintained a series of loosely connected regional units—the patriarchates—hierarchical at the local level, but internationally collegial. This was in fact closer to the arrangement of the first-century church than was the centralized, bureaucratized church of Rome. The Orthodox knew the lives and thoughts of the early Christian fathers, and they carried those saints with them in their daily spiritual walk. Throughout their history they

123

maintained a consistent emphasis on the monastic life, on the definitive role of church councils, on the mysteries of the sacraments, and on the power of icons to inspire awe and devotion. Finally, for Eastern Christians, church and state were always intertwined, whether under Rome, Byzantium, the Turks, or the Russian tsars.

Yet in some ways the Eastern Christians changed considerably. Of course, there were changes of theological understanding and emphasis. But beyond these, the Orthodox took in new peoples and cultures as they spread northward; they took on a new language in Church Slavonic; their modes of expression changed to fit the cultural characteristics of the peoples they embraced. The Middle Ages saw them add a much stronger emphasis on the mystical side of Christian faith than had previously been the case. Institutionally, the Christians in Constantinople operated very differently when the Byzantine emperor was the head of their church than when the patriarch served the Turks. Amid all this change, from time to time some people refused to adapt. Frequently, as in the case of the Russian Old Believers, they would spin off to form their own, conservative yet distinct, branch of the faith.

So, as with every other living faith, change was a constant factor. Yet there is at least one way in which the spirituality of Orthodox Christians did not change from the first generations to the most recent. Amid the ebb and flow of change, an intense piety, a personal sense of the transcendence of God and the power of Christ in everyday lives, acted as an anchor for the faith of the people.

Suggested reading

Bratsiotis, Panagiotis. *The Greek Orthodox Church*. Trans. by J. Blenkinsopp. Notre Dame, Ind.: University of Notre Dame Press, 1968.

Brumfield, William C., and Milos M. Velimirovic, eds. *Christianity and the Arts in Russia*. Cambridge: Cambridge University Press, 1991.

Campenhausen, Hans von. *The Fathers of the Greek Church*, trans. by S. Godman. New York: Pantheon, 1959.

"Eastern Orthodoxy."*Christian History*, 16.2 (issue 54, 1997).

Ellis, Jane. *The Russian Orthodox Church: A Contemporary History*. Bloomington, Ind.: Indiana University Press, 1986.

"John Chrysostom."*Christian History*, 13.4 (issue 44, 1994).

Meyendorff, Jean. *The Orthodox Church: Its Past and Its Role in the World Today*, 3d rev. ed. Crestwood, N.Y.: St. Vladimir's Seminary Press, 1981.

Miliukov, Paul. *Outlines of Russian Culture: Part I. Religion and the Church*. Philadelphia: University of Pennsylvania Press, 1942.

"The Millennium of 'Russian' Christianity."*Christian History*, 7.2 (issue 18, 1988).

Nouwen, Henri J. *Behold the Beauty of the Lord: Praying With Icons*. Notre Dame, Ind.: Ave Maria, 1987.

Paraskevas, John E., and Frederick Reinstein. *The Eastern Orthodox Church: A Brief History*. Washington, D.C.: El Greco, 1969.

Preobrazhensky, Alexander. *The Russian Orthodox Church: 10th to 20th Centuries*. Moscow: Progress, 1988.

Ware, Timothy. *The Orthodox Church*. Gloucester, Mass.: P. Smith, 1964.

Way of a Pilgrim, The. Trans. by H. Bacovcin. Garden City, N.Y.: Doubleday, 1978.

Zernov, Nicolas. *Eastern Christendom: A Study of the Origin and Development of the Eastern Orthodox Church*. New York: Putnam's, 1961.

Christians in the Non-Christian World to 1500

Western Christians are accustomed to thinking of Christianity as a European religion. But in its first few centuries it thrived mainly in the Middle East, North Africa, and Asia. Around A.D. 500 one-half of the world's 40 million Christians lived in South Asia, from India to Persia. By contrast, only one-third lived in Europe. One of the neglected truths of history is that where the church first flowered, it later almost ceased to exist. The early churches of Asia, North Africa, and the Middle East can be described under three categories:

1. long-term minorities (for example, the Copts in Egypt);
2. isolated majorities (the Ethiopian church); and
3. extinct churches (the Nestorians in Central Asia).

Chapters 1–3 told the story of the rise of Christianity to dominance in the Roman world. While Christianity was becoming identified with Rome, several of the Eastern and North African churches split away from the Roman Church and from each other, ostensibly over matters of doctrine. While no one can deny the sincerity of these theological quarrels, the disputes often masked underlying ethnic divisions and nationalist aspirations. Two major factors account for the decline (in some cases, the demise) of these churches. One factor was that the center of gravity in Christendom shifted to the north and west, beginning with the Roman acceptance of Christianity in the fourth century. The other was the rise of Islam three centuries later.

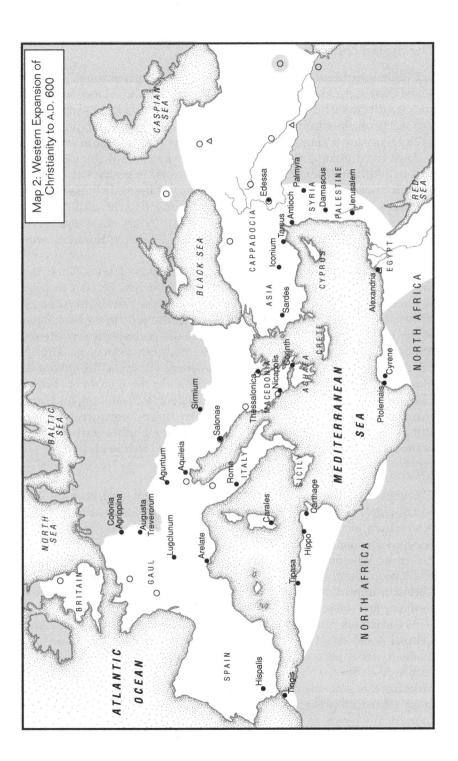

Map 2: Western Expansion of Christianity to A.D. 600

The Syrian church and its offshoots

Christianity began as a Jewish sect. In the early generations, it spread where there were Jews. When the apostles traveled abroad they frequently stayed with Jewish Christians and did their preaching in synagogues. Very early on, Alexandria, a center of Jewish learning in Egypt, became a Christian center. The same happened in other parts of the ancient world.

Jews lived throughout West Asia from the time of the captivities onward. Although some Hebrews were allowed to go back to the land of their ancestors when the Persians defeated the Babylonians in the sixth century B.C., far more stayed in their scattered locations throughout the Persian domains (the book of Esther tells the story of some of these). The Diaspora was made complete after A.D. 70, when Roman armies sacked Jerusalem and destroyed the temple.

As spiritual (and often biological) descendants of Jews, Christians found themselves spread throughout the Roman and Persian empires. Just as the church expanded northward and westward from Rome, so it also expanded eastward out of Edessa, a trading city in the Syrian part of the Persian empire. Edessa was under the ecclesiastical control of Antioch, a Greek-speaking city near the Mediterranean coast. But the Edessans spoke Aramaic, the Semitic language common throughout the Mesopotamian Basin, and they were oriented to the East. From Edessa Christianity spread to Nisibis, Artashat, Seleucia-Ctesiphon, and other cities in what are now Syria, Iraq, eastern Turkey, northwestern Iran, and Armenia. Several ancient Christian texts, including early versions of the New Testament, come from this so-called Syrian church.

Persia

Christianity soon spread throughout Persia (modern Iran), from the Tigris and Euphrates River Valley to the caravan routes of Central Asia. The magi, or wise men, who came to worship the baby Jesus are reputed to have been Persians. Persians and Medians are mentioned by Luke as witnesses at Pentecost. Whether either of these connections resulted in the formation of a Persian church is unknown, but it is certain that there was a substantial Christian minority—well-educated and respected for its knowledge of medicine and the sciences—in many parts of Persia by A.D. 200.

As Christians penetrated Persia they encountered Zoroastrianism, a Central Asian religion that taught both monotheism (one God) and dualism (two aspects of God, one good and one evil). In 224 the warrior-king Ardeshir seized power in Persia and founded the Sassanian dynasty. Ardeshir was a deeply committed Zoroastrian. His conquests brought many Christian prisoners into Persia, but he and his successors also sporadically persecuted the followers of Christ.

Persia repeatedly warred with the Romans. When Constantine's Edict of Toleration (or Milan, 313; see pp. 56–57) made Christianity the semi-official religion of the Roman Empire, patriotic Persians began to persecute their Christian neighbors, whom they accused of being agents of Rome. On Good Friday, April 17, 341, Persian authorities put to death Simon Bar Sabbae, the bishop of Seleucia-Ctesiphon, and about 100 others. The persecution went on for several decades, until the Christians could persuade their fellow citizens that they were loyal Persians despite their now-foreign religion.

Arabia

Like the Hebrews, the Arabs are a Semitic people who trace their ancestry to Abraham. Arabs are listed among the earliest Christians at Pentecost in Acts 2. Most Arab Christians lived near Israel in what is now Jordan. There they interacted with both the Syrian church to the north and the Egyptian church to the southwest. But there were also Christians in other parts of the Arabian Peninsula. In the fourth century Ethiopians brought Coptic Christianity down the Red Sea to Yemen, although a century later the Coptic form had been largely replaced by the Syrian rite. Syrian Christians from Mesopotamia also brought the gospel south through the Persian Gulf to Bahrain in the fourth century.

Arabian Christianity was thus a mixture of the Zoroastrian-influenced Syrian rite and the Coptic pattern of Egypt. Because of the nomadic nature of many Arabian groups, Christianity never achieved a solid foothold among them. When Islam swept across the Middle East in the seventh century Arab Christianity was quickly wiped out.

India

Ancient traditions hold that Christians brought the gospel as far as India in the first generation after Christ. *The Acts of St. Thomas*, an apocryphal book dating from the third century, says that the apostles divided the world among them and Thomas won the privilege of converting India. He was reluctant to go, however, because he could not speak any of the Indian languages. God overcame Thomas's hesitations by arranging to have him sold into slavery as a carpenter. He was bought by Abban, an official sent by the Indian King Gundophorus to buy skilled workers. Carried off to India, Thomas had a number of adventures and succeeded in winning the king and people to Christ.

All this could be dismissed as romantic fancy but for the fact that there was a King Gundobar in northwest India during the latter first century A.D. It certainly would have been possible for Thomas or other Christians of his era to sail to India via either the Red Sea or the Persian Gulf. A lot of trade moved between India and Rome in that era. An overland

Tradition credits the apostle Thomas with introducing Christianity to India. (From Edith Simon, *The Saints* [London: Weidenfeld and Nicolson, 1968])

journey would have been more difficult, but not impossible. The historian Eusebius reports that an Egyptian scholar, Pantaenus, made a missionary trip to India late in the second century. Other sources tell of a Christian community in the Punjab region of northwest India as early as the third century.

Armenia

The gospel also went to Armenia. Located on the southern slopes of the Caucasus Mountains and the plateau of what is now eastern Turkey, Armenia was forever being overrun by one great power or another. In the early centuries after Christ it served as the border battleground between Persia and Rome and later between Russia and Turkey. It became overwhelmingly Christian late in the third century and has held that identity ever since.

Gregory, an Armenian aristocrat, embraced Christianity while exiled from his homeland. When he returned he tried to share his new faith, without much success at first. Gregory then managed to convert the king and several nobles, and a mass conversion of the Armenian population followed. Priests of pre-Christian religions became priests of Christianity. Shrines of pre-Christian religions became Christian churches. Gregory and his descendants became bishops and patriarchs of the Armenian church, and the church eventually became the strongest emblem of Armenian nationalism.

The church was a chief source of cultural conservatism, constantly reminding the people of their history and the necessity of commitment to God and Armenia. It was a democratically inclined church; its main structural feature was decentralization. There were five more-or-less equal patriarchs, with bishops and priests below them. But most major decisions were made by mixed councils of priests and laypeople.

The Church of the Holy Cross reflects the Armenian Christians' desire to hold fast their own ecclesiastical tradition in the midst of occupation by various conquerors. (Atiya)

When Persia conquered Armenia in the fifth century and tried to enforce Zoroastrianism, the Armenians resisted and ultimately won religious liberty. They were equally independent of the Roman and Byzantine churches, rejecting the Council of Chalcedon and becoming monophysite doctrinally (see p. 132). In 491 the Armenian church finally split off from the churches of the West, as much to preserve the political independence of their country from Byzantium as to uphold their theological distinctiveness. In the fifteen centuries since then, Armenia has seldom been an independent nation and has frequently been a target for genocide, but it has always retained its national identity, focused primarily on the Armenian church.

Churches of North Africa

No church better exemplifies the theme of this chapter than that of North Africa. Here Christianity flowered most brilliantly in the first centuries after Christ and disappeared almost utterly with the rise of Islam. North Africa was the home of many of the most brilliant early Christian thinkers and church leaders: Augustine of Hippo; Tertullian and Cyprian of Carthage; and Clement, Origen, Arius, Athanasius, and Cyril of Alexandria. The North African church can be divided into three sectors: Egypt, western North Africa, and Ethiopia. Each had a very different experience with Christianity.

Christianity may have come to the region as early as the first generation after Christ's death. Simon, who carried Jesus' cross, was from Cyrene in what is now eastern Libya, and the Gospel of Mark may have been written in part to his two sons (Mark 15:21; Rom. 16:13). The Ethiopian government minister who became a Christian in Acts 8 presumably took his new religion home with him.

Egypt

While that early conversion does not seem to have resulted in an Ethiopian church, there was a thriving community of Christians farther down the Nile in Egypt by the late second century. Here monasticism was invented, and from here it spread throughout the Roman Empire (see pp. 88–91). At first this church was closely connected with the centers of Greek learning, such as Alexandria, and Christians were mainly Roman citizens. But after about 300, Christianity began to take hold among the indigenous Egyptians. Priests translated the Bible into Coptic, the Egyptian language, and theology and practice began to diverge from Roman standards.

This divergence came to a head in 451 after the Council of Chalcedon declared Jesus was one being with two natures—both fully God and fully human. People called *monophysites* disagreed, saying that Jesus was mostly God and less than fully human. The monophysites lost at Chalcedon, but their view became popular in many non-Roman parts of the church, especially among the Copts of Egypt. It may have been that the monophysite view was more compatible with preexisting Egyptian beliefs about the god Osiris. Certainly this theological dispute provided a vehicle for Egyptians to express resentments against their Byzantine overlords. The controversy continued for nearly two centuries and caused riots and sporadic persecutions.

Carthage

As in Egypt, the church in western North Africa came first to the Latin-speaking population of cities. But, unlike Egypt, here Christianity did not take lasting hold in the rural population. Throughout the empire there was a severe persecution from 303 to 313. After it was over the church was confronted with what to do about those who had denied their faith to avoid persecution. Some thought confession and repentance were sufficient; others demanded that apostates be rebaptized. Many laypeople who had remained true to the faith did not want to take the sacraments from priests and bishops who had recanted or otherwise cooperated with Roman authorities. (For a recent parallel, see the discussion of the Chinese church in Chapter 17, pp. 444–47). So in 312 they split off and appointed a bishop of their own.

This left two groups of Christians in western North Africa; one identified with the lenient treatment of repentant sinners, the other—called *Donatists* after their second bishop—rigorously asserted that some sins are unforgivable. Some historians also detect ethnic resentment from the descendants of the Phoenician-speaking Carthaginians who had been conquered by the Romans some 500 years previously. However,

Augustine, who was probably ethnically Carthaginian,[1] was among those who attacked the Donatists, who had no one of comparable brilliance on their side. At a bishops' conference at Carthage in 411, the Donatists were labeled heretics. They were violently suppressed; by 413 all had been killed or dispersed into hiding. Most of the Catholic population of North Africa died off when the barbarian Vandals sacked the cities later in the fifth century, but Donatists survived in rural areas. When Islam presented a faith as rigorous as the Donatists' some three hundred years later, most readily converted.

Ethiopia

If Christianity did not take hold in Ethiopia through the queen's minister mentioned in Acts, it surely did in the fourth century. Frumentius and Aedesius, two young sailors from Tyre, were on a ship returning from India via the Red Sea. When their ship put in for provisions along the Ethiopian coast, it was attacked and all but the two boys were killed. The king took them into his service at Axum. In time they convinced several people, including the king, of the truth of the message about Christ. Aedesius went back to Tyre, but Frumentius stayed on and ultimately was appointed bishop of Axum. At first only the upper strata of Ethiopian society became Christians. Then, in the fifth and sixth centuries, Syrian monks came to evangelize and translate the Bible into the local language. Soon the majority of Ethiopians were steadfast Christians. The Islamic conquest of Egypt in 638, however, cut them off from other Christians.

The dance of Ethiopian Christian priests is part of a distinct church that dates back to at least the fourth century. Through much of its existence Ethiopian Christianity has coexisted with a dominant Islam. (Zernov)

Muslim conquest

Islam exploded across the Middle East and North Africa in the seventh century. Its founder and prophet, Muhammad (570–632), was a well-born but poor resident of Mecca, a caravan town on the water route from Egypt to India. He began to have visions at age forty, and soon proclaimed a new religion to his fellow Arabs. This religion recognized one God, Allah, who was also the God of Judaism and Christianity. Muhammad recognized the law of Moses, David's Psalms, and the Gospels as all part of God's revelation. He regarded both Moses and Jesus as prophets of God, although he did not regard Jesus as divine. Perhaps building on Christian ideas, Muhammad propounded the idea of progressive revelation: each new revelation from God superseded those that had gone before. Thus, just as (in Muhammad's view) Jesus' gospel superseded Moses' law, so God's message to Muhammad, recorded in the *Qur'an*, superseded the Bible.

The *Qur'an* was more than just a theological document. Like *Torah*, it specified rules for religious observance and daily living and a strict set of penalties for those who failed at righteousness. Muhammad set up a theocratic state at Medina and soon won several Arab tribes to the banner of Islam. After his death in 632 Muhammad's disciples took the new religion on a campaign of conquest, converting whole populations in the process. By 634 the entire Arabian Peninsula was in Muslim hands. In 651 the Arab conquests stretched from the Nile Valley to the Persian Plateau. By 715 they had conquered the rest of North Africa and the greater part of Spain. From those limits, Islam stretched out in later centuries to become the dominant religion as far away as West Africa, India, and Indonesia.

Although the Arab conquerors quickly broke up into several warring factions, there were certain common aspects of Arab rule over Christians throughout most of the newly conquered territories. As has been noted, the Arabs allowed many Christians to retain their faith because they were "people of the book." But they had to pay special taxes, they had to wear badges or special clothing, and they were forbidden to build new churches or to evangelize Muslims. Borrowing a Persian practice, the Arab caliphs treated the Christian population of each country as a community under the control of its religious leaders and held those patriarchs responsible for the behavior of all Christians. In practice, Muslim religious fervor led to sporadic waves of persecution, especially when Muslims viewed the Christians' use of images in worship as idolatry. Under these disabilities, the Christian population of Arab-controlled countries either declined into a static, defensive minority or died out completely.

The Monastery of St. Antony is one of the last Coptic monasteries in the Egyptian desert. (Atiya)

Egypt

Coptic Christians had long chafed against the Catholicism of the Roman and Byzantine empires. Many Egyptian Christians welcomed the Arabs at first as liberators, and some served in the Arab administration of their country. But within a century they came to resent the poll tax, land tax, and other disadvantages of being Christians in a Muslim society. The numbers of Christians declined sharply when the government said converts to Islam would not have to pay the poll tax. Perhaps as many as 24,000 Christians converted in 744 alone. Egyptian attempts to throw off the Arab yoke failed, and persecution followed. Yet the Coptic Church has survived twelve centuries of Muslim domination, although vastly reduced in size and vigor, as a symbol of Egyptian nationalism.

Two aspects of Coptic church life deserve further description. One is the hierarchical nature of the Egyptian church. A strong structure of institutional leadership helped the Egyptian church survive persecutions while other groups of Christians disappeared. At the top was the pope of Alexandria and patriarch of the See of St. Mark. This Coptic ruler was one of four ancient patriarchs who traced their lineage to the apostles, the others being at Rome, Antioch, and Constantinople. This patriarch was not seen as infallible, but he could not be removed and was the supreme authority in church life. Since he was selected by lot from a group of elderly and pure monks, he was beholden only to God. Beneath him was a hierarchy of archbishops, bishops, abbots, archpriests, priests, archdeacons, and deacons. As in the Roman Church, all those above the rank of archdeacon were celibate and served for life. The monastic movement began in Egypt and continued to be central to Christian practice there long after it had faded away in Europe.

The center of Coptic Christianity was not the individual but the worshiping community. The Mass, heavy with ritual, emphasized God's people as a corporate entity calling on their Lord for cleansing, purification, preservation, and protection. Something of the aura of worship in a Coptic church comes through in this early twentieth-century description by Adrian Fortescu:

> Perhaps nowhere in the world can you imagine yourself back in so remote an age as when you are in a Coptic church. You go into a strange dark building; at first the European needs an effort to realize that it is a church at all, it looks so different from our usual association. But it is enormously older than the . . . chapels to which we are accustomed. In a Coptic church you come into low dark spaces, a labyrinth of irregular openings. There is little light from the narrow windows. Dimly you see strange rich colours and tarnished gold, all mellowed by dirt. In the vault above hang ropes bearing the white ostrich eggs [a symbol of watchfulness], and lamps sparkle in the gloom. Before you is the exquisite carving, inlay and delicate patterns, of the *haikal* screen. All around you see, dusty and confused, wonderful pieces of wood carving. Behind the screen looms the curve of the apse; on the thick columns and along the walls under the low cupolas are inscriptions in exquisite lettering—Coptic and Arabic.[2]

Western North Africa

In western North Africa the Christian church did not survive. When the Arabs arrived in 697, the majority of those Christians who could leave the region did so. There was a massive exodus of upper-class Catholics to Italy and Spain. The only effective resistance to Arab power came from Berber tribes, which had not been evangelized by Christians. The Donatists mostly embraced Islam as a welcome contrast to what they perceived as the wishy-washy leniency of the Catholics.

Ethiopia

The Ethiopian story is different. There, Christianity remained the majority religion, and it still is. Because there are so few reliable written records, historians know very little about Ethiopia from about 700 to 1270. But the Christian church emerged from centuries of isolation

6.1. Nestorius and Cyril

The career of Nestorius provides an example of the degree to which issues of regional loyalty and personal ambition became entwined in theological disputes, and the depth of passion such disputes could arouse. As the popular bishop of Constantinople, Nestorius was one of the most powerful figures in the fifth-century church. An orthodox trinitarian, follower of the Nicene Creed, and opponent of Arianism, Nestorius ran afoul of a dispute over the mixture of human and divine elements in Christ's person and died wearing the heretic's label.

On one side were such people as Cyril, bishop of Alexandria, who emphasized the divine nature of Christ almost to the exclusion of the human nature. Cyril was accused of embracing the Gnostic heresy by overemphasizing Christ's divinity.

Apparently deciding the best defense was a good offense, Cyril attacked Nestorius. Nestorius was accused, although he denied the charge, of saying Christ was both human and divine, but that his two natures were so distinct as to amount to two different beings.

Nestorius did say that the term "Mary, mother of God," was inappropriate, and he protested against the rising worship of Mary.

Cyril has been accused of acting against his rival largely out of a desire to aggrandize the see of Alexandria at the expense of Constantinople. The dispute grew so loud that the Roman emperor called a bishops' council at Ephesus in 431. Cyril and his supporters arrived first, started the meeting without Nestorius and his bishops, condemned Nestorius' supposed position, and removed him from office. Nestorius' people arrived, held their own council, and excommunicated Cyril. Cyril's people went on a rampage, physically attacking Nestorius and his supporters.

In time the emperor and Celestine, bishop of Rome, intervened on Cyril's side. Celestine's action may have stemmed as much from a desire to promote Rome's position at the expense of Constantinople as from theological conviction. Condemned as a heretic, Nestorius was exiled to a monastery, apparently in Egypt. There he lived out his days in great emotional and physical distress, praying and writing in defense of his position.

strong and unified, having fought off Islamic forces for centuries. As was the case in Armenia, Ethiopia as a nation depended on its particular brand of Christianity for its identity. After a nationwide revival around 1300, Ethiopian monarchs and church leaders began to reach out past the Muslim barrier to communicate with European Christians.

Nestorians

One of the places the Christian church survived Islam was in Persia. This was partly because in the fifth century a great change came upon the Syrian-derived churches—they embraced the Nestorian heresy (see box 6.1). The Roman Empire's church leaders reaffirmed their anti-Nestorian decision at the Council of Chalcedon in 451. This signaled a decisive break between the Syrian and Byzantine churches. Those priests who agreed with Nestorius went into exile. Many took refuge at Nisibis and other points in the Persian empire. From that time onward, Persian Christians came to be called Nestorians and were regarded as heretics. In return, the Nestorians regarded Catholics as heretics. The Nestorian Christians were able to prosper in Persia partly because they could point to this doctrinal controversy as convincing proof that they were loyal Persians and not agents of Rome.

Sometimes this separateness went to extreme lengths. In 484 Bar Sauma was Bishop of Nisibis and ambitious to move up to the position of patriarch, then held by Babowai. Using his connections at the Persian court, Bar Sauma managed to have Babowai condemned for treason because he had sent a letter to the Byzantine emperor. Babowai was executed: suspended by the ring finger with which he had sealed the letter, he starved to death. Although Bar Sauma may have demonstrated his loyalty to Persia, he never managed to ascend to the patriarchate.

One of the features that made Persian Christianity stand out was the fact that not all believers were baptized. Baptism seems to have been reserved for those—priests, nuns, and laypeople—who were prepared to lead a life of celibacy and self-denial. Believers who were not ascetic and celibate could not receive baptism, and perhaps not the other sacraments, either.

Some historians say this spiritual elitism is the reason Christianity never became the majority religion in Persia. But one must remember that Persia in that time was a melting pot of many religions—Judaism, Buddhism, Hinduism, Nazoreanism, Manichaeism, and Christianity, along with the state-supported Zoroastrianism. Soon all these would be overwhelmed by Islam. The Nestorians were zealous missionaries who carried their faith along the caravan routes deep into Asia. They converted both individuals and entire tribes. The Uighurs, Onguts, and Keraits all were Christian peoples in the thirteenth century, as were many Huns and other Turks and Mongols, several hundred thousand in all. Even Chinghis Khan (1162?–1227), founder of the Mongol empire, took a Christian wife in a marriage alliance with the Keraits. By 1500, however, most of this Christian growth had been lost. These Central Asian peoples turned to Islam or, among the Mongols, to Buddhism.

Mar Johanan, bishop of Ooroomiah. (Billy Graham Center)

India

One place where the Nestorian presence survived was India. There are reports of Christians in southern India, in Kerala and Sri Lanka, during the sixth century. These may have been descendants of a group that was reputed to exist in the Punjab in earlier times. They identified themselves by the name of St. Thomas. However, it is more likely these Christians were descended from Nestorian merchants who came later by sea. These Persian merchants doubtless married Indian women and over generations formed a native Indian branch of the Nestorian Church. Since that time they have been called "Syrians," for that is the origin of their faith, although they are ethnically South Indians. For centuries their bishops were sent from Persia; they conducted their services in Syriac even though few of the participants understood that language. In this they were similar to Europeans who retained Latin for worship.

Very little is known about the lives of these Nestorians of South India. Outside of Kerala their numbers were very small and their influence insignificant. Their ranks must constantly have been depleted, for it was easy to slip into the accommodating grasp of Hinduism. Hinduism did not attack other religions; it just ingested them by making room for their

The catholicos (patriarch) of the Nestorian Thomasite Church. (Leslie W. Brown, *The Indian Christians of St. Thomas* [New York: Cambridge University Press, 1982])

gods in its pantheon and gradually adulterating their practices. As for the Thomasite Christians reported in the first few centuries in the Punjab, it is possible they moved south to join Nestorian communities. More likely they were simply absorbed into Hinduism. Any vestiges that remained would have been wiped out after Islam took North India in the tenth century.

China

Nestorians also brought Christianity to China. There, as in India, they encountered one of the world's oldest civilizations. But Chinese society was much more unified and tightly organized than Indian society, and Chinese religion did not accommodate foreign faiths but rather overwhelmed them. The mainstay of Chinese philosophy and social organization has been Confucianism for more than 2000 years. Codified by the sage Confucius in the fifth century B.C., it is a practical, this-worldly religion stressing hierarchy, order, right behavior, and duty to family and state. Confucianism is the glue that holds Chinese society together. It is balanced by Daoism, a native Chinese religion with a more contemplative, mystical spirit, and by Buddhism, an import from India. Together, these three did a comprehensive job of satisfying the spiritual needs of the vast majority of Chinese people. Although foreign religions, from Christianity to Zoroastrianism, were tolerated in China at various times, none except Islam ever took hold, and that only among minority peoples on China's western fringe.

Small Christian communities, protected by the emperors, thrived in China wherever Middle Easterners traded. An exception to this protection was during the reigns of the Empress Wu Hou and her immediate successors (683–705). Several Turkish tribes of Central Asia—the Uighurs prominent among them—became Christians through the ministry of Nestorian merchants and priests. It is even possible the Chinese emperor, Xuan Zung, and his family may have become Christians. Some Daoist monks, however, felt threatened and persuaded the Emperor Wu Zung in 845 to persecute all the foreign religions, and Christianity was wiped out. It is unclear what became of the Chinese Christian population. Some people may have emigrated into Central Asia. Others may have converted to Buddhism, Islam, or Manichaeism. A tiny number survived down to the seventeenth century, when they were rediscovered in sad condition by Jesuit missionaries going through the motions of worshiping God but not understanding much of the content of their religion.

In the thirteenth century Nestorian Christianity again came to China along with the Mongol conquest. Mongol leaders had taken Christian wives from such Central Asian peoples as the Keraits, and their offspring spread throughout China as the Mongols consolidated their control of the country. After this second, propitious start, the church died again when in 1358 the Mongol dynasty collapsed, and Christians lost government protection.

Despite their ultimate failure to establish a lasting Christian presence in China, the Nestorians were more successful than any later group of missionaries at putting the gospel of Christ into Chinese idioms and at winning a measure of acceptance from the Chinese people and government. This seems to have been due partly to their habit of appropriating terms and concepts from native Chinese religions, such as Confucianism, Daoism, and the popular new religion, Buddhism. Also it was due to the patronage of pow-

6.2. Mark and Sauma

The careers of Mark and Rabban Sauma, two Chinese Nestorians, reveal the fluid nature of the contest between Christianity and Islam in Central Asia in the thirteenth century.

Both were members of the Uighur tribe, one of several largely Christian Central Asian peoples in those years. Sauma was born in Khanbalik (Beijing) about 1250 during the Mongol Yuan dynasty. He and his friend Mark became Nestorian monks and set off through Tibet for the caravan routes of Central Asia on a pilgrimage to Jerusalem.

On the way they stopped in Baghdad, capital of the Persian portion of the Mongol Empire, where they became friends of the Nestorian patriarch, Denha I. On Denha's death in 1280 Mark was chosen to be the new patriarch or supreme father of Nestorian Christianity and served for 36 years. Soon he sent Sauma off to the capitals of Western Europe to represent the Nestorian Church and the Persian Khan's domains, hoping to convince the Western leaders to join them in an assault on the Muslim powers. Sauma celebrated Mass with Pope Nicholas IV and visited King Philip of France, Edward I of England, and other European leaders; but he could not raise the help he needed. Thus a Christian member of a Turkish tribe, born in China, served a Persian monarch within the Mongol empire as ambassador to the courts of Europe.

In the decades that followed, however, nearly all the peoples of West and Central Asia surrendered to the inevitable and embraced Islam. Nestorian Christians fell into the role of a persecuted minority.

erful Chinese leaders. And still further it was due to the Nestorians' willingness to ignore those aspects of Christianity that the Chinese found objectionable, such as the crucifixion and death of Christ. Their ultimate failure may be attributed to three things: the absorptive powers of Confucianism—which over the centuries overwhelmed one cultural invader after another; Buddhism, which was new, extremely popular, and met many of the needs Christianity might have addressed; and their heavy reliance on the patronage of cosmopolitan emperors. When there was a change at the top, they easily came under attack.

6.3. The Nestorian Stele

The Nestorian writer Adam engraved a message in Chinese and Syriac on a stele near Changan (Xian) in 781, commemorating nearly 150 years of Nestorian Christianity in China. It read in part:

Then the Messias, one of the Three Persons, covered his true majesty and making himself a man, appeared unto the world. An angel came to minister the mystery, and a Virgin brought forth the Holy One. A star appeared which gave notice of his birth to those of the kingdom of Persia. They came to offer him Tribute, and all was done according to what had been foretold by the four-and-twenty saints. He published to the world the most true law. He purified their customs and rectified the faith. He cleansed the world. He perfected virtue and therein founded the three virtues. He opened the way to life and shut up that of death. He manifested the bright day and banished the obscure darkness. He conquered the obscure seat, at what time the devil remained wholly subdued, and succoured with his mercy the sinking world, that men might ascend to the habitations of light. After He had per-

fected his work, He ascended into the heavens at Midday. There remained 27 books of holy scripture [literally, 27 sutras, a Buddhist term]. There was opened the gate to conversion by means of that water which cleanseth and purifieth. His ministers made use of the holy Cross, they made their abode no more in one place than another, that they might illuminate the whole world. The world being thus reduced to union, men did walk after their example, and thus did they open the way to life and glory. . . .

By this means, at the time, when a king named T'ai Tsung did govern with famous prudence and sanctity, there came from Judea a man of high virtue, by name Alopen, who being guided by the clouds brought the true doctrine. And in the year A.D. 635 he arrived at court. The king commanded the Colao, Fang Hsuan-ling, that he should go and meet him as far as the West, and that he should treat him as his guest with all manner of kindness. He caused this doctrine to be translated in his palace, and seeing the law to be true, he powerfully commanded it should be divulged through the Kingdom, and presently after, he sent forth a royal patent, which contained that which followeth. . . .

The great emperor Kao-Tsung, the son of T'ai Tsung, continued with good decorum the intention of his grandfather, enlarging and adorning the works of his father. For he commanded that in all his provinces churches should be built and honours conferred on Alopen, bestowing upon him the title of bishop of the great law, by which law he governed the kingdom of China in great peace, and the church filled the whole country with the prosperity of preaching.

In the year 698 (699) the bonzes of the sect of the pagodas, using their wonted violence, did blaspheme this new and holy law, in this place of Eastern Chou; and in the year 712

some particular persons in the Western Hao with laughter and disparagement did mock it. . . .

*The king gave many honourable titles in his court to the priest I-ssu, a great preacher of the Law, and also a garment of red colour, because he was peaceable and took delight in doing good to all. He came from afar off into China from the country of Balkh. His virtue surpassed our three famous families; he enlarged the other sciences perfectly. He served the king in the palace and afterwards had his name in the royal book. . . . **

*Alvarez Semedo, The History of the Great and Renowned Monarchy of China (London, 1655), 158–63; reproduced in Columba Cary-Elwes, China and the Cross (New York: Kennedy, 1957), 285–90.

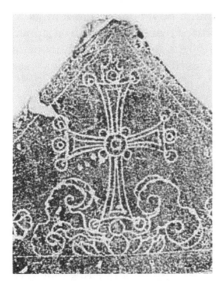

A rubbing from the Chinese Nestorian stele. (Arthur C. Moule, *Christians in China before the Year 1550* [London: Society for Promoting Christian Knowledge, 1930])

The Catholic Church in the East

Up to the thirteenth century nearly all Christian ministry in Asia, Africa, and the Middle East had been begun by Christians with origins in the Syrian or North African churches. Then two new Roman Catholic orders, the Franciscans and the Dominicans, were founded in Europe as efforts to reform European monasticism. Their members were not monks but friars, men who took monastic oaths of chastity, poverty, and obedience but who went out into the world to preach rather than into seclusion to contemplate.

143

Both orders were at the forefront of a growing Catholic missionary enterprise over the next few centuries. The Catholics had a long way to go to catch up to the Nestorians. St. Francis of Assisi (1182–1226), founder of the Franciscans, preached in Egypt. Other Franciscans and Dominicans went as missionaries to the Middle East. There, however, they seem to have concentrated more on prying loose Nestorian and Armenian Christians than on making new converts among the Muslim population.

John of Montecorvino was the first Catholic missionary to Asia. Born in Italy in 1247, he became a Franciscan friar and went to the Middle East, then on to India around 1292. After a year in India he journeyed to China, bearing a letter from the pope to Khubilai Khan, the Chinese emperor. John's mission was opposed by resident Nestorians who still regarded the Church of Rome as heretical, but the emperor allowed John to build a church in Beijing and to preach. By 1305 John had baptized 6000 converts. The Pope sent reinforcements, and the work continued to expand. But Rome's endeavors, along with Nestorianism, was destroyed when the nationalist Ming dynasty came to power in 1368.

Raymond Lull (1232–1315) was a wealthy Majorcan who ultimately became part of the Franciscan missionary effort. After having several visions of the suffering Christ he left his family to serve the Lord. He wrote and lobbied for missionary expeditions to the Mongols and Arabs, and devised and taught an evangelistic system at centers of learning throughout Europe. Late in life he made three attempts to bring the gospel to North Africa. Deported twice, he finally was stoned to death in 1315. Lull was a herald of the beginnings of European expansion and of the contentious, aggressive spirit that missions were to take in later centuries.

Conclusion

The Christian communities described in this chapter all fall into one of three categories: *long-term minority*, *isolated majority*, or *extinct church*.

In India, Egypt, and Persia, Christians were able to resist the crush of Hinduism and Islam and survive, but they could never manage to become more than a tolerated minority.

The Christians of Ethiopia and Armenia were isolated majorities. In both cases, they were cut off from regular contact with other varieties of Christians by political or ethnic forces, and in both cases they proceeded along paths of separate evolution. Their churches came to be closely identified with the ethnic feelings and national aspirations of their respective peoples.

The Christian churches of North Africa, Central Asia, and China became extinct when they were overtaken by other religions—particularly Islam, Buddhism, and Confucianism—that were exclusive in their claims.

It is important to note the key role politics played in each of these areas. The destruction of the church in western North Africa was influenced by Roman political schisms; the death of Chinese Christianity came with the fall of the Mongol dynasty; and the strength of Armenian Christianity was intimately related to Armenian nationalism.

Suggested readings

Atiya, Aziz S. *A History of Eastern Christianity*, rev. ed. Millwood, N.Y.: Kraus, 1980.

Brown, Leslie W. *The Indian Christians of St. Thomas: An Account of the Ancient Syrian Church of Malabar*, rev. ed. New York: Cambridge University Press, 1982.

Cary-Elwes, Columba. *China and the Cross: A Survey of Missionary History.* New York: Kennedy, 1957.

Falk, Peter. *The Growth of the Church in Africa.* Grand Rapids: Zondervan, 1979.

Hastings, Adrian. *The Church in Africa: 1450–1950.* New York: Oxford University Press, 1994.

Isichei, Elizabeth A. *A History of Christianity in Africa: From Antiquity to the Present.* Grand Rapids: Eerdmans, 1995.

Latourette, Kenneth Scott. *A History of the Expansion of Christianity:* Vol. 2. *The Thousand Years of Uncertainty, 500 A.D. to 1500 A.D.* Grand Rapids: Zondervan, 1966.

Neill, Stephen. *A History of Christianity in India: The Beginnings to A.D. 1707.* New York: Cambridge University Press, 1984.

Trimingham, J. Spencer. *Christianity Among the Arabs in Pre-Islamic Times.* New York: Longman, 1978.

Waterfield, Robin E. *Christians in Persia: Assyrians, Armenians, Roman Catholics and Protestants.* New York: Barnes and Noble, 1973.

7

Transformation and Renaissance

The Black Death

The relatively stable medieval society, unified at least in theory, was greatly shaken in the fourteenth and fifteenth centuries by a series of crises. Chief of these was bubonic plague, called the *Black Death*, an epidemic that began in 1347 and cycled through Europe for the next four centuries. It cut a swath that left a third of Europe's population dead.

By the late thirteenth and early fourteenth centuries, Europe was fully populated. All land that could possibly be tilled had been put under the plow and still the population grew more rapidly than its food supply. The continent was ripe for catastrophe.

Catastrophe struck—the "Little Ice Age." Europe became a few degrees colder and a little wetter. This shortened the growing season just enough to cause periodic famines and temporary shortages. Poor roads and limited transportation facilities meant that, even if one part of Europe had surplus grain rotting in storage, other regions suffered acute shortfalls.

Although few actually died of starvation, the weakened population became susceptible to a major epidemic, which came in 1347. The plague, transmitted from rats to humans by fleas, causes swelling and lesions in the lymph nodes, which then turn black and fetid. In Europe 90 percent of those infected within three weeks after a new outbreak died within the next three days, though the death rate declined to 30 percent thereafter. As late as 1660, after three centuries of continuous outbreaks throughout Britain and continental Europe, the Black Death killed 2000 people a week in London. No one understood the causes of the disease or how to prevent it, since even the most elementary sanitary precautions were completely unknown. Many viewed it as the wrath of God for the sins of the world and tried to deal with it in religious or ceremonial ways.

The nursery rhyme "Ring around the Rosie" was originally sung as a memorial to the children who fell to the Black Death. The "ring" refers to fever-flushed cheeks, "posies" to flowers the children put in their pockets to mask the nauseating smell of fetid lymph nodes, and "a-tishu, a-tishu" (with regional variants) to the final sneezing before the children all fell down dead. Some English children still sing it each May Day to remember the children who died by the plague.

In the *Danse Macabre* ("Dance of Death") there was a more extreme response to the plague—a person representing death and carrying a scythe led a marathon snake dance. Those who fell from exhaustion often were trampled to death by the remaining dancers. The *Danse Macabre* attempted to appease death, but like "Ring around the Rosie," it more truly recognized the plague's power over the dancers' lives.

Perhaps the most widespread of the popular plague-related cults, the bands of flagellants, tried to do penance on behalf of society to induce a punishing God to forgive their sins and spare them. The flagellants turned a normally private form of penance into a public and collective imitation of Christ on behalf of the entire body of Christ. Their processions, ranging from fifty to 500 participants, lasted for thirty-three and one-half days, a day for each year of Christ's earthly life.

7.1. *Ars Morienda*

The *Ars Morienda* ("art of dying") literature trained people to die well, giving them appropriate sentiments and words to speak to the family gathered around the deathbed. These little books were among the most popular forms of literature from the fourteenth through the seventeenth centuries.

Thank Him ever, while thy soul is in thy body, and put all thy trust in His passion and His death only, having trust in none other thing. To this death commit thee fully. In His death wrap all thyself fully; and if it come to thy mind, or by thine enemy it be put into thy mind, that God will damn thee, say thus:

Lord, I put the death of Our Lord Jesus Christ between me and mine evil deeds, between me and the judgment; otherwise I will not strive with Thee.

If He say: Thou has deserved damnation; say thou again: The death of our Lord Jesus Christ I put between me and mine evil merits, and the merits of His worthy passion I offer for merits I should have had, and alas have not. Say also: Lord, put the death of my Lord Jesus Christ between me and Thy righteousness. *

*F. M. Comper, ed., The Book of the Craft of Dying and Other Early English Tracts Concerning Death (London, n.p., 1917).

Each day they would travel to a different town, hear Mass in the church, then gather in the town square. There they stripped to the waist and formed a circle. Each in turn dropped to the ground with arms outstretched in the shape of a cross, while those still standing stepped over the fallen, lightly striking down with the whips they carried. When they were all on the ground, they arose together and began whipping themselves in earnest while singing hymns to celebrate Jesus' suffering. This happened twice each day in public. A third, private flagellation was conducted in the evening. The flagellants hoped their action would remind God that he no longer needed to punish Christians, since Christ had already suffered and died to redeem his children.

7.2. Flagellant

A foutheenth-century monk described a personal flagellation. One winter's night this man . . .

shut himself up in his cell and stripped himself naked. . . . and took his scourge with the sharp spikes and beat himself on the body and the arms and on the legs till blood poured off him. . . . One of the spikes on the scourge was bent crooked like a hook, and whatever flesh it caught tore off. He beat himself so hard that the scourge broke into three bits and the points flew against the wall. He stood there bleeding and gazed at himself. It was such a wretched sight that he was reminded in many ways of the appearance of the beloved Christ when he was fearfully beaten. Out of pity for himself he began to weep bitterly. And he knelt down, naked and covered in blood in the frosty air, and prayed to God to wipe out his sins from before his gentle eyes.*

*Norman Cohn, Pursuit of the Millennium, rev. ed. (New York: Oxford University Press, 1970),127.

The Black Death did have a positive effect. For serfs and townspeople who survived, it was a golden age. Game was plentiful in the forests, which reclaimed the cropland that could no longer be cultivated. Land could be rented cheaply, and labor was at a premium. Landlords often substituted animal crops, such as wool, milk, and meat, for grain crops. A few herdsmen could produce a respectable income on land that would have required many hands to cultivate grain. In Florence, workers' wages doubled in 1348 after more than a century of stagnation.

The population crisis also contributed to the end of the manorial and feudal systems, and new capital-intensive machines replaced labor-intensive ways to produce goods.

In England, however, landlords squeezed between rising labor costs and shrinking markets turned to the government for help. They managed to agree to freeze wages in 1379. This alienated the wage-earners, who saw their hopes for a better life blocked, particularly since the freeze was added to the "poll tax" of 1377 and 1381. The poll tax was levied on every man, woman, and child, rich and poor alike. The peasants responded by revolting in late May and early June of 1381. The revolt, though short-lived, shook English society to its foundations. Combining the ideals of religious and social equality, John Ball, the priest who led the revolt with Wat Tyler, summarized their feelings in the rhyme:

> *When Adam delved and Eve span,*
> *Who was then a gentleman?*

The rebels demanded equality before the law, abolition of serfdom, confiscation and redistribution of church lands not immediately supporting a parish priest, abolition of all lordships in the realm except that of the king, and abolition of all bishops but one. The rebels invaded London, looting and burning. They murdered the archbishop of Canterbury, the prior of the wealthy order of the Knights Hospitaler, and the royal treasurer before the fourteen-year-old King Richard II agreed to their demands. At a second meeting between the king and the rebels to iron out details, Wat Tyler was seized by the lord mayor of London, then killed when he drew his sword to defend himself. The rebellion immediately collapsed, but it left a lasting scar on the English ruling classes.

The Babylonian captivity

As society was reeling from the effects of the Black Death, the Church hierarchy failed to respond to the crisis. Innocent III (1160–1216) and Gregory VII (c. 1023–1085) had subdued kings and asserted the supreme power of the Church in the investiture controversy. But now King Philip the Fair of France managed to manipulate the appointment of a French pope, Clement V (1264–1314). Clement was concerned about political instability and physical danger in Italy, so he moved his headquarters to papal territory inside France at Avignon in 1305. There he and his successors ruled the Church for seven decades. Although the Avignon popes were less dependent on the French kings than the Roman popes had been on powerful Italian families, few Christians believed they were independent. This seventy years at Avignon was referred to as the *Babylonian captivity*, reminding pious church people of the seventy years Israel spent in Babylon.

The popes at Avignon were primarily administrators, not noted for their spiritual qualities. They believed their primary responsibility was to ensure the church's independence by making her financially secure and wealthy enough to meet secular rulers on equal terms. Therefore, any source of revenue the church could claim was exploited. Moneys

149

were funneled through Europe's largest bureaucracy, which was centered in a magnificent papal court. Avignon popes also began to centralize Church law to gain independence from secular rulers who were asserting control over national churches.

The great schism

In 1378, two years after Pope Gregory XI (c. 1329–1378) returned the papal court to Rome, the college of cardinals elected an Italian archbishop as pope. But he so thoroughly alienated the cardinals that they rescinded their decision six weeks later, declared the election void, and elected another French pope, Clement VII (1478–1534). Clement moved back to Avignon and the *great schism* began. Half of Europe's church leaders accepted Clement VII, while the other half remained loyal to the pope at Rome. Few based their choice on religious motives, but rather on what they thought politically advantageous to their nation or region. Godly laypeople who knew about the schism were heartsick and disillusioned. In response to the desire for a unified Church, the Council of Pisa met in 1409, deposed both popes, and elected a third. Neither of the sitting popes accepted the agreement, so now there were three.

In 1417 the Council of Constance met with more success, partly because it asserted its authority more firmly. The council accepted the resignation of one pope, declared a second deposed, and discounted the claims of the third entirely. Then they chose a new pope, Martin V (1368–1431). He lived to be the undisputed head of the European Roman Church, but not before great damage had been done to the Church and its prestige. The state of the Church in the aftermath of these troubles led to the widespread growth of heresy, opposition to the hierarchy, and strong calls for reform.

7.3. The Council of Constance

This holy Council of Constance . . . declares, first that it is lawfully assembled in the Holy Spirit, that it constitutes a General Council, representing the Catholic Church, and that therefore it has its authority immediately from Christ; and that all men of every rank and condition, including the pope himself are bound to obey it in matters concerning the Faith, the abolition of the schism and the reformation of the Church of God in its head and members.

Henry S. Bettenson, ed., *Documents of the Christian Church* (New York: Oxford University Press, 1961), 192–93.

Lay piety and mysticism

The nature of piety began to shift in the fourteenth century. Christians relied less on the clergy and the institutional Church than on direct access to God. Partly in response to the plagues, partly in response to the difficulties in the Church, but largely in response to sensitivity toward God's Spirit, a wave of mystical spirituality swept through Europe.

Early in the fourteenth century the great mystic Meister Eckhart (c.1260–c.1327) taught that the true goal of life was complete separation from the world of the senses by being absorbed into the "Divine Unknown." Eckhart had many followers, and as the century progressed several large mystical communities were formed in response to his teachings.

Eckhart Von Hochheim, or Meister Eckhart (c.1260–c.1327), was a preacher, writer, and mystic, the meaning of whose ideas still stir debate. After his death, he was judged to be heretical by the pope. (Billy Graham Center)

Although the Flemish word means "nuns," the *Béguines* (see p. 97) were pious laywomen who lived together to develop their spiritual lives. *Béguinages* ("convents") were formed to meet the need for mystical religious communities and also helped to resolve a major problem. Late medieval women were expected to commit themselves, either in marriage or to the nunnery, while the younger sons of upper-class medieval families were discouraged from marrying. Many women found the permanence and formidable cost of the nunnery forbidding, yet they were unable to marry. The *béguinages* provided an alternative for those women who were pious and mystical but who had no desire to commit themselves for life. Most *béguines* worked at a task, such as weaving, to support the community, or staffed hospitals for the sick and hospitality houses for the wayfaring. While they worked they devoted much of their time to prayer and contemplation.

But the movement justified the Church's reluctance to accept mysticism when it fell into serious heresy in the early fourteenth century. These women were formally independent of the discipline of local parish priests, and as a result fell under the sway of itinerant heretical mystical guides, who led the *béguines* through mystical contemplation and ascetic practices toward the goal of union with God. Union with God, however, turned the mystic *into* God on earth. Since God is the lawgiver, mystical union freed the mystic from both human and moral law. For example, an adherent to a seventeenth-century English version of the heresy said the test of true mystical union was to "commit all sin as if it were no sin."

151

The most convenient way to do so was to violate each of the Ten Commandments in order, to show that blasphemy, adultery, and murder were perfectly acceptable to one who was in union with God.

Once the hierarchy learned of the heresy of the *béguinages*, it closed them down. Yet the idea of a semi-monastic community of religious women remained alive and resurfaced later in the fourteenth century as the *Sisters of the Common Life*.

Devotio moderna

The Sisters of the Common Life, the successors to the *béguinages* in the Low Countries, formed a part of the popular revival known as the *devotio moderna*. The *devotio moderna* began when a book-loving preacher by the name of Geert Groote (1340–1384) started preaching in Dutch. Groote tried to combine genuine heartfelt piety with a deep appreciation for learning, and fostered that double appreciation in those he converted. A complex and multifaceted movement, the *devotio moderna* was primarily a great lay revival, though it was accompanied by monastic and educational reform.

The systematic meditations that were central to *devotio moderna* piety focused on episodes in Christ's life. Each meditation was intended to set the tone for the entire day, a constant refrain that was to be in the mental background of all the day's other activity. These thoughts were to slip into and occupy the mind at any moment when it was not otherwise occupied—while eating, walking, waiting, or in routine tasks. Literate practitioners of the *devotio moderna* kept a spiritual notebook or journal. Many monks and brothers in the *devotio moderna* copied books to earn money for the monastery or brotherhouse. As they copied they would jot down particularly stirring and uplifting passages. One of the all-time greatest pieces of devotional literature, Thomas à Kempis' *Imitation of Christ*, grew out of this practice (see box 7.4).

Thomas à Kempis was a *devotio moderna* monk in an Augustinian house, one of a large number of reformed monasteries that arose in response to the religious revival begun by Groote.

The *Brethren of the Common Life* served both the monks and the sisterhouses as priests. The Brothers also lived in communities, and when not on detached service to a sisterhouse or monastery or teaching weekend Bible classes for the laity, they too copied books and kept devotional journals. One dimension of the *devotio moderna* was its impetus for educational reform. Another was its organized meditations and notebook journaling. Through both of these components it contributed to the unique character of the Northern Renaissance.

7.4. The Imitation of Christ

Thoughts to Help with the Spiritual Life: Remember always your end, and how that time lost returns not. Without care and diligence you shall never get virtue. If you begin to wax lukewarm, it will be evil with you. But if you give yourself to fervor, you shall find much peace, and feel lighter toil through the assistance of God's grace and the love of virtue. A man fervent and diligent is prepared for all things.

Advice on Inward things: In the cross is salvation, in the cross is life, in the cross is protection against our enemies, in the cross is infusion of heavenly sweetness, in the cross is strength of mind, in the cross joy of spirit, in the cross the height of virtue, in the cross the perfection of holiness. There is no salvation of the soul, or hope of everlasting life, but in the cross. Take up therefore your cross and follow Jesus, and you shall go into life everlasting. He went before, bearing His cross, and died for you on the cross; that you also may bear your cross and desire to die on the cross. For if you be dead with Him, you shall also in like manner live with Him. And if you share his punishment, you shall also share His glory.

Spiritual Comfort: Without the Way there is no going; without the Truth there is no knowing; without the Life there is no living. I am the Way, which you ought to follow; the Truth which you ought to believe; the Life which you ought to hope for. I am the Way inviolable, the Truth infallible, the Life unending. I am the way that is straightest, the Truth that is highest, the Life that is truest, the Life blessed, the Life uncreated.

A Devout Exhortation to Holy Communion: Two things I perceive to be exceedingly necessary for me in this life; . . . food and light. . . . [T]he Word of God is the light of my soul, and Thyself the Bread of life.

—Thomas à Kempis

Anticlericalism

In England lay piety took a number of forms, of which anticlericalism was an important element. Actually this was true all over Europe, but in England the most popular book of the fourteenth and fifteenth centuries was William Langland's *Piers the Plowman* (see box 7.5). Langland combines great affection for the Roman Church as the body of Christ with severe condemnation of the clergy. He ties his anticlericalism to a wider social criticism. A major theme of this work, as stated in one English translation, is that "the clergy and others like them, speak readily of God, and His name is often in their mouths, but lowly men have Him truly in their hearts."[1]

While Langland was a popular poet, his contemporary at court, Geoffrey Chaucer, used his *Canterbury Tales* to portray a monk whose "sole pleasure lay in riding and the hunting of the hare (over which he spared no expense)" and a begging friar "adept with flattery and tittle-tattle . . . [who] knew all the taverns and innkeepers and barmaids better than the lepers and beggars, for it hardly befitted a man of his ability and distinction to mix with diseased lepers."[2] Chaucer also pilloried a pardoner who "had a brass cross set with pebbles and a glass reliquary full of pig's bones. Yet when he came across some poor country parson he could make more money with these relics in a day than the parson got in two months; and thus by means of barefaced flattery and hocus-pocus he made the par-

7.5. Piers the Plowman

Whereas Holy Church is the source of all holiness and truth, which spring from her through honest men who teach God's Law, yet equally, when she has a corrupt priesthood and time-serving preachers and teachers, she can also be the source of all manner of evils. For the Church is like the trees in the summer-time—some boughs are covered in leaves, while others are bare, and if the boughs are bare you know the roots of the tree are diseased. So the parsons and priests and preachers of Holy Church are the roots of the true faith, on whom the people depend; and where the roots are rotten, clearly the flowers, the fruits, and leaves will never be healthy.

—William Langland

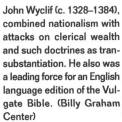

John Wyclif (c. 1328–1384), combined nationalism with attacks on clerical wealth and such doctrines as transubstantiation. He also was a leading force for an English language edition of the Vulgate Bible. (Billy Graham Center)

154

son and the people his dupes." Although Chaucer included a poor parson, "rich in holy thoughts and acts . . . who truly preached Christ's gospel and taught his parishioners devoutly," both Langland and Chaucer directed widespread cynicism toward the higher clergy and the Church as an institution.

John Wyclif (also spelled "Wycliffe," c. 1328–1384), a prominent English reformer and Oxford philosopher, gave a theological bent to this disaffection with the clergy when he taught that the spiritual blessing of the Eucharist depended on the faith of the believer who partook of it, not on the words of the priest as he elevated the host to become the body of Christ. He wrote that to meditate uprightly upon Christ

> . . . is infinitely better than to celebrate the sacrament. Nor is it out of keeping that Christ be sacramentally in the wine mixed with water or other liquid, nay, in the midst of the air, but preeminently in the soul, since the end of the sacrament is for Christ to dwell in the soul through virtues. In this way the layman, mindful of the body of Christ in heaven, more efficaciously and in a better manner than this priest who performs the sacrament, yet with equal truth (but in another manner), causes the body of Christ to be with him.

Wyclif alienated the Church by backing the government's right to confiscate the lands of corrupt clergy. He initiated a translation of the Latin Vulgate Bible into English (see box 7.6). Although he was condemned by the pope in 1377, Wyclif's powerful friends protected him from the Church's punishment for a time. His friends finally abandoned him by 1382, and he was driven out of Oxford, likely only escaping a heretic's execution because he died a natural death two years later.

7.6. Wycliffe Translation of the Lord's Prayer

Matt. 6:9–13:

Thus ye schulen preye. Oure fadir that art in heuuenes holowid be thi name, thi kyngdom come to, be thi wille don in erthe as in heuene, geue to us this day oure breed ouir other substaunce & forgeue to vs oure dettis, as we forgeuen to oure dettouris, & lede us not in to temptacioun: but delyuer us from yuel amen.

Luke 11:2–4:

And he seide to hem whanne ye preien: seie ye, fadir halowid be thi name, thi kingdom come to, geue to us to daie: oure eche daies breed, and forgeue to us oure synnes: as we forgeuen to eche man that owith to us, and lede us not in to temptacioun.

Although Wyclif escaped being condemned as a heretic in his lifetime, partly because of the disarray of the Church during the great schism, he was later condemned and his bones were exhumed and burned in 1427.

Lollards

English anticlericalism took a more organized form in *Lollardy*. The Lollards, basically followers of Wyclif's teachings, were so widespread in fifteenth-century England that the word *lollard* came to mean any overtly pious person.

Lollards believed that the direct relationship between the individual believer and God—not the institutional Church and God—is central to Christianity. The implications they drew from this emphasis threatened the entire position of the Church in society. Lollards took the Bible's teaching of the priesthood of believers to mean that wicked priests not filled with God's grace could not effectively administer the sacraments, while any Christian who had received grace could administer the sacraments as well as any priest. This doctrine later became central to the Protestant Reformation. The Lollards also taught that ordinary Christians could and should read and interpret the Bible for themselves, a position which challenged the role of the Church in solely guiding the moral life of all Christians.

As the Lollards circumvented the institutional Church in their theology they attacked the wealth and power of the Church directly. Most clerics, Lollards quipped, were more interested in the cure of hams than in the cure of souls. A Lollard suggested that if the Church's lands were nationalized and redistributed there would be enough for fifteen earldoms, 1500 knights, 6200 esquires, 100 almshouses, and fifteen universities, with 20,000 pounds left over for the king. Many English people liked the idea of curtailing the Church's power, and Lollardy had won widespread support by the opening years of the fifteenth century.

Unfortunately for their cause and safety, the greatest support for the Lollards came from the less powerful elements of English society, who turned to its teachings in droves. By the1420s, the Lollards were perceived as a political threat by the upper classes. Their egalitarian religious ideals were identified with social revolution and the ideals of the peasant revolt of 1381, which still rankled in the minds of the politically powerful.

King Henry V (1413–1422) set out to destroy Lollardy, and by 1422 the prisons were full of Lollard heretics awaiting trial or execution. By 1431 they had gone completely underground, not to surface again until the sixteenth century, when Lollardy became part of English Protestantism.

Bohemians

A fourteenth-century spiritual revival in Bohemia (what was to become the Czech Republic) also was influenced by the teachings of Wyclif. This movement encouraged frequent celebration of the Lord's Supper and fostered a great appetite for sermons. The demand for preaching led the Bohemians to build the 3000-seat Bethlehem Chapel in Prague. In 1400, six years after the chapel was built, Jan Hus (c. 1370–1415) took its pulpit and began delivering solidly biblical sermons in fiery Czech to overflowing congregations.

Hus attacked wealth and abuses in the Church, extending his attacks to the institution of the papacy, which he believed to be no older than the time of Constantine. The Church responded by burning him at the stake in 1415, despite a promise of safe conduct when he was called to defend his views at the Council of Constance.

Hus's execution rallied the Bohemians against the Church. A protest by 452 Czech nobles declared that Hus had been falsely burnt, and religious turbulence, largely associated with the growing Hussite practice of taking both bread and wine at communion, spread throughout the countryside. *Utraquism* (communion *sub utraque specie,* "under both kinds") symbolized the Bohemian revival's stress on lay Christianity and eucharistic mysticism.

In 1419 the Bohemian utraquists split into radical and moderate wings. The moderate utraquists pressed for reform along the lines of the Four Articles of Prague but did not challenge the social or political

---

7.7. The Four Articles of Prague (1420)

1. That the Word of God shall be freely and without hindrance proclaimed and preached by Christian priests in the kingdom of Bohemia.

2. That the Holy Sacrament of the body and blood of Christ under the two kinds of bread and wine shall be freely administered to all true Christians who are not excluded from communion by mortal sin.

3. That since many priests and monks hold many earthly possessions against Christ's commands and to the disadvantage of their spiritual office and also of the temporal lords, such priests shall be deprived of this illegal power and shall live exemplary lives according to the Holy Scripture, in following the way of Christ and the apostles.

4. That all mortal sins, and especially those that are public, as also other disorders contrary to the divine law, shall be prohibited and punished by those whose office it is so that the evil and false repute of this country may be removed and the well-being of the kingdom and of the Bohemian nation may be promoted.

structure of Bohemia. The more radical Taborites wanted to go beyond the Four Articles. They placed greater stress on the supremacy of the Bible. They followed the Sermon on the Mount literally, to the point of economic sharing and pacifism. The Taborites also expected God to speak to them directly at any moment. Eventually most Taborites turned from their pacifism to develop a theology of holy war in expectation of the end times. They developed one of the most powerful fighting forces in Europe, holding off foreign Catholic invaders for some fifteen years.

By 1434 the war-weary Bohemians reacted against the Taborites, and the utraquists made peace with the Catholic Church. Catholics and radical utraquists lived side by side until 1561. Then the utraquists, who had always been dependent on Roman Catholic bishops to ordain their priests, formally rejoined the Church, although their laity still partook of both wine and bread in communion.

The Renaissance

The Renaissance or "rebirth" of classical Greco-Roman culture, traditionally dated from 1300 to 1600, marks the transition between the Middle Ages and the modern world. Primarily an intellectual movement in the widest sense of that term—encompassing music, art, and literature as well as philosophy and theology—the Renaissance was dominated by the elites. The Renaissance began in Italy, then spread slowly through the rest of Europe during the fifteenth century. As the sixteenth century began, the Reformation, which should be considered part of the Renaissance, began to translate Renaissance ideas for ordinary people. Until the Reformation popularized those ideas, the few Renaissance intellectuals lived surrounded by a fundamentally medieval culture.

One of the most important factors to take into account in trying to understand the spread of Renaissance ideas throughout Europe is the invention of movable type, making possible the printing press, which entirely transformed the fifteenth-century intellectual world. In 1450 Johann Gutenberg (c. 1390–1468) perfected a process by which he could make lead castings of individual letters, arrange them to form a book page, print any number of copies of that page, then take the castings apart for reuse. Movable-type printing made mass-produced books inexpensive and accessible to large numbers of people. Before 1450 a book the length of the one you are reading would cost two months' wages for a professional scribe—the equivalent of $1600 at $5 an hour. Or the person could spend two months copying the book personally, and after all this effort the book would be unreliable, given the probability of scribal error. In a printed book even the typographical errors were consistent from copy to copy, so scholars could pass corrections on to their colleagues.

A folio from the Gutenberg Bible of 1456 may actually have been printed by Johann Fust, but it used the movable type technology developed by Johann Gutenberg (1398–1468). (Billy Graham Center)

7.8. The "Miracle" of the Press

Besides the restoration of learning, now almost complete, the invention of many fine new things . . . had been reserved to this age. Among these, printing deserves to be put first. . . . The invention has greatly aided the advancement of all disciplines. For it seems miraculously to have been discovered in order to bring back to life more easily literature which seemed dead.

Louis LeRoy, *?De la Vicissitude ou Variete des Choses en l'Univers* (Paris: 1575), trans. by J. B. Ross; quoted in Eliz Eisenstein, "Printing" in *Portable Renaissance Reader* (New York, 1958).

In the years between 1450 and 1500, printing gave scholars as many books as all of Europe had produced in the previous 1000 years. The cost of books declined proportionately. The family of a moderately successful merchant or craftsman (though not that of a peasant) could own a personal copy of the Bible and a few other works and train their sons, and occasionally even their daughters, to read them. This, in turn, supplied a ready market for the printers and encouraged them to produce and distribute even more books, which further reduced the cost.

These books contributed to the excitement of fifteenth-century discovery. Fifteenth- and sixteenth-century Europeans fanned out to expand the perimeters of the known world, returning with exotic and thrilling tales of unknown lands and people. While the Romans had known about China, the Greeks about India, and both something about parts of Africa and Asia, for most medieval Europeans the world reached little further than what the eye could see from the bell-tower of a village church. Some merchants traveled the great fairs of Europe, pilgrims and influential clerics might undertake the perilous journey to Rome, and pious or ambitious knights might go on a Crusade. But such travelers were exceptional. As the sixteenth century began, accounts of the lands and cultures discovered by Christopher Columbus, Ferdinand Magellan, Vasco da Gama, and Henry Hudson were printed, making them available to all literate Europeans. These books of travel tales broadened intellectual horizons and awakened Renaissance men and women to a new sense of the diversity of the world.

The Renaissance rediscovered nature and the natural world in Europe as well. Francesco Petrarch (1304–1374) may have symbolically opened the Renaissance by climbing the highest mountain in the region. He was one of the first European tourists, appreciating nature for its own sake. In his diary Petrarch recorded: "The only motive for my ascent was the wish to see what so great a height had to offer."[3] Medieval travelers avoided mountains, the home of robbers and demons, so Petrarch marks the beginning of a new attitude in a new era. This emphasis on nature comes through most clearly in the works of Renaissance artists. While medieval artists portrayed spiritual reality by painting two dimensional figures on gold foil backgrounds, Renaissance artists came to believe that nature and humanity *themselves* were spiritual. Petrarch claimed that when God took on a human body he affirmed its value. The incarnation, according to Petrarch, implied that artists could and should portray the human body. These new ideas, first displayed in churches and palaces in Florence and other Italian cities, were spread in the next century by printed books and single-page broadsheets. Therefore, these images and ideas affected men and women throughout Europe.

The Renaissance and the printed book changed European education. Scholars gained power and influence in princely courts, and rulers became educated. Scholarship was no longer just for clergy; it became a passport to a better life for everyone who wanted to be important. Renaissance intellectuals labored with the goal of making education available to many people. Where medieval scholarship relied heavily on commentaries, printing produced accurate editions of original texts, prodding scholars beyond the commentaries to the sources themselves.

7.9. Leonardo da Vinci

Leonardo da Vinci was a brilliant artist who combined careful observation of the details of nature with the search for an ideal form based on mathematics and geometry. In the *Vitruvian Man*, for example, he studied the proportions of a real human being in all its detail in light of the geometrically based proportions of the Greek mathematician Vitruvius.

In this drawing Leonardo also made a religious point about the human being. When the man stands in one position he touches the circle, an infinite shape symbolizing the spiritual dimensions of the human being, while in the other position he touches the sides of a square, the traditional human shape.

However, Leonardo also showed the Renaissance characteristic of diversity, describing himself to the duke of Milan as an inventor, an engineer, a man who could devise engines of war, cast cannon, and even build grand monuments to the duke. Leonardo's greatest works, however, are probably his notebooks full of drawings and notes on many subjects. Leonardo was a keen observer and drew everything he saw and many things he imagined or invented. Among the many things he dreamed up in the pages of his notebook were a helicopter with practical possibilities, a spring-powered horseless carriage that was less practical, a forced-air central heating system, portable bridges, and a machine gun.

This stress on sources prompted Europeans to reexamine their cultural roots. In Italy, scholars turned to their Roman (and Greek) heritage for inspiration. As the Renaissance moved north in the sixteenth century the Reformation turned to the sources of the Christian faith and emphasized the text of the Bible as the only authority for faith and life.

The Italian Renaissance interest in classical culture led educators to develop a new curriculum, the *studia humanitas* ("humanities studies"), derived from the Roman orator Cicero's educational proposals. The humanities included the study of Latin, Greek, and Hebrew grammar; practical rhetoric; ancient Greek and Roman poetry; history (which Cicero viewed as wisdom teaching by example); and moral philosophy, the practical application of ethical precepts. The *studia humanitas* prepared citizens for a productive and active political life. This marked a significant change in basic cultural aspirations. In the Middle Ages, the individual expressed what it meant to be fully human by contemplating and worshiping God. Renaissance writers called citizens, including Christians, to an active public life. They were to change the world, rather than merely to pray for the world. To be fully human during the Renaissance meant to become actively involved in *this* world.

The Renaissance ideal of the active life emphasized people as unique individuals, in contrast to the Middle Ages, in which people had importance in the context of the community. The Renaissance stress on the unique individual led to an emphasis on individual creative genius, particularly the genius of the architect, painter, or sculptor. The brightest and best Renaissance young people aspired to become artists, though genius implied diversity as well. The well-rounded individual has been hallowed in cliché as the "Renaissance man." Box 7.9 shows how this being was personified in Leonardo da Vinci (1452–1519).

Hand in hand with the Renaissance view of human potential and freedom came a sense of discontent, reversing the ideal of contentment cultivated in the Middle Ages, when all were encouraged to be satisfied with the place that God had ordered for them (see box 7.10).

Capitalism, one expression of Renaissance discontent, proved a mixed blessing for Europe. Though it clearly advanced the overall standard of living, especially for those who already had money, it also challenged basic, long-standing economic beliefs. Medieval economic ethics condemned lending money at interest, since Deuteronomy 23:19 forbids charging interest to a citizen of one's country. Capitalism, however, depends on raising borrowed money and cannot accept the biblical injunction. Capitalism challenged patterns of work, as well. Medieval laborers worked for a year or two, then took six months or a year off, until they ran out of money. Capitalism increased workers' wants while

7.10. Mirandola

The creative individual was a free individual. The Renaissance stress on freedom was perhaps most eloquently expressed by Giovanni Pico della Mirandola, when he had God tell Adam:

Neither a fixed abode nor a form that is thine alone nor any function peculiar to thyself have we given thee, Adam, to the end that according to thy longing and according to thy judgment thou mayest have and possess what abode, what form and what functions thou thyself shall desire. Thou shalt have the power to degenerate into the lower forms of life, which are brutish. Thou shalt have the power, out of thy soul's judgment, to be reborn into the higher forms, which are divine.*

*Pico della Mirandola, *Oration on the Dignity of Man;* quoted in Ernst Cassirer, ed., *The Renaissance Philosophy of Man: Petrarca, Valla, Ficino, Pico, Pomponazzi* (Chicago: University of Chicago Press, 1956).

reducing real wages, driving people into work—full-time and permanently. While raising the expectations of the lower classes, capitalism fueled the ambitions and achievements of the emerging middle classes and threatened the traditional position of nobility, turning them conservative and reactionary. These social stresses exacerbated traditional tensions between clergy and laity, upper and lower clergy, and village and agrarian peasants. Ultimately the emerging social reordering led to the widespread feeling that traditional institutions could be criticized and changed. Such discontent bore fruit during the Reformation.

Nationalism, a second manifestation of Renaissance ambition and discontent, strained the medieval ideal of cultural unity. Nationalism refers to the cluster of feelings that modern people associate with patriotism—being loyal to a country or king and identifying with those who speak the same language. Despite the common perception that national identification is natural, European nationalism developed and was cultivated (mostly by kings) during the transition between medieval and Renaissance times. Medieval thinking offered loyalty first to God, as embodied in the universal church, and second to the local lord and village, as opposed to the neighboring lord and village. The idea that one could justify killing a Christian from another area and language on the orders of some vague king would have left a medieval serf dumbfounded. Lords might fight for an overlord out of self-protection or mutual self-interest, but hardly for pride of country.

Three great national monarchies rose to dominate Europe after 1450, despite pressure and the struggles of many minor principalities to maintain a unified Christian world government. England, France, and Spain all developed strong monarchies and won the primary allegiance of their subjects.

163

The French king, Charles VII, won control over the French church in 1438 when he regulated church-state relations through the *Pragmatic Sanction of Bourges*. Charles severely limited the authority of the papacy to make Church appointments and collect revenue in France. His policy of *Gallicanism* fostered a virtually independent church within the Roman Catholic sphere.

As the Spanish monarchs Ferdinand and Isabella reconquered the Iberian Peninsula from the Muslims they used their resulting position as defenders of the faith to consolidate their position as absolute rulers and unify the nation. They, too, won the right to appoint bishops and control the Church revenues collected in their domain.

Nationalism led to smaller units in central Europe and Italy—duchies, counties, and independent cities—rather than strong monarchies, but that too came at the expense of the Church. Germans and Italians fought for their independence from the Church as much as from the emperor of their "Holy Roman Empire."

Renaissance papacy

Much of the criticism leveled at the Church was directed at the papacy. Spiritually it reached a low ebb in the fifteenth century, as powerful Italian families fought for control of the office. The Renaissance popes made their mark primarily as patrons of the arts, rather than as pastors of the church. They were highly cultured and educated devotees of Renaissance ideals with a superb eye for both architectural magnificence and artistic genius. Under their patronage Michelangelo (1475–1564) painted the Sistine Chapel and designed the dome of St. Peter's, while Raphael (1483–1520) executed the four wall paintings of the Stanza della Signatura.

These same popes, however, failed to provide the moral leadership that might have prevented the breakup of the Church in the Protestant Reformation. Under these vacillating popes the Church came under the well-deserved criticism of humanists and pious believers, for the Church

Girolamo Savonarola (1452–1498) anticipated the Reformation in his sweeping religious, moral, and government reforms of Florence, Italy. (Billy Graham Center)

was clouding any consistent understanding of what it meant to be a Christian. Nominal Christianity or even conscious secularity ran endemic through the administration of the Church. The political theorist Niccolò Machiavelli (1469–1527), for example, advocated naked, power-grabbing pragmatism in his advice to rulers, with no reference to or reverence for theological or biblical principles—an astonishing reversal of medieval priorities. Renaissance ideals, however, also led to several strains of vibrant and evangelical Christian reform.

7.11. Savonarola

You, Florence, heard with your ears not me but God, whereas other Italians always heard the words of others; and, therefore, you, Florence, will not have the slightest excuse if you do not mend your ways. . . . Believe it then, Florence, and change your ways and do not believe that your flagellation is ended, for I see the sword behind it. . . . [But] the renovation of the Church will come about, and many who are present here at this sermon will see it.

Savonarola

Late fifteenth-century Florence reacted against Church corruption and the Renaissance in a popular, prophetic reform movement led by Girolamo Savonarola (1452–1498). The moral corruption, both in the Church and in the world, distressed Savonarola deeply. In the early 1490s he began to preach against the vices of the Florentines and the de Medici government then in power in the city.

Savonarola's reading of the Bible focused on the prophetic books. He believed he stood in the line of God's prophets, inspired to pronounce judgment on the Church, on Italy, and particularly on Florence.

When Charles VIII of France invaded Italy in 1494, toppling the ruling Medici family, Florentines turned to Savonarola, who twice had persuaded Charles to spare the city. The priest interpreted the French invasions as God's "cleansing force" and the fulfillment of prophecy. This alienated the pope, who was organizing an alliance to drive the French out of Italy. By mid-1495 Savonarola virtually ruled the city from his cathedral pulpit.

Supported by the new "popular" regime allied with France, Savonarola organized a campaign for vigorous moral reform. Virtuous Florentines tossed their frivolous and useless possessions into a great "bonfire of the vanities." Sandro Botticelli (1445–1510), the great Renaissance artist, contributed large numbers of his unsold paintings to the flames. Savonarola believed that once Florence, the "watchtower of Italy," repented and changed, her example would lead Italy and the rest of Christendom to repent as well. This would begin the kingdom of God on earth.

As Savonarola became convinced that God's plan depended on him, he began to challenge the pope's authority over the Church. Pope Alexander VI excommunicated him in 1497. Savonarola responded by denying the pope's right to discipline him, publicly stating that whoever accepted the excommunication was a heretic.

Meanwhile, one of Savonarola's disciples had challenged a papal supporter to trial by the ordeal of fire. The two men agreed to walk into a bonfire, allowing God to vindicate the survivor. The two delayed and wrangled for most of the appointed day, leaving, much relieved, when God put a stop to the whole trial by sending a downpour to put out the fire. The waiting crowd, soaked by the same rain, turned against Savonarola. Without popular support, Savonarola was immediately arrested, tried under torture, then burned as a heretic.

Erasmus

In northern Europe Desiderius Erasmus (c.1466–1536), Europe's foremost scholar and one of its most influential reformers, used the insights of Renaissance humanism to work for change in the Church. Erasmus shared the emphasis on returning to the sources, and in particular to the Christian roots. He worked closely with the best printers in Europe to prepare a new and more accurate text of the Bible and editions of the church fathers, as well as classical texts.

The purpose of all his scholarship was to encourage piety. Erasmus had grown up in the *devotio moderna,* with its appreciation for learning as an important element in piety. He developed the connection between learning and piety as fully and deeply as has any Christian, especially in his most important work, the *Christian Soldier's Manual,* a guide for spiritual living. For Erasmus, learning was of little value if it did not result in greater piety and piety was shallow unless fortified by learning.

Erasmus also shared the Renaissance emphasis on the active life, believing that the Christian's life had to be filled with charity and good deeds. His view of the Bible reflected this, accenting the acts and advice of Jesus as recorded in Matthew, Mark, and Luke. The Synoptic Gospels, in contrast to the more systematic and theological writings of John and Paul, emphasize an active and obedient Christian life, he believed. Erasmus, however, rejected any mechanical or legalistic definition of obedience, believing it can only grow out of internal, heartfelt piety. He taught that Christianity was inadequate if its people were satisfied by pilgrimages to see relics of the saints, mechanical repetitions of prayers, and attendance at Mass. Along with the mystics, Erasmus believed that true piety was a matter of a personal, heartfelt relationship with God.

Humanism reached its pinnacle in the scholarship of Erasmus (c.1466–1536). While he remained steadfast to the Roman faith his attacks on clerical abuse and work on the Greek New Testament helped pave the way for others. (Billy Graham Center)

Erasmus partook deeply of the critical and reforming spirit of the late fifteenth and early sixteenth centuries. He struggled to reform abuses in the Church, attacked inconsistency in the lives of church leaders, and poked fun at foolishness. In his brief dialogue, "A Pilgrimage for Religion's Sake," Erasmus pointed out that "The Lord's Cross is exhibited publicly and privately in so many places that if the fragments were joined together they'd seem a full load for a freighter. And yet the Lord carried his whole cross." In *The Praise of Folly,* Erasmus pointed to the man who "was delivered from execution by the favor of the patron saint of thieves so that he could relieve those who are burdened with too much wealth."[4] He attacked members of religious orders who "shrink from the mere touch of money as if it were poison. They do not, however, retreat from the touch of wine or of women."[5] He described a monk who would tell Christ at the judgment day that "he hasn't touched any money in over sixty years unless he wore two pair of gloves to protect his fingers."[6] Erasmus also attacked the idea that a Christian could buy forgiveness of sins and then "thinks he can start on a new round of sinning with a clean slate."[7]

7.12. Erasmus

I would that even the lowliest women read the Gospels and the Pauline Epistles. And I would that they were translated into all languages so that they could be read and understood. . . . Would that, as a result, the farmer sang some portion of them at the plow, the weaver hum some parts of them to the movement of his shuttle, the traveler lighten the weariness of his journey with stories of this kind. *

Although Erasmus loved the teaching and example of the church fathers, and printed many editions of their writings, he also appreciated the Greek and Roman classics, though his advice was to read them selectively:

A sensible reading of the pagan poets and philosophers is a good preparation for the Christian life . . . [but] if the obscene passages in the ancients bother you, then by all means refrain from reading them. **

I would like to point out briefly two weapons that we should prepare to use in combating the chief vices. These weapons are prayer and knowledge. St. Paul clearly expresses the desire that men be continually armed when he commands us to pray without ceasing. Pure prayer directed to heaven is able to subdue passion, for it is, as it were, a citadel inaccessible to the enemy. Knowledge, or learning, fortifies the mind with salutary precepts and keeps virtue ever before us. These two are inseparable, the former imploring but the latter suggesting what should be prayed for. St. James tells us that we should pray always for faith and hope, seeking the things of salvation in Jesus' name. We may recall that Christ asked the sons of Zebedee if they really knew what they were praying for. We must always emphasize the dual necessity of both prayer and knowledge. Neither allow your knowledge to lessen nor your prayer to become sterile. ***

*Joseph Shaw, et al., *Readings in Christian Humanism* (Minneapolis: Augsburg, 1982), 293.

**John P. Dolan, ed., *The Essential Erasmus* (New York: NAL/Dutton, 1964), 321.

***The Essential Erasmus, 35.

Although Erasmus attacked abuses vigorously in print, he remained firmly committed to the Church when other reformers felt driven out. Erasmus based his commitment to the unity of the Church partly on his belief in the ambiguity of being human. As a human being, Erasmus believed his understandings were never exact, seldom consistent; he rarely could definitively know what was true. Issues, then, could only rarely be clear-cut. Since he could never be certain that he was right, he could not set his voice against the consensus that Christians had developed through the ages.

As human beings were essentially flawed in his view, they must be incapable of coming to salvation without the grace of God, though he thought they were able freely to cooperate with God in their salvation. Erasmus resolved this tension by examining the nature of the fall. The fall had deprived human beings of the grace that had enabled Adam and Eve to obey God perfectly and live forever, but sin had not changed their essential humanness. Human beings could still make good choices and could prepare themselves to receive God's grace. With the help of grace the Christian could obediently live the life of active faith that the Bible demanded.

Erasmus's most popular work, *The Praise of Folly,* clearly shows his ambiguity. Folly (personified) gives a speech to praise herself—a foolish thing to do. In the course of the speech Folly praises such foolishness as indulgences, pilgrimages, and other forms of Christian superstition Erasmus condemned. But she also praises eating, lovemaking, friendship, and even the ultimate foolishness of Christian charity and self-sacrifice—things Erasmus valued. By using such an ambiguous persona as Folly to deliver the speech, Erasmus could write a powerful, if gentle, manifesto for reform. His vision was of a church that is tolerant as it recognizes human ambiguity. *The Praise of Folly* is the work of a Renaissance humanist reformer, one very different in tone and spirit from the Protestant and Catholic Reformers who were standing in the wings.

Conclusion

The late Middle Ages and the Renaissance set the stage for the fragmentation of the Church in the sixteenth century by challenging, in various ways, the control that the institutional Church exercised over the people of Europe. The Church was simply not ready to withstand the onslaught of the Protestant movement. It had failed to respond to the crises of the fourteenth century and was unable to reform, despite the mood of anticlericalism from England to Bohemia and the open reforming attacks of Savonarola and Erasmus. Some of the blame may be given to the kings who controlled Church appointments. But the Renaissance popes, who spent their time building beautiful palaces while other Christians wrestled with God over salvation, deserve as much blame.

Suggested readings

Bainton, Roland. *Erasmus of Christendom*. New York: Crossroad, 1982.

Chaucer, Geoffrey. *Canterbury Tales*. Various editions.

Cohn, Norman. *Pursuit of the Millennium: Revolutionary Messianism in Medieval and Reformation Europe and Its Bearing on Modern Totalitarian Movements*. New York: Oxford, 1970.

"Columbus and Christianity." *Christian History*, 11.3 (issue 35, 1992).

Dickens, A. G. *Lollards and Protestants in the Diocese of York, 1509–1558*. Oxford: Oxford University Press, 1959.

Erasmus, Desiderius. *Christian Humanism and the Reformation: Selected Writings of Erasmus*, 2d ed., B. Rhenanus ed. New York: Fordham University Press, 1975.

Gottfried, Robert S. *The Black Death: Natural and Human Disaster in Medieval Europe*. New York: Free Press, 1983.

"John Wycliffe." *Christian History*, 2.2 (issue 3, 1983).

Kaminsky, Howard. *A History of the Hussite Revolution*. Berkeley, Calif.: University of California Press, 1967.

Lambert, Malcolm D. *Medieval Heresy: Popular Movements from the Gregorian Reform to the Reformation*. 2d ed. Oxford: Blackwell, 1992.

Langland, John. *Piers Plowman*. Various editions.

Mollat, Guillaume. *The Popes at Avignon, 1305–1378*, trans. by J. Love. New York: Nelson, 1963.

Peter of Mladenovic. *John Hus at the Council of Constance*, trans. M. Spinka. New York: Columbia University Press, 1965.

Thomas à Kempis, *The Imitation of Christ*. Various editions.

Weinstein, Donald. *Savonarola and Florence: Prophecy and Patriotism in the Renaissance*. Princeton, N.J.: Princeton University Press, 1970.

Wilcox, Donald J. *In Search of God and Self: Renaissance and Reformation Thought*. Boston: Houghton-Mifflin, 1975.

"William Tyndale." *Christian History*, 6.4 (issue 16, 1987).

Workman, Herbert B. *John Wyclif: A Study of the English Medieval Church*. Hamden, Conn.: Archon, 1966.

8

The Reformation

The Reformation was a complex, multifaceted response to the church experience of the fifteenth and sixteenth centuries. Many Christians realized that the Church was simply not serving the spiritual needs of the people. It had become corrupt, and abuses were widespread. At the same time, Christians were becoming more literate and articulate, so they expected more of the Church.

This seething discontent, which cut across national and class lines, led to no less than eight independent reforming movements in the sixteenth century (see fig. 8.1).

1. *Erasmus* attempted to reform the Church from within (see pp. 166–69).
2. *Martin Luther* began the Protestant Reformation in Germany.
3. *Ulrich Zwingli* began the Swiss Reformation in Zurich.
4. *John Calvin*, a Frenchman living in Geneva, Switzerland, developed a systematic Reformed theology.
5. A strong *Anabaptist movement* inaugurated what became known as the "Radical Reformation," a distinctive movement that grew out of Luther's thought, yet rejected the close ties Protestants had with the secular governments and called the church to separate from the world.
6. *Spiritualists*, another Radical Reformation movement, elevated subjective revelation over both church and Scripture.
7. The Roman Catholic *Council of Trent* (1545–1563) reformed the church, partly in response to the Protestant threat, but also prodded by internal Catholic pressure for reform.
8. *Reformation in England* took a uniquely national form and became a Protestant Erasmian church, attempting to combine the best of Protestant and Catholic traditions.

All of these movements were committed to reforming abuses within the Church, cleansing it, and persuading Christians to new levels of piety and devotion to God.

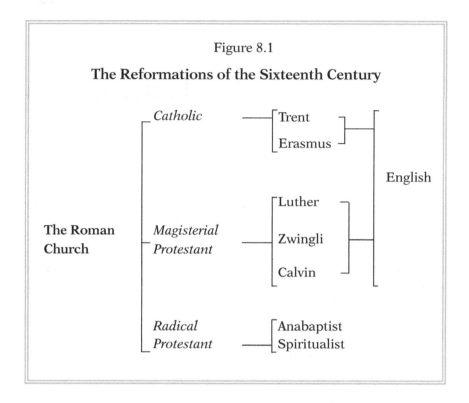

Figure 8.1

The Reformations of the Sixteenth Century

Martin Luther

The basic driving force behind Martin Luther's life was an overwhelming sense of his sinfulness and his corresponding desire to gain salvation. A narrow escape from a bolt of lightning while crossing a field in 1505 convinced him to leave the world and join a rigorous monastery in order to dedicate his life to gaining salvation. Entering full-time professional Christianity was the normal first step for a Christian worried about salvation. The devotional rhythm and prayers of the monastery, however, did not bring peace to Luther's soul or confidence that he was saved. He became, as one historian has put it, "the best damned monk in Christendom," rigorously doing all that could be expected of a monk but still feeling that he was damned, a sinner, and unworthy of heaven.

Luther turned to the sacrament of confession and penance, which, according to Church teaching, cleansed the sinner of any sin that was

Martin Luther (1483–1546) was born in Eisleben and was educated partly by the Brethren of the Common Life. His Reformation convictions grew over a period of a decade or longer from his doubts about his own salvation. (Billy Graham Center)

confessed before a priest, repented, and counterbalanced by some good work or freely accepted punishment. Luther burdened his confessor, Johannes Staupitz, with six-hour confessions, dredging up the most minor unkind thoughts and confessing them as sins. He was in agony for fear that he would forget to confess a sin, which would leave him liable for all the consequences of that sin, and probably damned forever. Staupitz worked hard to convince Luther that his scruples were excessive, but Luther refused to believe him.

Staupitz finally told Luther to work for his doctoral degree in biblical studies, reasoning that the time and energy Luther would spend on his studies would take his mind off his sinfulness. More important, he hoped that studying the Bible would give Luther a more personal, less legalistic faith. While Luther did not find the Erasmian faith that Staupitz hoped he would, he did find the solution to the problem of his sin in Romans, the dawn breaking when he read 3:21–22: "But now a righteousness from God, apart from law, has been made known, to which the Law and the Prophets testify. This righteousness from God comes through faith in Jesus Christ to all who believe." Here he found the concept of *passive righteousness*, which was to govern his understanding of Christianity from then on. In Luther's eyes human beings were helplessly evil until God's grace changed their essential nature. He believed that this change from being an evil person to being a Christian led to a gradual change in a person's life, a change that would not be completed until the day of judgment. For Luther, believers were entirely passive in this gradual transformation to a life of righteousness. Even their faith itself had been given by God's grace.

Later Luther wrote:

> Certainly I had been possessed by an unusually ardent desire to understand Paul in his Epistle to the Romans. Nevertheless, in spite of the ardour of my heart I was hindered by the unique word in the first chapter: "The righteousness of God is revealed in it." I hated the word "righteousness of God," because in accordance with the usage and custom of the doctors I had been taught to understand it philosophically as meaning, as they put it, the formal or active righteousness according to which God is righteous and punishes sinners and the unjust.
>
> As a monk I had led an irreproachable life. Nevertheless I felt that I was a sinner before God. My conscience was restless, and I could not depend on God being propitiated by my satisfactions. Not only did I not love, but I actually hated the righteous God who punishes sinners. . . . Thus a furious battle raged within my perplexed conscience, but meanwhile I was knocking on the door of this particular Pauline passage, earnestly seeking to know the mind of the great Apostle.
>
> Day and night I tried to meditate upon the significance of these words: "The righteousness of God is revealed in it, as it is written: The righteous shall live by faith." Then, finally, God had mercy on me, and I began to understand that the righteousness of God is that gift of God by which a righteous man lives, namely, faith, and that this sentence—The righteousness of God is revealed in the Gospel—is passive, indicating that the merciful God justifies us by faith, as it is written: "The righteous shall live

by faith." Now I felt as though I had been reborn altogether and had entered Paradise.[1]

Luther's theology of passive righteousness put him into direct conflict with the Church. The conflict became public on October 31, 1517, when Luther publicly invited debate on the practice of selling indulgences by nailing a list of 95 objections to indulgences to the Wittenberg cathedral door, which served as a community bulletin board. Indulgences were based on the idea that some Christians had done more good than they needed. They went directly to heaven when they died, and the surplus of good works could be used by the Church to balance the sins of the less virtuous through the indulgence. An indulgence was not forgiveness of sin, but a forgiving of the penalty due to sin. Theoretically an indulgence involved making a financial sacrifice to indicate the penitent's contrite heart. However, the Church had come to depend on the sale of indulgences to raise money for such projects as building St. Peter's Cathedral in Rome. When Luther wrote that good works were entirely the fruit of grace and did not cause salvation he undercut the entire theology behind indulgences, not to mention the Church's precarious financial position.

Luther and Erasmus shared a commitment to seeing all of the Bible in the hands of the laity, and Luther translated the entire Bible into German. Yet Luther interpreted the Bible rather differently than did Erasmus. Since the idea of passive righteousness came from Paul's New Testament writings, Luther saw the Epistles of Paul as the heart of the Bible and the lens through which the rest of the Bible should be read. For Erasmus the life and teachings of Jesus, recorded in the Gospels, were the center of Christianity. Their differences were a matter of emphasis, but ultimately those differences proved irreconcilable.

Luther summarized his theological position in three Latin phrases. The first of these was *sola fides* ("faith alone"), by which Luther meant that salvation did not depend on good works at all. Related to *sola fides* was Luther's second slogan, *sola gratia* ("grace alone"), in which Luther ascribed salvation entirely to grace, without any human cooperation at all.

The third of Luther's Latin slogans was *sola scriptura* ("Scripture alone"). Luther claimed that the Bible was his only source of authority and rejected the traditions of the Church as authoritative interpretations of the Bible. It was because of this view that Luther eventually felt compelled to leave the Church when his interpretation of the Bible clashed with that of the Church hierarchy.

In 1521 Luther was called before the diet (or assembly) of the German nation, meeting in the city of Worms. He was accused of heresy

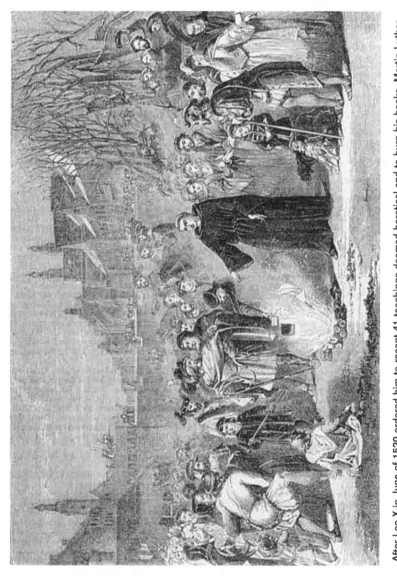

After Leo X in June of 1520 ordered him to recant 41 teachings deemed heretical and to burn his books, Martin Luther responded with a bonfire of Catholic books and the papal bull against him. This set the stage for his excommunication on January 3, 1521, and his climactic defense before the Diet of Worms. (Billy Graham Center)

and was asked to retract his opinions, but he would not. He responded by saying: "Since then our serene Majesty and your lordships request simple reply, I will give it without horns and hoofs and say: Unless I am convinced by the testimony of scripture or by plain reason (for I believe in neither the pope nor in councils alone) . . . I cannot and will not recant, for it is neither safe nor honest to violate one's conscience. I can do no other. Here I take my stand, God being my helper."[2]

Luther's defiance at Worms marks the beginning of the "Protestant" church, although the term was not coined until 1529 when a number of German princes and free cities "protested" against the decision of the Diet of Speyers to reaffirm the Diet of Worms. It was originally an epithet against the protesters but was eventually adopted by the Protestants as a badge of honor. Since then it has come to refer to Western Christians who are not Roman Catholic or Eastern Orthodox, and non-Western Christians who have ties to western Protestant churches.

Luther's reliance on the Bible alone, without reference to the interpretation of the Church, led him to reject many of the customs and practices of the Church. Luther found only two sacraments, baptism and the Lord's Supper, in the Bible, and so rejected the other five traditional sacraments (confirmation, penance, ordination, marriage, and extreme unction). He could not find the Bible teaching that priests had a special role in the church or that they must be celibate, so he rejected both ideas. Luther, like Wyclif, came to believe that all Christians were priests and needed no mediator other than Christ before God.

In 1525 Luther agreed to help nine refugees from a convent of nuns who had become Protestant to find husbands. He succeeded for eight, but finally agreed to marry Katherine von Bora himself, "to please his father, spite the pope, and give Katie a name." They had a remarkably happy and successful marriage and six children. In fact, Luther said "in domestic affairs I defer to Katie. Otherwise I am led by the Holy Ghost." Once he even joked that he relied more on Katie than on Christ.[3]

Luther's ideas were spread by mass media technology. The printing press had, by 1517, revolutionized communication. Between 1517 and 1520 more than 300,000 copies of his books and tracts were printed. Luther had a genius for writing to ordinary people, and his tracts became tremendously popular. Germans were just beginning to become literate, and Luther provided these new readers with cheap or even free reading matter—broadsides tacked to trees and buildings, illustrated four-page tracts, and political cartoons—attacking the Roman Catholic Church.

As Luther's message of the priesthood of all believers and salvation by grace alone radiated through Germany, a number of radicals took Luther's ideas to an extreme he found unsettling. The first of these were the Zwickau prophets, who argued that they had received direct inspirations from the Holy Spirit, and such revelations to individual believers had more authority than the Bible. Although a few of Luther's followers in Wittenberg accepted the Zwickau prophets and their Spirit-led faith, Luther believed they were dangerously uncontrolled and attributed their opinions to the Devil. These Spiritualists remained a splinter group within the wider Protestant Reformation, but they wielded an important influence on some segments of the Anabaptists; small groups of Spiritualists survived throughout Europe.

The *peasant revolts* took the egalitarian implications of Luther's idea of the priesthood of all believers to their logical conclusions. The year 1525 saw sporadic uprisings throughout southern and central Germany. These peasants turned to Lutheran doctrine and biblical teachings to justify their desire to choose their own pastors and put an end to serfdom: "Christ has delivered and redeemed us without exception, by the shedding of his precious blood, the lowly as well as the great. Accordingly it is consistent with Scripture that we should be free and wish to be so."[4]

Luther reacted sharply against the peasant revolts. In May of 1525 he wrote *Against Robbing and Murderous Peasant Bands*, in which he appealed to the princes to "smite, choke, and stab" the rioters. Luther depended on the support of the princes for his survival and the success of the Reformation. In turn, he gave the princes his political support. Luther's political theology supported the secular rulers in that he believed the church ought to stay out of politics completely and leave the ruling to the princes. The German princes, trying to gain independence from both the Holy Roman emperor and the pope, who supported the emperor, found these ideas satisfying.

Luther also believed churches ought to give up their vast properties and be satisfied with only the church buildings, though he thought that the government ought to pay priest's salaries in exchange for all the church lands. Gaining church lands gave Lutheran princes an enormous political advantage. Before the Reformation the princes' power had rested on their personal property holdings, which accounted for some 10–15 percent of the land in their principalities. Turning Lutheran allowed princes to double or even triple their power base, since the Church owned 15–30 percent of the land in most areas of Germany.

However, even when all the political advantages were added up, politics merely made it easier for a convinced Lutheran prince to follow his conscience and leave the Roman Catholic Church. It rarely persuaded a Catholic prince to become Lutheran. For a convinced Catholic prince, no temporary political advantage was worth spending eternity in hell.

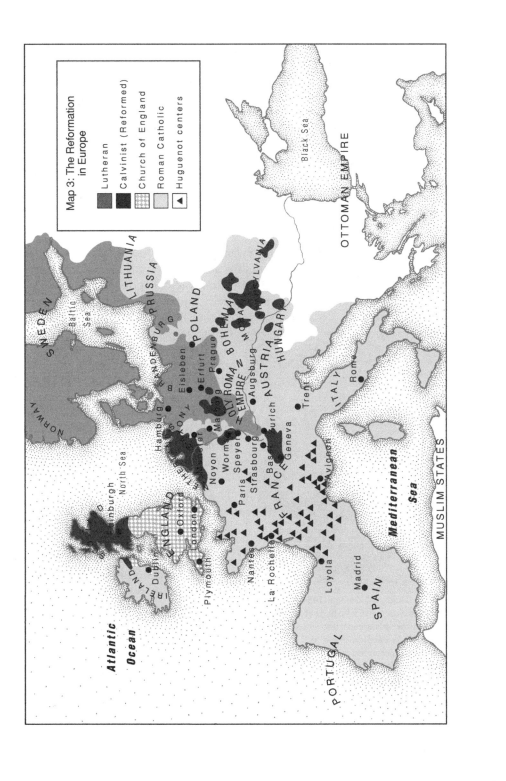

Map 3: The Reformation in Europe

Lutheran
Calvinist (Reformed)
Church of England
Roman Catholic
▲ Huguenot centers

Atlantic Ocean

NORWAY
SWEDEN
Baltic Sea
North Sea
LITHUANIA
PRUSSIA
BRANDENBURG
POLAND
Edinburgh
IRELAND
Dublin
ENGLAND
Oxford
London
Plymouth
NETHERLANDS
Hamburg
SAXONY
Eisleben
Erfurt
Prague
BOHEMIA
MORAVIA
TRANSYLVANIA
Münster
Magdeburg
HOLY ROMAN EMPIRE
AUSTRIA
HUNGARY
Noyon
Worms
Speyer
Augsburg
Paris
Strasbourg
Basel
Zurich
Geneva
Trent
Nantes
FRANCE
La Rochelle
Avignon
Loyola
SPAIN
Madrid
PORTUGAL
Mediterranean Sea
ITALY
Rome
OTTOMAN EMPIRE
Black Sea
MUSLIM STATES

The Holy Roman emperor, Charles V, technically ruled over a host of German principalities, but he was too busy holding together his far-flung empire against threats from the Turks to the east and France to the west to subdue the Lutheran princes. By the time the Catholic German princes took serious measures against the Protestant *Schmalkaldic League* it was too late. Division was complete. The two sides finally agreed to live and let live in the *Peace of Augsburg* in 1555. The Peace of Augsburg allowed each prince to choose the religion of his principality and marked official recognition that the split between Protestant and Catholic had permanently broken the Body of Christ apart.

Zwingli

Ulrich Zwingli (1484–1531), a Swiss reformer based in Zurich, became convinced by Luther's arguments for salvation by grace alone in 1519. An Erasmian humanist, Zwingli came to Protestant convictions through his study of the Bible, not experientially and viscerally as Luther had. In the same year, Zwingli announced that he would no longer preach

from the passages the Church had set for each Sunday, but would preach through the entire book of Matthew with the Greek text open in front of him. This caused considerable excitement in Zurich.

During Lent of 1522 Zwingli broke with the Church when a Zurich printer and his helpers ate sausages, with Zwingli's approval. The printer needed strength to finish printing a Swiss-German translation of the Bible by Easter, but eating meat during Lent had been strictly forbidden. From this beginning the Reformation in Zurich took on a distinctly political tone, led by the decisions of the Zurich town council, which Zwingli accepted. Zwingli himself served as a chaplain in the Swiss army. Zwingli viewed the reformed Zurich as the new Israel and the beginning of God's kingdom on earth. Part of his motivation for seeing Zurich as the new

Ulrich (Huldrych) Zwingli (1484–1531) was a Swiss nationalist, who had served as chaplain to Swiss mercenaries, and a humanist scholar. As people's priest at Zurich Great Church he organized the Zurich Reformation between 1519 and 1525. After failing to form an alliance with Luther at the Marburg Colloquy he was killed in the Battle of Kappel against Swiss cantons allied with the pope. (Billy Graham Center) nation of God came from his humanist belief in returning to "the sources," or the ancient models. In the Italian Renaissance the ancient models had been Greece and Rome. Zwingli took the ancient people of God—Israel—as a model for the new Christian nation, Zurich. As a result, Zwingli placed particular stress on the Old Testament.

Zwingli's patriotism influenced his doctrine of the sacraments, for which he is best known. He believed that the nation of Zurich was unified in part by its common profession of Christianity, symbolized by participating in the Lord's Supper. Zwingli recognized that some people participating in the Lord's Supper were not truly believing Christians. For them the sacrament could not really be the body and blood of Christ but merely a public testimony of adherence to a religious community, just like the Old Testament Passover.

This view led Zwingli to describe the Lord's Supper as merely a memorial meal, commemorating Christ's death. The bread and the wine symbolized, but did not literally *become*, Christ's body and blood. Zwingli rejected the idea of the *real presence* of Christ in the Eucharist partly because he believed transubstantiation to be scientifically impossible. With Luther, Zwingli did not believe in the existence of what Thomas Aquinas and the medieval philosophers had termed *substances*. Nothing could be changed into Christ's actual body and blood in the miracle of transubstantiation. Luther resolved the problem by saying that Christ is everywhere for the faithful, including in the bread and the wine of the Lord's Supper. Zwingli took a more radical approach and read the text, "This is my body," to mean "This signifies my body." That reading justified his view of the Lord's Supper as merely a memorial, and therefore an appropriate civil, as well as religious, ceremony.

Zwingli supported infant baptism for equally political reasons: Baptism was also a symbol that marked the infant child as part of Zurich. Baptism did not wash away original sin. Zwingli's patriotic concerns led him to reject the sacramental grace that the Roman Catholic Church preached, and he developed a theology of the sacraments more appropriate to a national Protestant church. Despite this theological creativity, Zwingli left no one specific tradition as his heir. Instead, his followers were absorbed by the other two important Swiss movements—the Anabaptists and the Calvinists.

The Anabaptists

A group of Zwingli's Zurich followers shifted his ideal of returning to the sources from the Old Testament to the New Testament church. These "Swiss Brethren" rejected Zwingli's state church. Partly in response to conflict with the Zurich government, though ultimately in response to widespread persecution throughout Europe, they became convinced that the ideals of the true church were radically different from and entirely opposed to those of the state.

These *Anabaptists* who scattered throughout Europe symbolized separation from lukewarm and ungodly state churches by practicing *believer's* baptism—baptizing adult believers (rather than infants) by pouring water over them. Since all sixteenth-century Anabaptists had already been baptized as infants, they were called "Anabaptists" or "rebaptizers" by those who hated them. The practice of believer's baptism symbolized a new, exclusive understanding of the church as a small brotherhood of heartfelt believers, rather than an institution serving the spiritual needs of the nation.

The Anabaptists modeled themselves directly after the New Testament church, which they saw as a small band of the persecuted faithful. They followed Christ's words—especially those of the Sermon on the Mount (Matthew 5–7)—to the letter. As one Anabaptist put it, "No one can truly know Christ unless he follow him in life."[5]

Following Christ in life, as understood through the Sermon on the Mount, had some momentous consequences. For one thing the Anabaptists absolutely refused to swear oaths, based on Christ's words: "Simply let your 'Yes' be 'Yes' and your 'No,' 'No'; anything beyond this comes from the evil one" (Matt. 5:37). In a Christian society, the judicial oath meant that God guaranteed that a statement was true. A person who lied under oath was expected to be struck dead almost immediately, with no chance of salvation. The judicial oath therefore served as a glue for the society and largely filled the role that contracts do in American society. Not only were court trials accompanied by oaths, but most business and land dealings were sealed similarly. However, since Jesus had told the Anabaptists not to swear oaths, they set themselves outside of the fabric of society. This led to immediate and widespread persecution, since the Anabaptists were perceived as dangerous anarchists for refusing to swear oaths. In many countries, simply admitting to being an Anabaptist was sufficient grounds for execution.

In 1527, Felix Manz of Zurich became the first Anabaptist martyr. He was found guilty of sectarianism and denouncing capital punishment. Manz's sentence read in part: "Manz shall be delivered to the executioner, who shall tie his hands, put him into a boat, strip his bound hands down over his knees, place a stick between his knees and his arms and thus push him into the water."[6] Other Protestants conducted much of the persecution against Anabaptists, and the preferred method of execution remained drowning, a cruel and macabre joke since it symbolized yet another "rebaptism."

Persecution reinforced the Anabaptist belief that the church and the state were entirely opposed to one another. In the Anabaptists' view, governmental authority was ordained by God, but only for unbelievers, to maintain order in a fallen world full of sinful behavior. The state, therefore, did not involve the community of saints. They did no evil. In fact, according to most Anabaptists, the state itself was under the control of Satan, which was why it persecuted true Christians. The kingdom of God had to be built without the help of the state. The Anabaptists had a very optimistic view of the Christian community and believed that Christians could be truly virtuous disciples of Christ.

One consequence of the Anabaptists' optimistic view of the church and pessimistic view of the state was an inclination towards millenarianism. This view, which has continually surfaced throughout church history, emphasizes that the world is evil and becoming steadily worse. However, there is hope, for at the point at which the evil is worst, a good king will come to conquer the forces of evil and establish true peace and prosperity. For most Christian millenarians, including the Anabaptists, Jesus has been identified as that king. Millenarians usually look for a literal reign of 1000 years (a millennium, hence the name), and saints can prepare the way for his return. Millenarianism is, in fact, a political solution to political injustice that appeals to those who are oppressed economically or socially.

Anabaptist millenarianism led to a lurid episode that discredited the entire movement in the eyes of some Christians and symbolized Anabaptism for generations. In 1534 a number of Anabaptists took over the city of Münster in western Germany. When the bishop who ruled the city brought his army to take the city back, the Anabaptists took up arms. Fueled by their leaders' prophetic claims, they pronounced themselves the new Israel preparing the way for the return of King Jesus. Jan van Leiden, one of the Anabaptist leaders, was crowned "King David" and gathered a harem around himself. The bishop's army starved the city into submission, forcing the people to eat grass, rats, and each other, before overrunning it.

Münster ran entirely counter to the Anabaptist principle that Christians are to avoid involvement in government. However, the Münster Anabaptists included Spiritualist elements, though not directly related to the Zwickau prophets. Jan van Leiden and other leaders had drifted from Anabaptism into Spiritualism, and they relied on direct revelations from the Holy Spirit to guide their acts. This accounts for their willingness to rule the city. However, many Europeans believed that Münster represented the hidden potential in all Anabaptism, and the episode permanently tainted the movement and was used to justify the continuing persecution.

Six refugees from Münster converted a Lutheran ex-priest by the name of Menno Simons in the far northern part of the Netherlands. Menno founded the Anabaptist *Mennonites*, with a pacifist interpretation of Jesus' injunction to "love your neighbor as yourself." He taught that this condemned all violence, including military service, so he entirely dissociated himself from Münster.

"The regenerated do not go to war, nor engage in strife," Menno wrote. "They are the children of peace who have beaten their swords into plowshares and their spears into pruning hooks and know of no war. . . . Since we are to be conformed to the image of Christ, how can we then fight our enemies with the sword?"[7]

In Moravia, to the east, other Anabaptists began to form economic communities that held all possessions in common, following the example of the church in Acts. These *Hutterite* communities proved successful and stable. The Mennonites, Brethren of Switzerland and south Germany, and the Hutterites survived as the only major groups holding to purely Anabaptist principles remaining in the twentieth century, although the idea of believer's baptism has won widespread acceptance. In a later century, a mild form of the Anabaptist view that the state is evil found its way into the American doctrine of the separation of church and state.

Calvinism

By the 1550s and 1560s, the energies of the original Reformers had begun to dissipate. The man who took the lead in the second generation of the Reformation was John Calvin (1509–1564). He set the Protestant Reformation on a firm intellectual basis. As *Calvinism* came to dominate the Protestant Reformation, Zwinglians, (though not Lutherans), began to merge with Calvinists to form the Reformed wing of Protestantism.

Calvin was a French lawyer who was converted to Protestantism and went to Basel, Switzerland, to publish his views. In 1535, on his way from Basel to Strasbourg—another Protestant center—he stopped off in Geneva for the night. As Calvin told it, the great, burly, red-bearded Guillaume Farel, leader of the Reformation in Geneva, accosted Calvin and told him that God needed him in Geneva. Calvin protested that he needed to be free to study, to which Farel responded that "God would curse [his] retirement and the tranquillity of the studies [he] sought."[8] Calvin interpreted this as a sign from God and remained to lead and shape the Genevan Reformation.

A well-trained lawyer and humanist scholar, Calvin brought his gift of critical and systematic thinking to the service of God and the Protestant church. His basic theology was centered on three major propositions: First, God is completely sovereign over his creation. Second, human beings after the fall are entirely tainted by sin. And third, the

For John Calvin (1509–1564) a one-night stopover at Geneva in 1536 proved decisive. The fiery Protestant preacher Guillaume Farel recruited the young scholar and together they spent two tumultuous decades reforming Geneva morally and ecclesiastically, while Calvin refined the theological system that came to bear his name. (Billy Graham Center)

Holy Spirit is active in the life of each Christian and, through Christians, he chooses to transform and redeem the world for the kingdom of God.

Since those who are entirely sinful will never turn to God on their own, God elected some before the foundation of the world, whom the Holy Spirit compels to salvation. Calvin became famous for this view of election, called *predestination*, although Augustine, Luther, Zwingli, and many Catholic scholars before the Reformation shared his view. For Calvin, predestination was a doctrine of comfort (see box 8.1), since it was the only way that anyone could be saved. Calvin believed that, given a free choice, everyone would choose to go to hell, unless God stepped in with his grace.

Calvin's stress on the Holy

8.1. On Ephesians 1:4

"Even as he chose us in him before the creation of the world":

Here [Paul] declares that God's eternal election is the foundation and first cause both of our calling and of all the benefits which we receive from God. If the reason is asked as to why God has called us to participation in the Gospel, why He daily bestows upon us so many blessings, why He opens to us the gate of heaven, we always have to return to this principle, that He chose us before the world was. The very time of the election shows it to be free; for what could we have deserved, or in what did our merit consist, before the world was made?

—John Calvin

John Calvin, *Commentary on Ephesians.*

Spirit also shaped his view of the Bible as the instrument through which the Spirit speaks to the elect. Therefore, gospel teachings are not meant as good advice for everyone, nor as the way to salvation; the Bible assumes that the reader is already saved. Its advice is meant to guide the choices of the saved. For those who do not have the Holy Spirit living in them the Bible is merely a set of dead letters, interesting but ultimately inconsequential.

For Calvin one of the most important channels that the Holy Spirit used to interpret the Bible was the sermon. The sermon not only provided a unified and consistent interpretation of the Bible; it also gave the Calvinist community a great deal of cohesion, particularly since the sermon was still the major form of mass communication. The average Calvinist in the sixteenth and seventeenth centuries probably heard about 15,000 hours of sermons in a lifetime.

The Netherlands became Calvinist largely because Calvinists began to preach throughout the country, often in open fields. Although these sermons were outlawed by the Roman Catholic government, these field preachers drew large Sunday afternoon crowds of peasants, apprentices,

John Knox (c.1514–1572) was a bodyguard for the Scottish martyr George Wishart and a galley slave after the fall of the Protestants at St. Andrews Castle. Freed in 1549, Knox attempted to lead a Reformation in England but fled to Geneva when Mary assumed the throne. He returned to Scotland in 1559 to help the Scottish lords organize a Calvinist national church. (Billy Graham Center)

wealthy merchants, and aristocrats. A picnic and sermon became the fashionable way to spend a Sunday afternoon.

One of the key messages Calvinists heard in these sermons, whether in the Netherlands, or in southwestern France, Scotland, or England, was the call to transform the world. Christians were called to respond to God's saving love by building his kingdom on earth in anticipation of its fulfillment in heaven. It is possible for Christians to build God's kingdom, Calvinists taught, because the Holy Spirit is living and active in them. Calvin believed that all Christians are called to full-time kingdom service, as had been the medieval monks and nuns. The medieval monastic ideals of prayer, study, and work became Calvin's ideals for all Christians in their vocations. Kingdom-building labor included virtually any respectable occupation, so long as it was done to the glory of God. Taking Luther's idea of the priesthood of believers even more positively, Reformed people believed that Christians called to be seamstresses, farmers, town mayors, or seamen could be just as blessed as those called to the preaching ministry. The idea of work as worship led many Calvinists to labor zealously at their vocation and earned them a reputation for industry, frugality, and sobriety. Sometimes the prosperity that followed hard work was viewed as a sign of God's special favor, but any theologically sensitive Calvinist would say that adversity was the same, for "the Lord disciplines those he loves" (Prov. 3:12a; see Heb. 12:6–13).

Some Calvinists were called to government service and became involved in the political process as part of their obligation to further God's kingdom. If the existing government willfully and flagrantly resisted being transformed for God's kingdom, however, Christians were not to obey the government but to resist its tyranny.

The "thundering Scot," John Knox (c.1514–1572), tested those principles in leading Scottish Calvinists against the rule of Catholic Mary Stuart, "Queen of Scots" (1542–1587). Knox invoked the right of Christians to resist "anti-Christian" (by which he meant anti-Protestant) tyranny. Knox, however, along with all other Calvinists, was careful to insist that only those called to government, the "lesser magistrates," could lead such resistance. Calvinists believed that government was entirely legitimate, and only governors could rebel against other governors. The leaders of the Scottish Reformation did not tolerate popular rebellion.

Calvinists were also concerned with making the church independent of the state. In Geneva, the church was governed by the company of pastors (the preachers) in conjunction with twelve lay elders. The church also had doctors, who were responsible for education, and deacons who administered the charities. These offices were formally distinct from the city councils, who governed the city of Geneva, though the two cooperated with each other freely.

Outside of Geneva, Calvinists developed a full-blown presbyterian form of church government, in which local congregations, governed by elders and deacons, sent representatives to regional bodies, who in turn sent representatives to national assemblies. Presbyterianism gave Calvinists a great deal of discipline and cohesion, since the various congregations remained in constant contact and were capable of concerted action, while retaining the responsiveness and flexibility that comes from centering authority at the local level. In the sixteenth century many people became Calvinists because of this ecclesiastical structure, rather than Calvin's theology.[9] Presbyterianism proved an effective means of gaining independence from state control and secular authority. Furthermore, it gave many who were not nobles experience in ruling and representative government (see fig. 8.2).

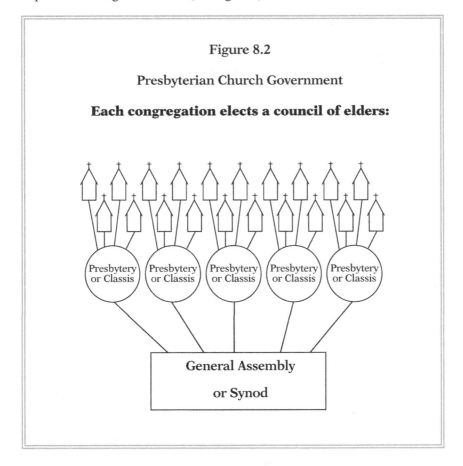

Figure 8.2

Presbyterian Church Government

Each congregation elects a council of elders:

Presbytery or Classis

Presbytery or Classis

Presbytery or Classis

Presbytery or Classis

Presbytery or Classis

General Assembly

or Synod

Church and state were not entirely separate in Geneva, however. Michael Servetus (1511–1553) was burned at the stake by the civil authorities for denying the Trinity in general and the eternal existence of Christ in particular. Calvin felt that denying the Trinity and the divinity of Jesus was not merely wrong, but attacked the very foundations of Christianity, as the Council of Nicea had determined in 325 when Arius had denied the divinity of Jesus. Calvin brought the accusation of heresy against Servetus; the city council tried him and sentenced him to burn, while Calvin pleaded for a more humane sentence of death by beheading.

For Calvin the doctrine of the Trinity was more important than Servetus's life, and he was willing to persuade the government of Geneva to support his view. His power in Geneva, however, was merely that of persuasion; he held no formal office. His influence over the Protestant churches in Europe was strong, and his ideas influenced most Protestants in the late sixteenth and seventeenth centuries.

English Reformation

The English Reformation began as an act of state but developed into an independent reformation that synthesized Erasmian humanism and continental Protestantism. Henry VIII (1491–1547; reigned 1509–1547), the English king, had just finished writing a book attacking Luther, which earned him the title "Defender of the Faith" from the pope. Henry knew, however, that one of his primary jobs as king was to produce an heir. Without an heir no king could prevent chaos and civil war upon his death; rival factions would immediately set up their claimants to the throne. Henry's father had come to the throne in the aftermath of just such a civil war. England at the time was politically fragile and could not afford another round of civil war.

In order to produce an heir, Henry wanted to annul his eighteen-year, sonless marriage to Catherine of Aragon (1485–1536) and marry Anne Boleyn (1507?–1536), a noted beauty who refused to allow Henry into her bed until she wore a wedding ring. Henry argued that the marriage had been invalid because Catherine had been married to Henry's elder brother Arthur until the groom's untimely death at fifteen years of age. Although the pope had granted a formal dispensation for that marriage, Henry argued that Leviticus 20:21, which prohibited marrying a brother's wife on pain of childlessness, meant that his marriage to Catherine was sinful and invalid. The difficulty Henry faced was that Catherine's nephew was Charles V, the Holy Roman emperor who had political control over Italy and, therefore, over the pope. Charles also had a claim to the English throne through Catherine if Henry produced no heir. After tortuous negotiations and various threats, Henry in 1535 simply renounced the authority of the pope over England and immediately secured his annulment, though not yet his heir.

Henry's archbishop, Thomas Cranmer (1489–1556), who had been confirmed by the pope before the break, led the English Reformation and founded the Church of England. Cranmer was both an Erasmian and a Protestant, and molded the new church to fit his vision. Cranmer was careful to change very little at the parish level; the weekly rhythm of worship, prayer, and the sacraments remained undisturbed. The one major transformation Cranmer did make was to change the church services from Latin into English, but that was a popular reform. Most of the changes took place in the upper administrative levels, where ordinary people did not notice them.

Cranmer was committed to continuity because, as a national church, the Church of England had to meet the spiritual needs of, and unify, all English people. His commitment to unity bore fruit in the Book of Common Prayer, which focused the church on worship and prayer (see box 8.2). Worship and prayer remain the central unifying forces of the Church of England. The first commitment the Church of England made was to an accessible Bible; King Henry had the Bible translated and had a copy put in every church in England. Cranmer further worked to unite humanist and Protestant convictions through his stress on a life of active virtue. For Erasmian humanists, being a Christian meant following Christ's example in a virtuous life; for Luther and the Protestants a life of active virtue was the result of God's grace working in the Christian's life. Cranmer was careful to define both grace and obedience in such a way that both Protestants and humanists could affirm his words.

A third key element in Cranmer's theological program for the Church of England was his emphasis on the concept of *adiaphora* or "things indifferent." Cranmer used this idea to keep the essentials of the faith to a minimum, allowing for a good deal of theological latitude among members of the Church of England, especially in specific forms used in worship. He also used this to justify the king's control over the church, allowing the king to determine adiaphora as he saw fit. Since none of these indifferent things threatened salvation, no one had an excuse for refusing to conform to the king's will.

Although Henry VIII was not a Protestant, he did not persecute Protestants, and he made sure that when he died his son Edward (1537–1553), who was nine years old at his coronation, had a firmly Protestant council of regents to rule for him. This was at least partly because Edward was illegitimate by Catholic law, though a legal heir in the eyes of the Protestants. During Edward's reign, the nation became solidly Protestant, in part because the government confiscated church lands and sold them to English people, who would have to give them back if the country became Catholic again.

Edward VI's reign was very short, and his half-sister, the daughter of Catherine of Aragon and a staunch Catholic, came to the throne as Mary I (1516–1558). Prominent Protestants were forced into exile in the hotbeds of Continental Protestantism, or they were martyred in England, where their blood kept hatred of Catholicism alive for generations. Cranmer himself, after a long period of solitary confinement, recanted his Protestant beliefs. But before he went to the stake he recanted his recantation, and he vividly dramatized his renewed stand at his death when he calmly thrust into the fire the hand that had signed the document denying his Protestant convictions.

"Bloody Mary's" reign lasted five years. When her half-sister, the daughter of Anne Boleyn, came to the throne in 1558 as Elizabeth I (1533–1603), she got the chance to remake the church as she saw fit. Ten of the twenty-four bishoprics were vacant when Elizabeth became queen, and all but one of the remaining bishops resigned when she declared herself Protestant.

The Marian exiles returned from the Calvinist lands of Switzerland and Germany, rejoicing that God had sent a "Deborah," who would prove just as godly as the Old Testament judge. They expected to help Elizabeth complete the Reformation in a Calvinist fashion. Elizabeth, however, chose not to follow the lead of these *Puritans*, but rather to continue in the Erasmian tradition of Cranmer. Her goal was to unify England through the Book of Common Prayer.

The English Puritans, who were Calvinists, pressed for further reform within the Church of England. They were far more conscious of doctrine than the Erasmian Anglicans; they stressed good preaching, as well as church discipline, to correct the wayward. The Puritans were unhappy with the Book Common Prayer because it stressed prayer rather than preaching. They were also

> ## 8.2. The Book of Common Prayer
>
> *Graunt that this day wee fall into no synne, neyther runne into any kinde of daunger, but that al our doings may be ordered by thy governaunce to do alwaies what is righteous in thy sight.*

> ## 8.3. "Of Good Works"
>
> *Albeit that good Works, which are the fruits of Faith, and follow after Justification, cannot put away our Sins, and endure the severity of God's Judgment; yet are they pleasing and acceptable to God in Christ, and do spring out necessarily of a true and lively Faith; insomuch that by them a lively Faith may be as evidently known, as a tree discerned by the fruit.*
>
> —"The Thirty-nine Articles," Article Twelve

unhappy with the Church of England's commitment to being a national church because it allowed religiously tepid people to jog along without being challenged.

The center of Puritan spirituality lay in what Puritan scholar William Perkins (1558–1602) called the *Practical Syllogism*:

> God plants faith in those he saves. I know this because the Bible says so.
> I believe. I know this because I experience it in my heart.
> Therefore, I am saved, and can know that for certain.

The practical syllogism led the Puritans to stress a warm, vibrant, glowing, and attractive faith.

When Anglicans refused to complete the Reformation of the English church, the Puritans became upset. While the majority of Puritans continued to work to reform both the church and the nation from within the church, some refused to "tarry for the magistrate" any longer and separated from the Church of England to become *congregationalists*. Congregationalists were Calvinists who believed the church should make decisions by a vote of the congregation, whereas other Calvinists elected representative elders to make decisions. Some of these congregationalists fled to the Netherlands and then to America, where they became the Pilgrim fathers and a part of the fabric of American religion. Other seventeenth-century congregationalists became the first Baptists.

The tension between Puritans and Anglicans came to a head in 1640 when the two found themselves on opposite sides of a civil war between the Parliament and King Charles I (1600–1649). The Puritans, bent on transform-

8.4. English Baptists

English Baptists grew out of the congregationalists in two ways. First, early in the century John Smyth and Thomas Helwys fled to the Netherlands where they were influenced by the Arminians and the Dutch Mennonites, and combined these two notions into the "General Baptist" movement, which argued for free will and human responsibility in salvation. In mid-century a group of Calvinist Separatists came to the conclusion that the practice of believer's baptism symbolized their belief in a gathered, rather than a national, church more ef-fectively than infant baptism. They also interpreted Scripture to teach baptism by immersion.

After the Restoration of the Church of England in 1660 the Baptists, with the other dissenting churches, suffered varying degrees of persecution but survived into the eighteenth century, when they were once again tolerated. The General Baptists of the eighteenth century tended to become Unitarian, or to adopt Unitarian theology, while the Particular Baptists continued within the dissenting tradition until today. Most British Baptists remain staunchly Calvinist.

8.5. John Bunyan

The conflicts during the English Commonwealth produced a writer whose work used to be one of the most popular and well-read English books. John Bunyan (1628–1688), a Baptist, spent many years in prison for his beliefs. While there, he wrote *The Pilgrim's Progress*, an allegorical account of the Christian's spiritual journey. In an intriguing and approachable style, Bunyan recounts the struggles and temptations of the Christian life. His work has enriched the language with such clichés as the "Slough of Despond" and "Vanity Fair."

ing their culture and trained in the methods of representative church government, began to run for governmental office in large numbers in the 1620s; they came to control the English Parliament. The king, on the other hand, supported an Anglicanism that had lost touch with the religious temper of the nation as a whole. It stressed rites, rituals, and gorgeous display and appeared more and more crypto-Catholic to the Puritans. As the king alienated a Parliament already upset at his religious policies by refusing to call it into session between 1629 and 1640, the nation became polarized. Finally, in 1640 the king, in desperate need of new tax revenue, was forced to call Parliament into session. This session became known as the "Long Parliament" and almost immediately took Charles to war.

Parliament and the Puritans won the war, but the Puritan experiment in completing the Reformation failed. Although united in opposition to the Anglicans and the king, they could not agree among themselves how to replace either. They initially fell out over the issue of religious toleration at the Westminster Assembly, (which met to form a new Puritan church). The conservative presbyterians wished to impose a national presbyterian church, while the independents fought for congregational independence and later outright toleration. The impasse meant that no church was established during the Puritan rule, and an astonishing variety of sects flourished. The Puritans muddled along until 1660, when Charles' son, Charles II (1630–1685), was restored to the throne. Since Puritan rule had tolerated such a great diversity of opinion, including some very radical and unconventional forms of religion, Puritanism was discredited. In the *Restoration*, the Church of England returned to its Erasmian Anglican model. The Puritan influence, however, more dramatically and permanently marked the English colonies in North America (see pp. 221–27).

The Catholic Reformation

The Catholic Reformation was a second-generation reformation that responded to the Protestants from within the Roman Church. Its ideas were rooted in the efforts of reformers who predated Luther. The Catholic Reformation moved to a double rhythm, stressing personal piety on the one hand and the pastoral function of the church on the other. The two themes reinforced each other. The Church, as pastor, tried to bring genuine piety to its parishioners, and pious laypeople demanded a Church able to meet their spiritual needs.

The Catholic Reformation began well before Luther. A good example of early Catholic reform is the *oratory* movement begun in Italy in the late fifteenth century. Oratories were lay groups whose members cultivated their spiritual lives by attending Mass frequently and practicing works of charity, especially aiding one another in time of need. If a member of the oratory fell sick, the group would support the family, and upon the member's death, the oratory would take care of dowries for a member's daughters and apprenticeship fees for sons.

The *Oratory of Divine Love*, founded in Rome in 1517, included

Ignatius of Loyola (1491–1556) was pursuing a military career when convalescence from a battle wound turned his thoughts in a spiritual direction. His manual of spiritual warfare, *Spiritual Exercises*, so fired a group of disciples in 1534 that Paul III in 1540 approved their Society of Jesus as an order of the church. (Billy Graham Center)

a number of eminent Reformers and spun off new religious orders and a more traditional path of renewal than that followed by those who became Protestants. *The Society of Jesus* or *Jesuits*, the most important of the new orders, became the shock troops of the Catholic Reformation and the Church. This group was founded in 1540 by Ignatius of Loyola (1491–1556) and demonstrated, as did no other organization, the power and concerns of the Catholic Reformation.

In 1521, while recovering from a war wound, Ignatius read all the romances his library contained and so was driven to read spiritual works. A professional soldier in the army of Ferdinand of Spain, Ignatius was moved enough by his readings to dedicate his life to Christ as a soldier for the Lord. While they shared some concerns about conditions within the Roman Church, Ignatius and Luther came to exactly opposite responses. The unity of the church was all important to Ignatius. He believed passionately that the body of Christ was not meant to be torn asunder and that the Holy Spirit was alive and active in the Roman Catholic Church.

8.6. The *Spiritual Exercises*

The core of Jesuit piety lay in Loyola's *Spiritual Exercises*, a set of principles and meditations designed to help a person make choices or reaffirm choices already made. These exercises also show the intense loyalty of the Jesuits; the famous Exercise 13 reads:

To arrive at complete certainty this is the attitude of mind we should maintain: I will believe that the white object I see is black if that should be the decision of the hierarchical church, for I believe that linking Christ our Lord the Bridegroom and His Bride the Church, there is one and the same Spirit ruling and guiding us for our soul's good. For our Holy Mother the Church is guided and ruled by the same Spirit, the Lord who gave us the Ten Commandments.

In 1534 Ignatius, with five like-minded men, agreed to offer their services to the Church, vowing poverty, chastity, and absolute obedience to the pope. They offered to become missionaries to Palestine to convert the Muslims to the Catholic faith. Transportation difficulties made it impossible for them to reach the Holy Land, but the Church redirected their energies, and their movement grew to become a world teaching and missionary order.

The Jesuits were characterized by an intensely active and personal spirituality. To become a Jesuit it was not enough merely to have a calling to the religious life. A Jesuit had to be converted, to be born again. Jesuit piety consisted in inner devotion, not just external actions.

The Jesuits became superbly educated and trained missionaries and teachers and the key to the success of the Catholic Reformation. The renewal movement as a whole was, indeed, a success. A believer faced with the old, unreformed Catholic Church and an aggressive and devout Protestantism found it difficult to choose. The same believer facing Protestant heresy and a reformed and vibrant Catholic Church did not. Spain, Italy, and France, where political factors allowed the Catholic Reformation to take hold, resisted Protestantism and remained Roman Catholic. The Jesuits take much of the credit for this, as well as for reconverting Poland, Moravia, and Bohemia to Catholicism.

The Catholic Reformation found its summary in the Council of Trent, a general council of the Church which met irregularly between 1545 and 1563. There were two main themes at the Council of Trent. It defined Catholic doctrine and reformed abuses in the Church. Ecclesiastical reform was largely independent of the Protestant threat, showing that the Church was trying to develop piety in its parishioners. It included decrees insisting that all priests live in the parish that supported them and preach the Word of God to their parishioners, and that bishops provide schools to help pastors learn how to preach. Defining doctrine was, by and large, a direct response to Luther and the Protestant Reformation.

Since there was genuine disagreement as to which was the more important theme, the fathers at Trent decided to take them by turns, issuing first a doctrinal decree and then a reform decree.

The Council of Trent began by defining the authority by which the Church could make decisions. Where Lutherans believed that only the Scriptures could be authoritative for the Church, the fathers at Trent included both Scripture and the continuous tradition of the church as authorities. They believed that God still spoke to the church through the Holy Spirit, and that the Bible itself had not been dropped intact from heaven, but had been selected by the church with the guidance of the Holy Spirit.

The Council declared that no one could be saved except by grace, but salvation by grace did not exclude preparing the heart to receive grace, and cooperating with God in the work of salvation. The Council of Trent consistently responded to Luther's "only" by saying "both and." Both faith and works cooperate in salvation.

The Council of Trent defended all seven of the traditional Catholic sacraments (baptism, confirmation, Eucharist, marriage, ordination, confession, and extreme unction), which Luther had cut to three (later two) and the other reformers had cut to just baptism and the Lord's Supper. The Council said that baptism washes away original sin completely, so that the baby is in a state of salvation until it deliberately sins. They also said that sacramental grace does not depend on the faith of the recipient but actually works through the elements of the sacrament.

The Council of Trent also affirmed the divinely inspired character of the Vulgate translation of the Bible against the new translations that were being brought out. It affirmed the central role of priests in the Church against Luther's view that all Christians are priests. And it affirmed that rites and rituals are helpful in strengthening piety.

8.7. The Council of Trent

They who by sin had been cut off from God, may be disposed through His quickening and helping grace to convert themselves to their own justification by freely assenting to and co-operating with that grace; so that, while God touches the heart of man through the illumination of the Holy Ghost, man himself neither does absolutely nothing while receiving that inspiration, since he can also reject it, nor yet is he able by his own free will and without the grace of God to move himself to justice in His sight. Hence, when it is said in the sacred writings: Turn ye to me, and I will turn to you, we are reminded of our liberty; and when we reply: Convert us, O Lord, to thee, and we shall be converted, we confess that we need the grace of God.

John H. Leith, ed., *Creeds of the Churches: A Reader in Christian Doctrine for the Bible to the present*, 3d ed. (Louisville: Westminster/John Knox, 1987), 442.

After Trent, Catholicism became modern—a denomination with a defined doctrine. It was no longer simply *the church*, with room for almost everyone. But at the same time it became a reformed Catholicism, with a great emphasis on personal piety and the pastoral function of the Holy Mother Church. In many ways the Church after Trent was a much greater, if also a diminished, Church.

Conclusion

By 1600 European Christianity had become thoroughly fragmented. Southern Europe, where the Catholic Reformation began, remained solidly Catholic; the Jesuits regained large areas of Eastern Europe for the Catholic Church as well. Lutherans dominated northern Germany and Scandinavia, while southern Germany remained Catholic. Calvinists had established themselves in pockets throughout Western Europe. England, of course, had established the Anglican Church, a blend of Erasmian and Protestant ideas, though Calvinist Puritans challenged Anglican moderation. Anabaptists survived in tiny congregations and communities scattered in various nooks and crannies throughout Europe.

The Reformation, in both its Protestant and Catholic forms, breathed new life into the church. During the seventeenth century, however, the fragmentation of Europe led to increasing religious warfare, while reformers found it increasingly difficult to pass on their fervor and piety to the generations that followed them.

The response of the average European Christian to these monumental religious changes depended to a large extent on location. In Italy and Spain, Protestants must have seemed distant bogeymen, vaguely associated with the nefarious enemy English and Dutch. Some social historians see very little change from the Middle Ages in southern Europe. In England and Scandinavia the thorough replacement of the Roman Church by varieties of royally proclaimed Protestantism seems to have excited interest, primarily among the intellectual elite. Most other members simply noticed the change in the language of the church service and the fact that the pastor now had a wife. Other changes were relatively gradual as the impact of brief sermons and catechism trickled down. In middle Europe—France, Germany, and Switzerland— real choice must have been presented to the average believer. Lutheran, Calvinist, and Anabaptist preachers and ideas swung through periodically, and the local political leaders might change affiliation suddenly. Making the wrong religious choice could be fatal.

Where Protestants, especially Reformed Protestants, succeeded, the church became a major social institution. Sermons, especially, became a major source of ideas, information, and entertainment. Reformed sermons used all the rhetorical devices to communicate powerfully to a mass audience. From them Westerners have absorbed the humanist habit of arguing on the basis of a text—in this case the Bible. The Calvinist requirement for godly, biblically-guided elders accelerated the growth of literacy among non-nobles. In addition, the experience of farmers and craftsmen in church government directed them to concerns in the realm of secular politics as well.

Suggested readings

Bainton, Roland H. *Here I Stand: A Life of Martin Luther*. Nashville: Abingdon-Cokesbury, 1955.

Dickens, A. G. *The English Reformation*. New York: Schrocken, 1968.

Dillenberger, John, ed. *John Calvin: Selections from His Writing*. Garden City, N.Y.: Doubleday, 1971.

Estep, William R. *Renaissance and Reformation*. Grand Rapids: Eerdmans, 1986.

Ignatius of Loyola. *Spiritual Exercises*, trans. by R. W. Gleason. Garden City N.Y.: Doubleday, 1964.

"John Calvin." *Christian History*, 5.4 (issue 12, 1986).

Luther, Martin. *Selections from His Writings*, J. Dillenberger ed. Garden City, N.Y.: Doubleday, 1961.

"Martin Luther: His Later Years and Legacy." *Christian History*, 12.3 (issue 39, 1993).

"Martin Luther: The Early Years." *Christian History*, 11.2 (issue 34, 1992).

McNeill, John T. *The History and Character of Calvinism*. New York: Oxford University Press, 1954.

"The Radical Reformation: The Anabaptists." *Christian History*, 4.1 (issue 5, 1985).

"Thomas Cranmer and the English Reformation." *Christian History*, 14.4 (issue 48, 1995).

"Ulrich Zwingli." *Christian History*, 3.1 (issue 4, 1984).

European Expansion, 1500–1800

In 1497 Vasco da Gama and a crew of Portuguese sailors rounded the Cape of Good Hope and sailed into the Indian Ocean. Their mission was just one part of the eruption of European people and involvements across the globe during the fifteenth and sixteenth centuries. Exploration and trade were set in motion by other developments in Europe: the Renaissance; the Reformation; the rise of the middle class; and the creation of nation-states.

There were several motives for such voyages. Partly these were trading expeditions, seeking such exotic goods as ivory and slaves. They were also attempts to outflank the Muslim powers that controlled the Eastern Mediterranean. They sought to make contact with the outside world, perhaps even with the fabled Christian kingdom of Prester John in Asia (see box 9.1). Such an ally might help crush the Muslims in a vast pincer movement. These voyages also attempted to satisfy the curiosity of European kings and princes about what lay beyond the borders of Europe. Some sailors went to discover and claim new lands in order to enhance the prestige and wealth of their sovereigns. And some went to spread the gospel of Jesus Christ. Christopher Columbus, for example, was a mystical and passionate Christian in addition to being a visionary explorer.

The main explorers of Africa and Asia were the Portuguese, who were inspired by the vision of Prince Henry the Navigator (1394–1460). In the New World Spain took the lead. In time the Portuguese overseas empire was largely swallowed up by the Dutch. The Dutch, in turn, gave way to the British in most parts of the world. But neither these nor other Protestants showed the missionary zeal of their Catholic rivals. In the centuries with which this chapter is concerned, most of the expansion of Christianity around the world was undertaken by Catholics, not Protestants.

9.1. Prester John

Prester John was the ruler of a legendary Christian kingdom who captured the imaginations of European travelers for several hundred years. He first appeared in the historical writing of the Cistercian bishop Otto of Freising (c. 1110–1158):

Not many years ago a certain John, a king and priest who lives in the extreme Orient, beyond Persia and Armenia, and who, like all his people, is a Christian although a Nestorian, made war on the brothers known as the Samiardi, who are the kings of the Persians and Medes. . . . At last Presbyter John—for so they customarily call him—put the Persians to flight, emerging victorious after the most bloodthirsty slaughter. . . . He is said to be a direct descendant of the Magi, who are mentioned in the Gospel, and to rule over the same peoples they governed, enjoying such glory and prosperity that he uses no scepter but one of emerald.*

European travelers tried to locate this Prester John and what they supposed to be a Christian kingdom of fantastic wealth and power. Otto's original account may have been a garbled reference to Yeh-lü Ta-shih, twelfth-century ruler of the Kara-Khitai, a Buddhist Mongol people of Central Asia.

Later interest focused on various of the Mongol khans, for there were usually Nestorian Christians at the Mongol court, and several descendants of Chinghis Khan were married to Keraits, a Christian people of Central Asia. Still later, European travelers went looking in India, where there were also Christians, but none found a Christian king of Prester John's fabled power.

Attention finally focused on Ethiopia. Its people were not Nestorians but Monophysite Christians. But their king was indisputably a Christian king. An Ethiopian embassy in 1306 offered Spain help against the Moors in return for help defeating Arabs in Northeast Africa; the Spanish rulers did not respond. As Portugal began to look outward from its shores in the 1400s, expeditions were sent across North Africa by land and sea, looking for Prester John in the hope of establishing a way to break the Arab monopoly on trade with the Indies. The search culminated in the mid-1500s, when a Portuguese mission did reach Ethiopia. They spent several years there, and brought back news to the pope of their discovery that Prester John was a very mortal ruler, one not likely to be much help in attempts to run the Arabs out of the Middle East.

*Robert Silverberg, The Realm of Prester John (Garden City, N.Y.: Doubleday, 1972), 7.

Typically, an explorer would bring news to Europe about what Europeans saw as a "new land," although all these lands had inhabitants already, many had complex civilizations, and most had enjoyed far more contact with the rest of the world than had Europe. Then a few Europeans would go to this new place and set up a small trading business. Along with the traders went missionaries, often even before the establishment of formal outposts by the European empire.

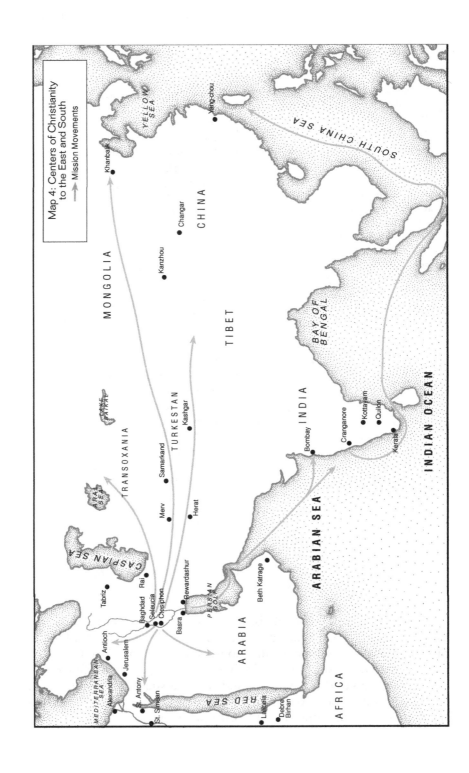

Map 4: Centers of Christianity
to the East and South
→ Mission Movements

While these missionaries spoke of evangelizing the local population, that goal eluded many. More often they primarily served the spiritual needs of Europeans in the foreign locations. In Ghana, French and Portuguese missionaries seldom ventured beyond the neighborhoods of coastal trading posts. When the Portuguese built the Castle of St. George at Elmina, Ghana, in the early 1500s, they intended to use it as a base for both commerce and evangelizing the surrounding peoples. But few priests survived the hot, humid climate. Those who remained became bogged down with orders from Portugal to say a daily Mass inside the castle and minister to the ritual needs of the Portuguese traders. Somehow, they never got around to making much of a connection with the local people.

This pattern resulted in the planting of Christian missions at several points in Africa south of the Sahara by 1700. Portuguese priests established missions in the Azores (1431), Cape Verde Islands (1450), Zaire (1491), Ghana (1501), and several spots on the East African coast in the sixteenth century. Yet only the post in Zaire attracted many African converts.

Perhaps this effort would have been more successful had the Europeans not become heavily involved in the slave trade. All told, Europeans bought or abducted more than 10 million Africans and forcibly shipped them to the New World before the 1860s. The strong association of Europeans with slavery in coastal Africans' minds cannot have helped the missionaries' cause. It was not until the nineteenth century that the number of African Christians began to climb. That increase was at least partly because missionaries in that century became the most prominent European opponents of the trade in slaves, as well as because they had pushed into the interior of the continent.

Catholic missions in Asia

Christianity spread more rapidly across Asia than across Africa, in part because European (particularly Portuguese) military and economic involvement in Asia was more extensive. Portuguese merchants established trading outposts at Goa, India, in 1510 and at Malacca on the Malay Peninsula in 1511. From there they followed Filipino and Okinawan pirate-traders north to the China coast. They began to trade at Kagoshima in southwestern Japan in the early 1540s and established a port at Macao on the China coast in 1557.

Missions were part of the Portuguese motive for seeking overseas possessions. Under the pope's grant of *padroado*, or patronage (*patronato* in Spanish), the king of Portugal had the right to appoint bishops and otherwise control the church within Portuguese dominions. This effectively subordinated the secular clergy to the crown's political and military agenda and set up a conflict between the secular clergy, controlled by the king, and members of the Jesuits, Dominicans, and other orders not under royal control.

India

India was the first Asian land to receive attention from Catholic missionaries, who followed close on the heels of the first Portuguese traders. Initially the priests at Goa ministered mainly to Portuguese men who lived in India and to their Indian families. The only major venture outside the Portuguese community set the pattern for the growth of Indian Christianity in future years.

India was divided into a few thousand castes, social groups set off from one another. These castes were arranged in a hierarchy of power and prestige. A person was born into a particular caste, could never change to another, and would likely have very few dealings with people outside his or her own caste. In 1536 the Bharathas, 10,000 pearl-fishing folk who lived along the Coromandel Coast in the southeast, accepted baptism. Thus at one stroke an entire caste of Indians became Christians. But there is doubt as to the depth of understanding many individuals had of their new religion. Moreover, since Christianity was now identified with the Bharathas, none of their neighbors of other castes would consider the new religion.

Then, in 1542, Francis Xavier (1506–1552) came to India (see box 9.2). Within a few years he and his Jesuit followers had begun missions in many parts of India. What is more, they worked hard to instruct their converts and incorporate them under a growing network of Jesuit priests sent out from Portugal. Still, Catholic Christianity remained confined to a few castes and the environs of Portuguese imperial outposts.

As had been the case in Armenia for several centuries, the Catholic missionaries had better luck recruiting non-Roman Catholic Christians than in bringing the gospel to the non-Christian populace. The Jesuits soon learned of the Church of St. Thomas in Kerala and elsewhere. These Christians had never heard of the pope and were indignant when the Romans called them heretics because of their historical link with Nestorius. The Thomasites regarded their own style of worship as purer than that of the Catholics, for they did not venerate Mary, nor use images. In fact, they clung to this distinctive as a way of setting themselves apart from the idol-filled culture of the Hindus around them. In 1599 a new Catholic archbishop, Aleixo de Menezes, came to Goa filled with the zeal of the Catholic Reformation. He took advantage of the death of the Syrian bishop, Mar Abraham, to force the Thomasites to join the Catholic Church and adopt its practices. At a stroke the Church of St. Thomas ceased to exist. Fifty-

Francis Xavier (1506–1552) was among the first followers of Ignatius Loyola in founding the Society of Jesus, and arrived in India in 1542 as a papal legate and missionary to Asia. He established thriving churches in India and Japan. (Billy Graham Center)

four years later about a third of the Thomasite Christians bolted from the Roman Catholic Church and reestablished an independent organization following the old ways.

Up to this point only a few lower-caste and outcaste Hindus had become Christians through Catholic missions. Then, in 1606, a Jesuit named Robert de Nobili arrived in Mathurai in South India with a bold new vision. Following Paul's injunction to be "all things to all people that by all means I might win some," he sought to evangelize high-caste Indians by becoming like them. He saw that Hindus of the higher castes identified Christianity with the lower castes and so were unwilling even to consider his religion. So de Nobili separated himself from other missionaries and their lower-caste converts. He learned Tamil, Telugu, and Sanskrit, wore Indian clothes, became a vegetarian, and generally took on the appearance of a Brahmin, or high-caste Hindu. Soon he had baptized about 600 high-caste converts. He allowed them to retain their old customs, including complete segregation even from Christians of the lower castes.

Robert de Nobili (1577–1656) became a Jesuit in 1596 and arrived in India as a missionary in 1605. He became the first European to have knowledge of Sanskrit, the Vedas, and Vedanta. In thirty-six years as a missionary he established a Christian community of several thousand. (P. Thomas, *Christians and Christianity in India and Pakistan* [London: Allen and Unwin, 1954], facing p.116)

In all this, de Nobili met fierce opposition from other missionaries, who tried to bring European culture along with Christ, or who sought to remake Indian social structure around more egalitarian goals. Such missionaries said he was compromising his faith, even denying Christ. De Nobili's methods resembled those of Matteo Ricci in China (see pp. 214–16). Ricci encountered similar success at winning converts, and similar opposition from non-Jesuits within the church. After de Nobili's death, the Catholic Church repudiated his attempts to bring Christianity into Indian culture. In the long run, however, he was proved to be ahead of his time, since most modern missionaries have paid at least lip service to his ethic of identification with the people he served.

The Jesuits were joined in India by Augustinians, Dominicans, Franciscans, and in time by secular clergy as well. Just a few Indians became priests. The only Indian bishop was a Brahmin convert from Goa named Matthew de Castro, consecrated in 1637. For the most part, the church was staffed by Europeans, as in Africa, Latin America, and most other parts of Asia, and it remained European culturally. De Nobili's attempt to make Christianity indigenously Indian was repudiated during the *rites controversy* (see pp. 215–16). The king of Portugal came to view the Jesuits as dangerous opposition and ordered them out of his domains in 1759. Fourteen years later Pope Clement XIV dissolved the order, and the Jesuit age of missions was over. At its height in 1750, the church in India numbered perhaps one-half million Christians—half of these in Goa and a quarter in Kerala. By 1800 this number had been cut in half, and a severely weakened church faced the Indian people.

Protestants came to India, too, but they came a century and a half later and in much smaller numbers. Protestants took part in other aspects of European expansion in these centuries—the rise of the middle class, the formation of nation-states, and exploration and conquest overseas. But they were slow to embark on missions, preoccupied as they were with the theological and political issues raised by the Reformation. Those Protestants who went to minister in India were part of the European imperial efforts—mainly chaplains sent to serve the men who worked for the Dutch and British East India companies. Most active Protestant missionaries to the Indians came at the behest of the Danish government to its tiny outposts at Tranquebar and Serampore. There, missionaries (particularly some Germans, such as Bartholomew Ziegenbalg) set the pattern for Protestant missions throughout the world in future generations. They took as their first task the translation of the Bible into Indian languages, so that converts could read it for themselves. But converts were not plentiful. Perhaps only 35,000 Indians were baptized as Protestants during the entire eighteenth century. The Protestant effort, here as elsewhere in Asia, was dwarfed by Catholic missions.

Japan's Christian century

One of the fastest-growing churches in Christian history was in Japan. Starting with a handful of believers in 1549, it grew to one-third of a million members at its height six decades later. Christianity took deep root in Japan and survived despite horrific persecutions in the middle of the seventeenth century.

Francis Xavier and his companions entered a country in chaos. The emperor had long been a powerless figurehead. Even the *shogun*, a military ruler who had held the country together in recent centuries, had lost effective control. Japan was divided into scores of warring fiefs, each headed by a *daimyo*, or feudal lord. Buddhism was the strongest cultural force, but it was fragmented into myriad sects and monasteries. Shinto, the native Japanese religion, was in decline, and Confucianism had not yet captured the Japanese ruling class. Amid such political, military, and cultural fluidity, the way was open for Christianity to prosper.

207

This was a Japanese church from the beginning. The number of Portuguese residents in Japan was never large. The key early figures in the church were nearly all Japanese. The first, Yajiro, had fled Japan after killing a man, but then he met Francis in India and came back with the Jesuits to introduce them to his homeland. Without such an intermediary the Christians might well have failed to connect with the Japanese population. *Daimyo* on the southwestern island of Kyushu, such as Shimazu Takahisa of Satsuma and Otomo Yoshishige of Bungo, gave the Jesuits and their converts protection, and in return they hoped their domains would receive the bulk of Portuguese trade. In fact, the Jesuits themselves became deeply involved in international trade, serving as interpreters and drawing the main part of their income from Japanese and Portuguese merchants.

9.2. Francis Xavier

Francis Xavier (1506–1552) was a missionary by accident, but he became, after the apostle Paul, perhaps the greatest missionary of all time. Born to a Basque aristocratic family, he was educated at the University of Paris. There, early in the Reformation, he fell in with an earnest band of young Protestants and nearly became one himself. But he was soon swept away by the charismatic personality and godly zeal of Ignatius Loyola, and became one of Loyola's first disciples in the Society of Jesus. In 1541, King John III of Portugal asked Loyola to give him four missionaries for his possessions in India. Loyola could spare only two of his small band. When one of those took sick, Loyola ordered Xavier to fill in, and on a single day's notice Xavier sailed for India.

Arriving alone in Goa in 1542, Xavier embarked on a decade of frenetic activity. He began by addressing the needs of the spiritually loose collection of rogues and adventurers in Goa. He ministered to the sick and prisoners, taught children, preached and encouraged, and founded a college to train Jesuit priests. He is credited with miraculously healing hundreds of ailments by making the sign of the cross over sick people, sprinkling them with holy water, or having them wear scraps of paper with Bible verses written on them. Soon Xavier expanded his work to the Bharathas and other low-caste fishing peoples in south India. Drawing a small army of European and Indian priests around him, Xavier concentrated on catechizing children and teaching them to spread the rudiments of the gospel to their families.

Soon Xavier's restlessness drew him on to new challenges. He visited and preached in Ceylon, at Malacca on the Malay Peninsula, in the Moluccas (Indonesia), and then back at Goa again in 1548. The following year he sailed to Japan with a Portuguese trading mission, two other Jesuits, and three Japanese to begin the conversion of that country. After two years there he left behind a church of 100 believers that would grow to 300,000 in the next half century. His next objective—to reintroduce Christianity to China—was frustrated. Xavier died in 1552 on Sanchuan Island off the coast of south China, still trying to gain entry into that country.

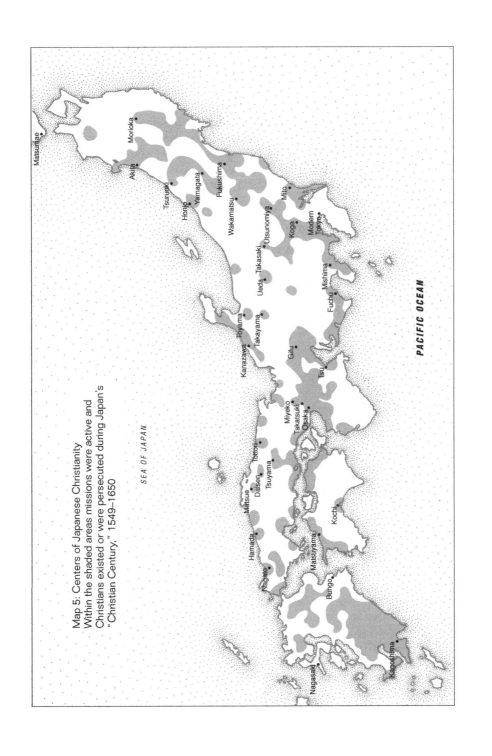

Map 5: Centers of Japanese Christianity
Within the shaded areas missions were active and
Christians existed or were persecuted during Japan's
"Christian Century," 1549–1650

SEA OF JAPAN

PACIFIC OCEAN

Matsumae

Morioka
Akita
Tsuruoki
Honjo
Yamagata
Fukushima
Wakamatsu
Utsunomiya
Ueda Takasaki
Mito
Koga
Modern Tokyo
Fuchu Mishima

Kanazawa
Toyama
Takayama
Gifu
Tsu

Miyeko
Takatsuki
Osaka

Tottori
Daisen
Tsuyama
Matsue
Hamada
Nagato
Matsuyama
Kochi
Bungo
Kagoshima
Nagasaki

Although Portuguese missionaries dominated the clergy and higher decision making, and although they worked sacrificially, there never were very many Portuguese priests. Effective leadership in the church fell to a large cohort of *dojuku*, native Japanese who taught their fellow believers about Christianity. Typically, a town or fief had a single church made up of several smaller, more intimate cells. Believers met on Sundays in church buildings and private homes to hear sermons given by *dojuku*, sing hymns written by Japanese Christians, and pray together. They also met as families for daily recitations of the Lord's Prayer, Apostles' Creed, and other prayers. They might see a priest for mass and confession only once every three or four years, when their turn on the Jesuits' rounds came up. These *Kirishitan* groups built hospitals and schools, served their fellow Japanese in time of flood and famine, and otherwise earned the respect of their neighbors.

The church grew by means of mass conversions. With society organized into tight, hierarchical fiefs, the involvement or at least the acquiescence of the *daimyo* was crucial. For example, when the *daimyo* at Nagasaki, Omura Sumitade, became a Christian in 1571, the church in Nagasaki numbered 5000; six years later it had grown to 60,000. Other fiefs, whose *daimyo* clung to Buddhism and opposed the new religion, had almost no converts.

At first the Japanese thought Christianity, which had come to them from India, was just another form of Indian Buddhism. Buddhist monks and nuns became converts, and even some who did not convert helped the new religion penetrate Japanese domains. But soon the Buddhists found out they were dealing with a hostile faith. Jesuits led their converts in sacking Buddhist temples and Shinto shrines, and in forcing some Buddhists to convert. Soon the more militant Buddhist sects began responding in kind.

Over the whole Japanese Christian period Japan was gradually unified by three great military conquerors: Oda Nobunaga (1534–1582); Toyotomi Hideyoshi (1536–1598); and Tokugawa Ieyasu (1542–1616). Oda treated Christians favorably and was on close personal terms with several Jesuits. This was also true of his successor, Toyotomi, at first. But suddenly, in 1587, quite without warning, Toyotomi turned on his erstwhile friends, banished the Christian *daimyo* Takayama Ukon, ordered the Jesuits out of Japan, and decreed that all Japanese Christians must recant, go into exile, or be killed. Toyotomi's reasons are obscure. Perhaps it was the influence of Buddhist advisors or the fact that several Christian women had refused to be his concubines—an unheard-of affront. But certainly part of Toyotomi's new rancor came from fear. Gaspar Coelho, a Jesuit official, had unwisely involved himself in Japanese politics and unwittingly had raised in Toyotomi's mind the specter of all the Christian *daimyo* uniting against him.

In time, Toyotomi calmed down and decided not to enforce the anti-Christian edicts, but soon another variety of threat presented itself. In defiance of a papal edict, Spanish Franciscan friars came to Japan in 1593, followed by Augustinians and Dominicans in 1602. The Franciscans did not understand the Japanese political situation and insisted on taking a prominent public posture, identifying themselves with Spanish imperial aims at the expense of both the Portuguese and the Japanese. Toyotomi reacted in 1597 by crucifying twenty Japanese priests (three of them Jesuits, the rest Franciscans) and six Spaniards in Nagasaki, then ordering both Franciscans and Jesuits out of Japan.

Before all had left, Toyotomi died in 1598 and was succeeded by Tokugawa Ieyasu in 1600. For a time, after unifying Japan with the help of several Christian *daimyo*, Tokugawa allowed Christians to remain unmolested, mainly because he valued the continued trade with Portugal. The church continued to grow. But soon Dutch and English traders appeared on the horizon. They told tales of Spanish empire-grabbing around the world that scared Tokugawa, and they offered to trade without any unsettling missionary activity. Soon the Dutch had supplanted the Portuguese as chief foreign traders and persecution of Catholics began in earnest.

In 1614 Tokugawa Ieyasu declared that all Christians were by definition subversive agents of foreign powers. He and *daimyo* at his command rounded up missionaries and Japanese priests and shipped them to Macao and Manila, destroyed churches, and ordered Japanese Christians to renounce their faith. Tokugawa declared that every Japanese must register with a local temple and have his or her religious life supervised by a Buddhist priest. After Tokugawa's death in 1616, his son Hidetara and grandson Iemitsu succeeded him and embarked on a campaign of terror. Probably five or six thousand Japanese Christians—2 percent of the total—died under torture in the next thirty years. This was surely the largest number of martyrs at any one time and place in Christian history. British and Dutch traders—Protestants and servants of their own countries' imperial ambitions—sometimes aided the Japanese government in persecuting Japanese and European Catholics. Most of the martyrs were *dojuku*, although some of the remaining clergy were also included. Christians suffered branding, beheading, burning at the stake, having their limbs sawn off—all the sorts of tortures that European Protestants and Catholics visited upon each other and on Jews at about the same time. The most gruesome torture was *ana-tsurushi*, in which a Christian would be suspended upside down in a pit filled with sewage, with cuts about the forehead. Most victims lasted only a few hours, but one Japanese woman suffered for fourteen days before she died from loss of blood.

211

Crucifixion of priests was part of the first wave of persecution to rock the Japanese church in the late 1500s. As a result the surviving Christians were driven underground. (Mark Dinely, courtesy C. R. Boxer)

The point of all this was to terrorize the Christian population into denying their faith, and some complied. But by far the majority of these were verbal recantations only. The strength of the Japanese Christians' continuing commitment is evident from the fact that the Shimabara Rebellion of 1637–1638, though it began as a dispute over economic and political oppression, quickly took on an openly Christian identification. Before it was over, 37,000 Christian men, women, and children had died at the hands of government troops.

Some Christians fled to northeastern Japan, where government control was less strong, but in time all were forced to go underground. Persecution of *Sempuku Kirishitan* ("hidden Christians") did not cease with the annihilation of the Shimabara rebels. Throughout the rest of the seventeenth century, Buddhist priests acted as government agents, ferreting out remaining groups of Christians and having them tortured and killed. In places that had had large numbers of Christians it became the custom that all residents must publicly trample a crucifix as part of the New Year celebrations. The descendants of any known Christian were watched down to the seventh generation.

Those Christians who remained complied outwardly with government edicts, for example registering with Buddhist authorities and allowing Buddhist priests to perform their funerals. The Japanese church lost contact with the West and ceased to exist in the eyes of Rome. The faith was diluted or destroyed by persecution, intermarriage, or simply inadequate nurture. Yet many Christian communities preserved their faith in secret for more than 200 years. Lacking priests, they maintained cells led by elders, baptizers, and catechists. They kept some Christian documents and observed the festivals of the church year. They venerated Mary, recited prayers daily, and kept their faith alive until the Japanese government finally allowed them to practice openly in the nineteenth century.

It may be that all this suffering inevitably accompanied the Tokugawa family's consolidation of national power. But if the Franciscans had left Japan to the Jesuits, if they had been more sensitive to the Japanese political situation, if they had been less eager to identify with Iberian imperial ambitions, or if the Dutch and British had not undercut the Portuguese and Spanish, the church in Japan might have been spared.

9.3. The Philippines

The Portuguese were not the only Europeans operating in Asia. Thanks to Spanish conquest, the Philippines quickly became the most thoroughly Catholic land in Asia. The first European to arrive there, Ferdinand Magellan (1521), was simply trying to sail around the world and did not plant a colony.

Colonization came in 1565 when Miguel Lopez de Legaspi arrived from Mexico with a conquering party. The Filipino people, lightly armed and politically fragmented, offered little resistance against the world's most powerful empire. Soon all the lowlands were under Spanish control. Unlike the situation in Latin America (see p. 216), Spain's first object in the Philippines was to win souls to Christ; extracting wealth was only a secondary goal. So the colonial regime was a bit less harsh than in the Caribbean or South America.

Legaspi's party included five Augustinian missionaries. They were soon joined by Franciscans, Jesuits, and others. Outside the southernmost islands, which had recently become Muslim, Filipino religions quickly gave way before the material superiority of Spanish Christianity. By 1610 more than 300,000 Filipinos—nearly half the population—had become Christians, and the church continued to grow in succeeding decades. Filipino converts received baptism readily and many took Spanish names, although they were slower to attend confession or to give up animistic practices. The church brought schools, hospitals, and export agriculture to the Philippines and contributed to a higher status for women.

Like other facets of Spanish imperialism it remained paternalistic. A native clergy grew only slowly and remained under the dominance of missionaries.

Jesuit scholars in China

Francis Xavier died without reaching his goal of a solid Chinese mission, but Christianity soon returned to China anyway. Three earlier efforts to plant the gospel—two by Nestorians and one by Franciscans—had each faded in turn. Then came the Jesuits, late in the sixteenth century, with a radical new approach: They sought to win China by becoming members of China's ruling elite. For centuries China had been governed by scholar-bureaucrats, whose deep learning in the Confucian classics fitted them for command. Like de Nobili in India, the Jesuits who came to China sought to convert members of the elite class and so convert the

nation. The experiment showed considerable promise before papal politics forced it to be abandoned.

The premiere figure in the Jesuit adventure in China was an Italian, Matteo Ricci (1552–1611). Sent originally to Goa, he moved on to Macao. Then in 1582 he and his friend Nichole Ruggieri became the first Jesuits to gain permission to reside in China proper (near Canton). There they made a few converts and attracted the attention of government officials with their systems for memorizing vast amounts of information and their knowledge of clocks and

A Jesuit astronomical observatory and other adaptation of European natural science gained the esteem of upper-class Chinese and gained many converts in the late 1500s and early 1600s under Matteo Ricci (1552–1611). Ricci wrote a catechism and a major doctrinal work in Mandarin.

astronomy. The last was especially important to the Chinese emperor, for his right to rule depended on the *Mandate of Heaven*. Such astronomical oddities as comets and eclipses were taken as evidence that the Mandate was slipping unless the emperor could predict them in advance. Obviously, sophisticated astronomical techniques were an invaluable asset, and Europe had recently taken the lead over China in that field.

After twenty years of trying, Ricci succeeded in winning an appointment to the imperial court in Beijing. He donned Chinese dress and became a member of the Chinese bureaucracy. From that vantage point he and his Jesuit colleagues not only displayed European scientific achievements, but also made systematic attempts to engage the best Chinese minds in philosophical debate. Few Chinese officials thought the Jesuits' learning superior to their own, but they did give a grudging respect to these scholars from the West. In time, quite a number of Chinese scholar-officials—and one imperial prince—became Christians. More Jesuits followed, as did Franciscans, Dominicans, and others. By Ricci's death in 1611, Chinese converts numbered about 2000. A century later the church had perhaps as many as 300,000 members and included people from all strata of Chinese society. There were Chinese priests and Chinese bishops.

The Jesuits strove to fit Christianity into Chinese culture. They made very little mention of the crucifixion, which would have repelled the Chinese elite. They used ancient Chinese words for God and Heaven, and thereby tried to convince the Chinese that knowledge of God went deep into their heritage but had somehow been forgotten. The Jesuits allowed their converts to continue the quasi-religious practices of venerating their ancestors. Without this it is doubtful they would have made significant inroads into the Chinese population, for respect for ancestors was fundamental to Chinese society.

The Jesuit success in China might have continued to expand had not politics intervened. Ricci had been eager to identify himself with the Chinese, but later missionaries came to be seen as tools of Portuguese imperial ambitions. In the early eighteenth century the Catholics lost favor with the emperor and other high officials. After several waves of persecution in various locations, an edict in 1724 prohibited Christianity entirely. By 1732 nearly all the missionaries had been evicted from the country and the church had been driven underground. There, like the church in Japan, it survived despite surveillance and persecution for over a century.

The rites controversy

The ultimate decline of the Jesuit mission in China must be laid partly at the door of the rites controversy. As noted, Ricci and other

Jesuits had used indigenous Chinese words and allowed their converts to continue traditional ceremonies so long as the converts understood these rites, not as worship, but merely as tokens of respect. Such accommodations to Chinese ancestral rites were critical to the Jesuits' success, just as were de Nobili's accommodations to India's caste system. Missionaries in other orders, perhaps jealous of the Jesuit success, complained to the pope, starting in 1643, that these accommodations cut the heart out of the Christian message. After nearly a century of acrimony, the pope ruled against the Jesuits in 1742 and demanded that they change their ways. Thirty-one years later the pope dissolved the Society of Jesus entirely (see p. 251).

Catholic missions in Latin America

If the Portuguese were the main propagators of Christianity in the Old World, in the New World it was the Spanish. Here, temporal differences made for a very different sort of encounter. In Asia a small, audacious, but relatively weak company of Portuguese adventurers confronted old, strong civilizations in India, China, and Japan. The major goal of the Portuguese was trade. They were neither inclined nor able to impose Christianity on the Asian peoples they met. Accordingly, Christianity took hold mainly on the margins of Asian societies.

In America, by contrast, Spain was the world's foremost naval power and encountered native peoples who were less unified and militarily weaker. The Spanish imposed their temporal authority and their religion on the masses of New World inhabitants and systematically annihilated all aspects of preexisting culture and social structure they could identify.

The Spanish and Portuguese dominions in America stretched over a vast area and encompassed many peoples. The general pattern of Christian development embodied (1) conquest, (2) frontier missions, and (3) the establishment of a settled church.

Conquest

The cross and the sword had gone together in Iberian thinking for centuries in the long-standing contest with Muslim Moors for control of the Iberian peninsula. *Conquistador* and priest often disagreed over methods, but both were bent on imposing their religion and their country's temporal dominance on the local inhabitants. Thus, Hernán Cortés brought friars with him when he invaded Mexico in 1519, and Francisco Pizarro did the same in Peru a decade later.

Religion helped justify conquest. Every *conquistador* carried the *requerimiento*, a summary of Christian history and an order to Indians to surrender, acknowledge the Spanish king and the pope, and become Christians. The *conquistador* read the *requerimiento* at the beginning of every battle, usually in Spanish and at such a distance as to be inaudible to the Indians under attack. By so doing, he absolved himself, his troops, and his sovereign of any responsibility for the bloodshed to follow.

Frontier missions

The Spanish first took the main centers of New World population, and then fanned out in succeeding generations, conquering farther into the hinterland. Sometimes soldier and priest worked together. On other occasions they were at odds.

A classic example of Spanish frontier missions is the career of Father Junipero Serra. Born in 1713, the son of a Spanish farmer, tiny Father Junipero embodied the dedication and strength of character typical of friars in New Spain during the frontier phase. At 35 he gave up a post in philosophy at the University of Majorca to seek martyrdom as a Franciscan missionary to the Mexican Indians. On his arrival in Vera Cruz he chose to walk rather than ride the 250 miles to Mexico City, despite a severe leg injury that brought excruciating pain at every step and left him hobbled for life. He scourged himself daily with chains to drive out sinful thoughts and beat his chest with a stone while preaching to impress Indian listeners. After two decades of fruitful ministry in Mexico, Serra accompanied an expedition of Spanish soldiers to California in 1769. Together they walked the length of that territory as far north as San Francisco Bay, arguing much of the way. They explored the land and founded military outposts and missions that eventually would encompass most of the California Indian population. Serra spent the last years of his life embroiled in the politics of the infant colony, in daily contact with the military authorities but ever at odds with them.

Similar missionary efforts were undertaken by Franciscans and members of other orders throughout New Spain and the Portuguese colony of Brazil. Typically the friars traveled in twos and threes into Indian areas, barefoot and unarmed to emphasize their peaceful intentions and to differentiate themselves from the soldiers. At first they would preach through interpreters, but after learning the local language they would preach directly to the people. They aimed special attention at chiefs, hoping for mass conversions. In fact, they frequently succeeded in bringing whole tribes to Christ. It has been estimated, for example, that more than 4 million Native Americans were baptized in the first fifteen years of Spanish settlement in the Caribbean. The priests tried to persuade Indians to embrace Christianity, but they were not above applying punishments, including death, to those who resisted.

Junipero Serra (1713–1784) was born in poverty on the island of Majorca but worked his way to a doctorate in theology. He gave up a university professorship to become a missionary to Native Americans of the American Southwest. He baptized 6000 and confirmed 5000 during his missionary career. (Billy Graham Center)

The missions took over total control of the Indians' lives, organizing them into villages modeled on Thomas More's *Utopia*. The goal was to bring the Indians what the friars saw as the benefits of Spanish civilization and to protect them from its evils. Property was communally owned and labor communally performed. The priests controlled the Indians' daily schedules, their food, clothing, and economic activities, and strictly limited their contact with the outside world. The intention here was not to punish the Indians so much as to keep them away from the corrupting influence of the coarser sorts of Europeans. They constructed Christian buildings on the sites of Indian temples to harness the power of preexisting religious commitments for Christianity. Theoretically all this was only for a ten-year period of tutelage, after which the Indians would receive title to their Hispanicized villages and control over their lives. But seldom did the friars give up control so soon.

The priests sought to annihilate every vestige of Native American religions, smashing idols and outlawing any preexisting practices. Yet they did not succeed in eliminating Indian beliefs. Frequently the result was a veneer of Catholic external categories imposed on a base of Native American religious assumptions. For example, multiple Indian gods found themselves transformed into Catholic saints with their powers and personalities largely intact. This was not an indigenization of Christianity so much as a debasement of both cultures.

Bartolomé de Las Casas (1471–1566) interceded relatively successfully for native rights on both sides of the Atlantic, although some of his reports of abuses are thought to have been considerably exaggerated to make his point. He was still pleading for the Guatemalans in the court of Philip II in his 90s. (University of New Mexico Press)

For Indian converts the changes must have been bewildering. One telling incident occurred in Guadalupe, Mexico, in 1531. An Aztec Christian named Juan Diego saw a vision of the Virgin Mary and miraculously a painting of her (as a dark-skinned Aztec maiden) appeared inside his cloak, assuring even the lowly of her tender care and compassion. The cloak is still exhibited in the church built on the location of the vision and the Virgin of Guadalupe became the patron saint of Mexicans. In 1990 Juan Diego himself was canonized.

The missions found themselves at odds with the *encomienda*. This was the other major form of Spanish colonial social organization, in which conquering soldiers were given control over lands and their inhabitants as serfs. Theoretically the *encomenderos* were supposed to evangelize their charges, but they seldom followed through on that responsibility. Bartolomé de Las Casas (see box 9.4) and other priests were highly critical of the ways *encomenderos* exploited their Indian workers. Conflicts also developed within the church. The various missionary orders were always at each other's throats. The regular clergy also came under severe criticism from the seculars. The latter were subject to *patronato*, that is, their policies and leaders were all subject to the king, whereas the missionary orders owed allegiance directly to the pope. As time went on and the number of seculars increased with the European population, the regulars found their activities more and more circumscribed.

9.4. Bartolomé de Las Casas

Bartolomé de Las Casas (1471–1566) was the first person to be ordained a priest in the New World. The son of a merchant who had sailed on Columbus's second voyage, young Las Casas came to Hispaniola as the governor's legal advisor and quickly became part of the colonial elite.

A spiritual crisis induced him to take holy orders in 1510 when he was in his mid-thirties. Within a few years he had come to understand that the Spaniards' treatment of the native population violated Christian imperatives. He spent the rest of his life fighting against exploitation of the Indians. He attempted an ultimately unsuccessful experiment in building a mixed community of Indians and Spaniards in which no one held total authority. He passed over richer sees to accept the position of bishop of Chiapas, an impoverished district in Mexico. He traveled to Spain several times to seek royal and church support for laws abolishing Indian slavery and limiting the degree to which colonists could exploit Indian labor.

Many Spaniards, both in Spain and in America, resented what they regarded as Las Casas's meddling. They defended Spanish methods of conquest on biblical grounds, citing Luke 14:23, "Go out into the highways and hedges, and compel them to come in," as divine authorization for the use of force in enslaving Indians and obtaining conversions. In their view Indians were inferior to Spaniards, resisted Christianity unreasonably, were probably better off dead, and, if they did live, could only benefit from contact with Christian civilization.

Las Casas defended Native Americans as a skilled and intelligent, if meek and childlike, people. In his *Defense Against the Persecutors and Slanderers of the Peoples of the New World Discovered Across the Seas* (1550), he wrote:

The Indians are our brothers, and Christ has given his life for them. Why, then, do we persecute them with such inhuman savagery when they do not deserve such treatment? . . . [They] will embrace the teaching of the gospel, as well I know, for they are not stupid or barbarous but have a native sympathy and are simple, moderate, and meek, and, finally, such that I do not know whether there is any people readier to receive the gospel. Once they have received it, it is marvelous with what piety, earnestness, faith, and charity they obey Christ's precepts and venerate the sacraments. For they are docile and clever, and in their diligence and gifts of nature, they excel most peoples of the known world.

Las Casas won this argument, but it is not clear just how much good that did. Starting in 1550 the king, exhorted by Las Casas and many other missionaries, began to limit the degree to which Spanish colonists could impose their will on the Indians. But by the time these laws had much effect the Indian population of the Caribbean and large parts of mainland Latin America had already declined sharply, the victims of Spanish brutality and European diseases to which they lacked immunity.

A new, hardier variety of labor—African slaves—was brought in and exploited as viciously as had been the Indians, but the friars did not object.

Settled church

As the European population grew and the institutions of empire proliferated, the church entered into a more settled phase. In this period, missions to the Indians declined—indeed, the Indian population decreased dramatically as enslavement and disease took their toll. The population of Mexico dropped from 17 million in 1532 to 1 million in 1608, a decrease of 94 percent.

This signaled not only the end of the missionary phase, but also a decline in the quality of the Latin American church. The orders lost numbers and influence, and in 1767 the Jesuits were ordered out of all Spanish dominions. The church became an institution primarily of wealth and power, the holder of half the agricultural lands in Latin America and the employer of countless lawyers and financiers. In the later colonial period the clergy declined to the point where many individuals abused the confessional, violated their oaths of celibacy, and otherwise brought their calling into ill repute.

By the eve of the continent-wide movement for independence at the start of the nineteenth century the church was deeply intertwined with the existing power structure throughout Latin America. It exerted a strong, but ultimately unsuccessful, pull against the tide of independence, assuring its irrelevance in the struggles for national self-determination.

Protestants in North America

Just as the Spanish and Portuguese made Catholicism the religion of Central and South America in the sixteenth century, so the English made Protestantism the religion of most European settlements in North America in the seventeenth century. In time this religion came to dominate the United States and Canada (with the exception of French-speaking Quebec). Most English colonists were Anglicans—members of the Church of England. But the colonies also included Presbyterians, Quakers, Baptists, and adherents to a host of other denominations and sects (see chap. 11). The Protestants who had the most dramatic, long-term effect on American society and culture, however, were the Puritans who founded New England.

The Puritans

As we saw in chapter 8, the English Reformation was initially less thoroughly infused with the principles of Luther and Calvin than was the Reformation on the Continent. The break with Rome occurred more because of Henry VIII's felt need for a male heir than because he or other English leaders were convinced of the rightness of Protestant theology. Only slowly and incompletely did Reformation views creep into the Church of England.

9.5. Black Robes in New France

Roman Catholic Christianity came to the far northern part of the New World as well. Chaplains accompanied the 1535 exploratory expedition of Jacques Cartier, and by the seventeenth century large numbers of missionaries, Jesuits prominent among them, were working in New France. Some ministered to the overseas French population, but a higher percentage than in the British colonies devoted themselves to Indian missions.

The fathers' initial objective was to make French farmers out of the Huron and, later, the Iroquois. Samuel de Champlain described this objective in terms of dual activities of church and state:

They are not savages to such an extent that they could not, in course of time and through association with others . . . become civilized . . . with the French language they may also acquire a French heart and spirit. . . . It is a great wrong to let so many men be lost and see them perish at our door, without rendering them the succour, . . . which can only be given through the help of princes, and ecclesiastics.*

Many Indians easily resisted this assimilating imperative for, unlike the Spanish, the French did not possess overwhelming military superiority. Although they might win some battles, their ultimate security on the North American mainland depended on alliances with Indian peoples, not annihilating or enslaving them. In that more equal power situation, some Indians chose to become Christians, but many did not.

The missionaries tried to place them on farms near mission stations, but most stuck with their ancestral hunting regimen. Except in the few areas of substantial French settlement it was French priests and traders who adjusted their styles of living to Indian ways more than the other way around.

*Cornelius J. Jaenan, The Role of the Church in New France (Toronto: McGraw-Hill Ryerson, 1976), 23.

The main advocates of Reformation ideas in seventeenth-century England were young, vigorous reformers who came to be called *Puritans*. This was a term of abuse at first, describing their intention to purify the Church of England of its popish residue. But soon they embraced the title as their own. Many Puritans stayed within their Anglican congregations and pushed for Calvinist reforms, biblical preaching, and individual awakenings through a conversion experience. Others split off into congregations of their own and so became known as *Separatists*.

Some Separatists left England in 1608 for the Netherlands, where they could worship among other Calvinists. Tiring of life in a foreign country, however, soon they were back in England, planning to go to the New World. There they intended to set up a godly "city on a hill" that would be a beacon to the corrupt and decayed regimes of Europe. In time, they hoped, all Europe would profit by this example and return to God.

In the fall of 1620 a band of separating Puritans aboard the ship *Mayflower* landed on Cape Cod in North America and set up the Plymouth Colony. In the next few decades hundreds and then thousands of Puritans joined them in Plymouth and nearby Massachusetts.

The New England towns they built were closed communities, dominated by clergy and filled in the early years with believing Puritans. They took seriously God's call to holy living and examined themselves and each other rigorously for evidence of sin. As in other parts of the North Atlantic world at the time, the Massachusetts Puritans did not tolerate deviation from their standards of theology or behavior. Outlandish deviants, such as Baptists and Quakers, were punished severely and sent from the colony. Because each individual who had been elected by God for salvation was supposed to undergo a conversion experience, individual Puritans looked deep inside themselves for signs of God's grace and anguished over the fate of their souls.

9.6. The Mayflower Compact

The Puritans set up what they regarded as a godly commonwealth in New England to promote Christianity, both within their community and in missions to the Native Americans. They based their laws on the Bible, particularly the Old Testament, and created government on a radical basis: popular participation and the common consent of the governed. Several of these themes can be seen in the *Mayflower Compact*, signed by the Plymouth colonists in 1620:

In the name of God, Amen. We whose names are underwritten, the loyall subjects of our dread sove-raigne Lord, King James, by the grace of God, of Great Britaine, Franc, & Ireland king, defender of the faith, &c., haveing undertaken, for the glorie of God, and advancemente of the Christian faith, and honour of our king and countrie, a voyage to plant the first colonie in the Northerne parts of Virginia, doe by these presents solemnly & mutualy in the presence of God, and one of another, covenant & combine our selves togeather into a civill body politick, for our better ordering & preservation & furtherance of the ends aforesaid; and by vertue hearof to enacte, constitute, and frame such just and equall lawes, ordinances, acts, constitutions, & offices, from time to time, as shall be thought most meete & convenient for the generall good of the Colonie, unto which we promise all due submission and obedience. In witness whereof we have hereunder subscribed our names at Cap-Codd the 11. of November, in the year of the raigne of our soveraigne lord, King James, of England, France, & Ireland the eighteenth, and of Scotland the fiftie fourth. Anno: Dom. 1620.*

*William Bradford, *Of Plymouth Plantation*, ed. by H. Wish (New York: Capricorn, 1962), 69–70.

The Puritans believed not only that God chose individuals for salvation, but also that God chose each person for a particular type of work. Because one was called by God to a vocation there was an obligation to work conscientiously in it. All this hard work, plus low taxes and cheap land, meant that, on the average, New England Puritans enjoyed a high degree of financial success compared to Europeans.

H. L. Mencken, a twentieth-century American social critic, wrote that "Puritanism is the haunting fear that someone, somewhere may be happy."[1] Many people today share his misunderstanding, but the Puritans of the seventeenth century bore little resemblance to the somber, repressed individuals that the adjective *puritanical* connotes. Mencken perceived inhibitions in his contemporaries and laid them at the door of the Puritans, when those inhibitions in fact stemmed more from the Victorian period, two centuries later. Although Puritans worked hard, they liked fun. They wore bright clothing—most often earth tones, such as green and russet, but sometimes red, yellow, or violet. Black was preferred for Sunday worship. Puritans insisted that a fulfilling sexual relationship was the joy and duty of every married couple. Puritans drank beer and complained bitterly when they could not get it. They loved family life and doted on their children.

The watchword for Puritans was not abstinence but moderation. All things belonged to God and were for God's glory. If God gave people good things they were to be enjoyed, but not to the point where the person became so enthralled with the gift that he or she ceased to perceive the Giver. So food or drink or play or sexual intercourse, each good in itself, should not be pursued for its own sake, but should be enjoyed in moderation and appreciated as a gift of God.

Puritan society was intensely intellectual. Most Puritans could read and write, for it was necessary for all of God's people to read Scripture for themselves. Puritans founded Harvard and Yale colleges, initially to train ministers, but later simply to educate young Puritans. They also laid the foundations for one of America's most important achievements: an effective public school system.

The New England Puritans are reputed to have been governed both by the people (democracy) and by the ministerial elite (theocracy). Neither was quite the case. Starting with the Mayflower Compact of 1620 (see box 9.6), rule was by a majority of adult free male church members in the New England colonies, or at least these were the franchised voters who elected governing officials. Puritans thought a social covenant among humans was the basis of society. Since all believers were spiritually equal, and all were called by God to their vocations, all had an equal responsibility to contribute to public management.

The idealized view of stern, pious Puritans has been almost universally presented. (Billy Graham Center)

But society was also based on a collective covenant with God. Christian principles must undergird every law and government action. Government was responsible to see that all people observed true religion and behaved in a godly manner. This extended to wage and price controls and laws against usury. The doctrine of vocation suggested that some people—not ministers but prominent laypeople—were the natural leaders of society. So, although the colonies held free elections with high participation, the same individuals—men such as William Bradford and John Winthrop—were chosen with monotonous regularity.

When the Puritans sailed to America they hoped to provide England with an example of a godly commonwealth. In time, they hoped, England would see the light and reform itself. Their hopes seemed to be realized in the 1640s, when a Puritan-influenced Parliament rose up and overthrew the increasingly autocratic King Charles I and proclaimed a Puritan state in England. Seven years of civil war tore the country apart, and the Puritan experiment in national government ended ignominiously with the restoration of royal government in 1660. During the dozen years of Oliver Cromwell's government in England, attention was torn away from New England and the sense of purpose of some American Puritans began to falter, along with the economy.

There were other signs of decline. The Puritan missions into the wilderness began to fall apart in the second generation as the holy zeal of the founders began to wear thin among their successors. The first sign of decline was the *Halfway Covenant*, reached in 1662. The Puritans baptized their children as infants but did not admit them to full church membership until they could testify to a conversion experience. The problem was that an increasing number of second- and third-generation people had not had such experiences, even though they believed the correct doctrine and lived righteous lives. Furthermore, they could not vote since they were not church members, and their children could not receive baptism. The Halfway Covenant allowed children to be baptized on the same terms as their parents, in the hope of preparing them for conversion experiences of their own.

This was the first public move to water down the requirements of Puritan theology, and it was much lamented by Puritan ministers. In ensuing decades the New Englanders were plagued by Indian wars, immigration of large numbers of people who did not care about Puritan theology, and outbreaks of witchcraft. The last culminated in the infamous Salem witch trials of 1692, in which hysterical preadolescent girls charged men and women with practicing evil arts. The only hope for an accused person was to confess, repent, and name other witches. To deny one was a witch was to insure one's doom. In four months twenty-seven people were convicted and twenty executed before the religious and civil authorities brought the panic under control. Anti-witchcraft episodes of this sort were common and sometimes bloodier in "enlightened" Europe in the same era, but that one occurred in New England signaled that the Puritan experiment was falling apart.

The Puritans have bequeathed to later generations much that is near to the heart of American culture. American universities and public schools got their start in the Puritan colonies. American democratic institutions owe a great deal to the New England town meeting and the Massachusetts legislature. The Puritans handed down an ethic of public service and civic responsibility that has helped provide the nation with effective leadership. On the negative side, some observers trace a certain intolerance in the American character to the Puritan legacy.

9.7. Puritans and Indians

The Puritan record of relations with the people who inhabited New England before them is not a pretty one. Their commitment to evangelize the Indians was soon forgotten. As more and more English people came, Native Americans were simply pushed out of their ancestral territory.

Although Puritans were more likely than other colonists to respect the Indians and pay for the lands they took, they took them nevertheless and sometimes fought bloody wars to get them. Both the Pequot War (1636–37) and King Philip's War (1675–78) were fought in part over land issues, as well as general English encroachment on Native American culture and freedom. These wars resulted in great loss of life on both sides and spelled doom for Native American civilization in New England.

John Eliot was one of a few exceptions to the Puritan neglect of missions to the Indians. Educated at Cambridge, Eliot came to Massachusetts in 1631 and soon became pastor of the Roxbury church. In 1644 he began to learn the Algonquian language. In a few years he was preaching in Indian villages and meeting a good response.

Like other Puritans, Eliot was convinced that Indians had to become English culturally before they could become Christians. He organized fourteen "praying villages," whose 11,000 residents were expected to adopt English manners, live in English-style houses, and engage in settled agriculture as they studied the Christian religion. Eliot translated the Bible into Algonquian and trained two dozen native evangelists to reach their own people.

When King Philip's War erupted, most Christian Indians fought on the side of the English, and their help was crucial to a narrow English victory. But by that time anti-Indian feeling ran high among the colonists. Many Christian Indians were imprisoned on a bleak island in Boston harbor without adequate supplies to survive the winter. Others were massacred by indiscriminate, vengeful whites. Massachusetts's Indian mission was in a shambles.

Linguistic training enabled John Eliot (1604–1690) to learn Native American language from a servant captured in the Pequot War of 1637. He not only preached to the Native Americans of Massachusetts but translated the Bible into Algonquian, the first Bible printed in the colonies. (Billy Graham Center)

Conclusion

While it is risky to draw generalizations across so many years and so wide a geographical scope, it is possible to discern themes in encounters between European Christians and the peoples of Asia, Africa, and America between 1500 and 1800.

One is the aggressive nature of nearly all the Europeans. The Spaniards were powerful and forced their religion on the people they met. Spanish power was so overwhelming that a whole continent was converted in short order. Others, such as the Portuguese in East Asia, had less military and economic power and so had to resort to persuasion to win small numbers of converts.

Second, the relationships between Europeans and indigenous peoples bred misunderstandings on all sides. Europeans tended to think of non-European peoples in one of three categories: (1) Some saw the peoples they encountered as noble savages in a childlike state, just waiting to receive peacefully the Word of God. This was the vision of Las Casas and many Puritans. (2) Others viewed them as hopeless heathens, vicious and perversely resistant to the gospel and other supposed blessings of European culture. This vision was common among Spaniards in Latin

9.8. Imperialism and Orthodoxy

For all the expansiveness of the Western European powers, it was the Russian church that expanded over the widest geographic territory in the sixteenth through eighteenth centuries. From the mid-sixteenth to the mid-seventeenth centuries, Russian trappers, followed by traders and soldiers, entered the vast, thinly-populated lands east of the Ural Mountains and brought them into the Russian empire. With them went Orthodox clergy to minister to the needs of resident Russians.

Some also went to convert the native inhabitants. In the decades around 1700 Filifei Leszczynski, Metropolitan of Tobolsk, sent several groups of missionaries across Siberia. Orthodox missionaries had success with some tribes. For example, by 1750 the Kalmyks in western Siberia and the inhabitants of the Kamchatka Peninsula on the Pacific were nearly all Christians.

In the second half of the eighteenth century, Russian adventurers took trade and Christianity across the Bering Strait into Alaska, the Aleutians, and down the Pacific Coast as far as what is now northern California. The southernmost Russian and the northernmost Spanish settlements were only about forty miles apart. But the empire was spread too far, was too thinly populated, and communications were too difficult to hold the whole operation together. There were never enough clergy to take the gospel much beyond the Russian settlements.

In time the Russians pulled back to within the borders of what was to be the USSR in the twentieth century. They left behind substantial pockets of Orthodox believers in such places as the Aleutian Islands.

America and helped justify the destruction of Indian culture and the killing of hundreds of thousands of people. (3) Still others held that these non-European peoples, though possessors of obvious material superiority and cultural richness, were fundamentally mistaken about the nature of the cosmos and needed to be persuaded of the rightness of Christianity. This image was common to Jesuit encounters with the rich civilizations of South and East Asia.

The first two images were silly stereotypes that made effective communication and understanding difficult. The third image, held by Europeans who dealt from a position of weakness rather than strength, was more realistic and resulted in more equal sharing between Europeans and their hosts. As centuries passed and European power increased, however, both this vision and the noble savage ideal faded before the heathen barbarian image, which came to characterize relations between Euro-American Christians and most non-Western peoples in the nineteenth and twentieth centuries (see chap. 13).

The non-Europeans made mistakes, too. The misidentification of Christianity with other, known religions was not new. Just as the Chinese had thought of Nestorian Christians as Buddhists during the Tang Dynasty, so many Japanese made the same mistake during Japan's Christian century. And Jesuit missionaries actually hoped they would be mistaken for Confucians as they tried to win the confidence of the Chinese.

A third theme was the recurrent tendency of European missionaries to fail in their intention to evangelize native populations. Instead, they frequently spent all their time ministering to overseas Europeans. This was substantially true for Puritans in North America, Portuguese in West Africa and Goa, and Spaniards in Latin America after the frontier stage had passed. It was less true, however, in other parts of Asia, such as Japan and the Philippines, and in Latin America in the early years. In those cases Europeans were few and the Christians present were full-blooded in their zeal for bringing the gospel to new peoples.

Suggested readings

General

Latourette, Kenneth Scott. *A History of the Expansion of Christianity.* Vol. 3: *Three Centuries of Advance, 1500 A.D. to 1800 A.D.* repr. ed. Grand Rapids: Zondervan, 1967.

Africa

Falk, Peter. *The Growth of the Church in Africa.* Grand Rapids: Zondervan, 1979.

Sanneh, Lamin. *West African Christianity: The Religious Impact.* Maryknoll, N.Y.: Orbis, 1983.

Asia

Boxer, C. R. *Japan's Christian Century.* Berkeley, Calif.: University of California Press, 1951.

Cary-Elwes, Columba. *China and the Cross: A Survey of Missionary History.* New York: Kennedy, 1957.

Covell, Ralph R. *Confucius, the Buddha, and Christ: A History of the Gospel in Chinese.* Maryknoll, N.Y.: Orbis, 1986.

Drummond, Richard H. *A History of Christianity in Japan.* Grand Rapids: Eerdmans, 1971.

Elison, George. *Deus Destroyed: The Image of Christianity in Early Modern Japan.* Cambridge, Mass.: Harvard University Press, 1988.

Endo, Shusaku. *Silence,* trans. by W. Johnston. New York: Taplinger, 1980.

"Hudson Taylor and Missions to China." *Christian History,* 15.4 (issue 52, 1996).

Mungello, David. E. *The Forgotten Christians of Hangzhou.* Honolulu: University of Hawaii Press, 1994.

Neill, Stephen. *A History of Christianity in India: The Beginnings to 1707.* Cambridge: Cambridge University Press, 1984.

———. *The Story of the Christian Church in India and Pakistan.* Grand Rapids: Eerdmans, 1970.

"The Paradox of David Livingstone." *Christian History*, 16.4 (issue 56, 1997).

Tuggy, Arthur L. *The Philippine Church: Growth in a Changing Society*. Grand Rapids: Eerdmans, 1971.

"William Carey and the Great Missions Century." *Christian History*, 11.4 (issue 36, 1992).

Latin America

Dussel, Enrique D. *A History of the Church in Latin America: Colonialism to Liberation (1492–1979)*, trans. by A. Neely. Grand Rapids: Eerdmans, 1981.

Gibson, Charles. *Spain in America*. New York: Harper and Row, 1966.

North America

Bremer, Francis J. *The Puritan Experiment: New England Society from Bradford to Edwards*. New York: St. Martin's, 1976.

Morgan, Edmund S., ed. *The Puritan Family: Religion and Domestic Relations in 17th-Century New England*, rev. ed. New York: Harper and Row, 1966.

———. *The Puritan Dilemma*. Boston: Little, Brown, 1958.

Ryken, Leland. *Worldly Saints: The Puritans As They Really Were*. Grand Rapids: Zondervan, 1986.

Simpson, Alan. *Puritanism in Old and New England*. Chicago: University of Chicago Press, 1955.

10

European Christianity
after the Reformation, 1600–1900

Luropean Christians fell to squabbling immediately after the Reformation. Puritan and Anglican, Protestant and Catholic—all warred against one another for dominance. Meanwhile, Protestant theologians systematized doctrine. Other Western thinkers experimented with ideas that emphasized the power of human reason to discover truth; they were skeptical of religious claims. Religious warfare and dry rationalism led Europeans to react in two related, though opposing, ways.

Some Christians responded to the "dead orthodoxy" of the theologians by developing a warmly devout brand of Christianity called *pietism*, which responded to the increasing secularity of eighteenth-century Europe by de-emphasizing the public arena and stressing the private, personal, and emotional experience of faith. At the opposite end of the spectrum, progressive Enlightenment thinkers called *philosophes* spurned historically agreed-upon doctrines of orthodox Christianity for a purely rational, scientifically-based religion, called *deism*, that could be shared by all people, of all creeds. Enlightened religion separated faith *from* reason, and subordinated faith *to* reason.

Before the end of the eighteenth century the Enlightenment spawned *romanticism*, which accepted the categories of rationalism but dethroned reason and celebrated the nonrational. Romantic Christians gloried in the emotional character of Christianity. The nineteenth century saw *liberal* Christians questioning traditional assumptions regarding the authority of the Bible and the authenticity of miracles, subjecting Christianity to a more sophisticated rational analysis than the deists. It also saw English Christians becoming respectable *Victorians*: sentimental, proper, and sterile.

232

Wars of religion

For most Europeans the Reformation led to war. Lutherans fought Catholics in Germany; Calvinists fought Catholics in France, the Netherlands, and Scotland; Puritans fought Anglicans in England. In each case religion was but one element in the conflict; social, economic, and political factors loomed large. But differences in faith provided the quickest and easiest means of identifying the combatants.

German Lutheran princes banded together in the Schmalkaldic League and went to war against the Holy Roman Emperor Charles V and the German Catholic princes in 1546. Catholic France helped the Protestants for political reasons. In 1555 the battered and war-weary Germans made peace based on the principle of *cuius regio, eius religio*—"he who rules, his religion"—which recognized the right of Protestants to exist. The formula still preserved some semblance of the idea of a unified Christendom, however, since only entire principalities or cities could become Lutheran or remain Catholic, depending on their ruler's choice.

Ten years later trouble flared up in the Low Countries, the modern kingdoms of the Netherlands, Belgium, and Luxembourg, where Calvinist preachers had begun to gather huge crowds in fields outside of town to hear their sermons. Charles V's son, Philip II of Spain, who also ruled the Low Countries, decided that the region was a hotbed of heresy. He sent Spanish Catholic bureaucrats to turn the region back to orthodox Catholicism. Resenting the foreign interference, Dutch nobles, Catholic and Protestant alike, protested in 1566. The Calvinist preachers interpreted the noble protest as support for the Protestant cause and decided to prove God Protestant, in one of the last manifestations of the medieval practice of trial by ordeal. The Calvinists hired men to knock over the images of saints in the Catholic churches, which the Calvinists viewed as idols. They believed that if God supported the Catholic faith he would protect the sacred images, but if he approved of the Reformation they would break. Within a week 400 churches were tested, and thousands of images smashed. Philip II, appalled by the sacrilege, sent in his troops, and the Dutch revolt began. The Calvinist rebels established a beachhead in the north, and consolidated it, while the Spanish Army maintained control in the south. The war lasted for eighty years, finally ending in 1648 with the permanent partition of the Low Countries into the Calvinist Netherlands and Catholic Belgium.

The French wars of religion, which began in 1559, pitted the *Huguenot*, or French Calvinist nobility of southwestern France, against the Guises, an ultra-Catholic noble faction based in central France. A series of weak teenage kings dominated by their Italian mother, Catherine dè Medici (1519–1589), were caught in the middle.

In 1572 the Huguenots seemed on the point of taking control when Catherine ordered the St. Bartholomew's Day Massacre, in which thousands of Huguenots, primarily in and around Paris, were dragged from their beds at night and murdered. In revenge, armed bands of Huguenots went on the rampage, and atrocities mounted on both sides.

Finally, in 1589, Henry of Guise and the reigning king, Henry III, were each assassinated by a supporter of the other. The throne then came to the Huguenot leader Henry (IV) of Navarre (1553–1610). His Protestant convictions did not run deep and he decided in 1593 that the loyalty of Paris "was well worth a mass," and amiably turned Catholic, which allowed him to consolidate his rule over France. To appease the Huguenots, Henry's *Edict of Nantes* in 1598 allowed Calvinist noblemen the right to hold services as long as they stayed more than twenty miles from Paris. The edict also allowed 100 Huguenot towns in southwestern France to fortify and maintain Protestant garrisons.

Germany, already battered by the religious wars of fifty years earlier, disintegrated between 1618 and 1648 in the Thirty Years' War. Seven "electors" held the right to choose the Holy Roman emperor: the three Protestant princes of Saxony, Brandenburg, and the Palatinate; the three Catholic archbishops of Mainz, Trier, and Cologne; and the king of Bohemia who broke the tie and was therefore almost always chosen to be the Holy Roman emperor. In 1618 the Protestant Bohemians revolted against their newly crowned king, the rabidly Catholic Ferdinand II (1619–1637), after he began rescinding their religious freedoms. They invited the Protestant elector Frederick V of the Palatinate to take the crown, upsetting the religious balance of the electors. Ferdinand's army overwhelmed the Bohemians in 1620 and the Palatinate in 1621, driving Frederick into exile and sending the agents of the Catholic Reformation flowing north to challenge Protestant strongholds.

Though the political issues had been resolved by 1622, the war continued, fueled by roving bands of mercenaries, who switched sides cheerfully and roamed the countryside, living off plunder. In 1630 the Swedish king Gustavus Adolphus (Gustav II, 1594–1632) rescued the Protestants, though neither Sweden nor its ally, Catholic France, accepted the pleas of the German states for peace. The Thirty Years War had become an international conflict, fought on German soil and only marginally connected with religion.

Finally, in 1648, an exhausted Europe came to terms in the Treaty of Westphalia, essentially dissolving the Holy Roman Empire, and confirming the principles of the Peace of Augsburg, though Calvinist rulers could now join Lutherans and Catholics. The Treaty of Westphalia marks the secularization of politics, an era in which Christian principles were

In "The Hanging" French artist Jacques Callot recorded the horror of a group hanging during the Thirty Years War, which was fought on German soil among Spain, France, and Sweden. (Princeton University Art Museum)

not the means for resolving conflicts. The representatives to the peace conferences were all secular, and the pope never signed the document. From that point, Christianity began to lose its relevance as the social cement of European society.

Protestant scholasticism

While Lutheran, Calvinist, and Catholic soldiers fought, Protestant theologians entered a new period of *scholasticism*, organizing and systematizing doctrinal orthodoxy. In the seventeenth-century German theological dynasties, sons followed their fathers in writing multi-volume definitions of what it meant to be an orthodox Lutheran. Their students, for whom the pastorate had became a lucrative and socially prestigious professional career like law or medicine, began to lecture on theological dogma from the pulpits. This did not meet the spiritual needs of parishioners.

Calvinism in England and the Netherlands, already systematized, also developed a more rigidly defined orthodoxy. Calvinism, however, was still a powerful and attractive movement. A leading voice in systematizing Reformed faith was the *Synod of Dordrecht* (or Dort) in the Netherlands in 1618 and 1619. This was an international Reformed synod, convened to answer the *remonstrants*, who were followers of Jacobus Arminius (1560–1609). Arminius had downplayed the work of God in salvation in order to protect the free will of the individual to choose Christ. The remonstrants affirmed that God's election of the saints was based on his foreknowledge of who would choose him and persevere. Christ's redemptive work is only for those who believe. A person called by the Holy Spirit is free to accept or reject the Spirit's leading.

10.1. *Epitome Credentorum*

Nikolaus Hunnius's the *Epitome Credentorum*, or *Summary of What We Believe*, was one of the most widely read religious books of the seventeenth century. The volume opened with these words:

It is said in scripture "that the just shall live by his faith," Habak. 2:4. It is therefore incumbent upon every believer, to acquaint himself with the means by which he might acquire a right perception of God and of the faith and confidence which are due to Him. And for all this he must be able to adduce proper evidence, which might strengthen him to confess the Son of God boldly before the world, and be ready always to "give an answer to every man that asketh him a reason of the faith that is in him" Pet. 3:15 and finally that he might be enabled effectually to resist the enemies of his creed and to defend his own faith.

Part of the motivation in calling the Synod was to unify the Dutch provinces into a monarchy, but theologians also were invited from Germany, Switzerland, and England. The Synod shaped the entire Reformed tradition. A doctrinal statement called the five *Canons of Dort* refuted the Arminian remonstrants, point by point (see box 10.2). The form of their reasoning placed the doctrine of predestination at center stage in Reformed theology, making it even more of a key to understanding salvation than it had been for John Calvin.

10.2. "TULIP"

The traditional Calvinist acronym TULIP has summarized the findings of the Synod of Dort (1620) for generations of Calvinists and students of Calvinism:

Total depravity (or inability) means that human beings, because of the fall, are entirely inclined to sin. Being spiritually dead, there is no "spark of goodness" or ability to please God in them. Therefore, no sinner could or would ever choose to accept Christ.

Unconditional election means that God places no conditions upon salvation. With perfect wisdom before the foundation of the world he chose those who would come to express saving faith in Jesus Christ. God does not merely foresee those who will accept of their own free will; he foreordains that some will believe, for absolutely none would choose God otherwise. The Calvinist denies that this means God is unfair, for all are worthy of hell, and for anyone saving faith is a sheer undeserved gift of grace.

Limited atonement means that the gospel is sufficient to cover the sins of all people universally, and the gospel message is for all the world. But Christ's atoning death is efficient in covering only the sins of the elect. In other words, Christ died only for the sins of those actually saved. If Christ had died to atone for anyone who died without salvation, then God's will has been thwarted, and he is not sovereign.

Irresistible grace means that the Holy Spirit irresistibly works to awaken faith and awareness of sin in the dead sinner, so that none of the elect finally reject God's offer of grace. The evangelism impulse grows then from love of God and a desire to be his servant, rather than an ability to convince others rationally.

Perseverance of the saints means that once a person is saved he or she cannot fall away from the Christian faith. Some may fall away because they never truly possessed saving faith, only an emotional experience. Others who are actually saved may sin grievously, but they will be restored in God's sovereign time.

Among those who accepted the Canons of Dort were the English Puritans. When they came to exercise political power during the years of the Long Parliament, the English Civil War, and the Cromwellian protectorship (1640–1660) they found that their movement, which had begun as a quest for more fervent piety, had deadened into mere theological orthodoxy. Parliament called the Westminster Assembly of Divines in 1643 to establish a national Puritan church to replace episcopacy in the Church of England. The Assembly struggled to keep the emphasis on genuine spirituality and the religious experience stressed in William Perkins' Practical Syllogism (see p. 193).

The first question and answer of the Westminster Shorter Catechism symbolizes the Assembly's commitment to genuine spirituality rather than mere orthodoxy. It says:

What is the chief end of man?

The chief end of man is to glorify God and enjoy him forever.

Yet the Westminster documents (the Confession, the Larger Catechism, and the Shorter Catechism) remained fundamentally doctrinal works that articulated correct belief and defined Christianity in terms of doctrines rather than actions. This was almost unavoidable since one can legislate correct doctrine, but one cannot compel correct experience.

As the seventeenth-century Puritans lost the stress on experience they also began to lose the power to move others, just when a significant element in the outlawed Church of England began to develop a dynamic and evangelical message. These Anglicans preached that God required heartfelt repentance from sin, true faith in Jesus, and sincere obedience to the requirements God set out in the New Testament. Although the Anglicans taught that only God's grace made it possible to meet these conditions for salvation, they emphasized human effort toward the strongly moralistic piety that characterized the Church of England from the restoration of the monarchy and episcopacy in 1660 on into the eighteenth century.

The Enlightenment

Tired of religious warfare and uninspired by scholastic sermons, cultured Europeans looked for something else to trust. They turned to nature and the human mind, particularly scientific thinking. Science had progressed mightily during the seventeenth century. By the end of the century Isaac Newton had formulated the law of gravity, which explained the workings of the entire universe—why an apple fell from a tree as well as how and why planets revolved around the sun. The law of gravity could even predict the existence of the planet Pluto before it was observed.

10.3. Francis Bacon, Galileo, and Isaac Newton

Sir Francis Bacon

Sir Francis Bacon (1561–1626) devised the scientific method in order to increase knowledge, since he believed that in the last days "many shall go to and fro, and knowledge shall increase" (Dan. 12:4). Bacon believed that the circumnavigation of the earth by Magellan and all the other voyages taking place in the sixteenth century fulfilled the first part of the prophecy but that science had to fulfil the second part. When it did, King Jesus would return to reign on earth.

The reason for this, Bacon believed, was that the fall had two consequences: First, Adam and Eve fell from their original innocence, a guilt that Christ removed on the cross. But they also fell from knowledge (for example, they could no longer name the animals). Science and the Christian community were responsible for reversing this second effect of the fall in order to enable Christ to return.

Galileo Galilei

Galileo Galilei (1564–1642) was a Christian astronomer who got into trouble with certain church leaders and theologians because his observations through a telescope conflicted with theories derived from their own understanding of the Bible about the way heavenly bodies ought to move. Some of these people accused Galileo of heresy. He responded to their challenges in his *Letter to the Grand Duchess Christina*, which reads in part:

I think that it is very pious to say and prudent to affirm that the holy Bible can never speak untruth—whenever its true meaning is understood. But I believe nobody will deny that it is often very abstruse, and may say things which are quite different from what its bare words signify. . . . Hence I think that I may reasonably conclude that whenever the Bible has occasion to speak of any physical conclusion (especially those which are very abstruse and hard to understand) the rule has been observed of avoiding confusion in the minds of the common people. . . . This being granted I think that in discussions of physical problems we ought to begin not from the authority of scriptural passages, but from sense-experiences and necessary demonstrations; for the holy Bible and the phenomena of nature proceed alike from the divine Word, the former as the dictate of the Holy Ghost and the latter as the observant executrix of God's commands. *

Isaac Newton

Isaac Newton (1642–1727) revolutionized the way in which Europeans looked at the world. In the late seventeenth century two major worldviews struggled for dominance:

Materialists argued that the universe is composed of matter and space. For them God, if He existed, had to be material. The vast majority of Christians rejected this view out of hand.

Vitalists argued that the world is a living organism; many of them viewed God as its soul. Believ-

239

ing the universe to be alive, vitalist scientists explored the secrets of the universe through such methods as astrology, alchemy, magic, and numerology. Virtually all respectable Christian scientists were vitalists.

Newton rejected both options, and he formulated the law of gravity with the idea that the universe is mechanical—partly material and partly spiritual. He conceived of both gravity and God as spiritual.

*Stillman Drake, *Discoveries and Opinions of Galileo* (Garden City, N.Y.: Doubleday, 1957).

Newton had discovered the law of gravity simply by using his human reason, and in doing so he had also discovered something genuinely new—something that Plato and Aristotle and the other ancient philosophers had not known. Newton's example led European progressive thinkers, the *philosophes*, to believe that human reason could discover and explain all facts and occurrences. After Newton, intellectuals became increasingly confident that they could duplicate Newton's achievements, not merely for physical nature, but also for society, politics, and even religion. Along with this confidence in reason as a means of solving problems, European intellectuals began to use rationality as the exclusive test for ideas. Any idea that could not be demonstrated using the scientific method was simply rejected. Their faith in reason led them to reject all other kinds of faith.

At the same time, the Enlightenment *philosophes* turned away from the traditional intellectual authorities: the Greek and Roman philosophers and the Bible. As they did so, European society as a whole began to reorient itself. Traditionally, people had imagined themselves backing into the unknown future, while facing a familiar and comforting past. During the Enlightenment, Europeans turned around to face the future, peering ahead blindly but confidently. They were certain that they could solve the future's problems by themselves. From this initial shift in intellectual attitude stems the cultural preference among Western people, especially Americans, for what is "new and improved," rather than "old-fashioned and out of date." This attitude tends to assume that today's people are in some way smarter than those in the past, so previous thinkers can be dismissed as irrelevant.

The *philosophes* turned their back on traditional Christianity, arguing that it was an unscientific and irrational religion. Though most *philosophes* agreed that religion itself was important and that God existed, they recast traditional religion to be more reasonable in their eyes. This search for a rational religion grew out of a number of concerns. First, of course, there was the desire to subject religion to scientific analysis, to find some sort of law that would explain religion the way the law of gravity explained the physical world. Second, the Enlightenment *philosophes*

A native of Pisa, Galileo Galilei (1564–1642) lectured in mathematics at the universities of Pisa and Padua and became philosopher and mathematician to Cosimo, duke of Tuscany, at Florence. His astronomical views were condemned in 1616, and he was sentenced to life imprisonment in 1633, but he remained under house arrest until his death. (Billy Graham Center)

were horrified by the wars of religion and were convinced that there must be some form of religion that did not cause such bloodshed and carnage. Third, they wanted to include the religious experience of non-Christians as well as Christians in their scientific religion, since Europe had just become aware of other cultures and religions in a big way.

When explorers, traders, and missionaries fanned out over the world, they returned with tales of exotic cultures that knew nothing of Christianity but were still orderly, moral, and well-constructed. When published, these travel tales instantly became best-sellers; people all over Europe became fascinated by China, India, America, Africa, and Turkey. The men and women who spent their afternoons and evenings in cultured Paris homes chatting about intellectual things and drinking tea (a fashionable, exotic beverage recently brought to Europe by the explorers—and all the rage at parties) began to think that they should be able to share a religion common to the Chinese.

The accounts of Chinese life and culture dealt a heavy blow to traditional European preconceptions. Europeans had long thought that Christian teachings were essential to ensure morality and decent civil behavior. The example of China contradicted these notions: Chinese were cultured, civilized, and moral, without any evidence of Christianity whatsoever.

The *philosophes* devised a new religion—not culled from a book but based on natural, rational principles deduced from human experience—and called it deism.

Deism claimed to represent a synthesis of the essential elements of all the world's great religions, subjected to rigorous rational and scientific scrutiny. In deism Christianity was shorn of nonessential and irrational ideas like Christ's resurrection from the dead, the virgin birth, and all of the biblical accounts of miracles. What was left, the essential religious core of Christianity according to the *philosophes*, were the moral teachings and example of a very good man.

This core of teachings, a morality Christianity shared with the other great religions of the world, was distilled out to develop a rationally-based, scientific morality. This natural morality, which could be used to measure all moral systems, was based on the concept of natural law. The *philosophes* believed that human behavior was governed by laws inherent in the universe, similar to those that held for the physical world. They believed that they could demonstrate that Christian moral principles tended to follow these natural laws and were therefore acceptable.

Enlightenment *philosophes* also tried to recast the traditional definition of the human person. Rather than describing human beings as created in the image of God and distorted by the fall, they preferred to think of the human being as an autonomous, rational self. That definition subordinated emotions, will, and faith to reason, and defined people in isolation from a community and from reference to God. This view has guided much of elite culture in the West since the Enlightenment.

The great enemies of the cultured and literate Enlightenment rationalists were superstition and the church, both of which kept people "ignorant, afraid, and cruel."[1] The *philosophes* believed that science and education could

10.4. The Theist

What is a true theist? It is he who says to God: "I adore and serve You"; it is he who says to the Turk, to the Chinese, the Indian, and the Russian: "I love you." He doubts perhaps, that Mahomet made a journey to the moon and put half of it in his pocket; he does not wish that after his death his wife should burn herself from devotion; he is sometimes tempted not to believe the story of the eleven thousand virgins, and that of St. Amable, whose hat and gloves were carried by a ray of the sun from Auvergne as far as Rome. But for all that he is a just man. Noah would have placed him in his ark, Numa Pompilius in his councils; he would have ascended the car of Zoroaster; he would have talked philosophy with the Platos, the Aristippuses, the Ciceros, the Atticuses—but would he not have drunk hemlock with Socrates?

—Voltaire

Herbert H. Rowen, ed., *From Absolutism to Revolution, 1648–1848* (New York: Macmillan, 1963).

eradicate the baleful influences of the church and superstition and pave the way to a gloriously new society composed of rational and enlightened individuals.

Pietism

Equally tired of religious warfare and just as uninspired by scholastic sermons as the rationalists, those in a movement known as *pietism* expressed its rejection of dead orthodoxy and Christian in-fighting by preaching a Christianity that was personal, emotional, and practical. The pietists saw themselves as completing the Reformation of the sixteenth century by reforming not merely doctrine, but life.

Pietist Christianity was rooted in a warm, emotional relationship with God—especially with Jesus. A pietist would begin a conversation with a stranger by asking "Do you love Jesus?" while a Calvinist or Lutheran might ask the more objective question "Are you a Christian?" or "Have you been saved?" "Do you love Jesus?" stated in present tense, is personal, stresses the relationship, and, above all, is subjective.

Another characteristic of pietism was a focus on small groups of Christians who agreed to be accountable to one another for their spiritual growth and development. These groups prayed together, studied the Bible together, and discipled one another. Such small groups powerfully cultivate spiritual maturity and spiritual discipline and remain one of the most exciting elements of the heritage of pietism.

10.5. Cherbury's Five Points

Lord Herbert of Cherbury suggested five points common to all major religions that he found to be compatible with reason:

1. The existence of a Supreme Being;
2. The need for worship;
3. The need for good conduct;
4. The need to repent of vices; and
5. The existence of rewards and punishments after death.

10.6. Benjamin Franklin

Benjamin Franklin, the American deist, wrote in a letter, possibly to Thomas Paine:

Weak and ignorant Men and Women . . . have need of the Motives of Religion to restrain them from Vice, to support their Virtue, and retainment the Practice of it till it becomes habitual.

Franklin advised Paine "not to attempt unchaining the Tyger by writing too well against Christianity."

An important aspect of the small groups was practical encouragement to a pure life. Pietists encouraged one another to live sober, godly, and pure lives, and did so in very immediate and practical ways. Practical religion included specified times of personal prayer and devotions; restraint in personal life, especially with regard to excessive eating and drinking; and works of personal charity, such as giving food or alms to the poor and unfortunate and visiting the sick or imprisoned.

This assumes a lay orientation, and pietism particularly encouraged Bible reading by the laity. Pietists did not emphasize theological training; they thought that everyone capable of reading the Bible could understand its message. For them the plain reading of the obvious sense of Scripture was an important antidote to the dry, dead orthodoxy they heard from their pulpits week after week. Lay reading of Scripture also led to a de-emphasis on doctrine and orthodox belief, to the extent that many pietists refused to apply any doctrinal tests whatsoever. It was enough that a person testified to loving Jesus and showed a transformed personal morality and lifestyle. Most pietists elected to remain in traditional churches, their pietism supplementing rather than replacing traditional religious practices.

Finally, pietism stressed the personal, even private, character of Christianity. Pietism and Enlightenment religion complemented one another in privatizing Christianity: the *philosophes* attempted to push Christianity out of public life, since it led to fighting and religious warfare, while pietists withdrew voluntarily because public life was less important. Since the end of the eighteenth century, Christianity in Europe has remained essentially personal and private.

Orthodox clergy often opposed pietist groups, fearing that they might fall into heresy without trained theological guidance. In many countries it became illegal to study the Bible without a licensed clergyman present, so pietists either went underground or emigrated to more tolerant areas.

10.7. Jacob Spener

Jacob Spener was, in many ways the father of pietism, and, in fact, the movement was named after his book *Pia Desideria*, in which he writes:

If only we Evangelicals would make it our serious business to offer God the fruits of his truth in fervent love, conduct ourselves in a manner worthy of our calling, and show this in recognizable and unalloyed love of our neighbours, including those who are heretics, by practicing our duties. There is no doubt that God would then allow us to grow more and more in our knowledge of the truth and also give us the pleasure of seeing others, whose error we now lament, alongside us in the same faith. . . . Holiness of life itself contributes much to conversion.

Herrnhut

Although pietists' Christianity was essentially personal, the stress on group support occasionally led them to the formation of intentional Christian communities. One of the earliest of these communities grew up on the estate of Nikolaus Ludwig, Count von Zinzendorf (1700–1760), a German nobleman. At the age of ten Zinzendorf, with a group of friends, had founded the "Order of the Grain of Mustard Seed," pledging to love the whole human family and spread the gospel. By 1722 Zinzendorf had given his life to the service of Christ and had welcomed a group of Moravian refugees to his estate.

By early in 1727 the community of about 300 people was deeply divided and bickering. The count and a number of concerned community members began to pray, and on May 12 the Holy Spirit descended on Herrnhut; the dissension ended as the community began to glow with new life. On August 27, 1727, twenty-four men and twenty-four women began a "prayer watch" of constant intercession. Each of them agreed to spend one specific hour of each day in prayer. This Herrnhut prayer vigil lasted for over 100 years and led, among other things, to a powerful concern for world missions, which continued to characterize both the Herrnhut community and the Moravian Brethren, as the group came to be known.

The community consisted of 200 family houses, a single brethren

Nikolaus Ludwig, Count von Zinzendorf (1700–1760), was an Austrian nobleman, trained in law, who served as a legal advisor to the king of Germany. His Moravian community at Herrnhut became so successful that he once was charged with enticing Moravian citizens to leave their homeland. Zinzendorf wrote two thousand hymns and produced a Bible translation for children. (Billy Graham Center)

house, a single sisters house, and a children's boarding house that was especially for the care of children whose parents were off in the mission field. The children's house also educated all the Herrnhut children. An elected council of twelve worked with the count to regulate every aspect of Herrnhut life. No one could marry or start a trade without first consulting the elders.

The community believed that its primary duty was to provide Christian nurture for its members. In order to do so the Moravian Brethren at Herrnhut established a system of small groups, called *choirs*. Choirs were grouped according to age, sex, and marital status. They met daily for mutual encouragement, sharing, confession, prayer, and discipline. Choir leaders met with Zinzendorf frequently, allowing him to keep track of the spiritual growth of each individual at Herrnhut.

Moravian spirituality was focused on the choirs, but was also guided by two important practices begun at Herrnhut. Zinzendorf started choosing a Scripture "watchword" for each day to serve as the devotional focus for the entire community. Zinzendorf, a gifted poet and composer, also com-

10.8. Zinzendorf's Hymns

"Jesus, Still Lead On"*

Jesus still lead on
Till our rest be won
And although the way be
    cheerless,
We will follow calm and fearless
Guide us by thy hand,
To our Fatherland
If the way be drear
If the foe be near
Let not faithless fears o'ertake us
Let not faith and hope forsake us
For through many a foe
To our home we go
When we seek relief
From a long-felt grief
When temptations come alluring
Make us patient and enduring
Show us that bright shore
Where we weep no more
Jesus still lead on
Till our rest be won
Heavenly leader still direct us,
Still support, console, protect us,
Till we safely stand
In our fatherland!

"The Saviour's Blood and Righteousness"**

Jesus, thy blood and
    righteousness
My beauty are, my glorious dress
Midst flaming worlds, in these
    arrayed,
With joy shall I lift up my head
Bold shall I stand in that great
    day,
For who aught to my charge shall
    lay?
Fully through thee absolved I am
From sin and fear, from guilt and
    shame
Lord, I believe thy precious blood,
Which at the mercy-seat of God
Forever doth for sinners plead,
For me, e'en for my soul, was
    shed
When from the dust of death I
    rise
To claim my mansion in the skies,
E'en then shall this be all my plea
Jesus hath lived, hath died for me

*Translation by John Borthwick
**Translation by John Wesley

posed hymns to accompany the daily watchword. Their hymn singing distinguished Moravian spirituality from that of most other churches of the time. The Moravians sang constantly, though, interestingly enough, rarely used hymnbooks, since Zinzendorf believed that a hymn had to be sung from memory in order to express an individual's Christian experience.

By its example, by its prayer, and especially through the missionaries it sent out, the Herrnhut community has had enormous world-wide influence. It particularly influenced the Wesleyan tradition through its contact with John Wesley (1703–1791).

Methodism

Wesley was already an English missionary when he met a group of Moravian Brethren missionaries in October of 1735. Both were on the way to America to evangelize the Indians. Wesley was struck by their calm faith as he despaired in the middle of a severe storm at sea. Wesley's mission failed, and he returned to England. There he made contact with another Moravian, Peter Bohler, who advised him to "preach faith until he should get it." He did and found his "heart strangely warmed." Later Wesley founded the Methodists, an English pietist movement.

> In the evening I went very unwillingly to a society in Aldersgate Street, where one was reading Luther's preface to the Epistle to the Romans. About a quarter before nine, while he was describing the change which God works in the heart through faith in Christ, I felt my heart strangely warmed. I felt I did trust in Christ, Christ alone, for my salvation; and an assurance was given me that He had taken away my sins, even mine, and saved me from the law of sin and death.[2]

The English church in the early part of the eighteenth century preached a rigorous holiness and morality but usually lacked an understanding of the spiritual power needed to meet its standards. Pious English became increasingly frustrated as they desperately tried to develop the holiness demanded by their theology. Many of them sought help through joining societies. One such society, called the Holy Club, had both John Wesley and his brother Charles as members. The members of the club spent an hour each morning and another each evening in private prayer, in addition to prayers at 9 A.M., noon, and 3 P.M. They competed with one another in self-examination, watching for signs of grace, and pushing themselves to religious fervor. Results were noted in coded diaries. They spent an hour each day in meditation, fasted twice a week, and received the Eucharist every Sunday. Before meeting anyone they thought through what they were going to say, so that their words might not be without purpose.

The Wesleys could not sustain the demands of the Holy Club until John's heart was warmed, and the pietist emphasis on a warm, personal relationship with Jesus gave the Wesleys the power to be holy. John Wesley believed that his conversion to pietism was a conversion to genuine Christianity, and he felt that he was called to go out and preach. His vibrantly evangelical preaching made staid English worshipers uncomfortable, and they barred him from Anglican pulpits. This left Wesley in a dilemma. He had the call to preach, but no place to exercise his call. So he went outside the church, to the fields and marketplaces, where he found a huge urban audience of unchurched miners and factory workers. Eighteenth-century England was in the middle of the Industrial Revolution. Men and women who had been driven off the land by the earlier Agricultural Revolution swarmed into the cities to compete for jobs. Those who were fortunate enough to find work toiled from sunup until sundown, falling exhausted and filthy into their beds as soon as they got home to snatch a few hours of sleep before they had to get up for the next day's work. On Sundays, the only day they had off, they were too dirty and too poor to be comfortable in an Anglican church. Wesley's outdoor preaching reached and converted these people. Revival swept England, churning out itinerant Methodist circuit preachers who had neither the time nor the inclination for proper Church of England seminary training but who did have a burning zeal for Christ and the unsaved.

But preaching was far less significant to Methodism than the follow-up organization. Initially a movement within the Church of England, Methodists worshiped in their local parish church but met in small classes with twelve to fifteen other Christians. The class encouraged spiritual growth and discipline, and met for structured Bible study. The class leader, a mature Christian, kept in close touch with each member. These were the keys to the success of Methodism.

Some mature Christians wanted a more intimate group than the relatively informal class and formed bands of six to eight people that met more frequently than classes and practiced encouragement and mu-tual confession of sins. Class membership was a prerequisite for the bands, and bands consisted largely of class leaders.

The third level of Methodist organization was the select society, which was part of Wesley's thinking but did not take root in Methodism. The select society was intended to allow Methodists

10.9. Wesley's Diary

John Wesley kept a daily diary of his spiritual walk. The entry for Tuesday, June 28, 1774, reads:

This being my birth-day, the first day of my seventy-second year, I was considering, How is this, that I find just the same strength as I did thirty years ago? That my sight is considerably better now, and my nerves firmer than they were then? That I have none of the infirmities of old age, and have lost several I had in my youth? The grand cause is, the good pleasure of God, who doth whatsoever pleases him. The chief means are, 1. my constantly rising at four, for about fifty years; 2. my generally preaching at five in the morning, one of the most healthy exercises in the world; 3. my never travelling less, by sea or land, than four thousand five hundred miles a year.

John Wesley (1703–1791), founder of the Methodist movement, was the fifteenth child of Samuel and Susannah Wesley. After his Aldersgate Street awakening he found churches closed to him and turned to field preaching. Thereafter he averaged eight thousand miles a year on horseback. The first Methodist lay ministers were organized in 1742. (Billy Graham Center)

to form an intentional community, sharing a common purse on the model of Herrnhut. Only a few select societies were formed in the early years of Methodism, and none survived. No Herrnhut developed in English pietism.

These Methodist organizations existed primarily to nurture Christian maturity toward Christian perfection. "Faith working by love" was Wesley's definition of Christian life, and he retained the stress on holiness and morality he inherited from Anglicanism, as well as its emphasis on cooperating with God in working out salvation. He added a driving concern for the poor people, who formed the bulk of his audience. Methodists, prodded by Wesley's preaching and the encouragement of class leaders, became thrifty, clean, sober, and upright folk. Wesley made no attempts to challenge the structures of society, but he did change the lives of individual people. Taken together, these individual changes, altered eighteenth-century English society and eventually brought the reforms in both personal behavior and politics that characterized the Victorian age.

10.10. Charles Wesley's Hymns

Charles Wesley (1707–1788) was one of the great hymn writers of Christian history. Here are the opening stanzas of some of his best-loved hymns:

O for a thousand tongues to sing
My great redeemer's praise
The glories of my God and king
The triumphs of his grace

Rejoice the Lord is King!
Your Lord and King adore;
Rejoice, give thanks and sing'
And triumph evermore
Lift up your heart, lift up your voice
Rejoice again I say, rejoice

Come thou long-expected Jesus
Born to set thy people free

From our fears and sins release us,
Let us find our rest in thee
Israel's strength and consolation,
Hope of all the earth thou art
Dear desire of every nation
Joy of every longing heart

Christ whose glory fills the skies
Christ the true the only light
Sun of righteousness arise
Triumph o'er the shades of night
Dayspring from on high be near
Daystar in my heart appear

Jesus, Lover of my soul
Let me to thy bosom fly
While the nearer water flow,
While the tempest still is high
Hide me O my savior hide,
Till the storm of life is past
Safe into thy haven guide
O receive my soul at last

Roman Catholicism

Although some Catholics accepted Enlightenment ideology, the church as a whole resisted it. The most important issues facing the church in the eighteenth century arose in France. The first of these was *Gallicanism*, an old issue that intensified during and after the religious wars of the seventeenth century. The Gallican idea asserted that the church should be subject to the nation rather than to the foreign pope, even while it remained orthodox in other respects. In an era of absolute monarchs, advisers to the French king wished to revive the practice that allowed kings to choose major church officials.

Jansenism, the second French controversy, arose in opposition to the teachings of the Jesuits and the Council of Trent on human free will. The Jansenists sided with St. Augustine's doctrine of predestination and resembled Protestant pietists in many ways. Blaise Pascal (1623–1662), the developer of the mathematical theories of probability, wrote one of the most influential Christian devotional works, *Pensées* (Thoughts), while living in a Jansenist commune. Politically powerful Jansenists combined with Gallicans to oppose the Jesuits in France, but in 1713 the pope declared Jansenists heretical, and most went into exile in Holland. There they comfortably became part of the Reformed tradition.

Many groups besides the Jansenists opposed the Jesuits. Political leaders in France, Spain, and Portugal believed the Jesuits had attained too much power and political influence, especially in those countries' colonial empires. In addition, the willingness of Jesuit missionaries to adopt local customs and costumes and to adapt local traditions for Christian purposes rendered them theologically suspect. When Jesuits allowed Chinese converts to continue rites honoring their dead ancestors (see p. 215–16, cf. p. 76), for example, their opponents argued that this was yielding to pagan religion. In 1764 the Jesuits were expelled from France and its territories overseas. In 1773 the pope dissolved the order entirely, responding to general fears among Catholics of Jesuit power. Although the Jesuits were restored in 1815, the fear they aroused was a symptom of another trend of the Enlightenment—anticlericalism.

The peak of resentment against clergy arose in response to the French Revolution. Starting in 1789, the revolution quickly became venomously intolerant of church officials, especially Roman Catholics. Revolutionaries perceived the church to be a hotbed of superstition, while they themselves advocated reason. Furthermore, they believed that the clergy were in firm alliance with the aristocracy, since most of the bishops and leaders were drawn from the ranks of the nobility. The revolutionaries promulgated the *Civil Constitutions of the Clergy*, which placed the church under the National Assembly, and confiscated church lands, thus establishing a secular, republican form of Gallicanism. This move split the church in France since most clergy refused to sign it, and it weakened popular support for the French Revolution.

The eventual heir of the Revolution, the Emperor Napoléon Bonaparte (1769–1821), mended relations with the church in the *Concordat of 1801*. Napoléon recognized Catholicism as the religion of France and permitted its free exercise. In return, the church allowed its confiscated lands to remain in lay hands and agreed that its clergy be appointed and paid by the state. Clergy would swear loyalty to the state before being invested with the symbols of their spiritual office by a bishop or the pope.

Romantic Christianity

Towards the end of the eighteenth century, various people, reacting against the sterile intellectual rationalism of the Enlightenment, began to stress the importance of feelings and emotions, as well as reason. At the same time, they were reacting against the increasingly mechanical rationalism of the Industrial Revolution. These *romantics* looked back longingly at the medieval past, which was not as caught up with rationalism and industry, a past which was exotic and exciting. Sir Walter Scott began to write the *Ivanhoe* novels, which exalted the romantic medieval knights. Lord Byron wrote poems extolling the passions and the exotic excesses of life. This general stress on feelings and emotions, as well as the return to the past, was reflected also in Christianity.

Responses to romanticism

The Oxford Movement

In the Church of England one of the powerful responses to romanticism was the Oxford Movement, begun in the 1830s. The Oxford Movement, which included such distinguished men as John Henry Newman (1801–1890), stressed the catholicity and traditional character of the church. These "Anglo-Catholics" looked back longingly to the medieval church, which had been undivided and traditional. The central emphasis of the Anglo-Catholics lay on grace, channeled through the sacraments. In their attempts to witness to the poor and the illiterate, they turned to the beauty of holiness, expressed in ritual and the Catholic tradition. They reasoned that it had been forged by Christians responding to the needs of illiterate medieval Christians. Anglo-Catholics promoted religious communities that were patterned after medieval monasteries and nunneries. They attended spiritual retreats and pilgrimages, participated in disciplined prayer and devotional book reading, and elevated the sacraments of Eucharist and confession.

Although the Oxford Movement became a vital part of the Church of England, their attempts to minister to the poor and the barely literate met with less success. Anglo-Catholicism appealed primarily to intellectuals and highly educated Christians who were looking for greater emphasis on feelings, emotions, worship, and adoration, rather than on doctrine. An elite movement, it did not replace Methodism as the religion of the poor.

German theology

In Germany theologians led by Friedrich Schleiermacher (1768–1834) responded to romanticism in quite a different way. Heavily influenced by German philosophical ideas, Schleiermacher took the separation of faith from reason and the privatization of religion several steps further than either the pietists or the deists. Schleiermacher defined religion primarily as a nonrational feeling. To be a Christian meant that the believer had experienced something that could not be scientifically analyzed.

Though many students assume that Schleiermacher's emphasis on religious feelings was like pietism's stress on religious experience, the two were quite different. Pietists believed that religious experience was the fruit of the Holy Spirit working in the life of the Christian, while Schleiermacher thought every human being experienced God and that "God-feeling" was at the basic core of human nature. Christians had the God-feeling more strongly than most, but in other respects they were no different than non-Christians. In this respect Schleiermacher was heavily influenced by the ideas of the Enlightenment. His was a religion that could be shared by everyone in the world. Schleiermacher's stress on the nonrational experience of God as the core of humanity was romantic, as was his insistence that this stress did not conflict with, but merely supplemented, the claims of reason.

Schleiermacher also contributed a method of doing theology to nineteenth- and twentieth-century Christianity. Rather than focusing on God, Schleiermacher insisted that theology should be done from the bottom up to study the God-feeling in human beings. Schleiermacher then went on to subject the Bible and the Christian tradition to scientific analysis, since that posed no threat to authentic Christianity. This theological tactic allowed liberal Christians to participate in both worlds. They could claim to be rational and scientific in their theology, while at the same time claiming to experience Christianity with traditional Christians.

Liberal Christianity

Schleiermacher's theology was in part a response to higher biblical criticism, an attempt to interpret the Bible "scientifically" by looking behind the words of the text to uncover the events as they really happened. Higher critics believed this was the only authentic way to interpret the Bible. As a result, they discerned four authors for the first five books of the Bible, which earlier Christians believed had been written by Moses. They also questioned the historical reliability of the Gospel of John and doubted that the apostle had written it. But more important than any specific doubts cast by the higher critics was the general questioning of the authority of the Bible. Furthermore, the critics left the impression that they were molding the Bible to fit their own scientifically-oriented notions of what it should have said.

One of the most important aspects of higher criticism was the "quest for the historical Jesus." Higher critics assumed that the real Jesus was different than the Jesus portrayed in the Gospels, asserting that early church theologians had embellished the accounts of those who had known Jesus. Higher critics tried to sift out the later additions and get at the real Jesus. The *questers*, as they were called, wrote scores of such lives of Christ through the nineteenth century, each portraying a different "real Jesus." They agreed only that Jesus was a simple carpenter's son and moral teacher who performed no miracles, never claimed to be God, and did not say that he had come to save the world or set up a kingdom.

Schleiermacher's stress on Christianity as the God-feeling allowed those who could no longer accept traditional beliefs to recast their faith in ways acceptable to modern intellectuals. Liberal Christians welcomed the freedom from an authoritative text that higher criticism gave them, and they drew two conclusions. First, with the higher critics they attempted to mod-

---

10.11. Lyman Abbott

I acknowledge myself, then, a radical evolutionist—it is hardly necessary to say a theistic evolutionist. I reverently and heartily accept the axiom of theology that a personal God is the foundation of all life: but I also believe that God has but one way of doing things; that His way may be described in one word as the way of growth, or development, or evolution, terms which are substantially synonymous; that he resides in the world of nature and in the world of men; that there are no laws of nature which are not the laws of God's own being; that there are no forces of nature, that there is only one divine, infinite force, always proceeding from, always subject to the will of God: that there are not occasional or exceptional theophanies, but that all nature and all life is one great theophany; that there are not occasional interventions in the order of life which bear witness to the presence of God, but that life itself is a perpetual witness to His presence: that He transcends all phenomena, and yet is the creative, controlling, directing force in all phenomena.

Lyman Abbott, *The Theology of an Evolutionist* (New York: Houghton Mifflin, 1897).

ernize Christianity, recasting ideas that were presented to the ancient mind in the Bible for modern scientific and rationalistic readers. Second, they refused to accept religious beliefs solely on the basis of authority, but insisted that any idea or belief had to meet the test of their own reason and experience.

Liberal Christians preferred to experience God in the day-to-day miracles of the creation. For them the law of God for the creation, or natural law, was God's primary revelation, though they did not deny that God was also beyond the world. This of course meant that liberals, far from being threatened by Charles Darwin's new theory of evolution, rejoiced as they found God at work in the evolutionary process.

The liberals, who found God in the birth of every child, were embarrassed by the thought of the virgin birth of Christ, since that diminished the special character of every other birth, and they were equally embarrassed by the exclusive claims that Christianity had traditionally made. Following Schleiermacher, they believed that all people are religious to a greater or lesser degree, and each person's God-feeling is as valuable as any other's.

Although they studied theology, most liberals firmly subordinated theology to Christian action. They believed that the authentic sayings of Jesus taught ethical behavior and a concern for social justice. They threw their energies into charity work and raising funds for good causes.

Although the ideas of the romantic and liberal Christians initially affected only a small coterie of theologians and philosophers,

10.12. Albert Schweitzer

Albert Schweitzer (1875–1965) was a musician, theologian, and humanitarian. After achieving international reputation as a Bach organist, he felt a call to become a physician so that he could address the problem of human suffering. In 1913 he left Europe for Gabon in Africa with his wife, also a physician. They spent the next fifty years in a hospital there.

Between surgical sessions Schweitzer spent his time writing theology and philosophy. Schweitzer summarized his philosophy in the phrase "reverence for life," which instilled in him a great reluctance to kill bees, beetles, or even disease-carrying mosquitoes. In his theology, Schweitzer attacked the "quest for the historical Jesus," showing that the German scholars had merely found a Jesus made in their own liberal image. Rather, the biblical Jesus was, for Schweitzer, an apocalyptic zealot who thought that God would start his kingdom any day, and when God failed to do so, tried to force God into it by his own sufferings.

There was no way that anybody in the twentieth century could relate to this sort of figure. Schweitzer himself, however, still wrote in almost mystical terms about "following Jesus" and clearly tried to fit his "reverence for life" and commitment to alleviating human suffering into a Christian framework.

in the long run their ideas trickled down to the middle level of church-goers, who vaguely understood that the objective basis of Christian faith was in some way being undermined. Since, however, the most fervent of these also believed in the pietist emphasis on the inner life, they did not object to these ideas until it was too late, and the assumptions of the liberals dominated Christian intellectual work into the mid-twentieth century.

The cult of respectability

"Victorian Christianity," a third way in which romanticism influenced Christianity, began twenty years before Victoria (1819–1901) ascended to the British throne in 1837, but continued throughout the nineteenth century. An influential group of evangelical Anglicans known as the *Clapham Sect*, led by William Wilberforce (1759–1833) and writer Hannah More (1745–1833), worked to extend the pietist revolution in morals begun by the Methodist movement to the middle and upper classes as well as the poor. The Clapham Sect founded the Church Missionary Society, the British and Foreign Bible Society for work overseas, and the Religious Tract Society to work in England. Door-to-door salesmen sold thousands of copies of cheap tracts written by More, and 7500 copies of Wilberforce's tract to the aristocrats were sold in six months. Few books have had a greater impact on a society. Wilberforce and his associates successfully got Parliament to abolish slavery and the slave trade in the British empire after 1807, and secured funds to pay the Royal Navy to enforce the ban. Wilberforce preached a revival of manners and saw examples of it in society: cock-fighting and bull and bear baiting died out, book shops selling obscene books had to close down, and English people became polite and respectable.

This respectability, however, often masked hypocrisy, and a self-seeking concern for morality at the expense of spirituality. Victorian evangelicals focused on such relatively trivial issues as Sunday observance—protesting the Sunday opening of parks, museums, and zoological gardens, and the running of trains on Sunday.

Indicative of the attitudes of the day is an advertisement for a coachman in *The Record*, an evangelical magazine: "High wages not given. A person who values Christian privileges will be preferred." "Christian privileges" probably meant permission to go to church and attend family prayers.

The evangelicals also attempted to gain control of the Anglican clergy by buying up the right to appoint priests. They endowed parishes with trusts, placing them on the boards of trustees, with the right to nominate priests when the parish posts were vacant. Through that and other means, one in twenty Anglican clergy was evangelical by 1820, and one in eight by 1830. Higher offices followed suit, and by the 1850s the episcopal bench was dominated by Victorian evangelicals. Their success led them to become essentially optimistic: they believed that they could convert the world and bring about the kingdom of God on earth through their mission societies before Christ returned.

The sentimental character of Victorian Christianity was firmly rooted in romanticism, which had cultivated sentiment as a virtue, particularly

10.13. The Plymouth Brethren

Always referring to themselves as simply *Christian brethren*, the Plymouth Brethren met for weekly communion and tried to model, as closely as they could, the New Testament Church. In their meetings preaching was on the spur of the moment: "It was the vessel, not the message that was prepared." Yet the Brethren were steeped in Bible study and developed theologically sophisticated exegetical techniques. Foremost among the Brethren Bible teachers was J. Nelson Darby, a prolific writer and teacher who developed the system of biblical interpretation known as *dispensationalism* (later popularized in the *Scofield Reference Bible*).

The central elements in the dispensation method of reading the Bible included, first, the principle that the Bible must be interpreted as literally as possible. This view can be summarized in the slogan, "When the plain sense makes good sense don't look for another sense." For example, all references to Israel are to the literal political nation of Israel, and never to the new Israel or to the church. Linked to that view is the understanding that God's revelation is progressive: He reveals more of himself and his law with each succeeding revelation.

These revelations, *economies*, or *dispensations* are usually seven in number:

1. "Innocence," the period before the fall.

2. "Conscience" or "moral responsibility," the period from the fall to the flood.

3. "Human government," the period from the flood to Abraham.

4. "Promise," the period from Abraham to the revelation of the law at Mount Sinai.

5. "Law," the period of the Mosaic law and the sacrificial system, which governed God's relationship with his people Israel until the atonement.

6. "Grace," the age of the church. At Pentecost God began the economy that will last until Christ's victory over the Antichrist in the battle of Armageddon.

7. "The millennium," the age in which the prophecies regarding Israel will be fulfilled and end with the last judgment and the new heavens and new earth.

among women. Victorian sentimentality looked mainly at the ordinary episodes of Christ's life. The Victorians enjoyed paintings depicting Jesus at work in his father's shop, with a suitably sentimental and pious glow about him, while Mary gazed on him sweetly. Another favorite was the image of "gentle Jesus, meek and mild," which grew out of the romantic emphasis on the medieval ideal of the knight who was strong in battle, but gentle in society. The Victorian sentimentalists recognized that Jesus was the great champion in battle against Satan. But they stressed the gentleness of Christ's life on earth, which soon deteriorated into a sentimental stress on the most trivial aspects of his earthly life.

Conclusion

By the end of the nineteenth century the Reformation had effectively been tamed, and religion, now the private purview of feelings and sentiment, no longer identified the antagonists in war. But pacifying Christianity also limited and diminished it as the nineteenth century became increasingly secular in tone.

Suggested readings

Altick, Richard D. *Victorian People and Ideas*. New York: Norton, 1973.

Gay, Peter. *The Enlightenment: An Interpretation*, 2 vols. New York: Knopf, 1966–69.

Hall, Marie Boas, ed. *Nature and Nature's Laws*. New York: Walker, 1969.

Harnack, Adolf. *What is Christianity?* 1901; repr. ed. New York: Harper and Row, 1957.

Hempton, David. *The Religion of the People: Methodism and Popular Religion, c. 1750–1900*. London: Routledge, 1996.

Houghton, Walter E. *The Victorian Frame of Mind*. New Haven, Conn.: Yale University Press, 1957.

"John Knox and the Scottish Reformation." *Christian History*, 14.2 (issue 46, 1995).

"John Wesley." *Christian History*, 2.1 (1983).

Niebuhr, Richard R. *Schleiermacher on Christ and Religion: A New Introduction*. New York: Scribners, 1964.

Parker, Geoffrey. *Europe in Crisis, 1598–1648*. Ithaca, N.Y.: Cornell University Press, 1980.

"Pietism." *Christian History*, 5.2 (1986).

Snyder, Howard. *The Radical Wesley*. Downers Grove, Ill.: InterVarsity, 1980.

Welch, Claude. *Protestant Thought in the Nineteenth Century*, 2 vols. New Haven, Conn.: Yale University Press, 1985.

"William Wilberforce and the Abolition of the Slave Trade." *Christian History*, 16.1 (issue 53, 1997).

Zimdars-Swartz, Sandra L. *Encountering Mary: From La Salette to Medjugorje*. Princeton, N.J.: Princeton University Press, 1991.

"Zinzendorf and the Moravians." *Christian History*, 1.1 (1982).

11

Early America

Religion in eighteenth-century America was characterized by heterogeneity. The story of the founding of New England by the Puritans has often been told, but many other groups were established in the colonies. The Anglican church, against whom the Puritans dissented, was represented when Jamestown was established in 1607. Anglicanism spread throughout the thirteen colonies, but was most prevalent in New York, Virginia, and other southern colonies. Indeed, the Anglican church became the officially established church in most of the southern colonies.

The Pennsylvania colony was founded by William Penn (1644–1718) as a haven for English Quakers who desired to escape the persecution they faced from the Church of England. Quakers, or *Friends* as they preferred to be called, were followers of George Fox (1624–1691) and inhabited Puritanism's radical fringe. A zealous, highly self-disciplined group, they believed that God spoke directly to believers through the inner light of Christ. Those who sought to share this view with the more hierarchically inclined Massachusetts Bay Puritans found themselves ejected from that colony, imprisoned, even executed for their presumption. Persecuted in England and America, many Quakers turned to Penn, an aristocrat and Fox disciple, for protection. Penn convinced the British king to cede him land in the North American interior. He and his followers set up Pennsylvania—"Penn's Woods"—with a constitution that explicitly welcomed any who believed in one God.

Philadelphia was the center of Quaker power as well as the commercial and intellectual capital of the middle colonies. Pietistic groups from Germany were attracted to the tolerant atmosphere of Pennsylvania.

Mennonites and Moravians were the most numerous early arrivals. The pietists were excellent farmers and gave Pennsylvania a reputation as the breadbasket of colonial America. The Moravians, who established the towns of Bethlehem and Nazareth, also brought their rich musical tradition to both Pennsylvania and Winston-Salem (in what became North Carolina). While the frontier was still being established, they were composing and performing marvelous instrumental and choral works in the classical tradition. *Dunkers*, a name given because of their mode of baptism, also came from Germany, as did the only Protestant monastic order in the colonies, the *Ephrata Cloister*.

Scotch-Irish Presbyterians also migrated to Pennsylvania, but for different reasons. They bypassed the eastern counties and centers of toleration, preferring the frontier where they were free from interference from landlords or tax collectors. They became legendary in frontier history because of their woodsman skills. They employed the famous flintlock rifles, made by German craftsmen in Pennsylvania, with equal ferocity against animals and the Native Americans. As they penetrated south down the Shenandoah Valley and eventually further west, the guns they used became known as Kentucky rifles. Maryland was organized for the protection of Catholics from the Church of England by George Calvert, Baron Baltimore (1580?–1632), although Roman Catholics were a minority even there. Lutherans were attracted to the colonies, and at first settled most prominently in Pennsylvania.

Dutch Reformed, Methodists (particularly from England), and other smaller groups made up the remaining colonial religious population. The Baptists in North America had their origin in Rhode Island, a colony led by Roger Williams after he was expelled from Massachusetts Bay Colony for denying the authority of the civil magistrates over religious matters.

The two great events of the eighteenth century were the Great Awakening and the revolt by the colonists against England. Both events turned loose forces that had far-reaching impact, and both events demonstrate the influence of religion on the direction of history. Indeed, both events also demonstrate that revolution followed emancipation from a particular mindset. The Great Awakening may be seen as a revolt against Calvinism as it had come to be practiced by New England Puritans and the American Revolution as a revolt against the restrictions of Parliament.

The Great Awakening

The Great Awakening, an intense movement characterized by religious activity throughout the colonies, had an anti-Enlightenment aspect. The Enlightenment emphasized the primacy of human reason and gave prominence to natural law. From Copernicus to Locke, the

George Whitefield (1714–1770) was a member of the Oxford University "Holy Club" with John and Charles Wesley and followed the Wesleys to Georgia, where he established an orphanage. His power, however, was as an open-air evangelist. His ambitious crusades in the colonies and throughout England, Scotland, and Wales eventually broke his health and contributed to his early death. (Billy Graham Center)

ability of human beings to use reason to resolve dilemmas was emphasized. The Great Awakening opposed the outward religiosity and rationalism that had infected American Calvinism, as well as the liberal attitudes of the Enlightenment. It called for a return to simplicity of faith and trust in God.

One source of the Great Awakening was the pietistic sects from Germany. The Moravians, for example, sponsored and supported by Nikolaus Ludwig, Count von Zinzendorf, settled in colonial Pennsylvania. Their contribution was an emphasis on lay participation in worship services, simplicity of worship, the necessity for heartfelt conversion, and an emphasis on Psalm singing in their gatherings. The Mennonites had a similar style and impact.

Another source was the rise of Methodism in England. John Wesley had been strongly influenced by Moravians while a missionary to North America and carried their call for warmhearted conversions to the urban masses of England. His disciple George Whitefield entranced the masses on both sides of the Atlantic.

Theodore Frelinghuysen (1691–1747), pastor of a Dutch Reformed Church in the Raritan Valley of New Jersey, began preaching to crowds of interested people, as did Presbyterian William Tennent (1673–1746) in Pennsylvania. Tennent, a University of Edinburgh graduate, not only preached to his congregation but established a training school for lay evangelists known as the *Log College*. The Log College was intended to help promising revivalist preachers bypass lengthy training.

George Whitefield (1714–1770) was the great preacher of the evangelical revival in England and in America. Initially under the leadership of Charles Wesley, Whitefield undertook several preaching missions to the colonies between 1739 and 1770. Whitefield started in Georgia and preached his way north.

On one of these missions, he traveled 800 miles on horseback, delivering 130 sermons. Benjamin Franklin once estimated that 30,000 people were gathered to hear one of his sermons, a huge crowd in the era before microphones.

Whitefield's voice and energy matched that of his friend Wesley, though Wesley was the better organizer. Whitefield preached in so many places to so many people that hearing a Whitefield sermon was probably the single experience shared by more people of his era than any other experience. His sermons were tremendously effective, causing people to weep and moan and turn to the Lord.

Franklin, himself a skeptic, described the impact he felt from Whitefield's preaching. At a Georgia rally to raise money for an orphanage, Franklin disapproved the choice of site and resolved not to contribute. Soon, however, Whitefield's words began to take effect:

I had in my pocket, a handful of copper money, three or four silver dollars, and five pistoles in gold. As he proceeded I began to soften, and concluded to give the copper. Another stroke of his oratory determined me to give the silver; and he finished so admirably that I emptied my pocket wholly into the collector's dish, gold and all.

Although Whitefield and the Wesleys remained friends throughout their lives, Whitefield's Calvinism and the Wesleys' belief in free will led to a split between the Calvinist and free-will Methodists.

If George Whitefield was the revivalist of the Great Awakening, Jonathan Edwards was the theologian. Edwards was the son of a Calvinist minister, a graduate of Yale, and minister of the Congregational Church at Northampton, Massachusetts, all by the age of twenty-three. Edwards, who was learned in languages and literature, possessed a brilliant mind. He Americanized Calvinism by emphasizing that it was not just that persons were sinful, but that they were weak in the midst of such a cruel environment as the frontier. His most famous sermon, "Sinners in the Hands of an Angry God," has been the subject of thousands of lectures and stories; his impact on his congregation and others was powerful. An unimpressive public speaker, Edwards read his sermons in a high-pitched monotone from a prepared text. When revival broke out, with some people falling to the floor, moaning and weeping in repentance, Edwards concluded that it had to be the work of the Holy Spirit, for his listless preaching could hardly move sinners to such emotion. His account of the revival, *A Faithful Narrative of the Surprising Works of God . . .*, was read by Wesley in England and probably played a part in Wesley's decision to send Whitefield to America. Although criticized for his determined defense of Calvinist theology against colonial Arminian and Unitarian movements, and although he was not really appreciated by his contemporaries in New England, Edwards stands today as the towering philosopher and theologian of the Great Awakening.

The Great Awakening brought a side-effect of discord and rancor to the lives of American Christians. A few revivalist preachers, particularly William Tennent's son, Gilbert Tennent, and a mentally disturbed preacher named James Davenport, cast aspersions on the salvation of local ministers and made disparaging remarks concerning those who read their sermons from a prepared text rather than depending on divine inspiration. Even Whitefield denounced "dead men" (who opposed his work) preaching to dead congregations. Factionalism within the churches inevitably resulted. Nearly every denomination suffered a division between New Lights (awakeners) and Old Lights, with both sides claiming to hold a corner on truth. Other disagreements were involved in these factions, but Awakening revivalism was the precipitating irritant.

11.1. "Sinners in the Hands of an Angry God"

Thus it is that natural men are held in the hand of God, over the pit of hell; they have deserved the fiery pit, and are already sentenced to it; and God is dreadfully provoked; his anger is as great towards them as to those that are actually suffering the executions of the fierceness of his wrath in hell, and they have done nothing in the least to appease or abate that anger, neither is God in the least bound by any promise to hold them up one moment; the devil is waiting for them, hell is gaping for them, the flames gather and flash about them, and would fain lay hold on them, and swallow them up; the fire pent up in their own hearts is struggling to break out: and they have no interest in any Mediator, there are no means within reach that can be any security to them. In short, they have no refuge, nothing to take hold of; all that preserves them every moment is the mere arbitrary will, and uncovenanted, unobliged forbearance of an incensed God. . . .

O sinner! Consider the fearful danger you are in: it is a great furnace of wrath, a wide and bottomless pit, full of the fire of wrath, that you are held over in the hand of that God, whose wrath is provoked and incensed as much against you, as against many of the damned in hell. You hang by a slender thread, with the flames of divine wrath flashing about it, and ready every moment to singe it, and burn it asunder; and you have no interest in any Mediator, and nothing to lay hold of to save yourself, nothing to keep off the flames of wrath, nothing of your own, nothing that you ever have done, nothing that you can do, to induce God to spare you one moment. . . .

God seems now to be hastily gathering in his elect in all parts of the land; and probably the greater part of adult persons that ever shall be saved, will be brought in now in a little time, and that it will be as it was on the great out-pouring of the Spirit upon the Jews in the apostles' days. . . .

Therefore, let every one that is out of Christ, now awake and fly from the wrath to come. The wrath of Almighty God is now undoubtedly hanging over a great part of this congregation: Let every one fly out of Sodom: "Haste and escape for your lives, look not behind you, escape to the mountain, lest you be consumed."

—Jonathan Edwards

Clarence H. Faust and Thomas H. Johnson, eds., *Jonathan Edwards: Representative Selections* (New York: Hill and Wang, 1962),161,165,172.

On the other hand, it was a creative time as well. Both the Baptists and Methodists established a foothold as substantial denominations and began to spread their ideas, particularly on the frontier. There was an increased interest in missionary work among Native Americans, an activity that had previously elicited little interest. Charitable institutions were started as well. Some scholars have credited the Great Awakening with bringing a steadying moral influence to the frontier. By far the greatest achievement of the Great Awakening was educational, in the founding of colleges to train a ministry: the Log College (which became

Jonathan Edwards (1703–1758) was the first American-born theologian of note. Educated at Yale College he became his grandfather's (Solomon Stoddard) assistant at Northampton, Massachusetts, in 1726 and assumed the pastorate when Stoddard died in 1729. Dismissed in a controversy in 1750, he became missionary to the Housatonnocs near Stockbridge, Massachusetts. Appointed president of the College of New Jersey in 1758, he died of smallpox a month later. (Billy Graham Center)

11.2. Not All Awakeners

While the Great Awakening invigorated the faith of thousands, thousands of others did not share their enthusiasm. Charles Chauncy (1705–1787) viewed the revival with a jaundiced eye in 1743 and concluded it went little beyond emotional excess:

The true Account to be given of the many and great Mistakes of the present Day, about the SPIRIT's Influence, is not the Newness of the Thing, the not having felt it before; but a notorious Error generally prevailing, as to the Way and Manner of judging in this Matter. People, in order to know, whether the Influences they are under, are from the Spirit, don't carefully examine them by the Word of GOD, and view the Change they produce in the moral State of their Minds and their Lives, but hastily conclude such and such internal Motions to be divine Impressions, meerly from the Perception they have of them. They are ready, at once, if this is unusual, or strong, to take it from some Influence from above, to speak of it as such, and to act accordingly. This is the Error of the present Day; and 'tis indeed the proton Pseudos, the first and grand Delusion. . . . How often, at other Times, and in other Places, has the Conceit been propagated among People, as if the Prophecies touching the Kindgom of Christ, in the latter Days, were now to receive their Accomplishment? And what has been the Effect, but their running wild?

Mark A. Noll, et al., eds., *Eerdmans' Handbook to Christianity in America* (Grand Rapids: Eerdmans, 1983), 122–230.

Princeton) founded by Presbyterians in 1746; Brown by Baptists in 1760; Queens (later Rutgers) by Dutch Reformed in 1764; Kings (later Columbia) in 1766; and Dartmouth by Congregationalists in 1769.

Revolution and nation-building

As the impact of the Great Awakening diminished, the political tensions between England and the colonists heightened between 1763 and 1775. Most U.S. history textbooks carry the story of the Stamp Act, Writs of Assistance, Continental Congress, the Boston Tea Party, and an incident between a British patrol and a Boston mob that was described by Samuel Adams as the "Boston Massacre."

The clergy of that era, particularly the Congregationalists and Presbyterians, began to preach sermons that cast Parliament and King George III in the role of tyrants and oppressors. These preachers increasingly associated virtue with the colonists and their cause and established a rationale for ignoring the biblical injunction to obey those in authority. Liberty was at stake in the minds of the revolutionary leaders, and they were glad to have the support of those Christians who identified the cause of freedom with separation from England. The danger of identifying virtue with the cause of revolution, of course, was that the seeds of civil religion were being planted. Just as the Puritans had perceived their commonwealth as a city on a hill for all to see, so the Christians of this era identified their revolutionary cause with divine providence. Robert Smith, a Presbyterian minister, put it simply in a 1781 sermon: "The cause of America is the cause of Christ."[1]

The theme of a "Christian America" arose from this notion and remains alive and well today. Those today who think in terms of a Christian America and identify virtue with, for example, U.S. foreign policy, draw their ideas from revolutionary era origins. Hence, the civil religious song, "God Bless America," assumes that providence is guiding the leaders and destiny of the United States of America.

Most members of the Anglican Church retained their loyalty to the British king—the head of the Church of England—and suffered because of their identification as Tories. Moravians, Mennonites, and members of other pietistic groups refused to take sides and bear arms in the conflict. Jesse Lee, a North Carolina Methodist, was torn between his patriotism and a growing conviction that a Christian ought not kill: "I weighed the matter over and over again, but my mind was settled; as a Christian and as a preacher of the gospel, I could not fight. I could not reconcile it to myself to bear arms, or to kill one of my fellow creatures; however, I determined to go, and to trust in the Lord."[2] Lee ended up in a noncombatant's role, driving a baggage wagon for the American army.

Once the lines were drawn, both by the early clashes between British soldiers and the colonists and by the adoption of the Declaration of Independence in 1776, a new set of problems faced the Christians of that era. Indeed, the new question concerned not only home rule, but who would rule at home. This phase of the revolution within took place simultaneously with the struggles between the soldiers of George Washington and the British. The social impact was most evident in the constitutions written by former colonies who now assumed an identity as new states. Some state constitutions abolished slavery, some began the process of breaking up large estates owned by Tories, and all of them addressed the issue of an established church.

The procedure known as *disestablishment* took place slowly from Maine to Georgia. The most heated debate took place in such states as Massachusetts and Virginia where

11.3. Loyalist and Patriot

Isaac Wilkens, Anglican layman (New York) on leaving America in 1775:

It has been my constant maxim through life to do my duty conscientiously and to trust the issue of my actions to the Almighty . . . I leave America and every endearing connection because I will not raise my hand against my Sovereign, nor will I draw my sword against my Country.

Abraham Keteltas, Presbyterian minister (Newburyport, Massachusetts) in a 1777 sermon:

[This war is] the cause of truth, against error and falsehood, . . . the cause of pure and undefiled religion, against bigotry, superstition, and human inventions. . . . In short, it is the cause of heaven against hell—of the kind Parent of the universe against the prince of darkness and the destroyer of the human race.

Mark A. Noll, et al., eds., *Eerdmans' Handbook to Christianity in America* (Grand Rapids: Eerdmans, 1983), 138, 140.

the established church was well entrenched. Religiously plural Rhode Island, on the other hand, accomplished the process with little discussion at all. The stakes in this process were very large for the predominant Protestant church groups. In Massachusetts, for example, the expenses for church maintenance, as well as the salary of the minister, were covered by funds derived from a state-supported levy. Disestablished churches would have to find a way to solicit such funds from voluntary contributions. An even more serious issue was that of church attendance. What would be the consequences if everyone opted not to attend church services now that they were voluntary? It is no wonder that some sermons foresaw death, abomination, and desolation for the new American nation. Other Christians took heart in the prospects, however, predicting that true religion would flourish as never before now that it would spring from proper inner motivation, rather than state compulsion.

If the American Revolution presented a mixed set of problems for Christians of that era, events from abroad presented even more. The

French Revolution, starting in 1789, was blamed for unleashing infidel ideas, and the Enlightenment was bringing in fresh challenges. Some clergy, at least, saw deism as the greatest single competitor to the Christian faith. As much as the denominations might disagree with each other over doctrine, the discussion took place within common Christian boundaries. Deists, on the other hand, were outside the faith—indeed "infidels"—since they defended a natural religion and an impersonal God who started the universe and left it to run by itself. They were criticized constantly in sermons and tracts. Thomas Paine's *Age of Reason* was regarded as dangerous heresy, and deist statements about errors in the Scriptures were constantly being refuted. The frequently tolerant attitudes of the

---

11.4. Rational Religion

The ideas of the Enlightenment came to American religion in the form of deism. This belief, subscribed to by most of the founders of the American republic, took God off the center stage he had occupied in the minds of Puritans and Awakeners and focused on human abilities instead. Insofar as God is the subject of the deists' attention, God is not personal and involved in the affairs of humans but is an abstract principle behind the operation of the universe. Sometimes the words of the deists were strident, as with Thomas Paine (1737–1809), firebrand of both American and French revolutions, quoted here in *The Age of Reason*:

The most detestable wickedness, the most horrid cruelties, and the greatest miseries, that have afflicted the human race, have had their origin in this thing called revelation, or revealed religion. It has been the most dishonourable belief against the character of the divinity, the most destructive to morality and the peace and happiness of man, that ever was propagated since man began to exist. It is better, far better, that we admit-

ted, if it were possible, a thousand devils to roam at large, and to preach publicly the doctrine of devils, if there were any such, than that we permitted one such impostor and monster as Moses, Joshua, Samuel, and the Bible prophets, to come with the pretended word of God in his mouth, and have credit among us. . . .

It is incumbent on every man who reverences the character of the Creator, and who wishes to lessen the catalogue of artificial miseries, and remove the cause that has sown persecutions thick among mankind, to expel all ideas of a revealed religion as a dangerous heresy, and an impious fraud. What is it that we have learned from this pretended thing called revealed religion? Nothing that is useful to man, and everything that is dishonourable to his Maker. What is it the Bible teaches us?—rapine, cruelty, and murder. What is it the Testament teaches us?—to believe that the Almighty committed debauchery with a woman engaged to be married; and the belief of this debauchery is called faith.

More frequently, however, the deists adopted a more congenial tone, albeit with much the same substance. John Adams (1735–1826), the second American president, wrote:

> God has infinite Wisdom, goodness, and power. He created the Universe. His duration is eternal, a parte Ante, and a parte post. His presence is as extensive as Space. What is Space? an infinite, spherical Vaccuum. He created this Speck of Dirt and the human Species for his glory: and with the deliberate design of making, nine tenths of our Species miserable forever, for his glory. This is the doctrine of Christian Theologians in general: ten to one.

> Now, my Friend, can Prophecies, or miracles convince You, or Me, that infinite Benevolence, Wisdom and Power, created and preserves, for a time, innumerable millions to make them miserable, forever; for his own Glory? . . . The Love of God and his Creation; delight, Joy, Tryumph, Exultation in my own existence, 'tho but an Atom, a Molecule Organique, in the Universe; are my religion.*

*Edwin S. Gaustad, ed., A Documentary History of Religion in America, Vol. 1, To the Civil War (Grand Rapids: Eerdmans, 1982), 294–96.

deists stood in sharp contrast to the sometimes dogmatic beliefs of the dominant Protestant groups. These attitudes, along with the rationalism and atheism set loose by the French Revolution, added to the burdens on the new voluntary religion that arose from the Revolutionary era.

The deist challenge was supplemented by the ideas of such leaders as Thomas Jefferson. He regarded religious leaders and many religious ideas as dangerous to freedom of thought. Indeed, he made the assertion that the goal of much of organized religion was to restrict free inquiry and to try and inhibit those groups who did not subscribe to orthodox ideas. Jefferson rejected the Scriptures for the most part and issued a book known as Jefferson's Bible, which contained all of the sayings of Jesus but omitted any references to miracles or the supernatural.[3]

The long-term impact of all this was the appearance of the Unitarians and Universalists. In brief, Unitarians rejected the idea of the Trinity as contrary to reason if there is just one God, with neither Son nor Holy Spirit. They stressed toleration in doctrinal matters. Universalists rejected what they viewed as the harsh doctrines of Calvinism and the idea of eternal punishment in hell. They taught that Christ's death atoned for the sins of the whole world and that eventually all would be saved.

If the Revolution posed dilemmas for Christians to ponder, so did the Constitution. In the first place, the founders had to deal with those factions that wanted to reestablish state-supported religion in some form. The First Amendment proscription against the establishment of a national religion dealt with that issue. Baptists, Methodists, and other minority denominations were particularly in favor of the First Amendment dictum that Congress could make no law interfering with the free exercise of religion. Both freedoms have been important in American history. The first part allowed for what Thomas Jefferson described as a "wall of separation" between churches and the state. As a result, Congress has never in American history attempted to establish a national religion. The Supreme Court decisions regarding that part of the Constitution have dealt with a wide variety of issues, such as prayer in public schools or attempts to get federal funds to support private religious education. The second dictum has protected groups from being punished for not saluting the flag, serving in the military, or performing in some fashion in violation of their religious conscience.

It appears that the Christians of that period did not regard the framers of the Constitution as being particularly religious people. But the mystique of the founders has grown with the years until some Christians have regarded many of the participants as evangelical Christians (certainly far from the case) or see the document itself as having been

11.5. Contagion of Liberty

The libertarian impulses of the revolutionary era extended, in the minds and actions of a few people at least, to the situation of African-American slaves. American rebels protested the "slavery" they suffered at the hands of British King George III; it can hardly have escaped their notice that they kept other human beings in a bondage far more real than their own metaphorical servitude.

Jacob Green (1722–1790), a New Jersey Presbyterian, put the issues well in 1776:

What a dreadful absurdity! What a shocking consideration, that people who are so strenuously contending for liberty, should at the same time encourage and promote slavery! . . . However we may be free from British oppression, I venture to say, we shall have inward convulsions, contentions, oppressions, and various calamities, so that our liberty will be uncomfort-

able, till we wash our hands from the guilt of negro slavery.*

The revolutionary decades did see a limited movement in the direction of liberty for slaves. All the northern states of the new republic gradually put an end to the slave institution within their borders. Manumissions jumped in the South as some masters found their consciences could no longer harbor the hypocrisy of holding slaves while fighting a war in the name of liberty. The international slave trade temporarily came to a halt.

But the North could afford to end slavery because there were few slaves in the North and slavery was not very important to the Northern economy. By contrast, Southern slave holders, such as Patrick Henry and Thomas Jefferson, though bothered about slavery on moral grounds, still found it inconvenient to free the people they held in bondage.

Mark A. Noll, et al., eds., *Eerdmans' Handbook to Christianity in America* (Grand Rapids: Eerdmans, 1983), 146.

divinely inspired. Compared to the rather optimistic Declaration of Independence, the U.S. Constitution has a more "Christian" view of humanity in that it reflects deep pessimism about human nature (like original sin) and calls for a series of checks and balances to keep natural human depravity from running amok. The discussion will continue, but there is little evidence of an explicit Christian influence in the document or in the lives of most of the people who deliberated in Philadelphia.

11.6. Religious Liberty

Freedom of religion had several roots in early British America, most notably in the multiple religious colonies of Pennsylvania and Rhode Island. In the era of the War for Independence, the principle of freedom of choice in religion was embraced across the land and became enshrined in the founding documents of the republic. It was championed by deists like Thomas Jefferson in the Virginia Bill for Establishing Religious Freedom in 1779:

Well aware that the opinions and belief of men depend not on their own will, but follow involuntarily the evidence proposed to their minds; that Almighty God hath created the mind free, and manifested his supreme will that free it shall remain by making it altogether insusceptible of restraint. . . . That to compel a man to furnish contributions of money for the propagation of opinions which he disbelieves and abhors, is sinful and tyrannical. . . .

We the General Assembly of Virginia do enact that no man shall be compelled to frequent or support any religious worship, place, or ministry whatsoever, nor shall be enforced, restrained, molested, or burthened in his body or goods, nor shall otherwise suffer, on account of his religious opinions or belief; that all men shall be free to profess, and by argument to maintain, their opinions in matters of religion, and that the same shall in no wise diminish, enlarge, or affect their civil capacities.*

From the more deeply worshipful point of view of pietism, Isaac Backus came to the same conclusion in 1779:

As God is the only worthy object of all religious worship, and nothing can be true religion but a voluntary obedience unto his revealed will, of which each rational soul has an equal right to judge for itself, every person has an unalienable right to act in all religious affairs according to the full persuasion of his own mind, where others are not injured thereby. And civil rulers are so far from having any right to empower any person or persons, to judge for others in such affairs, and to enforce their judgments with the sword, that their power ought to be exerted to protect all persons and societies, within their jurisdiction from being injured or interrupted in the free enjoyment of this right.**

The result of these trends was the First Amendment to the U.S. Constitution, which reads in part: "Congress shall make no law respecting an establishment of religion, or prohibiting the free exercise thereof."

*Edwin S. Gaustad, ed., A Documentary History of Religion in America, Vol. 1, To the Civil War (Grand Rapids: Eerdmans, 1982), 259–60.

**Ibid., 268.

By the 1850s, when this camp meeting was held in Queen Anne's County, Maryland, the preaching conventions were becoming more formalized affairs. In the earliest years on the frontier, however, they were not so well controlled. (Billy Graham Center)

The Second Great Awakening

What the Great Awakening did for the American Revolution and the writing of the Constitution, the Second Great Awakening did for the age of Jackson and the American Civil War. Emancipating forces were set loose by both movements that had far-reaching effects. John Adams said that revolution in the minds and hearts of individuals (in the Great Awakening) anticipated the actual, political revolution with England. In the same manner, a great, Protestant benevolent empire set the stage for the reforms of the Jacksonian era.

There is no one beginning point to the Second Great Awakening; waves of spiritual fervor rose and fell from the 1740s through the 1840s. The frontier camp meetings, especially at Cane Ridge in Bourbon County, Kentucky, were a colorful and much-remembered episode in the early 1800s. There was abundant emotion, frenzied excitement, and outlandish behavior by certain individuals. Reportedly, some in the throes of religious emotion barked like dogs. There were also solemn meetings, rejoicing by new converts, and a tangible increase in church membership. Camp meetings were common to several denominations; more often they were nondenominational in their early years, but eventually they were dominated by the Methodists, who set up regular campgrounds as summer conference centers and held annual revival meetings.

11.7. Report from Kentucky

At the sacramental solemnities of a Presbyterian church on the circuit of the Reverend James M'Gready, two brothers named John and William McGee, one a Methodist and the other a Presbyterian minister, were in attendance. The two brothers preached, and such a stirring experience followed that when the time came for the next meeting the ministers appointed to preach were unable to do so. There were cries and sobs all over the house and excitement indescribable. The inhabitants round about, on hearing of the stirring times, flocked in in such numbers that the church house was unable to accommodate the crowd. The people were so anxious about their salvation that these woodsmen soon cleared out the underbrush, felled the pine trees for pews, improvised a platform of poles, and erected an altar in the forest. After enjoying the spiritual refreshing, the people did not want to go home, and while some went foraging for provisions, others began the erection of temporary abodes made of poles and boughs. Such bedding as had been brought was used to improvise tents. Near-by farms were visited to secure straw for beds. This gave the meeting a new impulse; others flocked in bringing camp equipage. People came fifty to one hundred miles in carriages and wagons and on horseback. The meet-

ing lasted several days in spite of the fact that it was harvest time. . . .

The "falling exercise" appeared at the McGee meeting. . . . In this experience the individual felt the constriction of the large blood vessels, a shortness of breath, an acceleration of breathing, and dropped prostrate. The hands and feet were cold. He lay from one to twenty-four hours. Upon returning to normal he was sometimes in a state of despair and felt he was such a sinner he could never be saved. More often he rejoiced that his sins were forgiven and immediately began to exhort others to give their lives to Christ. Timid people without apparent talent often showed great ability in praying and exhorting at that time. Scoffers and unbelievers as well as those seeking salvation were "struck down." Whole families at home, individuals in bed asleep, on the road, or plowing in the field, were stricken. Children at school where there were no religious exercises were seized. John McGee in speaking of it said: "The people fall before the word like corn before a storm of wind; and many rose from the dust with Divine glory shining in their countenances. . . ."

The next most common phenome-non was known as "the jerks." . . . Like the falling exercise, it frequently fell upon people at meetings, but those far from the meetings were stricken. Elder Jacob Young said he had often seen ladies take it at the breakfast table as they were pouring tea or coffee. They would throw the whole up toward the ceiling, sometimes breaking both cup and saucer. As they left the table their heads would be so violently jerked that their braided hair, hanging down their backs, would crack like a whip. Witnesses say that some were taken up in the air, whirled over on their heads, coiled up so as to spin about like a cartwheel. They endeavored to grasp trees or saplings, but were carried headlong and helplessly on. J. B. Finley said that as many as five hundred of these subjects might be seen in one congregation in west Tennessee, bending the whole body first backward and then forward, the head nearly touching the ground forward and back alternately.

Everett Dick, *The Dixie Frontier*, quoted in John H. Cary and Julius Weinberg, eds., *The Social Fabric: American Life from 1607 to 1877*, 4th ed. (Boston: Little, Brown, 1984), 135–36.

Such individuals as Timothy Dwight (1752–1817) also played a part in the phenomenon. As president of Yale College, Dwight launched a bold attack to stir up the students at Yale and to demonstrate that there was an alternative to freethinking, deism, and other heresies. That he was successful can be measured by the fact that some of his students became leaders in the Second Awakening. Nathaniel W. Taylor (1786–1858) provided the theological base for New School Presbyterianism, one of the leading forces in the movement. Lyman Beecher, father of Henry Ward Beecher and Harriet Beecher Stowe, was the great organizer of the movement in New England. The new revivalism promoted by Taylor, Beecher, and others differed markedly from that of the first Great Awakening. The earlier preachers regarded the outpouring of God's spirit as a by-product of faithful preaching. Results in the lives and commitments of hearers were in God's hands. By the latter years of the Second Great Awakening most leaders were focusing on a revival "technique." These revivalists employed *new measures* evangelism to bring their hearers to the point of an immediate decision.

The towering figure of the new measures was the revivalist Charles Grandison Finney (1792–1875). Born in Connecticut, he moved to upper New York state and was determined to pursue a career in law in the early 1820s. But his conversion in 1821 pointed the way to what was to be an eventful and dramatic career. After making up his mind to become a Christian he went to an isolated spot in the woods, prayed aloud, and experienced a "mighty baptism" that overwhelmed him. This scene caused him to be impatient in later years with anyone who had difficulty defining their own conversion experience. Finney pursued theological studies under George W. Gale, the pastor of the Presbyterian Church at Adams, New York, but he rejected many of the doctrines Gale taught him. In 1824 he had dramatic success in a series of missionary meetings, and by 1825 he was ready to inaugurate a new era in American revivalism and to continue in the revival business for the rest of his life.

Finney began operating in a geographic section of New York state. This area had become known as the "burned-over district" because it was subject to so many emotion-laden movements. The area also promoted religious "ultraism."[4] The religious eccentricity of the era spawned such diverse movements as Shakerism, Mormonism, Spiritualism, Millennialism, perfectionism, sexual communism, abolitionism, and a dietary fad known as Grahamism. The energy connected with each of the ultraisms was tremendous. Energized by the religious enthusiasm of the burned-over district, these movements spilled over into the Jacksonian era and had a marked influence.

Finney insisted that a revival could be brought about by the right use of the proper means. This was heresy to many orthodox Protestants who looked back to the Calvinist precedents of the Great Awakening. Finney's new measures also scandalized many. These measures included:

the practice of praying for people in public by name;

women praying in public meetings;

extreme familiarity with the Deity in public prayer;

protracted meetings;

the use of an "anxious seat" for heightening the emotions of inquirers;

inquiry meetings; and

the admission of new converts to church membership immediately after conversion.

11.8. Charles Grandison Finney

Early in the nineteenth century, many New Englanders migrated along the "psychic highway" to the "burned-over district" of upstate New York. There, from the 1810s through the 1850s, wave after wave of fiery revival swept over the villages and farms, engulfing thousands in ecstatic new commitment to Jesus Christ. The most renowned and effective of the revival preachers was Charles Grandison Finney (1792–1875). Finney combined blunt preaching with sophisticated psychology and organization techniques to draw hundreds of thousands of listeners and thou-sands of converts over four de-cades of ministry in the United States and Europe. Like other preachers of the Second Great Awakening, Finney preached a perfectionist doctrine heavily influenced by Methodism. He ignored his own Calvinist roots and embraced the Arminian idea that a person had free will to choose God; thus, all people were free to come to Christ. This implicit repudiation of predestination greatly increased the numbers of people who would come to Christ through the ministries of Finney and subsequent evangelists.

Some historians have portrayed revivalism as the folk movement of the Jacksonian period. If that is true then Finney was the folk hero of the movement. Finney offered a liberalized Calvinism to a generation who wanted to become participants in the conversion process. By calling common people to "vote" on their own salvation, he fit in with the democratic tendencies and frontier individualism of his era.

Christianity and reform

Finney taught that conversion was not the goal, but actually the beginning, of the Christian life. The goal of the new convert must be to get rid of selfishness and to incorporate a *disinterested benevolence*, an idea that Dwight first explored as a theme of Christian living. As it was popularized by Finney and other revivalists, the feelings of compassion bore practical action in the formation of dozens of Christian associations—all of which were dedicated to doing good. Among the elements of this Christian *benevolent empire* were: the American Bible Society and American Education Society, 1816; the American Colonization Society, 1817; the American Sunday School Union, 1824; the American Tract Society, 1825; the American Temperance Society, 1826; the American Peace Society, 1828; and the American Antislavery Society, 1833.

This empire of idealism contributed much to the Jacksonian era. One of Finney's best-known converts was Theodore Dwight Weld (1803–1895), one of the most prominent antislavery lecturers of the time. Two sisters, Angeline and Sarah Grimké, daughters of a slave owner, moved to the North from Charleston so that they might be free to speak

The piercing eyes of Charles Grandison Finney (1792–1875), and his canny understanding of emotion, swept upper New York state and the major cities of the 1820s and 1830s. After contracting tuberculosis in 1832, he settled into pastoral ministry and became professor of theology at Oberlin (Ohio) Collegiate Institute in 1835. His *Lectures on Revival* remains influential among evangelists. (Billy Graham Center)

out against slavery. Both on the revival circuit and in his church in New York City, Finney (and other preachers) taught that slave owning was a sin. He moved to Oberlin College in 1835, with the help of two leading Christian reformers from New York City, Arthur and Lewis Tappan. Oberlin then became a center of antislavery agitation and later was a station on the informal network of aid to runaway slaves known as the *underground railroad*.

Not all Christians agreed with groups who were involved in the abolitionist movement. Southern white Christians used the Scriptures to defend the institution of slavery as moral. The Apostle Paul had urged Christian masters to be kind to their slaves, but he did not recommend that those slaves be freed. Abraham had owned bond servants. In historical context, when the taking of slaves as one of the fruits of victory was common, servants were assumed to be slaves. Some slave owners pointed out that the Afro-Americans under their care would never have heard the gospel had they not been brought to the plantation South. Christians taking sides in the antebellum era can be somewhat compared to the contemporary controversy over abortion: both sides identified their cause with truth and proved unwilling to compromise. Indeed, the abolitionist John Brown killed slave owners in the name of God and was immortalized in song for his alleged heroic deeds. Although Christians were at the heart of the early antislavery movement and other Christians spoke out early in defense of slavery, Christians soon lost control of the slavery controversy. By the mid-1850s it had been taken over as an issue by politicians on the national scene.

Many Protestant leaders shared a concern for the growing Western frontier, particularly that the forces of either barbarianism or Roman Catholicism might engulf the region. Lyman Beecher left New England to become president of Lane Seminary in Cincinnati so that the Ohio Valley could be saved for the kingdom of God. Indeed, Marcus and Narcissa Whitman went to the Oregon Territory in 1836 to make converts of the Native American population before Roman Catholic priests were able to do so. The Mormons were probably the only major group who moved west out of a desire to be left alone.

Christians were not as involved in the women's rights movement of that day as in the abolitionist and temperance movements. Oberlin College pioneered the way as the first coeducational institution. Finney was married three times and widowed twice. Each of his wives made a rather unique contribution to the role of women in the ministry. Some holiness groups encouraged the careers of women as preachers, and Phoebe Palmer brought the holiness movement to the Wesleyan tradition in the late 1850s and 1860s. For the most part, however, women were silent partners at best when it came to promoting the cause of women.

Most Protestants in the Jacksonian era were postmillennialists. Their view of the world was optimistic, even during such times as the financial Panic of 1837, when life in America was distressing. They were progress-oriented and reform-minded because they believed that the kingdom of God on earth could be hastened by the betterment of society. The disinterested benevolence idea was attractive because it was a means to bring the kingdom to fruition, perhaps in their lifetime.[5] Followers of William Miller (1782–1849), the founder of Adventism, were disappointed when his prediction of the second coming of Christ was not fulfilled in 1843, yet they were not looked upon by most American Christians as persons who were mentally deranged. The yeasty exuberance of the Jacksonians accommodated that idea as readily as they accepted the idea that a utopian community could produce a heaven on earth; that a Graham diet of fruits, vegetables, and coarsely ground grains—including "Graham crackers"—could cure the most deadly disease; that the cold water treatment could cure the worst of headaches; or that the organizing of institutions could solve the many social problems that were arising.

The Jacksonian Christians cannot be faulted for not trying to solve the problems facing them. At times they appeared to be trying too hard.

They neglected certain problems, such as the growing plight of Native Americans; however, many of them in the North did pursue the abolition of slavery. They supported Andrew Jackson as a President for the ordinary people, but could not see the value of fair wages or eight-hour days. Their successors, in the period of urban revival led by Dwight L. Moody, did not do much better. The post-Civil War generation would be faced with a host of problems arising from the twin processes of industrialization and urbanization.

Suggested readings

"The American Puritans." *Christian History*, 13.1 (issue 41, 1994).

Bonomi, Patricia U. *Under the Cope of Heaven: Religion, Society and Politics in Colonial America*. New York: Oxford University Press, 1986.

Bushman, Richard L. *From Puritan to Yankee: Character and the Social Order in Connecticut*. New York: Norton, 1970.

Gaustad, Edwin S. *The Great Awakening in New England*. New York: Harper and Row, 1957.

————, ed. *A Documentary History of Religion in America*. Vol. 1: *To the Civil War*. Grand Rapids: Eerdmans, 1982.

"George Whitefield." *Christian History*, 12. 2 (issue 38, 1993).

Hackett, David G., ed. *Religion and American Culture: A Reader*. New York: Routledge, 1995.

Hatch, Nathan O. *The Democratization of American Christianity*. New Haven, Conn.: Yale University Press, 1989.

"Jonathan Edwards and the Great Awakening."*Christian History*, 4.4 (issue 8, 1985).

Marsden, George M. *Religion and American Culture*. New York: Harcourt Brace Jovanovich, 1990.

May, Henry F. *The Enlightenment in America*. New York: Oxford University Press, 1976.

McLoughlin, William G. *Isaac Backus and the American Pietistic Tradition*. Boston: Little, Brown, 1967.

Noll, Mark A. *Christians and the American Revolution*. Grand Rapids: Eerdmans, 1978.

12

Nineteenth-Century Europe and North America: Mission and Uplift

The dominant fact of the nineteenth century in Europe and North America was the industrial revolution. Begun in England in the eighteenth century, this cataclysm remade the face of the two continents. It created a numerous, poor industrial proletariat and a sizable middle class. It brought the goods of the world to Europe and the United States, and sent a flood of European and American businesspeople abroad. The industrial revolution was the engine behind the creation of European and American overseas empires late in the nineteenth century, as industrializing nations tried to gain exclusive control of cheap raw materials and captive markets.

European politicians and generals carved up Africa and Southeast Asia into colonies and maintained less formal spheres of influence in China and Latin America. The Christian experience in Europe and North America in the nineteenth century was defined mainly by these two great, interlocking developments: the industrial revolution and imperialism.

The industrial revolution

After 1500, Western Europe experienced four revolutions that dramatically separated Westerners from their ancestors' experiences.

1. The *religious revolution* that we call the Reformation ended both the idea of Christendom and any hope for visible Christian unity.

280

2. The *scientific revolution* replaced God and the Bible with natural law and sciences as the primary sources of intellectual authority.
3. The *democratic revolution* replaced the despotism of a hierarchical authoritarian state with a stress on individual liberties.
4. The *industrial revolution* changed the nature of human work and of economic interchange in ways that continue to affect the world.

The industrial revolution occurred as machines replaced human or animal muscle in the production of goods. The first steps in the process occurred in eighteenth-century England, then spread rapidly to Europe, North America, and Japan. In England the industrial revolution was preceded by an agricultural revolution, wherein new crops (especially potatoes from the Americas) and more scientific methods of farming greatly increased yields. This resulted in the rapid growth of rural population as more, better nourished babies survived to adulthood. At the same time, fewer farm workers were needed to produce the crops, so many had to look elsewhere for livelihood. The burgeoning factories absorbed much of this surplus labor.

In those factories workers spent their time tending machines. Although initially the machines were similar to those that had been developed in the Middle Ages, the eighteenth century saw innovations increase the efficiency of the machines, making centralization and integration of machinery throughout a manufacturing process feasible and profitable. The increased use of water power tended to cause factories to cluster at places where water made a significant descent; falling water spun wheels, which powered other machines. When steam engines came along, factories were freed from the necessity of locating near falling water, but now they became chained to locations where fuel—at first wood, and later coal—could be easily and cheaply obtained.

Mechanization was accompanied by a shift in economic philosophy that paralleled changes in political philosophy. Economics spurred the ongoing trend of democratic movements to limit control by the state over the individual. In the eighteenth century *mercantilism* developed, the view that private business should serve the economic interests of the state and be subject to oversight and regulation. In the nineteenth century mercantilism was replaced by *laissez-faire* capitalism. *Laissez-faire* insisted that businesspeople should be allowed to pursue profit in whatever way they saw fit, with minimal government interference. The unregulated market would be the most efficient way to direct investment, provide for most people to prosper, and have the state benefit from the general prosperity.

A new form of business organization, the *corporation*, also dramatically altered the relation of capital, labor, and management. Partnerships and joint-stock companies—the dominant means of organizing economic activity before the industrial revolution—had been used since antiquity to raise more funds than one individual could invest in a business. Both assume fairly direct involvement by the investors in managing the business. Each investor can be held personally liable for all the debts and obligations of the company. In a corporation (or "limited company" in the British Commonwealth), the investor only risks the amount of money invested. Furthermore, the investing shareholder can be relatively distant from the day-to-day operations; that is done by a management team hired by the stockholders. Management's primary responsibility to the owners is to ensure profits. The corporation allows hundreds, even thousands of investors to pool money, enabling economic enterprises to grow many times larger than any that had existed before. In contrast to a small, preindustrial workshop where the owner and employees worked side by side, the owners of a corporation are unlikely to know any of their employees below the top management level.

Great increases in productivity accompanied industrialization. Before the industrial revolution a farmer could harvest about two acres of wheat in a day, cutting with a scythe. After the industrial revolution, using a McCormick reaper, he could harvest ten acres.

More important, industrialization brought major changes to the human condition that remain a source of struggle. First, change became normal. Whereas, prior to 1800 the average person could expect to live and work pretty much as his or her grandparents had, people have since expected things to change definitively and dramatically. Within one person's life span, from the 1880s to the 1960s, travel in a covered wagon was replaced by a jet airliner. The speed and scope of change sets the generations born after 1800 off from the rest of human history.

There were many other changes. The home largely changed from a place of production to a place where goods purchased in the market were consumed. Before the industrial revolution people produced most of what they needed in food, soap, clothing, tools, and building materials. With the industrial revolution, goods became more homogeneous; factory-produced goods are uniform and have no individual style. Craftsmanship was moved from the product to the machines that produced the product. Gradually, people in industrialized countries lost their preindustrial attitude of frugality, based on an assumption of scarce goods.

However, conditions of life worsened for many people. The family came under severe stress when, for the first time in human history, large numbers of fathers began to work outside the home and became more distant from the daily lives of their wives and children. Whereas in 1800 the whole family worked together on the farm or in a small family shop, by mid-century declining wages often demanded that everyone work long hours separately in factories. The father might work in one factory,

A hard-working plowman and a family walking to church are the ideals of a late-nineteenth-century temperance engraving. Among the fruits on the "Tree of Temperance" are industry, riches, virtue, self-denial, true friends, a good temper, religion, and business success. (Billy Graham Center)

the mother in another, and their children in a third. Rarely would they all be home at the same time. Furthermore, "home" often meant a dark, overcrowded, ill-ventilated room in a tenement building in an urban slum. A by-product of industrialization was the concentration of people into cities, close enough so that they could walk to work. Overcrowding led to the rapid spread of cholera and typhoid, especially through contaminated water supplies. The combustion of coal in factories and homes sent great amounts of soot and other contaminants into the air. Despair, ill-health, long hours of monotonous work, and uprootedness often led to abuse of alcohol and other drugs.

Christian responses to industrialism

The Christian church as an institution was ill-prepared for these changes. In Europe the rural parish remained the functional ideal. Yet a declining portion of the population lived in rural settings. Long hours of factory work made Sunday truly a day of rest to catch up on sleep and family matters; few working folk placed priority on attending a church that did not relate to their lives during the week. We have seen how the Wesleyans in England tried to meet this need by preaching outside of the church. The Sunday school movement began as an effort to teach literacy to children who worked in factories the rest of the week; the Bible was the text. Gradually, Christian organizations recognized the need for different kinds of ministry to the urban dweller. The response *par excellence* was the Salvation Army (see box 12.1).

Nineteenth-century Western Christians were at the forefront of a vast array of reform movements, by which they attempted to ameliorate the worst consequences of the industrial revolution, as well as other ills of their age. The leading edge of reform in England and America was the movement to end

> ## 12.1. Salvation Army
>
> Founded in the slums of East London in the 1860s by holiness evangelist William Booth (1829–1912), the Salvation Army rapidly spread across the globe, coming to America in 1880.
>
> Uniformed salvation soldiers entered city slums to lead the poor to Christ and soon found themselves called to aid their people in countless ways. They provided housing, set up soup kitchens and medical stations, organized job training and placement, gave legal assistance, tracked down missing persons, sold ice and coal at low prices, visited prisoners, and entertained potentially delinquent children with camps and athletic leagues. Salvationists sometimes characterized their mission as "soup, soap, and salvation"—an expression of their attempt to meet the needs of the whole person.

slavery. It began in the era of the American Revolution, when Quakers and other people of conscience freed their own slaves and outlawed slavery in several American states. Not long afterward, a group of Anglican evangelicals known as the *Clapham Sect* became the chief moral voice in the British Parliament. Led by William Wilberforce (1759–1833), by 1807 they succeeded in forcing England to outlaw the trade in slaves, and spent the next several decades trying to get the rest of the world to comply.

Americans motivated by Christian convictions—for example Theodore Dwight Weld (1803–1895) and Harriet Beecher Stowe (1811–1896), the author of *Uncle Tom's Cabin*—were at the core of the American antislavery movement. Using organizing techniques and networks of committed people borrowed from the evangelical revival movement, Christian abolitionists and their less explicitly evangelical colleagues pressured American society to abandon slavery. By the 1840s several denominations had organizational splits that pitted North against South regional factions over the issue of slavery. Ultimately the antislavery task was taken over by the state in the American Civil War. But the initial impulses, techniques, and personnel all came from the Second Great Awakening.

Evangeline Cory Booth (1865–1950) devoted her life to service in the Salvation Army. A sergeant at age fifteen, at twenty-three she was principal of the Army's International Training College. She became field commissioner for Canada in 1896 and commander of operations in the United States in 1904. She was named the first woman general in the international organization in 1934. (Billy Graham Center)

12.2. Antislavery Impulse

James Russell Lowell (1819–1891), poet, author, political reformer, and antislavery activist, wrote the poem (later hymn) "Once to Every Man and Nation." In it he called Americans to repudiate slavery and embrace the Northern cause in the Civil War. His words vibrate with the sense of heroic mission of nineteenth-century Protestantism on both sides of the Atlantic.

Once to every man
  and nation
Comes the moment to
  decide,
In the strife of truth with false-
  hood,
For the good or evil side;
Some great cause, God's new
  Messiah,
Offering each the bloom
  or blight,
And the choice goes by
  forever
'Twixt that darkness and that
  light.
Then to side with truth is noble,
When we share her wretched
  crust,
Ere her cause bring fame and
  profit
And 'tis prosperous to be just;
Then it is the brave man chooses,
While the coward stands aside,
Till the multitude make virtue
Of the faith they had denied.
By the light of burning
  martyrs,
Christ, Thy bleeding feet
  we track,
Toiling up new Calvaries ever
With the cross that turns not
  back;
New occasions teach
  new duties,
Time makes ancient good un-
  couth;
They must upward still,
  and onward,
Who would keep abreast
  of truth.
Though the cause of evil prosper,
Yet 'tis truth alone is strong;
Though her portion be the scaf-
  fold
And upon the throne be wrong;
Yet that scaffold sways
  the future,
And, behind the dim
  unknown,
Standeth God within
  the shadow
Keeping watch above
  His own.

The impulse to improve society spilled over from antislavery (see box 12.2) to other problem areas. Frequently, one individual would be involved in several sorts of reform. The English evangelical Anthony Cooper, Earl of Shaftesbury (1801–1885), for example, worked tirelessly to improve factory conditions, regulate labor by women and children, and establish slum schools. Other reforms that stemmed from Christian convictions and revivals included movements for temperance, peace, women's rights, world distribution of the Bible, child welfare, and prison reform. Not all of these activities would be thought liberal today; anti-Catholicism was a cause that animated many of the Protestant reformers.

All these movements for reform were motivated by Christian principles, energized by revivalist passions, and staffed largely by committed Christian people. But one nineteenth-century Christian movement went beyond reform to express revolutionary aspirations. This was the Christianity of African-American slaves. For several generations after slavery was introduced to North America, Christians made little attempt to share their faith with their slaves. But in the awakenings of the eighteenth and nineteenth centuries, the vast majority of black Americans came to embrace Protestant Christianity. The master class tried to turn Christianity to their own advantage. They attempted to make slaves docile by preaching from such Pauline texts as Ephesians 6:5: "Slaves, obey your earthly masters with respect and fear, and with sincerity of heart, just as you would obey Christ" (NIV). Arkansas slave Lucretia Alexander recalled, "The [white] preacher came and . . . he'd just say, 'Serve your masters. Don't steal your master's turkey. Don't steal your master's chickens. Don't steal your master's hawgs. . . . Do whatsomever your master tells you to do. Same old thing all the time."[1]

Slaves, for their part, used their faith in God to help them endure their bondage. Slaves prayed and sang eagerly of the rest that would be theirs in Heaven. Slave preachers also emphasized such Old Testament themes as lamentation, exodus, and the visitation of God's wrath on oppressors. South Carolina slaves at the beginning of the Civil War were jailed for singing:

12.3. Angelina and Sarah Grimké

Sarah (1792–1873) and Angelina Grimké (1805–1879) were pioneer activists in the fight to end slavery and establish the rights of women—two causes the sisters saw as one. The daughters of a prominent South Carolina family, the Grimké sisters abandoned the South in the 1820s because they could not tolerate a slave society any longer. In the 1830s they joined the growing abolitionist movement. Because of their intellect, their passion, and their origins in the Southern aristocracy, they commanded special attention when they wrote and spoke against slavery.

That intellect and passion carried over into speaking and writing on behalf of women's equality, as well. Angelina's 1836 antislavery pamphlet, *Appeal to the Christian Women of the South*, was followed two years later by Sarah's *Letters on the Equality of the Sexes and the Condition of Women*. The Grimké sisters conceived both antislavery and feminism to be explicitly Christian callings.

> We'll soon be free
> We'll soon be free
> We'll soon be free
> When the Lord will call us home.[2]

Others were more explicit:

> Oh! Fader Abraham
> Go down into Dixie's land
> Tell Jeff Davis
> To let my people go[3]

It was no accident that Nat Turner, the leader of North America's bloodiest slave revolt, and Henry Highland Garnet, the most militant free black opponent of slavery, were both preachers.

Christian social reform movements of the nineteenth century were founded on a postmillennial view of the future. Most Protestant evangelists—European and American—were convinced that Jesus would come again, although there was some disagreement about whether that would be soon or quite far off in the future. In either case, nearly all agreed that their jobs in the meantime were to save as many souls as they could, and to prepare for Christ's return by perfecting both individuals

Masters and slaves sometimes mingled in slave religious meetings on the plantations, at which black preachers spoke. Slaves also attended white churches (seated in segregated galleries), and sometimes gathered in secret. (Billy Graham Center)

Richard Allen (1760–1831) began preaching while still a slave. His master enabled him to purchase his freedom, and he taught himself to read and write. After an incident at St. George's Methodist Church in Philadelphia, Allen and Absalom Jones organized the Negro Episcopal Church, which grew into the African Methodist Episcopal Church, with Allen its first bishop, in 1816. (Billy Graham Center)

12.4. Richard Allen and Black Christianity

Richard Allen (1760–1831) rose from slavery to found the first African-American denomination in the United States.

When Allen was converted at about age seventeen by an itinerant Methodist preacher, his changed life so impressed his master that the master also embraced Christ, then allowed Allen to work to buy his freedom. Freed in 1783, Allen soon began circuit preaching himself. He joined a Methodist church in Philadelphia where he taught the Bible and led prayer meetings in a mostly white congregation.

When the church decided to segregate its black members, Allen and other blacks walked out and formed their own congregation, calling Allen to preach. Two decades later, in 1816, Allen's church and other congregations of free black people joined together to form the African Methodist Episcopal denomination, with Allen as bishop. From that decade on, it was black churches that formed the main institutional support for black communities, and pastors who formed the largest contingent of black leaders.

and society as much as they could. Some thought that they were playing an instrumental part in ushering in the kingdom of God on earth in their own lifetimes. American Protestants especially held the opinion that the United States occupied a unique place in God's plans. In the words of historian and Nazarene preacher Timothy L. Smith, there was a new world coming, and America would play a central role in it: "Christianity and culture seemed to be marching together, onward and upward toward the 'grand consummation of prophecy in a civilized, and enlightened, a sanctified world. . . . the transformation of society into the kingdom of Christ was to be the great work of the American churches." [4]

This view clashes sharply with the more recently common idea of pre-millennialism—of Christ returning before the world is perfected. But in the mid-nineteenth century, the postmillennial interpretation—that Christians must perfect the world in anticipation of Christ's

12.5. Phoebe Palmer and Holiness

The Christian who, more than any other, created the Holiness Movement out of Wesleyan Methodism was an American, Phoebe Palmer (1807–1874). John Wesley had based his distinctive understanding of the Christian walk on what happened *after* conversion. Even after one was saved, one still committed sin. Wesley found this an intolerable state of affairs. He preached a life of self-discipline that would lead in time to "perfect love"—gradual perfectionism.

Palmer went Wesley one better. The earnest Christian, she said, could be made holy in a flash, by appropriating a "second blessing" that was available if one committed everything to God. In the revivalist atmosphere of the mid-nineteenth century, Palmer's message had enormous appeal. She is credited with personally assisting the salvation of 25,000 people, and then ushering thousands into "perfect love." She taught and exhorted from the 1830s

to near the end of her life, including a triumphal four-year revival tour of England in the 1860s.

But she was more than a preacher. She exemplified the nineteenth-century Protestant synthesis of evangelism and good works. She was the moving force behind innumerable urban social service projects. The most widely known was the Five-Points Mission in New York City, which provided housing, education, and religious instruction for poor families. Five-Points was a prototype for the settlement house movement of the early twentieth century.

Palmer never claimed the title of *preacher* for herself. Like many Christian women leaders of her generation she believed that God ordinarily called only men to spiritual leadership. She regarded herself, like Deborah in the Old Testament, as an exception—called specifically by God to ministry. She always was careful to give her husband, Walter, a lay preacher and homeopath, first billing, even though audiences came primarily to hear her.

Phoebe Worral Palmer (1807–1874), was an author, woman's rights advocate, and influential force in the early holiness movement through such books as *The Way to Holiness* and *The Promise of the Father*. She also was active in visiting prisoners and distributing tracts in the slums of New York. She established the Five Points Mission in 1850, which originated several settlement houses. (Billy Graham Center)

return—carried the day. It drew on the perfectionism of John Wesley and the Methodists, and it informed the later Holiness and Pentecostal movements. It encouraged enthusiastic Christians to go to all lengths to improve the lot of humankind, through a vast variety of good works and movements for social reform. It preached a synthesis of evangelism and social commitment that was lost in the next century.

Some historians argue that revivalist Protestantism was a tool used by the business class in Europe and America to make the new working class docile. They point out that many revival leaders and sponsors were owners of the new factories that needed cheap workers who would appear at work on time and sober and who would work without complaint at boring, repetitive, and dangerous jobs (see "Currier and Ives" lithograph promoting both business and religious values p. 283).

Even granted that the particular brand of Christianity most typical of nineteenth-century revivals helped to inculcate docility rather than rebellion in the people who suffered most from the industrial revolution, it is difficult to deny the power of the Holy Spirit in the revivals. The revivals were enormous in scale: they touched millions of lives on thousands of occasions in widely scattered locations on two continents, over a period of more than three-quarters of a century. They inspired Christians and organized them to carry out projects to ameliorate the pains of the early industrial era, and to usher in the kingdom of God.

A babble of new voices

On various radical fringes of the nineteenth-century revival and reform movements there sprang up new religions that have lasted a century and more. Some regard these as heresies or cults, others as variant forms of Christianity. The divergences of these groups from orthodox Christianity took off in several directions. Followers of Ellen White (1828–1915), called *Seventh-Day Adventists*, sought to obey God's medical, as well as his moral, laws by eating only grains and vegetables, exercising, drinking lots of water, and abstaining from sex and other excitements. Mary Baker Eddy's (1821–1910) disciples called themselves *Christian Scientists*. They believed that there is no material world, only the spiritual. Sickness, then, is the result of a mental failure to comprehend God and that infirmity can be overcome by focusing one's attention on Christ.

Numerous utopian communities appeared in nineteenth-century Europe and America. Some, such as cotton manufacturer Robert Owen's New Lanark factory town in Scotland, were mainly secular in inspiration and embraced the industrial age even as they sought to soften its negative consequences. Others, including the Shakers, who began several American communities, and the Harmonists at New Harmony, Indiana, were fervent believers who desperately awaited Christ's second coming. The Shakers and the Oneida community in New York followed their unique theology into unorthodox sexual practices of celibacy and communal marriage, respectively. None of the religious communities expanded beyond a small membership—they were by nature inward-looking. But they testify to the extraordinary fluidity of the European and American religious scene in the nineteenth century.

Imperialism

Since the end of World War II, the predominant theme in international politics has been decolonization, the breakup of the great empires that came together in the nineteenth century to dominate much of the globe (see chap. 17). Twentieth-century conflicts in India, Vietnam, the Middle East, Eastern Europe, and Central America had roots in those empires. The more recent liberation of Eastern Europe from Soviet domination has later origins but should be seen as part of the same process.

12.6. Latter-day Saints

The most spectacularly successful of the new religions born in the ferment of nineteenth-century revival was the Church of Jesus Christ of Latter-day Saints, more commonly known as the *Mormons*. The central figure was Joseph Smith (1805–1844), a poor upstate New York farm boy from a family of eclectic religious enthusiasms. Smith experienced a series of visions, beginning in the 1820s, from which he concluded that the other varieties of revival—indeed, all the other religions—did not have it quite right. Like Hong Xiuquan in China in the 1850s (see pp. 330–31) and Sun Myung Moon in Korea in this century (see p. 448), Smith concluded that God had called him to restore the true gospel of the early church.

Smith dictated *The Book of Mormon*, he said, from golden tablets he found buried in the woods, translating their ancient Egyptian language under the power of the Holy Spirit. The book told of two Hebrew peoples who came to the Americas before the time of Christ, and of their subsequent spiritual and temporal struggles.

In this and other writings, in passionate speech and charismatic presence, Joseph Smith offered new answers to most of the questions troubling the hearts of farmers and industrial workers in the United States and England. Quickly, thousands of disciples came together to form a disciplined, worshipful community. But the very success of the Mormons and their unorthodox theology offended their neighbors. Persecuted without mercy, the Mormons were forced to move again and again—from New York to Ohio to Missouri to Illinois and, after Smith was murdered, to the arid wastes of Utah. There, under the powerful organizational talents of Smith's colleague Brigham Young, they made the desert bloom.

For all the exotic theology the Mormons embraced, their manner of community and style of worship had much in common with other Christians, particularly with the evangelical wing of Protestantism. The Mormons studied the Bible and prayed to an infinite-personal God not very different from the one to whom Charles Finney and Phoebe Palmer prayed. They practiced rigorous righteousness and self-examination like Calvinists. Their intense commitment to communal self-help echoed the chords of other utopian communities, from Puritans to Anabaptists to the inhabitants of New Harmony. Like Catholics, the Mormon church was hierarchical, male-dominated, and, in some respects, rather secretive.

One much-noted Mormon innovation, polygamy, was faithfully practiced for two generations and then discontinued in the 1890s under pressure from the United States government. Thereafter, Mormons were distinguished by social insularity, material prosperity, mutual self-help, and missionary enthusiasm. Mormons dominated public life in the mountain region of the western United States and, in the twentieth century, spread across the globe. In the decades after World War II, their rate of worldwide growth was exceeded only by Pentecostals.

Most simply, *imperialism* is control by one nation over a dependent area or people outside its borders. In one form or another empires have existed since the time of the ancient Babylonians, but the most extensive and significant episode of imperialism occurred during the nineteenth century (to 1914), when as much as 85 percent of the world's population lived in countries that were or had been parts of European empires.

The proud English cliché, "The sun never sets on the British Empire," was quite literally true—British holdings extended around the globe. Virtually all the nations of Western Europe ruled empires at one time or another, and their rivalries make up much of the history of international conflict in the eighteenth and nineteenth centuries. While the course of those conflicts is beyond the scope of this survey, the motives for acquiring overseas territories are pertinent. Those motives included trade, military materiél and strategy, and nationalistic conceit.

Some analysts emphasize the economic motive. Rivalries before the industrial revolution aimed at control of the sources of valuable trade goods. Thus the Spanish, Portuguese, and Dutch fought over access to the East Indies to control sources of valuable spices. French and British rivalry in North America was over furs. One country, at least in part, sought to keep another from gaining undue advantage in this way. Later, with the development of industry, the argument goes, nineteenth-century colonial powers (especially Britain) sought to control raw materials, to monopolize markets for their manufactured goods, and to monopolize investment in their colonies.[5]

In the nineteenth century especially, colonies also had strategic importance. When ships changed from wind to steam power, they needed places to refuel. Since coal was the primary fuel, naval powers needed networks of secure coaling stations around the world, with safe havens where their fleets might pause unthreatened. As might be expected, Britain, with the largest fleet, required many of these coaling places. But even the United States, a meager imperialist, acquired Wake Island in the mid-Pacific and other isolated spots to fill this need.

Perhaps a more important, though ineffable, motive was national pride. Imperialism was popular with the masses within the imperialistic country. European countries who joined the imperial game late—Germany and Italy—referred to themselves as the "have-not countries" until they, too, acquired colonies after the 1885 Berlin Conference. The era of empire-building matched that of the spread of *Social Darwinism*, which theorized an innate superiority of one race over another and stressed the rule of strength and supremacy in the survival of societies. It should surprise no one that enthusiasm for conquering foreign lands was accompanied by racism and color prejudice. In its most benign

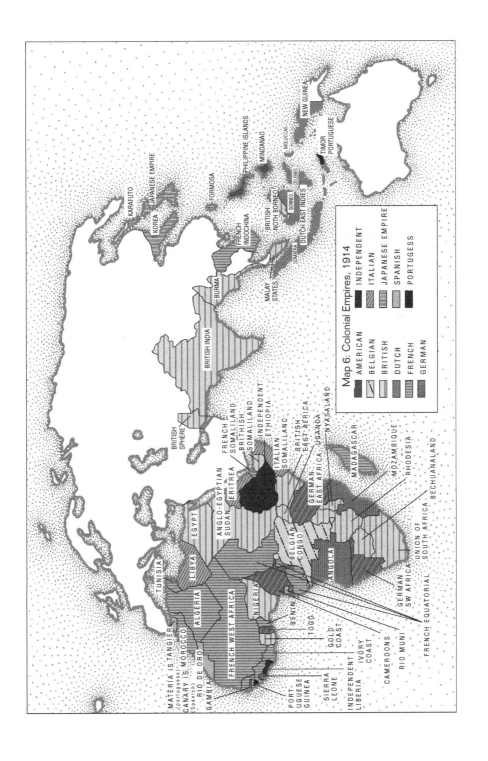

Map 6: Colonial Empires, 1914

AMERICAN
BELGIAN
BRITISH
DUTCH
FRENCH
GERMAN
INDEPENDENT
ITALIAN
JAPANESE EMPIRE
SPANISH
PORTUGESS

KARAFUTO
JAPANESE EMPIRE
KOREA
FORMOSA
BURMA
BRITISH INDIA
FRENCH INDOCHINA
PHILIPPINE ISLANDS
MINDANAO
MOLUCCAS
BRITISH NOTH BORNEO
BORNEO
CELEBES
SUMATRA
DUTCH EAST INDIES
MALAY STATES
TIMOR PORTUGUESE
NEW GUINEA

BRITISH SPHERE
TUNISIA
LIBYA
EGYPT
ANGLO-EGYPTIAN SUDAN
ERITREA
FRENCH SOMALILAND
BRITHISH SOMALILAND
INDEPENDENT ETHIOPIA
ITALIAN SOMALILAND
BRITISH EAST AFRICA
UGANDA
NYASALAND
MADAGASCAR
MOZAMBIQUE
RHODESIA
GERMAN EAST AFRICA

MATERIA IS TANGIER
(portuguese)
CANARY IS.
(Spanish) MOROCCO
RIO DE ORO
ALGERIA
FRENCH WEST AFRICA
GAMBIA
PORT-UGUESE GUINEA
SIERRA LEONE
INDEPENDENT LIBERIA
IVORY COAST
GOLD COAST
TOGO
BENIN
NIGERIA
CAMEROONS
RIO MUNI
FRENCH EQUATORIAL
BELGIAN CONGO
ANGOLA
GERMAN SW AFRICA
UNION OF SOUTH AFRICA
BECHUANALAND

form, the *white man's burden* condescendingly legitimized colonialism as a way to train indigenous people in civilization and democracy and then set them free when they were ready. This is what many British believed they were doing. Others, buttressed by the then well-respected teachings of pseudoscientific racism, believed that colonial subjects were perpetual children who needed the benevolent administration and guidance of kind-hearted Europeans to move them slowly toward more enlightened patterns of life.

Contemporary aversion to imperialism should not blind us to some of its positive achievements—even though these may be linked to some negative effects. In British areas especially, law and order prevailed more widely than previously. The British, possessors of overwhelming force, prohibited tribal warfare, enforced abolition of slavery, and everywhere advanced the rights of women—for example, forbidding ritual suicide by widows in India. Modern medicine assuaged plague, malaria, cholera, and other diseases. New crops, especially potatoes and maize from the Americas, brought better nutrition to parts of Asia and Africa. The colonial regime brought some peoples an opportunity to participate in the world market. Western technology brought dams, reservoirs, roads, railroads, telegraph systems, and harbors. Though designed to benefit the colonial power, these also frequently made travel and communication easier for natives and helped them develop a sense

12.7. The White Man's Burden

Many of the works of English journalist, poet, and story-teller Rudyard Kipling (1865–1936) describe British imperialism and express the condescending attitudes and sense of civilizing mission with which Europeans went overseas.

None does this more vividly than "The White Man's Burden," written in 1899, part of which reads:

Take up the White Man's
burden—
Send forth the best ye breed—
Go bind your sons to exile
To serve your captives' need;
To wait in heavy harness,

On fluttered folk and wild—
Your new-caught, sullen
peoples,
Half-devil and half-child.

Take up the White Man's
burden—
And reap his old reward:
The blame of those ye better,
The hate of those ye guard—
The cry of hosts ye humour
(Ah, slowly!) toward the light:—
"Why brought ye us from
bondage,
Our loved Egyptian night?"
By all ye cry or whisper,
By all ye leave or do,
The silent, sullen peoples
Shall weigh your Gods and you.

of nationhood that would be valuable later on. Education and literacy were advanced, though usually in the language of the colonial power, and a corps of native-born teachers emerged to take up the task. Most of these were trained in mission schools, for one of the other realities of the colonial venture was access to the gospel.

Each of these achievements had negative consequences, however. The imposition of European law and order often disrupted delicately balanced social patterns that had developed over centuries of experience. Surviving widows in India were often driven to prostitution because the traditional family support systems did not account for them. Also, Europeans did a notoriously bad job of setting political boundaries. Often they combined several traditionally hostile groups into one country, as the Hausa and Yoruba in Nigeria, or split a group into two countries, as the Ibo between Nigeria and Cameroon. Western medicine and sanitation meant that more children survived, so population growth outstripped available resources of food, land, and housing. The introduction of cheap Western manufactured goods led to a decline in local craftsmanship and put many people out of work. Growing crops for the world market proved perilous for growers who had no control over pricing or fluctuations in demand by the consuming countries. It also concentrated land ownership in the hands of a colonial elite and reduced formerly self-sufficient peasants to poorer, landless agricultural laborers. The enthusiastic applications of Western technology often led (and still lead) to the destruction of ecosystems, pollution, and other environmental disasters. Even literacy caused a kind of cultural imperialism, whereby Western values and standards led local educated elites to denigrate or abandon their own oral literature. Christianity tended to be identified with the outward paraphernalia of Western culture rather than the inward truths to be found in a relationship with God. In West Africa for example, there are places where women customarily wear nurses' uniforms to church, because that was how the Christian women who introduced the religion to the area dressed. While identity with the West may have been advantageous to missions during a colonial era, when a country fought its way toward independence from the West and a reassertion of indigenous values, Christians often have been viewed, at least vaguely, as collaborators.

Yet missions were the primary response of Protestant Christians to the imperial reality. In nineteenth-century Britain missionaries became folk heroes, with some of the charisma that would be attached to astronauts a century later. In an empire so vast there were many fields to which missionaries might be called. Two nineteenth-century British missionaries exemplify differing ways the gospel could be proclaimed to non-European cultures. David Livingstone (1813–1873) believed

Western patterns could accompany the gospel to enhance the lives of converted people. Modern missiologists (students of missions) would call him a *Westernizer*. James Hudson Taylor (1832–1905) believed he could strip the gospel to its essentials and remove most elements of Western culture associated with it. Missiologists would say he was *contextualizing* the gospel to its appropriate cultural context.

The life of Livingstone illustrates many trends in nineteenth-century Protestantism. Born and reared in a Glasgow industrial slum, Livingstone was one of seven children of factory workers. The family all lived in a single room. Typical of his station at the time, Livingstone worked in the thread factories from an early age. A typical day's schedule saw him working in the mills from 6 A.M. to 8 P.M., attending school from 8 P.M. to 10 P.M., and then studying. Livingstone's job required him to shift thread bobbins as they filled up, and he found that he had 90 seconds between each required shift. He brought his Latin book to the factory, propped it on the machine, and studied in the 90-second intervals. Converted at age fifteen, he became burdened for China and decided to study medicine in order to be admitted into the country. Most of his medical education was acquired at night while he continued to work in the mills.

When Livingstone finished his medical training, China was closed to Westerners because the First Opium War was raging. The London Missionary Society, one of a growing number of independent, inter-denominational agencies, offered him a post in South Africa. Once in South Africa, Livingstone was gripped by a desire to reach areas where no other missionaries had been, to preach the gospel and heal the sick. So he hired guides and porters and trekked far into the interior, to places and peoples Europeans had never seen. During his wanderings he explored much of southern and central Africa and recounted his discoveries in letters eventually published in the British press. Livingstone's dedication is evident: Sick himself with malaria and dysentery for thirty years, he lost his wife and three of his children to disease in Africa as well.

When he returned to England on a furlough to raise funds, he was greeted as a hero by great crowds and paraded through the streets. In 1871, when Livingstone had not been heard from for some time, the New York *Herald Tribune* sent reporter Henry M. Stanley to "find" Livingstone. After wandering about Africa for months, Stanley extended his hand to the first European he had seen and said, "Dr. Livingstone, I presume?" In 1873 Livingstone died. He was found kneeling by his bed in prayer. His body was buried in Westminster Abbey, but his heart was buried in Africa—a poignant reminder of his love for the continent and its people.

James Hudson Taylor (1832–1905) used medical training to enter the almost closed land mass of China, landing in Shanghai in 1854. When his own sending organization folded and no other would sponsor him, Taylor founded China Inland Mission in 1865. By 1891 he led 641 missionaries, nearly half of all Protestants working in China. All were encouraged to adopt Chinese dress and customs. (Billy Graham Center)

Livingstone's work in Africa's interior brought him into contact with the Arab-dominated slave trade that had been abolished in British-controlled territory in 1808. Slavery appalled Livingstone and he continually sought its extermination. Livingstone believed that the interior tribes resorted to the slave trade because they lacked other economic resources to exchange for manufactured goods. He hoped European economic connections would help abolish slavery. He believed that the introduction of crops for export would provide an economic alternative to the trade in humans. His slogan was that "commerce and Christianity" would end slavery. Thus, Livingstone did not hesitate to introduce and prescribe Western solutions to African problems, and he felt little tension between his roles as evangelist, healer, and promoter of international trade.

Taylor was a distinctly less heroic figure in the eyes of his British countrypeople, for he was not a champion of British culture and economic forms. In contrast to Livingstone, Taylor came from a middle-class family in a small town where his father was a pharmacist. Like Livingstone, at age fifteen Taylor felt a call to China and set about preparing himself. He began to practice an austere way of life, on the assumption that China would present him with many hardships. He practiced sleeping on a board, reducing his food consumption, and exercising to build up his stamina. He spent Sundays in evangelistic work and helping the poor. He tried to teach himself Chinese, while he also studied the usual pastoral regimen of Latin, Greek, and Hebrew. Like Livingstone, he chose to study medicine and obtained a scholarship to do so. By subsisting mainly on oatmeal and rice, Taylor found he could give away two thirds of his stipend and still survive. He frequently gave away more than was prudent but trusted God to provide for his needs, sometimes miraculously.

Sent to China before he completed his degree, Taylor ran into conflict with the missionaries there. They primarily stayed in port cities where the British navy could protect them against antiforeign rioting. They maintained European dress, worship, and culture and were quite cut off from the Chinese people. Taylor believed he could get a better hearing if he appeared less obviously foreign. He resolved to wear Chinese-style clothing and let his hair grow into a queue. He preached directly in Chinese, rather than using a translator, so his hearers would focus on the gospel message, not on the funny Western clothes or language of the messenger.

Fellow missionaries were horrified; they thought he was derogating the prestige and power they enjoyed. Eventually their quarrels led Taylor to leave their company and go into the interior of China where he resolved to be as Chinese as possible, while still being true to the gospel. Part of this entailed using women to minister and preach to women. This was appropriate in Chinese custom, but not the common practice among nineteenth-century European Protestants. When British gunboats penetrated up the rivers into China's interior, ostensibly to protect Taylor, he protested to no avail. Taylor tried to present the gospel with as little overlay of Western culture as possible.

12.8. Missionary Hymns

The convictions of the great age of European missions were evident in the hymn, "Hasten, Lord, the Glorious Time" (1830), by Thomas Hastings:

Hasten, Lord, the glorious time
When beneath Messiah's sway
Every nation, every clime
Shall the Gospel call obey.
Mightiest kings its power shall own,
Heathen tribes His name adore,
Satan and his host o'erthrown
Bound in chains shall hurt no more.

A similar theme was struck by "Ye Christian Heroes, Wake to Glory," though gentility was stripped away and impulses to combat and dominate were laid bare (sung to the tune of the "Marseillaise"):

Ye Christian heroes, wake to
  glory:

Hark, hark! what millions bid
  you rise!

See heathen nations bow before you,

Behold their tears, and hear
  their cries.

Shall pagan priests, their errors
  breeding,

With darkling hosts, and flags
  unfurled,

Spread their delusions o'er the
  world,

Though Jesus on the Cross
  hung bleeding?

To arms! To arms!

Christ's banner fling abroad!

March on! March on! all hearts
  resolved

To bring the world to God.

A more benign spirit, giving rather than taking, yet still condescending, is evident in "Speed Away! Speed Away!"

(1890) by the giant of nineteenth-century hymnody, Fanny Crosby:

Speed away! speed away on
  your mission of light,

To the lands that are lying in
  darkness and night;

'Tis the Master's command; go
  ye forth in His name,

The wonderful gospel of Jesus
  to proclaim;

Take your lives in your hand, to
  the work while 'tis day,

Speed away! speed away!
  speed away!

Speed away, speed away with
  the message of rest,

To the souls by the tempter in
  bondage oppressed;

For the Saviour has purchased
  their ransom from sin,

And the banquet is ready. O
  gather them in;

To the rescue make haste,
  there's no time for delay,

Speed away! speed away!
  speed away!

The scope of European and North American missionary activity in the nineteenth century was extraordinary. Wherever empire went, there too went missionaries. At the end of the eighteenth century the British East India Company had succeeded in taking over the Indian subcontinent, and English Baptist William Carey began the spread of Protestant Christianity there. After the Opium Wars pried open the Chinese economy in the 1840s through 1860s—beginning China's political dismemberment—hundreds and then thousands of missionaries (mainly British and American Protestants but also French and Belgian Catholics and even some Russian Orthodox) poured in to share Christ with Chinese people. When the nations of Europe carved up Africa among them in the 1880s (see p. 309) there soon were major French missions in French West Africa, German missions in Tanganyika, British missions in Kenya, and Belgian missions in the Congo.

Much of the missionary activity was in the hands of denominational boards. But new forms of church organization arose specifically to pursue the missionary task. These were similar in many ways to the Sunday School Union and temperance groups that arose in Europe and North America to pursue domestic reform. Numerous nondenominational missionary societies appeared on the international scene, such as Taylor's China Inland Mission, as well as societies devoted to printing and distributing the Bible in all the languages of the world.

Conclusion

In the nineteenth century, Europe and North America were in an optimistic and expansive phase. The industrial revolution brought enormous productivity but also serious social problems. Carried along by the self-confidence of the age, Christians preached individual redemption, even as they worked for reforms that would ameliorate the social problems that attended industrial development. As the search for markets, raw materials, and international prestige drew Western soldiers and traders abroad, missionaries went with them. They took many different postures toward the indigenous peoples, some overtly imperialistic, others sympathetic, but all convinced of the superiority and inevitability of Western civilization, including Christianity.

Suggested readings

Davis, David Brion, ed. *Ante-Bellum Reform*. New York: Harper and Row, 1967.

Handy, Robert T. *A Christian America: Protestant Hopes and Historical Realities*, 2d ed. New York: Oxford University Press, 1983.

Johnson, Paul E. *A Shopkeeper's Millennium: Society and Revivals in Rochester, New York, 1815–1837*. New York: Hill and Wang, 1978.

Latourette, Kenneth Scott. *History of the Expansion of Christianity*. Vol. 4: *The Great Century: Europe and the United States, 1800 A.D. to 1914 A.D.*; Vol. 5: *The Great Century: The Americas, Australia and Africa, 1800 A.D. to 1914 A.D.*; Vol. 6: *The Great Century: North Africa and Asia, 1800 A.D. to 1914 A.D.* reprint ed. Grand Rapids: Zondervan, 1970.

May, Henry F. *Protestant Churches and Industrial America*. New York: Harper, 1967.

Neill, Stephen. *A History of Christian Missions*. Baltimore: Penguin, 1964.

Raboteau, Albert T. *Slave Religion: The Invisible Institution in the Antebellum South*. New York: Oxford University Press, 1980.

Sandeen, Ernest R., ed. *The Bible and Social Reform*. Chico, Calif.: Scholars, 1982.

Smith, Timothy L. *Revivalism and Social Reform: American Protestantism on the Eve of the Civil War*. Baltimore: Johns Hopkins University Press, 1980.

Walters, Ronald G. *American Reformers, 1815–1860*. New York: Hill and Wang, 1978.

13

Christianity As a Worldwide
Phenomenon, 1750–1950

The two centuries from 1750 to 1950 witnessed the rise and maturation of the industrial capitalist economies of Western Europe and North America (see chap. 12). As those economies expanded, they sought markets for their goods and dependable sources of raw materials in countries outside the North Atlantic orbit. So the Third World was created; that is, nations and peoples outside Europe and North America (and later Japan) became part of a single world market system dominated by the industrialized nations.

Typically, a Western power would establish military or political hegemony over a region, directly through military conquest or political usurpation, or indirectly through gradual economic domination. When fully developed, colonial or quasi-colonial economic arrangements meant that Third World countries switched from subsistence farming to production of minerals or agricultural products for export. This amounted to an extractive economic relationship, with Asian, African, and Latin American countries supplying raw materials at low prices and buying manufactured goods at high prices, effectively draining their wealth into the coffers of the colonizing countries.

Within many colonized countries, land and political power became concentrated in the hands of an oligarchy connected to European or North American colonizers. Societal status was divorced from traditional patterns of hereditary hierarchy; even where the same families held authority they did so for new reasons. And often this new elite was composed of previously despised or outcast groups who had no status to lose by collaborating with colonial authorities. Along with that relationship went a certain cultural dependency, as European manners and customs frequently came to characterize the colonial elite. Christianity was often among those aspects of Western culture adopted by Third World elites. But cultural domination of the colonial elite was sown with the seeds of its own destruction. For it was among members of these elites, frequently those educated in Christian schools and infused with Western democratic ideals, that nationalism flowered in the twentieth century. Ultimately this resulted in at least formal independence for nearly all colonized peoples.

The encounter between Christians and non-Western peoples between 1500 and 1750 exhibited several common themes (see chap. 9):

1. the specter of aggressive Westerners seeking trade and total political and economic dominance;
2. a propensity for European Christians to misunderstand non-European peoples;
3. a reciprocal tendency to misjudge Westerners' intentions, motivations, and capabilities; and
4. a persistent habit of European missionaries, sent out to minister to Third World peoples, to concentrate on the overseas European population instead.

In the era of capitalist colonialism that followed 1750, the first three of these tendencies continued, while missionaries began to break out of confinement in international settlements and make contact with large numbers of local people. In these centuries, three new themes were added:

5. missionaries often were implicated in Western colonialism and lost credibility;
6. Protestants came to the Third World in force for the first time;
7. large and enduring Third World churches came into existence.

Church and revolution in Latin America

Latin America was the one region outside Europe and North America that was predominantly Christian in 1750. The Roman Catholic church was the established religion of both Spanish and Portuguese domains. It was not entirely an indigenous church. Although there were vast Catholic masses and a significant number of American-born priests, bishops were nearly all from Europe. That, together with the church's immense wealth (chiefly from land holdings), meant that the church was one of the pillars of the colonial regimes.

Political independence came in the nineteenth century, largely at the expense of church interests. In many newly formed countries, nationalism took the shape of anticlericalism. The nineteenth century was a period of prolonged political instability throughout much of Latin America. The two major contenders were conservatives and liberals. Conservatives were dedicated to hierarchy, land-owning, a strong central government, the established Church, and close ties with Iberia. Liberals pursued a more democratic and nationalistic agenda, favoring decentralized government. The liberals' strategy for the future was keyed to business rather than land owning and the interests of American-born, aspiring whites. When liberal, anticlerical regimes came to power the church lost lands and political influence and fell into decay. By the end of this period the Catholic Church had begun to recover, as it became used to functioning in a more pluralistic system without much support from politicians.

The changes in the Latin American church can best be explained by example. The most radical case of anticlericalism occurred in Mexico. There, as elsewhere in Latin America, bishops and parish clergy split over independence. Although the church hierarchy supported Spain, many priests, such as Father Miguel Hidalgo, were prime movers of the revolution. When independence was achieved, the constitution of 1814 enshrined Roman Catholicism as Mexico's official religion. But soon an assault on church prerogatives began. The *patronato* (see pp. 203–4) had tied the church to Spain. The new government appropriated the *patronato* and began to exercise its own authority over church business. Liberals who replaced conservatives and wrote the constitution of 1857 separated church from state and confiscated most church lands.

The conservative-liberal split was complicated by Freemasonry. This secret society claimed the allegiance of most of Mexico's elite, including quite a number of priests, even though Masonry had many qualities of a competing religion—oaths of allegiance and quasi-religious rituals among them. In much of Latin America most Masons were liberals and therefore opposed to the church. But in Mexico nearly all the elite, whether conservative or liberal, were Masons. There the split was between different branches of Masonry. Conservatives tended to be members of the Scottish Rite, while liberals mainly joined the York Rite. With the Masons so entrenched in both branches of the elite, perhaps the anti-Catholic tendencies of Freemasonry in general had something to do with the extremes to which Mexicans took their anticlericalism.

In time positivism and then socialism became Mexican national doctrines, and Roman Catholic leaders were persecuted. The number of foreign priests dropped sharply, so in the process of disestablishment the church also became decolonized, though in a most disorderly fashion. A dichotomy between bishop and priest evolved. In time the church hierarchy made its peace with the powers of the new order, while some parish clergy began to identify with the struggles of the lower classes. For example, priests joined with lay leaders to form the Catholic Workers' Union in 1903. By the twentieth century, the bishops had become a bulwark of the liberal party. They were middle-class and European in ancestry, but Mexican-born. Meanwhile, some parish priests were becoming advocates of the Indian and Mestizo (mixed European and Indian) masses.

Something similar happened in nearby Guatemala. Starting in 1871, the liberal regime of Justo Rufino Barrios tried to secularize Guatemalan society. Barrios disestablished the Roman Catholic church, seized most of its property, and sent the archbishop and other leaders back to Spain. Education was made secular, priests were forbidden to teach school, civil marriage was prescribed, and religious processions were banned. Barrios, like liberals elsewhere, became entangled in the growing British and U.S. economic intrusion in Latin America. To support plantation agriculture for export, his government rounded up Indians and forced them to work for wages. The devout Indian population and their priests resisted, setting the stage for conflicts that persisted to the end of the twentieth century. In Guatemala, as elsewhere in Latin America, the tendency was for the church hierarchy to become identified with dictatorial national governments tied to foreign neocolonial domination, while some parish priests and the urban and rural Catholic masses began to move into opposition.

To be sure, Mexican and Guatemalan nationalist anticlericalism was extreme. Each nation had its own national church history, in marked contrast to the colonial era, which was characterized by a common Latin American church. At the other end of the spectrum, the church in Ecuador seems to have avoided most of these class and ethnic conflicts.

Another noteworthy development of the nineteenth century was the introduction of Protestantism into a formerly Roman Catholic milieu. Protestant missionaries from Britain and the United States came to Argentina in 1820, to Brazil in 1855, to Peru in 1891, and to other Latin American nations at various times in-between. Representatives of all sorts of Protestant denominations took part, although in many countries the Methodists or Presbyterians led the way, followed by Baptists and members of smaller churches (including the Church of the Nazarene in the twentieth century). Although Protestants paid increasing attention to Latin America as the twentieth century progressed, not until the 1950s and the rise of indigenous Pentecostal movements did Protestantism became a major part of Latin American Christianity (see chap. 17).

For the most part the religion practiced by Latin American Catholics did not differ much from that of European Catholics. The official theology, liturgy, and teaching of the church were common throughout Catholicism. Exceptions to this rule were groups that blended European Christianity with African or Native American religions. Some Peruvian Indians, for example, blended their worship of "Holy Mother Earth" with Catholic veneration of the Virgin Mary. Cuba, Brazil, Haiti, and other places with large African populations blended elements of European and African folk religions. Christian saints became identified with West African *orisha* or spirits. In Trinidad pictures of John the Baptist were revered alongside those of Shango, god of thunder and lightning. Likewise, Oshossi, god of the hunt, was identified with the archangel Michael. This did not amount to complete syncretism, because the main structures of Christian worship and church life were kept separate from African-derived religious practices. But many people felt that recourse to two kinds of magic was more powerful than one. Similar accommodations have been made throughout Christian history (see, for example, pp. 76–77).

Africa

David Livingstone was the most famous European ever to be associated with Africa (see pp. 297–99). A doctor, missionary, and explorer, for more than thirty years he walked great distances in the bush where no Europeans had gone before, plying his medical trade and telling about Christ. He made two trips back to England to tell people about Africa. But it was his letters, published and circulated in England, that caught the imagination of thousands of English people with tales of the "dark continent" and what Livingstone regarded as its need for the blessings of European civilization.

Livingstone is important because he and his followers, such as Henry M. Stanley, the New York reporter who journeyed into Africa to write Livingstone's story, framed the understandings that Europeans and Americans had of Africa for generations thereafter. Africa, in their eyes, was a disease-ridden, backward, and miserable place, filled with child-like, superstitious people who desperately needed Western guidance and uplift. Livingstone's vision was that Africa would be saved from itself by being opened to the gospel and to intercontinental trade. Livingstone believed that legitimate commerce would offer Africans a profitable alternative to selling each other to Arab slave traders. One African is reported to have said to Livingstone, "To be plain with you, we should like you much better if you traded with us and then went away, without forever boring us with preaching that word of God of yours."[1]

If such a conversation actually took place the African speaker made a mistake: In the long run commerce disrupted African society more than did Christianity. Explorers such as Livingstone were followed by missionaries and especially traders, who increasingly demanded that their governments intervene in African politics to guarantee them protection and access to African souls, consumers, and sources of raw material. This fit well with the ideas about state power current in late nineteenth-century Europe. A European country, in order to feel like a first-rate power, had to possess an empire from which to extract wealth.

At a conference in Berlin in 1884–85, representatives of the major European powers began a process of dividing up Africa into more-or-less arbitrary spheres of influence. Belgium claimed the Congo River Basin. France got most of west and northwest Africa, plus Madagascar. The British claimed Egypt, the Sudan, parts of the Guinea Coast, and large stretches of south and east Africa. Germany took Namibia, Tanzania, Togo, and Cameroon. Portugal got Angola and Mozambique. Italy took Libya and Somalia. Missionaries and traders of the colonizing nations had been involved in most of these places for decades, although in some new colonies missionary contact did not start until after the Berlin Conference.

The European powers set about incorporating their African spheres into formal colonies by threat, conspiracy, and conquest. By 1900 the transition was complete: All of Africa except Liberia in the west and Ethiopia in the east was in European hands. The colonizers brought such benefits as Western education and medicine, but they also brought extractive economic arrangements that continued the drain of African resources. From the diamond and copper mines of South Africa to the cotton plantations of Egypt, the wealth of the colonies was set up for export. But the colonial regimes did not last long—in two-thirds of a century nearly all of Africa had returned to at least formal independence. In order to understand some of the ways African Christians experienced the colonial era, we will look at three countries: Ivory Coast, Uganda, and South Africa.

Ivory Coast

Like much of French West Africa, Ivory Coast did not become a Christian country under colonial rule. Catholic missionaries were active in West Africa from the 1490s on, but they were less active in Ivory Coast than in some other French domains. French influence (and therefore Christianity) was confined mainly to the coast. The northern part of the country, as in much of West Africa, was culturally in Muslim hands. In West Africa Islam was preferable to Christianity for many people, for they associated Christianity with the slave trade and colonial domination, while they associated Islam with the learning, culture, and refinement of the cities and universities of the savanna immediately to the north. French Catholic missionaries brought formal education to parts of Ivory Coast, but they did not succeed in raising up a corps of African priests to carry on their work. Beginning in 1910, large numbers of Ivory Coast people turned to Christianity, not through the Catholic church, nor through its Protestant adversaries, but through the enthusiastic ministry of William Wade Harris, an unaffiliated African evangelist (see box 13.1).

13.1. William Wade Harris

William Wade Harris (c. 1865–1929) was a Liberian of the Grebo tribe who felt called to prophesy. In 1913 and 1914 he toured Ivory Coast, dressed in a white robe and turban, preaching powerfully about Christ. It is estimated he personally converted 100,000 people in those two years. He went among the people, accepting their hospitality but shunning donations. He set up his followers in churches and appointed pastors to lead them. He sent missionaries into the interior to evangelize people there. After two years the French colonial government arrested Harris and deported him for fear his followers would rise up and demand political independence. His movement continued, however, both in independent churches and in congregations tied to the Wesleyan Methodist Church. By 1950 perhaps 2 million Christians in Ivory Coast, Ghana, and Liberia could trace their spiritual ancestry to William Wade Harris.

Gordon Haliburton helps explain some of the reasons for Harris's phenomenal success:

His identification with the people he converted was complete: he was a black man like themselves, familiar with their social structure, familiar with their moral and religious ideas, eating the same food and satisfied with the same material standard of living. There was no serious gap in the flow of ideas between him and them. . . .

[In addition] Harris claimed to be a prophet with all the special powers which God bestows on those He chooses. These powers enabled him to drive out demons and spirits, the enemies of God. He cured the sick in body and mind by driving out the evil beings preying on them. Those who practised black magic had to confess and repent or he made them mad. He had all the power of the fetishmen and more. . . .

He believed God had given him other powers, more dramatic assertions of their relationship, notably the power to call down fire and rain from heaven. These powers gave him an advantage over the missionaries because he showed his power over the spirits and did not ask people to act on blind faith. He completely discredited the old gods as he introduced his God. He kept his converts in the new faith by modifying their practices in intelligent ways, rather than by condemning them outright. . . . He did not have to drive wedges into the social body, as missionaries commonly did, to win over individual souls. Rather he won over the whole community and preserved its social structure intact. This meant that whereas mission converts had to leap over a great gulf separating their old beliefs and activities from the new ones, the Harris converts had only to take a step—a substitution of God for the former pantheon of gods and spirits, and an observance of God's taboos in the place of theirs. The men who had led the community in observing the old faiths led them in the new; it was not those who followed Harris who defied community feeling but those who held to the old ways.

*Gordon McKay Haliburton, The Prophet Harris (London: Longman, 1971), 2–3.

Other parts of West Africa followed a similar pattern, with some adoption of Christianity along the coast where the colonial regime was strong but much less to the north, in Muslim territory. In some places a large number of Africans became Christians. This occurred in Liberia and Sierra Leone, which were populated largely by repatriated former slaves and their descendants. Even in those countries, however, Christianity was limited mainly to urban areas and left inland peoples untouched.

Uganda

The church in Uganda was born out of conflict between British and Arabs for control of the country. Arab sultans had long controlled trade along the Swahili Coast of East Africa from the island of

---

13.2. Samuel Ajayi Crowther

Bishop Samuel Ajayi Crowther (c. 1806-1891) was the first African Anglican priest. A member of the Yoruba people of northern Nigeria, he was captured by Muslim slave traders at fifteen and sold to a Portuguese ship in 1822. The British were by this time no longer in the slave trade themselves; indeed they positioned ships off the African coast to intercept others (especially Portuguese) who tried to continue the trade in slaves. A British naval vessel stopped that ship and returned the captives to Sierra Leone and freedom. Ajayi was given a missionary's name and educated by Anglicans to be a school teacher. He became a Christian with a burning desire to bring the gospel to the interior of Africa. He was sent to the Church Missionary Society training school in London and ordained in 1843. Back in Africa he preached and taught.

Together with the missionary Henry Venn, Crowther conceived and instituted the Niger Mission, one of the first missionary attempts to penetrate the African interior, and the only one in that era staffed by Africans. The idea was to use African Christians to build an African church. Crowther was consecrated a bishop in 1864. In the succeeding decades the Niger Mission met fierce resistance from English traders on the Niger River, who accused Crowther's people of encouraging competition on the part of African traders. In the 1880s, as the British government took firmer control over the whole territory, some from the trading community plus a new generation of European missionaries imbued with the new ideas of pseudo-scientific racism tried to discredit the Niger Mission and Crowther. They accused the mission of mismanagement and syncretism, neither of which seems to have been true. But in the frenzy of imperialism, the era of mutuality between Europeans and Africans in the church came to an end and white missionaries reigned supreme.

It has been suggested that here were the beginnings of the movement toward independent churches in West Africa. When some African Christians saw the European church turning its back on their work and discrediting their spiritual maturity, they began to look to other institutional manifestations of the church.

Zanzibar. In 1844 Johann Krapf, a Swiss missionary working for the Anglicans, first began to share the gospel in Zanzibar, without much success. Thirty years later, Livingstone's disciple Stanley, while looking for the source of the Nile, had several conversations about Christianity and European culture with Mutesa, king of Buganda. Arabs were trying to convert Mutesa to Islam. In the end, Mutesa chose Christianity because he perceived the Europeans as potentially militarily stronger than the Arabs (they were not stronger yet, but soon would be). Further, he admired Western technology and appreciated that Europeans had given up collecting African slaves while the Arabs were still active in the trade.

As one would expect in a close-knit society, when the king converted so did many of his people. But conversion to Christianity did not bring harmony to Mutesa's domain. British, French, and Arabs clamored for trade and plotted ways to increase their respective countries' power in Uganda. When Mutesa died in 1884, his son Mwanga did not fully embrace his father's Christianity; Mwanga also continued some of the ancestral rites of previous kings. When some Christian Bugandans refused to participate, he became enraged at their disloyalty. Mwanga had several prominent Christians beaten, tortured, and burned alive in 1885–86. The rest of the decade was taken up with fighting among Bugandans who advocated the ancestral way, those who wanted Arab rule, and the clients of the British. By 1890 the troops of the British East Africa Company had prevailed, and four years later Britain took Uganda as a colony.

British rule brought peace, and integration into a growing network of international trade. The British built schools, roads, and a railroad to the coast. They also gave large tracts of African land to British subjects, on which African labor grew crops for export that made those British landowners wealthy. The period 1890–1914 also brought an expansion to the Ugandan Anglican church: it grew from 200 members after the persecution to about 65,000 on the eve of World War I.

Church growth continued across the denominations throughout the colonial period. Perhaps 20 percent of Uganda's 660,000 people were Protestants in 1911. About 200,000 more were Catholics. Largely through the growing ministries of local African catechists and evangelists, the church grew to 10 million by 1980—80 percent of the country's population. Almost all of these Christians were members of European denominations; very few joined the independent African churches that were so popular elsewhere. Less than 1 percent of Uganda's Christians were members of independent churches in 1980, compared to 18 percent in Zaire, 22 percent in Nigeria, 24 percent in Kenya, and 28 percent in South Africa.

The situation in Tanzania, just to the south of Uganda, during World War I illustrates the complex effects international politics had on African Christians in the colonial era. Tanzania was a German colony and large numbers of local people had become Christians through the ministry of German missionaries. But suddenly in 1916 the British came and put these Germans in concentration camps. African Christians were shocked to find out that European, avowedly Christian, nations would go to war with one another and commit vicious acts against other Christians in the name of petty nationalism. This realization demoralized Tanzanian Christians and contributed to the very slow growth of Christianity in the European denominations there. Independent African churches, by contrast, grew very rapidly.

South Africa

To most observers, South Africa's story is one of conflict between a large black African majority and a small white minority that has dominated and exploited the majority. But to most *Afrikaners* or *Boers*, the descendants of early Dutch colonists, the contest has been between Afrikaners as the oppressed minority and their British colonial overlords—or between God and the forces of evil.

Dutch rule began in 1652 when the Netherlands East India Company parked some sailors and soldiers at the Cape of Good Hope to raise provisions for ships passing on their way to the Indies. The Dutch soon began driving the native Khoikhoi and bushmen out of the Cape area and bringing in slaves from other parts of Africa and Asia. Dutch Reformed Church pastors served the European population, but no significant mission work was done until the 1790s when Moravian missionaries began to evangelize the non-Europeans. Britain conquered the Cape colony in 1795, lost it in 1803, and conquered it again in 1806. Under British rule a great variety of missionaries, from Roman Catholics to members of the Dutch Reformed Church, began to spread Christianity among the native peoples of South Africa.

The Afrikaners deeply resented British rule, not least because the British government unilaterally abolished slavery in 1836. A Boer woman, Anna Steenkamp, expressed her group's resentment:

> It is not so much their freeing which drove us to such lengths, as their being placed on equal footing with Christians, contrary to the laws of God, and the natural distinctions of race and color, so that it was intolerable for any decent Christian to bow down beneath such a yoke; wherefore we rather withdrew in order to preserve our doctrines in purity.[2]

So that same year 5000 Boers took off in wagon trains on the Great Trek, northward out of British-controlled territory and into the lands of the expanding Zulu nation. They saw this exodus in biblical terms as analogous to the patriarchs leaving Egypt and conquering Canaan. Their sense of being a chosen people was only heightened in 1838 when a party of Boers won the battle of Blood River, in which thousands of Zulus were slaughtered. The Afrikaners attributed their victory to God's miraculous intervention.

Ever after, the Boers thought of themselves as people with a divine mission to conquer the Africans and resist the British. In time Britain extended its hegemony over the Boer free states through bloody conquest. But then the British turned around and relinquished sovereignty to a British-and-Boer dominated Union of South Africa in 1910. For nearly four decades, various coalitions of Boer and British descent ruled the country and kept the black African population in subjection. In 1948 the National Party, made up almost entirely of Afrikaners who felt oppressed by the British minority, came to power on an explicit platform, called *apartheid*, of total racial segregation, white domination, and exploitation of Africans. Apartheid began in the Dutch Reformed churches, which maintained separate branches for the black, white, Asian, and mixed race populations. Dutch Reformed theology (in a mutant form) made up the ideological base for the apartheid regime. Most other denominations acquiesced in the racial arrangements, although in later years the Anglican and Methodist churches began to breed dissent. The black and mixed race churches, for their parts, served as incubators for the beginnings of black nationalism.

Independent African churches

Two trends of the colonial era, common across many parts of Africa, deserve particular mention: the rise of independent African churches outside missionary control and the peculiar role that Christian educational institutions played in raising up a generation of black nationalist leaders.

Independent churches appeared in several parts of Africa late in the nineteenth century. These were not churches started by Western missionaries. Rather, African independent churches had separated from the mission-related churches at the start or as a result of schisms. Their number and variety were enormous. Some sprang from Roman Catholic roots, others from Protestant traditions. Some seem to have had almost no connections with Western missionaries at all, while some were direct reactions to missionary activities. There were prominent independent church movements in western, central, eastern, and southern Africa by 1950, with communicants numbering in the millions. If one adds in the several million Egyptian and Ethiopian Orthodox adherents who were the remnants of ancient churches rather than new reactions to

Photo 1

Photo 2

Photo 3

African independent churches blend cultural and religious expressions into the Christian experience. Believers offer ecstatic prayer in an independent church (photo 1). In Ghana, women of the Musama Disco Christo Church parade through the village streets in a Christian celebration (photo 2). An evangelist of the African Apostolic Church of Johane Maranke conducts a service in Zimbabwe (photo 3). (David Barrett, *Schism and Renewal in Africa*, Nairobi: Oxford University Press, 1968)

European imperialism, the independent church rolls encompassed perhaps a quarter of the total Christian population by 1950, and their number was climbing sharply.

African independent churches frequently expressed yearnings for national freedom. It is no accident that there was a particular blossoming of such churches in South Africa. But more important, the independent churches expressed the efforts of Africans to take Christianity into their own cultures and make it African. Typically, a prophet (male or female) would be given a vision and recruit followers. Sometimes the vision included separation from the European mission church. Other times it was the missionaries or African leaders of the European-linked church who drove the prophets out. Often prophets and their followers practiced healings and spoke in tongues. Usually they blended elements of traditional African cultures with European Christianity. For example, some independent churches turned traditional memorials to the dead into Christian ceremonies honoring father, mother, and other ancestors.

Independent church movements frequently took on the culture and boundaries of particular tribes. Such was the case with the Legion of Mary Church, which came out of Roman Catholicism among the Luo people of western Kenya. But in other instances the movements crossed tribal and national boundaries. The revivals led by Harris on the Guinea Coast (see box 13.1) and Simon Kibangu in Zaire, for example, lasted decades, took in millions of people from various tribes, and spawned several independent churches.

Colonial governments often tried to suppress independent churches and arrested their leaders. They saw these movements as dangerous portents of a lack of docility that might grow to threaten colonial rule. Missionaries sometimes shared those views, though they more often worried that the independent churches might stray from European-defined orthodoxy. Certainly they must have felt uncomfortable when power over Christians was in the hands of African visionaries rather than European missionaries. Sometimes the differences were over theology. Some independent churches emphasized the Holy Spirit more and Jesus less than made missionaries comfortable. However, many others achieved a balance.

Conflicts also arose between Europeans and some African independent churches over the continuation of such traditions as polygamy and female circumcision. Many Africans tended to see these as indispensable parts of their culture and social structure. The ability to provide for more than one wife established a man as a person of stature in his community. A Kenyan woman had to be circumcised (i.e., have her clitoris surgically removed) before she could expect to attract a marriage partner. Christians who defended these and other native practices pointed out that nothing in the Bible prohibited them. Yet polygamy seemed at least uncouth to the missionaries and female circumcision seemed downright barbaric.

Such differences were not universal between missionaries and independent church adherents, for the variety of beliefs and practices among independent churches was tremendous. Insofar as it is possible to generalize, one may say that independent churches tended to emphasize prayer, sermons as dialogues rather than speeches, the Holy Spirit, healings, dreams, emotion, and informal structure more than did the missionary churches.

African nationalism

While Africans chafed under European rule, Christian missionaries were busy about their various tasks: evangelism, church planting, medical work, and education. All these activities lay near the heart of Christian charity. Yet they were also seen by some Africans (and some missionaries) as part and parcel of erecting and sustaining colonialism. J. Philip, superintendent of the London Missionary Society in South Africa, wrote in 1828:

> While the missionaries have been employed in locating the savages among whom they labour, teaching them industrious habits, creating a demand for British manufactures, and increasing their dependence on the colony, there is not a single instance of a tribe thus enjoying the labor of a missionary making war against the colonists, either to injure their persons, or to deprive them of their property. Missionary stations are the most efficient agents which can be employed to promote the internal strength of our colonies, and the cheapest and best military posts a government can employ.[3]

In view of sentiments like these, it is ironic that mission schools should have been fountainheads of African nationalism in the twentieth century. This was true in many parts of Africa. Patrice Lumumba (1925–1960), the father of independence for the Congo (Zaire), came from a Roman Catholic family, attended Catholic schools, and at one point intended to become a priest. Jomo Kenyatta (c. 1890–1978), the founder of independent Kenya, was raised near a Scottish mission station where he was educated and, in 1914, baptized. Kwame Nkrumah (1909–1972), prime minister of Ghana and prophet of pan-African nationalism, was a lifelong Catholic and one-time seminary teacher, even though he came to embrace a soft-core socialism as the most appropriate system for Africa's needs. South African nationalists Abel Muzorewa of Zimbabwe, and Desmond Tutu and Allan Boesak of South Africa, were Protestant ministers.

How is it that mission schools gave birth to anticolonial leaders? Partly, it is just because leaders needed to be educated. In many countries the only educational institutions under colonialism were church-run. Also, the schools taught in common, rather than tribal, languages—for

317

example, English and Kiswahili in Kenya. This brought people together across tribal boundaries and made possible the rise of national, rather than tribal, identity and organization. Then, too, the missionaries taught about universal love and the brotherhood of all people, that "in Christ there is neither Jew nor Greek, neither slave nor free" (Gal. 3:28). This whetted many an appetite for freedom. Erasto Muga draws a direct connection between missionary education and the Mau Mau revolt in Kenya: "Christianity may be said to have contributed to the development of Mau Mau in that the Africans saw that the European missionaries who taught love, brotherhood, equality, and justice for all, were so complacent, quiet, and not outspoken against these injustices during the African struggle for freedom and justice."[4]

Most Christian-educated Africans did not become revolutionaries, but a majority of revolutionary leaders were probably educated in Christian schools.

13.3. Kenneth Kaunda and Julius Nyerere

Julius Nyerere and Kenneth Kaunda are examples of nationalist leaders who were educated in Christian schools in Africa. Kaunda (1924–), son of a Christian minister and schoolmaster, led the people of Zambia to independence from Britain and served as president from 1964 to 1991. His theology would in America be called liberal Protestant, and he described himself as a "Christian humanist." He attempted to lead the United National Independence Party and later the state of Zambia according to Christian principles, as can be seen from these excerpts from his writings:

We are all brothers, for we are all children of God, and we should work together. No man can hate his fellow man or try to stop his progress, or keep him from enjoying all the fruits and rights of his country and of salvation in Christ.

While we are all children of our earthly parents by physical birth, we become by spiritual birth, in a special sense, the children of God. And in that spiritual relationship, all men should live in peace and love. If people do not belong to our race, colour or nation we must not hate them, for we are all God's children, and God's children must work together to banish sin from the heart and not to work against one another. . . .

Christian principles can never be split, they have either to be accepted, or sacrificed as they are. In our opinion, for Christian Churches not to condemn racial discrimination, whether practised by black or white governments, or any other groups, is to sacrifice Christian principles. What is immoral cannot safely be passed as Christianly right. . . .

It is my firm belief that we need an increasing number of Christian men and women in all political parties. It was our good Lord who said that his disciples should be the salt of the *earth, but I am sorry to say that many Christians are prevented from joining political parties. For example, many Christian teachers fear to join our U.N.I.P. openly because they fear that they will be put on a black list either by the missionary managers or by Education Officers. . . .*

For all my optimism about Man's possibilities, I do not make the mistake of forgetting that he is God's creature, with all that this means both in limitation and in dignity. Nor do I deny the reality of sin. The besetting sin of the humanist is Pride. The significance of Jesus Christ is surely that He spells death to our pride by showing us how far short of God's design for us we are. He is the Man against whom all men must measure themselves when they try to live the life of love. Then they will discover that He lived the perfect life of love not by

His own unaided ability but because He was totally submissive and obedient to the Will of God.

Julius Nyerere (1922–) was an equally fervent Christian, a Roman Catholic. He was educated in Christian schools and abroad, and later taught school in Tanganyika (present-day Tanzania). As the prime mover in Tanganyika's bloodless independence movement, Nyerere ascended to the presidency of his country in 1962 and served until his retirement in 1985.

Animated by Christian ideals, as well as desires for freedom and national unity, Kaunda and Nyerere showed passionate devotion to social justice for all their people. They fought against tribal rivalries and welcomed people of all races to participate in building their countries.

Asia

Nowhere was the power of European and North American industrial expansion felt more deeply than in Asia. Between 1750 and 1950, nearly all of the Indian subcontinent and Southeast Asia became part of one or another Western empire. China and Japan also were forced to submit to Western influence. Imperialism was not only political and economic. More missionaries, Protestant and Catholic, went to Asia in this period than to any other part of the globe in any era.

Despite this massive effort, only tiny percentages of Asia's huge population became Christian. Yet, toward the end of the era, small, independent Asian churches began to expand in numbers that remade Christianity into an Asian religion.

India

The predominant fact framing the Christian experience in India in these two centuries was the British Empire. Starting about 1750, the British East India Company began piecemeal to extend its power over Indian states and principalities. By 1857 it controlled nearly the entire subcontinent, either directly or through subservient Indian princes. The

Garmooch Bible Women and their students are shown in this photo from the period of British colonial rule of India. (Billy Graham Center)

British brought trains and telegraphs, bureaucracy, and an educational system to organize their domain and extract its wealth. All these superimposed a veneer of European culture, but did little to change the underlying Indian culture and social system. An elaborate system of caste continued to stratify society into discrete groups. The amorphous mass that is Hinduism continued to absorb people's religious energies.

Translation and education

The East India Company discouraged Christian missionaries because it did not want anything to disturb its economic position. Early Protestant missionaries, such as William Carey (1761–1834), had to either battle the East India Company or surreptitiously avoid it if they wanted to do their jobs. Beginning in 1793, Carey, together with a string of assistants, built a mission station at Serampore, a Danish territory near Calcutta that was out of the reach of the Company. There they popularized a new model for missions, based on work in Bible translation and education. They tried to interfere with Indian customs as little as possible, with the exception of *sati*, the practice of burning a wife on her husband's funeral pyre. Carey and later missionaries tried to eradicate this practice without success.

In the 1850s, the British government took over direct control of India from the East India Company. Among its first acts was to proclaim religious freedom. In the preceding decades, in anticipation of crown rule, missionaries had come to India in bunches. They found the Roman Catholic Church in decline, although it had perhaps 1 million members; the Syrian church limited to 250,000 people in a few castes in the south; and the Protestants, with fewer than 100,000 believers, just beginning to make headway. A century later, the Catholic Church had multiplied itself three times, the Protestants had grown tenfold, but the Syrians had increased only slightly. For one thing a schism had split the Syrian Christians into two churches. Protestants progressed by applying large numbers of missionaries and building schools, hospitals, and other social service outposts. The Catholics reversed their decline by belatedly supporting the growth of an Indian clergy.

One particularly noteworthy development of the half-century after 1850 was a tremendous rise in the number of women in ministry in India. Women missionaries came to India as doctors and church planters, although they were largely shut out of such occupations in Europe and North America. Thus missions provided a legitimate arena of achievement for women whose career aspirations were frustrated by Victorian-era gender role limitations. In India, as in China and elsewhere, the majority of missionaries were women, and many missionary women turned extraordinary energy toward reaching and supporting local women. Perhaps the greatest example of a woman ministering to women was Pandita Ramabai. Ramabai was the daughter of an unusual Brahman who believed both his sons and daughters must be educated. Left a widow in 1882, Ramabai went to England where she became a Christian. On her return she began to serve Indian widows and orphans, then branched out into education and the development of craft and agriculture industries to support impoverished Indians.

The cost of discipleship

Conversion to Christianity was no easy thing for Indians, especially those of high caste. Most Indians regarded conversion as capitulation to a foreign encroacher and treated converts as anathema. New Christians were driven out of Hindu villages and took refuge near mission stations. There, as in John Eliot's praying villages in seventeenth-century New England and Vietnam's strategic hamlets in the 1960s, those who consorted with the imperial power were cut off from families, friends, sources of livelihood, and cultural moorings.

Added to the difficulty was the stigma of caste. Evangelists met their greatest success among low-caste and outcaste Indians—people who had little to lose by adopting the foreign faith. The same had been true of Islam in India centuries earlier. And missionary hearts, animated by compassion, particularly reached out to the poor and downtrodden. A few entire castes became Christian. But this meant Christianity was branded as a religion of the lowest orders. In a society so sharply stratified as India, this insured that almost no members of higher castes would dare to convert.

Some attempts to mitigate this difficulty appeared in the late nineteenth and twentieth centuries. Parallel to the rise of an Indian national political consciousness in society at large, Christians sought more recognizably Indian ways to interpret their faith. These often cut across caste, as did the nationalist movement, in trying to express Christianity in Indian terms. Thus Sundar Singh (see box 13.4) became a wandering holy man in the Indian fashion, rejecting Western ways but preaching Christ. H. W. Krishna Pillai composed *Rakshanya Yathrikam* ("The Pilgrimage of Salvation"), a stirring epic poem, and N. V. Tilak wrote hundreds of hymns that expressed Christian messages in Hindu idioms.

Others began to work out Indian theologies and formed Christian *ashrams*, communities of people devoted to lives of simplicity, worship, and service. These were modeled on Hindu ashrams, but with Christian content, to show non-Christians that Christianity did not have to take Western shapes. These were mainly places of meditation, where anyone, Christian or not, could come to meet God in prayer and pursue the Christian faith in a wholly Indian context.

13.4. Sadhu Sundar Singh

The career of Sundar Singh (1889–1929?) demonstrates the difficulties faced by Indian converts to Christianity, but also the possibilities open to Christians as they moved out of European cultural idioms and into Indian patterns.

Singh was the son of a well-to-do Sikh farmer in northern India. Although raised in an anti-Christian atmosphere, he attended a school run by missionaries. At fifteen, during a period of despondency, Singh had a vision of Christ in a ball of light and promptly proclaimed himself a Christian. Driven out by his father, he at first took refuge with Christian missionaries. But soon he determined to become a Christian version of the *sadhu*, a wandering teacher. Dressed in a saffron robe and turban, Singh walked possessionless throughout the subcontinent, speaking about Jesus. Sometimes he was made welcome and given a place to stay, sometimes he was stoned and driven out. In his later years he made trips abroad and wrote about his experiences in India. On a preaching trip to Tibet in 1929 Singh disappeared. Thousands of Indian Christians trace their faith to his teachings.

Keshub Chunder Sen

Christianity also had some effect on Indian society and culture. Not only did Christians such as Ramabai work to ease the burdens of India's unfortunates, Christian ideas also began to creep into Hinduism. In 1820 the Hindu philosopher Raja Rammohun Roy published a book called *The Precepts of Jesus the Guide to Peace and Happiness* in which he embraced Christ's ethical teaching even as he denied his divinity. He founded the Hindu Theistic Church to propagate this teaching. He was succeeded by Debendranath Tagore, the prominent Hindu cultural nationalist and father of the poet Rabindranath Tagore, and then by Keshub Chunder Sen. Keshub would never admit that God could become a man, but he showed a powerful devotion to the person of Jesus. In 1880 he challenged his countrymen: "Gentlemen, you cannot deny that your hearts have been touched, conquered and subjugated by a superior power. That power, need I tell you? is Christ. It is Christ who rules British India, and not the British government. . . . None but Jesus, none but Jesus, none but Jesus, ever deserved this bright, this precious diadem, India, and Jesus shall have it."[5]

Despite such emotion, Keshub could never bring himself to become a Christian because, he said, the Christianity of the missionaries was distorted and Westernized and not true Asian Christianity at all.

China

"Christian missionary activities are the opening wedge for Western imperialism," wrote Tang Liangli. "The Opium War was merely one aspect of the foreign invasion of China: the Missionary War was its logical complement."[6] This was not an isolated sentiment. Most Chinese throughout modern history have regarded Christianity with suspicion as the cultural arm of Western imperialism.

Robert Morrison

The Christian religion was not extinct in China when the Protestant missionary Robert Morrison (1782–1834) reached Guangzhou (Canton) in 1807. Chinese and foreign Roman Catholics continued to worship and spread their faith, despite intense persecution for propagating an illegal religion. Anti-Catholic activities continued through the nineteenth century. For example, in Fujian in 1836, Father Perboyre, a Lazarist priest, was hanged. Such martyrdom devastated a church which for 200 years had depended on foreign leadership. With only a tiny fraction of the mainly foreign priesthood still functioning, China's Catholic church fell into a decline from which it had not yet fully recovered toward the end of the twentieth century.

Unlike their Catholic predecessors, Protestant missionaries did not march boldly into the heart of China making converts. For several decades, they merely hovered on the fringes. Morrison never went farther than Guangzhou, and he and his contemporaries spent most of their careers in Singapore, Penang, and other centers of overseas Chinese population. There they hoped to reach some expatriates who would take their faith into China proper. Only with the rise of European military intervention in the mid-1800s did Protestant missionaries begin to penetrate the interior.

In 1793, Lord McCartney went as the British king's emissary to Beijing, intent on opening up trade with the Middle Kingdom. After requiring McCartney to prostrate himself, the Qian Long Emperor wrote back to George III:

> Entrusted by Heaven to govern all men, the Emperor wishes to inform the King of England as follows:
>
> Admiring the great civilization of China and wishing to partake of it, you, as King of England, have sent envoys across the high seas to congratulate me on my birthday and present a memorial to express your obeisance. Being fully aware of your sincerity in this matter, I granted your envoys the privilege of an audience, gave a banquet in their honor, and provided them with generous gifts. In a previous decree I mentioned the fact that you, as King of England, would receive from me silk, jade, curios, and other valuables. I did this in order to show how much you have been kindly regarded. Yesterday my ministers reported to me that your envoys had made requests on trade matters. Since these requests are clearly a violation of Chinese law, I wish to inform you

that they have been rejected. Since the beginning of trade between China and Western countries, including England, Macao has always been the place where the trade is conducted. Were we only interested in our own welfare, this trade would not have occurred, since China, being so rich in products of all kinds, has no need of foreign trade. However, taking into consideration the fact that some of the Chinese products, such as tea, porcelain, and silk, are important to the material well-being of Westerners, including the British, we have established trading firms in Macao, so that not only Western consumers will be provided with these daily necessities but Western traders themselves will also make a good profit. Your envoys' extraordinary requests indicate clearly that many of you Westerners have failed to appreciate our kindness and generosity.[7]

It was true. China was a self-sufficient empire, the center of the world as the Chinese knew it. As it turned out, the Chinese misjudged Britain's newly acquired military power. But they were right in asserting that the British had nothing to trade that interested them (they preferred cotton and silk to British woolens, for example). Yet silver was draining rapidly out of the British economy to pay for tea and other Chinese goods. In desperation, the British East India Company hit on opium—a powerful, addictive drug that is the basis for heroin—and recruited a network of south Chinese pushers. When the Chinese government tried to stop this illegal narcotics traffic the British sent gunboats and soldiers. At the end of the First Opium War in 1842, Britain claimed access to five Chinese ports for trade, a permanent colonial outpost at Hong Kong, and affronts to the Chinese such as extraterritoriality, which meant a British citizen was not subject to Chinese laws when on Chinese soil. Subsequent gunboat diplomacy by the British, French, Americans, and others resulted in the opening of many more treaty ports and the economic prostration of China before a horde of Westerners.

A colonialist, "Western" Christ

Among those Westerners were Protestant missionaries. In the vanguard was Karl Gutzlaff (1803–1851), a Prussian-American who made several illegal trading and evangelism trips along the south Chinese coast in the 1830s. Etched in the minds of many Chinese is the picture of Gutzlaff standing in the shallows distributing Bible portions while opium was also being unloaded, all under the guns of a British warship. Gutzlaff and other missionaries frequently acted as interpreters for European and American military and trading ventures.

325

Photo 1

Native perceptions of missionaries in colonial states have sometimes been hampered by the Western lifestyles of the missionaries and pressure on them to conform to the colonial lifestyle. Photo 1 of a missionary being carried in a sedan chair and photo 2 of an opulent missionary "bungalow" are near caricatures of this image. More successful, especially in such areas as China, have been natives, perhaps trained by missionaries, who reach out like the elderly Bible teacher in photo 3. (Billy Graham Center)

Photo 2

Photo 3

Not all Protestant missionaries were directly implicated in colonialist exploitation. Many, such as Peter Parker (1804–1888), toiled for years as doctors and educators, as well as seekers after converts. But they, too, enjoyed the special rights of foreigners under the unequal treaties, and they communicated their conviction of the inherent superiority of all things Western. Many Chinese resented them for it. Only a few, such as James Hudson Taylor (see pp. 299–300), were willing to step across cultural boundaries to meet the Chinese on something like equal terms. Although Taylor may have remained convinced of Western superiority, at least he did leave the comfort of the treaty ports, don Chinese clothing, and attempt to adapt his style of presentation (though not his message) to Chinese culture.

Negative images of Christians spread throughout China. One common stereotype was of the "rice Christian." This scoundrel, it was said, converted only in order to receive food or the protection of their extraterritoriality from missionaries. Another misperception was that Christians were cannibals. The idea of the "body and blood" of the Eucharist seemed a bit bizarre and threatening. As in the Roman Empire (see pp. 43–44), tales spread that the orphans taken behind the walls of mission compounds were served for dinner.

At the end of the century, Chinese people, led by martial arts instructors, rose up to try to throw off the foreign yoke in what Westerners called the *Boxer Rebellion*. Among the Boxers' special targets were Christians; scores of missionaries and thousands of Chinese believers were killed. Yet when foreign troops counterattacked, it was to save Europeans, not Chinese Christians.

The number of Western missionaries jumped sharply in the first few decades of the twentieth century. Throughout the first half of the century China was in political and economic chaos. Some missionaries (and some other foreigners) turned to economic construction—helping build roads, and financing irrigation and similar development projects, as well as more usual missionary pursuits.

Before the Revolution

In this chaotic period, some of the foremost leaders of China were associated with missionary Christianity. Sun Yat-sen (1866–1925), first president of the Chinese republic, was a Christian who had obtained his medical education in Hawaii. His successor, Chiang Kai-shek (1887–1975), was apparently not a Christian, but Chiang's wife, Soong Mei-ling, and her powerful family were devout Methodists. Feng Yu-xiang was a Christian warlord reputed to have baptized his troops with a fire hose. Missionaries and other Western Christians took heart in the existence of such people in powerful positions in China in the 1920s and 1930s, hoping that the world's largest country would soon become a Christian nation. However, committed Christians were few in number despite the prominence of Soong and Sun. As China was trying to bring itself together as a modern nation and ward off European and American domination, many young intellectuals studied the idea systems of the West in search of possible models. Mao Ze-dong (1893–1976), for example, studied Christianity in the 1910s before deciding that Marxism had more to offer his country.

Alongside the expansion of missionary numbers and activities there grew an independent Chinese church. The first manifestation of independent development on the part of Chinese Christians was the somewhat heretical *Taiping* movement (see box 13.5). Because the Taiping Rebellion brought immense suffering to China (upwards of 20 million lives were lost), it did little to enhance the reputation of Christianity in Chinese eyes.

Sun Yat-sen (1866–1925) led an unsuccessful coup in 1895 and the revolutionary movement that overthrew China's monarchy in 1911. As leader of the Kuomintang political organization and president, Sun was unable to assemble a governing coalition nor put into place the political and social reforms he had sought. (Embassy of the People's Republic of China)

13.5. The Heavenly Kingdom of Great Peace

Hong Xiuquan (1814–1864) led what must be regarded as the largest Christian movement in China's history. Hong, a native of Southeast China and a member of the Hakka ethnic minority, grew up in a time of intense political turmoil as Europeans pushed for entry into China and the southeast coast became increasingly unstable. A bright young man, he tried and failed three times to pass the civil service examinations that would have guaranteed him and his family a position of power, wealth, and prestige.

After one of these failures, in 1837, Hong suffered an apparent nervous breakdown. He spent forty days in bed, during which time he had a vision. In the vision he was carried to heaven where he was instructed by an old man called the Creator and by an Elder Brother to return to the world and destroy demons. The vision lay fallow for six years, until Hong and his cousin Li read some Christian tracts that had come into their possession. Then the meaning of the vision became clear. The old man was God and the Elder Brother was Jesus. The demons were idols worshiped by Chinese people. Since Jesus' work on earth had not been completed, God was sending Hong to finish the task.

Hong and Li baptized each other and began to preach. Soon their converts numbered thousands who cast off their Buddhist and Confucian origins, smashing idols and ancestral tablets. Local leaders opposed all of this activity. Hong and his followers formed the Society of God-Worshipers (*Bai shangdi hui*) and fled to a remote, mountainous area. There they were joined by a motley assortment of outcasts—ex-bandits, dispossessed peasants, and members of ethnic minorities and secret societies. Hong's lieutenants welded them into a tight organization based on radical principles: (1) Christian faith; (2) a primitive communism; (3) the equality of men and women; and (4) a strict code of moral behavior.

Taking a theme from previous anti-government, millenarian movements, Hong proclaimed the Heavenly Kingdom of Great Peace (*Taiping tianguo*) and began to attack government armies. The Taiping army marched north to establish a capital at Nanjing, and might well have conquered the entire country had not Hong and his lieutenants fallen to fighting among themselves, and had they not been opposed by Western-backed government armies. In 1864 they were finally extinguished in a blood bath at Nanjing.

The Western response to the Taiping movement was positive at first, since it appeared a Christian king might come to power in China. But when it became clear that the rebels intended to overturn property rights and renounce the unequal treaties, Europeans and Americans in China— even missionaries—began to defend the *status quo ante*.

Taiping theology was orthodox in its emphasis on Scripture, its allegiance to God the Father, and its dependence on salvation through faith in Jesus Christ. It broke new ground in asserting that another savior after Jesus was needed to complete the task. In this respect, Taiping Christianity resembled some later Asian sects, such as the Unification Church (see p. 448).

One of the remarkable facts about Chinese Christianity in the twentieth century is the rise of a profusion of independent churches. Many of these were offshoots of Western missionary efforts, but many, like the Taipings, had only the most tenuous connections with outsiders.

By Western labels, these movements ranged from quasi-Roman Catholic to fundamentalist, from Presbyterian to Pentecostal. Some emphasized healing, some evangelism, some the social gospel. The proper dichotomy for understanding indigenous Chinese Christianity is not liberal versus fundamentalist, for China had experienced neither the Enlightenment nor the Industrial Revolution, which were the fountainheads of that split. Rather, these movements divided according to Chinese categories. At one pole were people infused with a Confucian spirit, such as Zhao Zi-chen, who took an activist role in trying to perfect

13.6. Watchman Nee

Watchman Nee (Ni Duosheng, 1903–1972) is the Chinese Christian best known by Westerners. His devotional classics, such as *Sit, Walk, Stand* and *The Normal Christian Life*, have sold hundreds of thousands of copies in Chinese and in translation. What is less well known is his role as the leader of an antiforeign Christian sect.

Ni was founder in 1922 of the Assembly Hall or "Little Flock" movement, which numbered perhaps 70,000 communicants in 700 congregations by 1949. Assembly Hall Christians shunned missionaries and foreign contact, emphasizing the Chineseness of their movement. They did not recognize denominational divisions. They pursued high standards of individual righteousness. Their theology, which drew heavily on the Plymouth Brethren tradition, was individualistic, otherworldly, and pietistic. They emphasized the inner voice of intuition over rational Christianity, and practiced such charismatic gifts as healing and speaking in tongues.

Yet Ni and the Assembly Hall Christians were no mere Chinese analog to fundamentalism. Western categories do not seem to fit the Chinese situation. Most of the vast profusion of Christian groups that have emerged in China in recent years owe their origins to groups similar to the Assembly Hall.

Ni refused to cooperate with the new government after 1949. He was arrested in 1952 and spent twenty years in prison. He died shortly after his release in 1972.

human society in the sight of God along the lines of biblical principles. Such people were active, for example, in the YMCA and in social reform movements. At the other extreme were mystics, such as Ni Duo-sheng (Watchman Nee, see box 13.6) who, like Taoist sages, retreated from the world into pietistic contemplation.

By the time of the 1949 Communist Revolution the church had grown to more than 750,000 Chinese Christians, most of them in church groups independent of missionary activity. In the years after Mao Ze-dong assumed power this Chinese church exploded in numbers and variety.

Korea

If China was typical of the impact of imperialism on Christian witness, Korea was the exception that proves the rule. In Korea imperialism was Asian, not Western, and that made all the difference. Christianity came to be identified, not with imperialism, but rather with active opposition to it. Largely as a result, Christian churches today claim more than a quarter of the Korean population. The spectacular growth of Korean churches after World War II lies outside the scope of this chapter, but the roots of Korean church growth happened in this period.

Christianity was first planted in Korea, not by foreigners, but by a Korean. In 1784 Yi Sung-hun, a Confucian scholar, returned from Beijing a Christian convert and began to tell others about Christ. The first missionaries—Chinese—followed, and were joined by French priests. The government persecuted Christians as had the Japanese government a century and a half earlier, and the church stayed underground. There it became a magnet for dissidents—dispossessed peasants and would-be revolutionists who found a support network among Christians.

Korea was not officially open to Christian missions until the 1880s. Horace Allen came to Seoul in 1884 as a doctor. He healed a prince, whereupon he won toleration for missionary activity. Soon other Protestant missionaries poured in, Presbyterians most prominent among them. The northwest part of the country, around Pyongyang, was the most fruitful ground for the new religion, partly because of its class structure. A marginal economic zone, it was not dominated by wealthy, conservative—and anti-Christian—landlords as was the more prosperous south. Christian missionaries worked mainly in education and medicine, along with church planting.

The Korean Awakening

In 1907 a religious revival swept over Korea much like the Second Great Awakening in the United States a century earlier (see box 13.7). This came at a time of despondency for many Koreans, for their country had just been made a Japanese protectorate. In 1910 it would be annexed. From then until the end of World War II, Christians were outspoken in opposing Japanese rule. In 1919, for example, fifteen of thirty-three signers of the Korean Declaration of Independence were Christians, and Christians organized demonstrations across the country.

A church under persecution

For their pains Christian leaders were jailed and beaten. In one instance the authorities locked the doors of a church and set it afire, burning the congregation alive. During World War II nearly all foreign missionaries except German Benedictines were jailed or forced to leave the country. The Japanese occupiers tried to force all Koreans—Christians included—to revere the Japanese emperor and observe Shinto rituals. Some Christians regarded this as merely a civil requirement and went along; others, who saw it as bowing down to Baal, refused, and were persecuted. As in Europe, out of such situations there arose divisions that would plague the church for generations (see pp. 372–74).

13.7. The Korean Awakening

A series of revival meetings in Pyongyang in 1907 caused Christianity to spread rapidly throughout Korea. An eyewitness account gives some of the flavor of those meetings:

After a short sermon Dr. Lee took charge of the meeting and called for prayers. So many began praying that Dr. Lee said, "If you want to pray like that, all pray," and the whole audience began to pray out loud, all together. The effect was indescribable. Not confusion, but a vast harmony of sound and spirit, a mingling together of souls moved by an irresistible impulse to prayer. It sounded to me like the falling of many waters, an ocean of prayer beating against God's throne. . . .

As the prayer continued, a spirit of heaviness and sorrow came upon the audience. Over on one side, someone began to weep and, in a moment, the whole congregation was weeping. . . .

Man after man would rise, confess his sin, break down and weep, and then throw himself to the floor and beat the floor with his fists in a perfect agony of conviction. . . . Sometimes after a confession, the whole audience would break out in audible prayer and the effect . . . was something indescribable. . . . And so the meeting went on until two o'clock a.m., with confession and weeping and praying.*

*William Newton Blair, Gold in Korea (New York: Presbyterian Church in the U.S.A., 1957), 66–67.

The war forced churches to rely on Korean leadership; they had no missionary overseers. The church had strong native leadership when the war ended. Although missionaries returned after the war and many attempted to resume their positions of dominance, the Korean church was extraordinarily effective at incorporating Western helpers within its structure without letting them dominate.

After the war Korea was divided into Soviet and American spheres of influence. The north, where Christianity had been strongest, now actively persecuted Christians, even though its leader, Kim Il Sung (1912–1994), had been raised in a Christian home. Christians fled south in huge numbers and have opposed the communist regime in the north ever since.

Thus, Christians in Korea were identified with Korean nationalism to the extent that they opposed Japanese rule, then Western missionary domination, and finally Russian-backed communism. In that identification lay their strength and vitality.

Japan

Christians reappeared in Japan in the 1860s from two directions: across the ocean and up from underground. The Tokugawa government's persecution had been very efficient, but it had not eradicated the *Kirishitan*

Young men such as Hiodayu Shimanuki were trained in the late 1800s at the height of missionary influence in Japan. A Bible study class in Harrisburg, Pennsylvania, funded this seminarian's studies under missionaries at Sendai, Japan. (Billy Graham Center)

movement completely. A few thousand covert Christians continued to worship, particularly in southwestern Japan around Nagasaki, a region that was never tightly controlled by the central government.

In 1853 and 1854 U.S. warships forced the Japanese to open their country to trade with the West. For the next few decades the government was in turmoil. The government was completely restructured after the Meiji Restoration of 1868 in an attempt to strengthen the country and repel the Western barbarians.

Some foreigners came to Japan, including some missionaries, although Christianity was still outlawed. In 1863 a group of French priests arrived in Nagasaki and tried to make contact with the remnants of the Japanese church. They succeeded in 1865 when a small group of

334

Christians from Urakami visited the priests. Cautious contacts proceeded for two years but were cut off in 1867 when police arrested 600 Urakami Christians and demanded that they renounce their faith. Three years later the government sent 3400 Christians into exile, scattered across twenty-one provinces. Not until 1873 were they were allowed to return home. An unofficial tolerance began, largely because of pressure from Western governments.

From that point Roman Catholic missions from Europe resumed, with a full complement of priests, schools, hospitals, and other ser-

Niijima Jo. (Billy Graham Center)

vices. Most native believers in time came out of hiding and rejoined the international church. A few, however—the *Hanare Kirishitan*—steadfastly refused to recognize the Europeans' authority and maintained a separate identity.

As in other parts of Asia, large numbers of Protestants poured into Japan with the opening of trade. Medical and educational missions began as soon as treaties allowed, in 1857. From then through the

13.8. Niijima Jo

Niijima Jo (1843–1890) was a young samurai who had no part in the Meiji Restoration. Bound by traditional duty to his parents and his lord, Niijima was troubled and unsure of his identity. Then in 1864 he read some missionary tracts and books about the West and began to see Christianity as a way out from under his yoke.

Shortly thereafter he stowed away on an American ship and ultimately landed in Boston. There he was befriended by ship owner Alpheus Hardy, who sent him to school, then to Amherst College, and finally to

Andover Theological Seminary. In the process Niijima became a Christian and decided to spend his life for Christ and for the Japanese nation.

Greatly impressed by the moral vigor of American education, Niijima determined to create something similar in his home country. When he returned to Japan, he founded Doshisha University for the purpose of educating morally diligent and civic-minded people who would strengthen their homeland. At Doshisha, Niijima was associated with a generation of social activists, many of them Christian socialists, who acted as the conscience and opposition to the dominant forces in Japan's government.

1930s Protestant missionaries played important roles in Japan's development, particularly in the founding of such key educational institutions as Doshisha University. Initially, most converts were former samurai who had been stripped of their positions by the new Meiji government and who had no part in remaking Japan. Throughout the modern era the church was identified with marginal dissident and outward-looking elements, including the Christian Socialist movement at the turn of the century.

The failure of Christianity in Japan

Very few Japanese ever became Christians. Perhaps this was because Christianity stood in a different light in Japan than elsewhere in the Third World. The Western imperial adventure was never as complete in Japan as in Africa, Latin America, or even China. Japan never became anyone's colony. It managed to rid itself of unequal treaties and other quasi-colonial disabilities sooner than did China, and it never suffered neocolonial economic domination as did much of Latin America.

The Japanese were always able to assert a degree of national strength of identity that eluded other Third World peoples. Although there were periods of attraction to things foreign, they were brief. Western culture—Christian or not—never held the allure for Japanese intellectuals that it did for their counterparts in other countries. Japan's emerging economic and military strength from the 1880s through World War II was built on an explicit celebration of the value and uniqueness of Japanese culture. This included veneration of the emperor in the state Shinto cult that emerged in the 1890s. Christianity just did not carry high prestige socially or intellectually. Although Christians were sometimes appreciated for their contributions to Japanese society, they were more often seen as marginal characters and political malcontents—sometimes even as agents of foreign powers.

Southeast Asia

The Malay Peninsula exhibited a pattern of religious succession that was shared to greater or lesser degrees by other parts of South and Southeast Asia. Located at a crossroads for seaborne trade, the peninsula received wave after wave of foreigners. The original inhabitants were animists. In ancient times, Hinduism and Buddhism from India claimed some adherents. From the fifteenth century Arab traders brought Islam and converted the bulk of the Malay population. Portuguese Catholics came in the sixteenth century, followed quickly by the Dutch, who supplanted Catholicism with Reformed Protestantism on the peninsula and throughout the Indonesian island chain. Finally, in the nineteenth century, the British brought a variety of Protestant denominations and official religious toleration. Christianity found few converts among the Malay population, which remained resolutely Muslim, but it did considerably better among Indians and Chinese who came in the nineteenth century with the British to pursue expanding opportunities. But, as in most of Asia outside the Philippines, Christianity remained the religion of only a tiny minority: the colonial masters and a small group of local people affiliated with them.

The Philippines proved to be an exception. There were no Christians in the Philippines when the colonizer Miguel Lopez de Legaspi arrived in 1565 (see p. 213). Thirty years later there were 300,000—about one-half the islands' population. By 1750 virtually every Filipino was a professing Catholic. That startling metamorphosis was achieved by the relentless labors of hundreds of Spanish friars, who not only preached to Filipinos but relocated them out of dispersed villages and into settled towns where they could be supervised and taught (some would say coerced). Masses of people were baptized upon the conversions of their village leaders. The work substantially converted an entire nation in a generation.

Spain lost control of the Philippines in the 1890s, as much because of the rise of Filipino nationalism as because of the U.S. military intervention of 1898. Thereafter, the United States imposed itself on the Philippines as a colonial power (after a long and bloody war) for nearly half a century. Although American-style political institutions and the English language became parts of Filipino culture, American religions did not take root. For a time it appeared Roman Catholics might lose control. Protestant missionaries poured in with the American army of occupation, and they made some converts. Far more significant was the formation of the *Independent Church* in 1902, a secession from the Roman Catholic Church and a repudiation of Spanish domination. The Independent Church won over large numbers of Filipinos, and began to move away from Catholic theology toward Unitarianism. But the Catholic hierarchy fought back. It sued successfully to keep control of church buildings, retired a lot of Spanish priests, and replaced them with Americans and Filipinos. The Filipino Independent Church remained larger than the combined Protestant denominations throughout the twentieth century, but never threatened Catholic dominance again.

Protestants made a dent in Southeast Asia only among certain tribes, such as the Karens and Kachins of Burma, which became almost entirely Protestant in the nineteenth and twentieth centuries, while other peoples around them remained untouched by Christianity.

The Pacific Basin

Christianity—and Western people generally—came to the islands of the Pacific abruptly in the nineteenth century. Europeans and North Americans found out about the islands and quickly came to trade, to convert, and to colonize. But the Christian story here was different than in many other places affected by Western imperialism. Whether because there was less commercial interest, because local societies were too small to resist the power of Western culture, or because native cultures rapidly incorporated Christianity without losing their own distinctives, in much of the Pacific, conversion to Christianity was quick and complete.

Movement of the faith proceeded from east to west. Christianity was planted in Tahiti in 1797 and quickly became deeply intertwined in Tahitian culture. The last place to receive missionaries was New Guinea in 1871. Especially in the early part of the nineteenth century, when island kings became Christians their populations followed. In Tonga, for example, the first missionaries came in 1826. In 1830 Taufa'ahau Tupou, chief of some outlying islands, became a Christian and took the name King George. He extended his power over the rest of Tonga until he had conquered it all by 1852. By that time Tongan missionaries had already gone out to several other island chains.

Christianity and Pacific island cultures fit well together, and Christianity quickly became incorporated into Polynesian culture. Most Pacific people were used to the notion of sacred time, because they were accustomed to taboo days, so they proved to be strict observers of the Sabbath. They spent all day Sunday at worship, prayer, and communal activities. In the eastern islands, a village's entire population would observe prayers morning and evening each day. Traditional village elders became leaders of the new religion. Christian festivals dominated the social life of many communities—not just Christmas, Easter, and saints' days, but traditional occasions such as Melanesia's new-yam festival became part of the Christian calendar. Many European Christian values, such as honesty and generosity, fit well with Pacific virtues. And traditional ideas about marriage were in accord with European marital norms.

But other aspects of Christianity did not fit quite so well. Most islanders were practical, concrete people who did not separate the sacred and secular, nor the natural and supernatural, the way post-Enlightenment Europeans did. What seemed to Europeans to be hopeless materialism—believing in God because he would bless them with good crops—seemed like simple practicality to Pacific peoples. So, too, missionaries were frustrated with Polynesians' lack of concern

These scenes of the Cook Islands, drawn by W. H. Sterndale, appeared in about the 1870s, when Christianity had swept through Polynesia. The "before" scene was captioned "heathen reveling" and more accurately depicts European and North American perceptions of life under paganism than the reality. Even the mode of dress is inaccurate, for Polynesians never wore grass skirts. In the "after" scene only the trees have withstood change, and a trim mission lady finds it prudent to restrain a pig on a leash. (Phaidon Press)

for European obsessions about timeliness and unremitting hard work. They never succeeded in getting Pacific peoples to stop dancing, and they were unable to make Pacific sexual mores—which had been loosening since contact with non-missionary Westerners—conform to missionary rules.

Unlike most other parts of the Third World, no nationalist movement grew up in the Pacific islands, except in Tonga, Samoa, and Fiji, before World War II. But after that war, independence from European governments came to most of the Pacific. At the same time churches were gaining their independence from foreign missions, generally without the kind of struggle that occurred elsewhere. As island cultures and economies connected with the outside world, island Christianity melted into international ecumenical movements and lost much of its island flavor.

Conclusion

The dominant fact of the two centuries from 1750 to 1950 was the spread of European and North American power around the globe. Empire brought extractive economic relationships and political domination to the Third World. It also brought cultural domination, and Christian missions were part of that. During this period Protestants took missions seriously for the first time. They joined their Roman Catholic rivals in spreading the Word of Christ wherever the sword of empire and the ship of commerce went.

Missionaries brought schools and modern medical care to common people in Asia and Africa. They reduced many languages to writing for the first time so that converts might read the Bible in their own tongue. The literacy thus gained was essential to economic progress. Frequently, Christianity meant an improved position for women in traditionally patriarchal societies.

However, the close identification of missionaries with the colonial regimes—sometimes their direct involvement in the colonial enterprise—meant they were much resented by many peoples. A tendency to denigrate local cultures and identify Christianity with Western culture was also resented, as it put pressure on converts to give up their national and ethnic identities for marginal positions in a European-defined social world.

One offshoot of all this was the rise of Third World nationalism, surely the dominant trend of the twentieth century. Missionary educators, often inadvertently, abetted this movement by educating the future leaders of revolutionary movements. Parallel to the rise of nationalist political movements in the late nineteenth and twentieth centuries was the rise of independent, indigenous church movements in much of Africa and Asia.

Suggested readings

General

Latourette, Kenneth Scott. *A History of the Expansion of Christianity.* Vol. 5: *The Great Century: The Americas, Australia and Africa, 1800* A.D. *to 1914* A.D.; Vol. 6: *The Great Century: North Africa and Asia, 1800* A.D. *to 1914* A.D., repr. ed. Grand Rapids: Zondervan, 1970.

Stavrianos, L. S. *Global Rift: The Third World Comes of Age.* New York: Morrow, 1981.

Latin America

Dussel, Enrique. *A History of the Church in Latin America: Colonialism to Liberation (1492–1979),* trans. by A. Neely. Grand Rapids: Eerdmans, 1981.

———, ed. *The Church in Latin America, 1492–1992.* Maryknoll, N.Y.: Orbis Books, 1992.

Willems, Emilio. *Followers of the New Faith: Culture Change and the Rise of Protestantism in Brazil and Chile.* Nashville: Vanderbilt University Press, 1967.

Africa

DeGruchy, John W. *The Church Struggle in South Africa.* 2d ed. Grand Rapids: Eerdmans, 1986.

Desai, Ram, ed. *Christianity in Africa as Seen by the Africans.* Denver: Alan Swallow, 1962.

Falk, Peter. *The Growth of the Church in Africa.* Grand Rapids: Zondervan, 1979.

Hastings, Adrian. *The Church in Africa: 1450–1950.* New York: Oxford University Press, 1994.

Hope, Marjorie, and James Young. *The South African Churches in a Revolutionary Situation.* Maryknoll, N.Y.: Orbis, 1981.

Isichei, Elizabeth A. *A History of Christianity in Africa: From Antiquity to the Present.* Grand Rapids: Eerdmans, 1995.

Moodie, T. Dunbar. *The Rise of Afrikanerdom: Power, Apartheid, and the Afrikaner Civil Religion.* Berkeley, Calif.: University of California Press, 1975.

Muga, Erasto. *African Response to Western Christian Religion.* Nairobi, Kenya: East African Literature Bureau, 1975.

Sanneh, Lamin. *West African Christianity: The Religious Impact.* Maryknoll, N.Y.: Orbis, 1983.

Asia and Oceania

Bays, Daniel H., ed. *Christianity and China: From the Eighteenth Century to the Present.* Stanford, Calif.: Stanford University Press, 1996.

Clark, Donald N. *Christianity in Modern Korea.* Lanham, Md.: University Press of America, 1986.

Covell, Ralph. *Confucius, the Buddha, and Christ. A History of the Gospel in Chinese*. Maryknoll, N.Y.: Orbis, 1986.

Drummond, Richard H. *History of Christianity in Japan*. Grand Rapids: Eerdmans, 1971.

Elsmore, Bronwyn. *Manna from Heaven: A Century of Maori Prophets*. Tauranga, New Zealand: Moana, 1989.

Forman, Charles W. *The Island Churches of the South Pacific: Emergence in the Twentieth Century*. Maryknoll, N.Y.: Orbis, 1982.

Garrett, John. *To Live among the Stars: Christian Origins in Oceania*. Suva, Fiji: Institute of Pacific Studies, 1982.

———. *Footsteps in the Sea: Christianity in Oceania to World War II*. Suva, Fiji: Institute of Pacific Studies, 1992.

———. *Where Nets Were Cast: Christianity in Oceania Since World War II*. Suva, Fiji: Institute of Pacific Studies, 1997.

Kang, Wi Jo. *Christ and Caesar in Modern Korea: A History of Christianity and Politics*. Albany: State University of New York Press, 1997.

Lutz, Jessie, ed. *Christian Missions in China: Evangelists of What?* Lexington, Mass.: Heath, 1965.

Neill, Stephen. *A History of Christianity in India, 1707–1858*. New York: Cambridge University Press, 1985.

———. *The Story of the Christian Church in India and Pakistan*. Grand Rapids: Eerdmans, 1970.

Tuggy, Arthur L. *The Philippine Church*. Grand Rapids: Eerdmans, 1971.

14

The Context for the Modern Church

The meaning of secularity

For many modern Christians the word *secular* conjures up images of militant atheism, libertinism, and perversion. A writer once participated in a panel on "secular literature" at a religious conference prepared to discuss Hemingway and Faulkner, only to discover that the intended topic was pornography. Unfortunately, many Christians do not understand secularity, in spite of the fact that it is the pervasive social and cultural attitude of the modern Western world.

As the Christian message penetrated diverse cultures around the globe it adapted to their distinct thought-forms and ways of life. Such adaptation of Christianity is generally accepted and understood by missionaries and Christian leaders. Yet there is inadequate understanding among Western Christians of their own native cultural context. This chapter explores the meaning of secularity as both the result and basis of modern Western thought. It will examine three approaches Christian thinkers who really understood secularity have taken in relating the Christian message to the world.

According to a popular story, the Emperor Napoleon once asked the astronomer Pierre-Simon Laplace where God fit into his new theory of the universe. The scientist is supposed to have replied with an expression of the secular mindset: "Sire, I have no need of that hypothesis." A very general definition of secularity might be "the non-necessity of God." To a great extent, modern movers and shapers of culture follow Laplace in claiming to have no need of the God-hypothesis to understand and explain the world. The German martyr and theologian Dietrich Bonhoeffer responded to this situation by commenting that God has let himself be edged out of the world as humanity has "come of age" and learned to live without God. Whereas God and the supernatural were once universally considered indispensable by European and American thinkers, that is no longer the case. The average person may still need God to live his or her life with a sense of meaning and fulfillment, but the great public institutions of education, science, politics, and the arts proceed in their works as if God does not exist. That is the meaning of secularity in its most profound sense.

People living in modern Western societies cannot live anything like a normal life without being deeply affected by this secular mindset. Limiting the practitioners of secularism to the few militant atheists or purveyors of pornography simply misunderstands culture. One of secularity's most significant manifestations is the pervasive privatization of religion in Western society. Secularity is not necessarily opposed to God and religion, but only to taking them very seriously in spheres of shared social life where public culture is shaped.

A few vestiges of Western society's presecular era, when religion was the dominant cultural force shaping public life, can be seen in the various forms of civil religion in European and North American countries. For instance, the U.S. Senate opens its sessions with prayer by an official chaplain. While that may be good in the eyes of most religious people in the United States, it does little to change the fundamentally secular process by which Congress works. At no point may a member's personal religious beliefs intrude into the deliberations in an overt way—even if they happen to represent the religious sentiments of the majority of a legislator's constituents. Privatization of religion goes far beyond the so-called separation of church and state, which is also a manifestation of secularity. In almost every sphere of public policy-making, from the highest echelons of government down to the local neighborhood arts council, it is considered inappropriate to raise the issue of God seriously.

Another way secularity deeply affects most modern people, including Christians, without their awareness, is the expectation among members of modern Western society that most of life's problems can be solved by purely secular means. Until a couple of hundred years ago people almost universally considered religious belief integral to individual and social life. Church or synagogue directly or indirectly affected almost every aspect of life. The priest, minister, or rabbi was as necessary as the doctor when illness or injury struck. Religious authorities sanctioned entertainment. The arts (literature, music, painting) were saturated with spiritual symbols and theological themes. The Bible was considered necessary as a guide to social and individual fulfillment and all of life was related to God, since it was a prelude to eternity in heaven or hell. In the modern Western world most people's lives are much more "this-worldly" in the sense that the solutions to life's problems, both large and small, are sought in technology and psychology. Even many Christians see the world as a godless place in the sense that God is relegated to heaven and a few sacred places, such as the church. The world goes on, and life can be lived quite successfully, with or without God.

The seeds of this secularity were sown in the unbelievably destructive religious conflict of the seventeenth century known as the Thirty Years War. This war was partly a result of the Reformation, and it turned Europe into a slaughterhouse. Some scholars estimate that one-half the population of the continent was killed, starved, or sent into exile during the war. As a result, many of the educated elite of Europe became disillusioned with revealed religion and dogmatic theology. They concluded that the religious conflicts of the Reformation gave rise to this chaos and destruction. Enlightenment thinkers believed that if society was to avoid such wars in the future and recover unity, it must base its common life and public institutions on purely nonsectarian, rational philosophies. Critics of traditional Christianity, such as Francois Marie Arouet de Voltaire (1694–1778), heaped literary scorn on the kind of dogmatic arguments and sectarian power-struggles that led to the religious wars of the seventeenth century. Voltaire was not an atheist, but the official church vilified him as an infidel because he promoted a kind of generic religion based on universal religious truths and moral ideas he called *theism*. This natural religion, based entirely on reason, came also to be known as *deism*—belief in a god stripped of all supernaturally revealed doctrines and elaborate trappings of the formal church. Many men of letters and leaders of European and American culture adopted this secularized religion during the eighteenth century and attempted to make it part of the basis for a new order in Western society.

Other factors besides the wars of religion sowed the seeds of secularism in Western culture. Modern scientific discoveries gave rise to a picture of the world as a great machine ruled by natural laws. Political science began to suggest ways in which society could govern itself without recourse to God's laws or any appeal by rulers to their divine right. During the Enlightenment, God and religion seemed to become irrelevant to the worlds of nature and society.

Of course, the harvest of these seeds of secularity would be a long time in coming. The intellectual centers, such as universities, became secularized long before the masses felt the impact of the new worldview.

With rare exceptions it was not until the late nineteenth century that the issue of secular influences in the church and among Christian theologians began to arouse controversy in the pews. Even then, few church members had much understanding of the true nature of secularity. Long before they were aroused to indignation by such secular influences as socialism, evolution, and higher biblical criticism, they were already accepting secularity unawares in the middle-class cultural values of individualism, nationalism, materialism, and privatized religion. Secularity crept up on Western Christians and deeply infected their lives before they noticed. The average Christian of Europe or America around the turn of the twentieth century was much more this-worldly in attitude and aspiration than his or her counterpart of 1600 or even 1800.

Secular views of human nature

The non-necessity of God is the essence of the secular mindset and the hallmark of modern Western life and thought. What does this mean for secular people's understanding of themselves? Can human nature and existence be explained and adequately understood without reference to God? This is one of the crucial questions for both secular and religious thinkers in the modern world. Once God has been excluded as an object of human knowledge, advocates of the secular view say, philosophy can turn to its most important task of understanding human nature. The great Enlightenment poet Alexander Pope (1688–1744) expressed this turn to the human subject in his famous couplet:

Know then thyself, presume not God to scan,
The proper study of mankind is man.

What have the best and brightest secular thinkers of the modern world said about humanity? What does humanity turn out to be without God?

During the nineteenth century various answers to these questions were offered by secular philosophers. Ludwig Feuerbach (1804–1872), the father of modern atheism, said that *"Man ist was er isst"* ("Man is what he eats"). Another German atheist philosopher of the nineteenth century, Friedrich Nietzsche (1844–1900) proclaimed that God is dead, and humans must take the place of God by becoming "Supermen" or masters of their own fate.

These and other secular thinkers have tried to present an alternative to the classical Christian account of human nature and existence. It is necessary to briefly summarize the latter in order to understand the modern secular alternatives. Blaise Pascal (1623–1662) summarized the classical Christian view of humanity with the memorable metaphor: "Man is a king with a broken scepter sitting on a crumbling throne." In other words,

Christians have traditionally defined humanity as the crowning glory of God's creation, bearing God's image, yet fallen into corruption through sin. Pascal emphasized the paradoxical quality of human nature and existence. The human person is both a glorious being of great dignity and value as created in God's image and a miserable wretch as fallen into sin (compare Psalm 8 and Psalm 53). According to Pascal, this inner contradiction is not only biblical, but also corresponds perfectly with real human experience.

To sever the umbilical cord between God and humanity, secular thinkers use the scalpel of Enlightenment scientific reasoning. No reasoning that considers God can correspond to modern science's account of the natural universe. Therefore, so long as one must refer to God in order to understand humanity, they argue, no respectable and responsible account of humanity can be given. The basic impulse of modern secular thinking about humanity, then, is to make God superfluous. Yet beyond this there is no consensus among secular thinkers about how to understand humanity without God.

An autonomous rational self

One of the earliest and most influential secular answers to the question of the human person was that he or she is an *autonomous rational self*. No single thinker gave this answer, exactly; rather it was an assumption among Enlightenment philosophers of the eighteenth century.

This consensus considered the human person capable of discovering truth through the use of innate rationality, without the guidance or authority of tradition, supernatural revelation, or worship center. The roots of this answer go back at least to René Descartes (1596–1650), French philosopher, mathematician, and scientist. Puzzled by the problem of certainty (or lack of it), Descartes closeted himself in a room by a stove one day in the winter of 1619–20 and vowed not to emerge until he had discovered at least one absolutely indisputable truth through sheer thinking. Finally he hit upon it: "Cogito, ergo sum" ("I think, therefore I am"). Unable to doubt his own existence, for the act of doubting presupposes it, Descartes believed he had discovered one item of indubitable truth from which many more clear and distinct ideas could be deduced and proven. What makes Descartes relevant to a discussion of secular thought is his revolutionary method of discovering and justifying knowledge. He began with his own individual experience of thought (including doubt) and based everything else—including his own existence, the existence of the external world, even God's existence—on his own rational subjectivity. This method of knowledge tended to make everything revolve around the individual. Furthermore, it tended to establish the individual's reasoning ability as the touchstone of all truth. These tendencies may not have been intended by Descartes, but they are consequences of

347

his day by the stove that have dominated Western philosophy and popular culture ever since. Beginning with Descartes, the human person became the center around which all things revolve, the "measure of all things." The individualistic and optimistic view of humanity has left an enduring mark on Western thinking in spite of incisive criticism and challenge from other secular thinkers in the nineteenth and twentieth centuries.

A product of forces

Classical Christian thought has seen the individual human person as, first and foremost, a creation of God, dependent on him and in a state of sinful rebellion against him. Secular Enlightenment philosophy has seen the human person as the product of his own will and reason, basically good but not yet fully in control of himself. Both views were radically challenged in the nineteenth century—never more radically than by the German-born social philosopher Karl Marx (1818–1883). Although most people today associate his name only with a socialist utopian economic arrangement, his social theory of human nature represents one of the most profound and influential secular answers to the question of humanity in the modern world.

Marx believed that the human person is the product of social and economic forces. He believed neither in God nor in the autonomous rational self, and so looked elsewhere for determining factors in human life. What he did believe in was the power of an individual's social environment. What really makes a person tick, so to speak, are social and economic class interrelationships. The individual is but a small part of the great drama of history, whose script is written by economic forces of labor, means of production, money, and class warfare. In fact, theologies and philosophies are products neither of divine revelation nor of human reason, but are invented by oppressors to justify and protect their economic interests. Marx believed that a purely scientific account of human nature and existence could be given, once one discovered the laws that govern the economic relationships of people and societies.

Marx's philosophy was forged in the crucible of the Industrial Revolution, which gave rise to extremes of poverty and wealth. He believed that the root problem of society was the economic system underlying the Industrial Revolution—*capitalism*. In one of the most important works of secular philosophy, *Das Kapital* (1867), Marx theorized that the real injustice and source of human misery lies in the exploitation of the working class by the owner class. The chief end or true purpose of humanity, he posited, is realized in production, for humans are basically workers. They are meant to enjoy the products of their labor in a cooperative society where the means of production (such as natural resources and land) are shared by all. Only in such a system can the individual receive the full benefit of his own labor and feel at home in the social and natural environment. Capitalism, he theorized, forces the laborer to sell his labor, and thus himself, to another for less than full value. After all, the essence of capitalism is profit and the way profit is made is by paying workers less than the full value of the goods they produce and then selling those goods at their full value. Marx saw several evil consequences resulting from this economic system: It alienates the worker from labor and its products, alienates the person from self and society, exploits workers at the hands of owners, and develops a two-class society—workers (proletariat) and owners. He predicted that the inevitable result of such a situation would be class warfare. Human nature cannot tolerate indefinitely such an economic and social arrangement. In a burst of utopian optimism, Marx predicted the emergence of a classless society out of the collapse of capitalism because of capitalism's contradiction of human nature. In such a classless society the individual would enjoy perfect freedom from economic exploitation.

Even those who do not accept Marx's specific economic theories often agree that human beings are determined by social and economic forces. Under the influence of Marx many modern secular men and women have come to interpret themselves and all human beings as controlled and shaped by the social and economic conditions into which they were born. They tend to interpret salvation as a change in these conditions that abolishes exploitation and alienation. They are followers of Marx without being communists.

A product of evolutionary process

Another modern secular answer to "What is humanity?" is: *A product of evolutionary processes*. This answer also challenges both the classical Christian view of humanity and the Enlightenment emphasis on human reason and individual dignity. In 1831 English scientist Charles Darwin (1809–1882) began a five-year voyage on the ship HMS Beagle. He was already convinced that species now living in nature evolved over great eons of time from earlier, now-extinct species. On this voyage to exotic places he sought the key to unlock the mystery of evolution—a purely natural mechanism by which species evolve from earlier ones. On the Galapagos Islands in the Pacific Ocean, west of Ecuador, he found evidence that competition for survival causes some species to die out and others to survive. He explained in *The Origin of Species* (1859) that evolution takes place by natural selection. Those species of plants and animals whose inherited or acquired characteristics fit them to their environment survive. Weaker, less adaptable species die off because their inherited physical characteristics are not as advantageous to survival and reproduction. Although Darwin himself did not coin the phrase, "survival of the fittest" aptly describes his theory of natural selection.

Charles Robert Darwin (1809–1882) originally studied at Christ's College, Cambridge, with the thought of entering ministry, but he vacillated throughout his life between agnosticism and faith. He wrote his first views of an evolutionary hypothesis in 1837 but waited until 1859 to publish *Origin of Species by Means of Natural Selection*. (National Portrait Gallery)

In 1871 Darwin published what has become one of the most controversial books of the modern Western world: *The Descent of Man.* Here he applied his theory of natural selection to the question "What is humanity?" *Homo Sapiens*, he argued, is biologically a product of the same process of natural selection that gives rise to all other species. All human characteristics, he believed, can be accounted for by the process of gradual modification of human-like ancestors. Darwin did not shy away from the conclusion that there is only a difference of degree, not of kind, between the minds of humans and the minds of other highly evolved animals.

Darwin himself only applied his secular account of human nature and existence to the physical and mental make-up of human beings. Others applied his idea of natural selection to human social and cultural life. A friend of Darwin's, philosopher Herbert Spencer (1820–1903), theorized that the dominance of certain individuals and groups of humans over others can be explained in survival-of-the-fittest terms. This particular application of the concept of natural selection, ironically and tragically, found great acceptance in conservative religious circles that generally rejected Darwin's theory of biological evolution. Many Protestant preachers of the late nineteenth century railed against Darwin's theory of the origins of species, while defending extremes of poverty and wealth with Spencer's social Darwinism. They interpreted the tendency of the rich to become richer and the poor to become poorer as a law of nature and therefore a law of God. God, they suggested, has made human social life so that those most spiritually and morally fit to lead tend to prosper economically, while those least fit for leadership sink into poverty. A leading advocate of social Darwinism was oil magnate John D. Rockefeller, a Baptist layman. He reportedly used such arguments to justify his cutthroat business tactics to build Standard Oil into a huge monopoly by driving smaller firms out of business.

For many Western people, naturalistic evolution has become the secular alternative to the Christian doctrines of creation and providence. They believe that there is no need of the "God hypothesis" to account for the origin and development of human life. Perhaps more than any other secular viewpoint, naturalistic evolution has forced Christianity onto the defensive in the modern Western world.

The struggle within

The depth-psychological revolution begun by Sigmund Freud (1856–1939) provided another secular answer to "What is humanity?" *The human is a product of unconscious drives.* Freud was an Austrian physician who specialized in nervous conditions. He is the father of *psychoanalysis* and is generally regarded as the father of mod-

Sigmund Freud (1856–1939), the father of psychoanalysis, became a lecturer and later professor of medicine at Vienna University in 1885, where he developed his theories of the mind and emotions. In response to criticism of his approach from religious leaders he became increasingly hostile to theism.

ern psychology. Disillusioned with traditional approaches to diagnosing and treating patients with serious mental and nervous disorders, he began using a new approach. With patients in a state of relaxation he would ask questions, probing deeply into their forgotten memories. He encouraged them to express any and all thoughts that came to their minds. Through this process of "free association" Freud discovered that many neurotic symptoms had roots in deeply repressed bad memories going all the way back to childhood. The person had unconsciously chosen to forget these disturbing events, filing them away in deeply hidden recesses of the mind. Those able to bring these memories to conscious expression and recognize them as the source of their mental illness seemed to experience some relief.

Drawing on his scientific work with mental illness, Freud constructed a total theory of human behavior based on the interplay between conscious and unconscious forces. Every person, he suggested, is, to a great extent, controlled by the unconscious. Freud posited three distinct levels or processes of the psyche to explain human behavior: the *id*, the *ego*, and the *superego*. The id is the unconscious aspect of personality and is ruled entirely by the desire for pleasure. The ego is partly conscious and partly unconscious and is governed by the desire for personal survival.

351

It keeps the id from impulsively doing destructive things in its search for pleasure. It is the id's governess, so to speak. The superego is built upon society's demands and expectations, the social conscience that forces the ego to restrain and repress the id in its hedonistic search for pleasure. Every individual personality is the result of struggle between the id, ego, and superego. In some people this conflict becomes so severe that it causes neurotic behavior or mental illness. However, since it is universally present in human beings there are really no qualitative differences among normal and sick personalities.

Freud's secular version of human personality and behavior is seen by many as a major assault on both the classical Christian and Enlightenment views of humanity. The traditional Christian doctrine of sin is replaced by repression. Guilt is largely reduced to a by-product of the conflict between the id and the superego. Fullness of redemption—wholeness—is an illusion. The Enlightenment idea of humanity fares no better than the Christian view at Freud's hands. Reason is not the governing faculty of human personality. That role is played by the unconscious. Far from being basically good and infinitely perfectible, Freud represents the human individual as fundamentally selfish and controlled by dark forces that can erupt at any moment into pathological behavior. Few of Freud's theories have survived decades of psychological research. However, his basic insights into the role of the unconscious in human life have left an indelible mark on Western culture, revolutionizing everything from education to criminology to advertising.

A self-realizing individual

A final secular answer to "What is the human person?" is: *a self-realizing individual*. As should be obvious from the theories of Marx, Darwin, and Freud, modern secular thinking about humanity has been dominated by explanations that reduce the person to a product of uncontrolled forces and processes. Is the individual then nothing more than an insignificant by-product of society, nature, and the unconscious? What of freedom, dignity, and self-determination? In protest against all views that reduce the individual to a product of blind forces, Jean-Paul Sartre (1905–1980) developed a secular philosophy centered around the radical freedom of the individual.

Sartre's name has become virtually synonymous with *existentialism* in the twentieth century. Reclusive and eccentric, he wrote a massive book of existentialist philosophy, *Being and Nothingness*, while actively participating in the French resistance against Nazi occupation in World War II. He believed that the world humans live in is literally absurd, because God does not exist. He considered the absence of God in modern culture quite obvious. Both the horrors of modern warfare and the freedom of humans to become something through their own will disproved the existence of God to Sartre's mind.

Sartre considered God a product of wishful thinking. Since life in the world would be absurd without God, people create God to give their lives meaning and purpose. Without God, Sartre argued, the human task is to *become* God—to create meaning and purpose in the world for themselves.

The nature of human existence is to transcend all status quo of the social and natural environment through intentional action. Sartre rejected appeals to heredity, or the unconscious, or God as having no validity, for explaining an individual's life situation. Insofar as individuals see themselves as determined by forces or processes outside their control, they are living below the level of consciousness, in inauthentic ex-

Jean-Paul Sartre (1905–1980), an atheist and philosophical communist, was among a group of German philosophers who applied the thought of Søren Kierkegaard in the existentialist movement. Martin Buber, Karl Jaspers, Gabriel Marcel, and Nikolai Berdyaev developed religious forms of existentialism.

istence or "bad faith." The nature of human personhood is not some predetermined set of characteristics, but questioning. The proper human mode of reality ("being-for-itself") is to establish one's own life situation through a freely chosen project of action.

To be authentically human is to create a world—a reality—which one has chosen for oneself. The authentic person refuses to be locked into someone else's reality. Sartre's own project involved living a life of radical, even revolutionary, activism while shunning publicity and society's acclaim. In 1964 he was awarded the Nobel Prize for Literature, but refused to accept it. His life of intentional nonconformity was his way of realizing his own individual selfhood through freedom.

Sartre's existentialist philosophy has had great appeal to many people in the modern Western world who cannot accept God or the deterministic versions of secular thought. If Marx, Darwin, or Freud was right, humans are to a very large extent mere products of forces beyond their control. Freedom is an illusion and the dignity of the individual is a myth. But secular men and women who fly to existentialism as the savior of freedom and individual dignity should realize that Sartre considered true freedom an awful burden. The kind of freedom he envisioned could exist only in an absurd world and would always coexist with nausea—a feeling of vertigo like a pilot whose plane is lost in thick clouds, who cannot tell which direction he is going or whether he is upside down or right side up. In a world without God—a truly secular world—this is the experience of many people and so they are drawn to the gospel of existentialism with its message of the individual's power to create a realm of meaning and value.

The influence of secularism

Secular ideas such as these permeate all aspects of life in the modern world. One does not have to study the Enlightenment philosophers, (Marx, Darwin, Freud, or Sartre), to be deeply affected by them. Their ideas, sometimes badly vulgarized, are the common stock of literature, art, journalism, politics, educational theory, and even religion. The average Christian is greatly influenced, consciously or not, by these secular philosophies. The pastor likely was trained in a theological seminary in which modern thought and its relation to the gospel was a major focus of study. Preaching, worship, pastoral counseling, methods of church growth, even Sunday school curricula are inevitably affected in some way by secular thought. As noted, fundamentalist preachers and churches have often accepted social Darwinism while railing against Darwin's theory of biological evolution. Pastors and chaplains have been trained in "clinical pastoral education," based on the theories of Freud and other secular psychologists. The *social gospel* and *liberation theology*, both influenced by Marx, have exerted extreme pressure in Christian thought and church life. A richly diverse school of modern theology is called *Christian existentialism*.

How should the church and thoughtful, reflective Christians relate faith to secular culture? That question is as pressing as the one early Christians faced in the Roman Empire 100 years after Jesus: How should Christians relate this new faith to pagan culture? Pagan thought and life (Hellenism) was the context in which early Christianity found itself, and secular thought and life is the context in which modern Western Christianity finds itself. Finding the proper way to relate the old message to the new context is one of the most urgent ongoing projects for Christians.

Christian responses to secularity

Modern theologians have tended to follow three main patterns of relating Christianity to secular thought: (1) accommodation; (2) reaction; or (3) mutual transformation. Three notable Christian thinkers—Paul

Tillich, Karl Barth, and Reinhold Niebuhr— illustrate these patterns. Each was something of a celebrity in mid-twentieth century Western culture. Each one was featured on the cover of *Time* magazine, a hallmark of celebrity status in Western society.

Accommodation

Paul Tillich (1886–1965) appeared on *Time*'s cover in March 1959. The story about him was entitled: "A Theology for Protestants." It might better have been: "A Modern Theology for Secularized Protestants." Tillich's theological system is one of the most creative and controversial modern attempts to adapt the Christian message to secular culture.

Paul Tillich (1886–1965)

Tillich's father was a pastor, and eventually an important official, of the Lutheran state church of Prussia. Young Tillich grew up in Berlin, where he received the finest education possible, eventually earning a Ph.D. in theology. He was ordained into the ministry in 1912 and served as an army chaplain during World War I. The horrors of war, the post-war political chaos in Germany, and his study of modern existentialist philosophy convinced him that Christians must rethink and even radically revise traditional concepts of God and his activity in the world. As a professor of theology at the University of Frankfurt during the 1920s, Tillich came into conflict with the National Socialists (Nazis) then beginning their rise to power in Germany. He openly warned German Christians against this new paganism and called them to recognize the cross and the swastika as absolutely contrary symbols. When Adolf Hitler came to power in 1933 Tillich was forced to flee Germany to avoid arrest by the Gestapo. He settled in America, teaching theology at three of the most prestigious theological institutions: Union Theological Seminary, Harvard Divinity School, and the University of Chicago School of Divinity.

Between 1955 and his death in 1965, Tillich gained a reputation as one of the world's most creative and ingenious religious scholars. Harvard appointed him University Professor, a special post that allowed him to teach any subject he wished. He drew enormous crowds to special lectures around the country, and students flocked to study under him, arriving at his classes up to an hour early to be assured a seat. He published numerous books, including a massive, three-volume *Systematic Theology*.[1] His homeland of Germany recognized Tillich's greatness and awarded him the Hanseatic Goethe Prize, a high national honor, in 1958. In 1965 the U.S. Supreme Court quoted from Tillich's theology in a decision ruling that one does not have to believe in God in any traditional sense to be a conscientious objector to military service. His influence on American and European intellectual life cannot be overestimated.

As a Christian thinker Tillich's primary concern was to communicate the content of Christian faith to modern secular people in a way they could understand and accept. Toward the end of his life he told an audience that "My whole theological work has been directed to the interpretation of religious symbols in such a way that the secular man—and we are all secular—can understand and be moved by them."[2] He aimed to be an apostle to intellectuals and always tried to show how Christianity and modern secular thought do not have to conflict. He attempted to bring them together in a synthesis through the method of correlation. In correlation Tillich looked to philosophers and scholars of contemporary culture to discover the questions modern men and women were asking. Then he looked to divine revelation, as he framed it, to provide the answers. The questions, he argued, must determine the *form* of the answers theology gives, while divine revelation must determine the *content*. Thus, theology should not choose between secular culture and the gospel, but should bring both into a creative synthesis.

Tillich's method of correlation might be illustrated by returning to the question, "What is humanity?" He believed that this question was being asked in the modern Western world in terms of existentialism: "What is the cause of alienation and what can overcome this experience of despair and give wholeness and meaning to the individual's life?" One of the most profound areas of Tillich's thought is his careful analysis of the human predicament. He listened attentively to existentialist philosophers, depth psychologists, and sociologists and concluded that an overwhelming anxiety in the face of life's apparent absurdity and inevitable death leads people to ask about the possibility of avoiding total despair. What people seek, he said, is a power that gives them "courage to be" in the face of the threat of "non-being." In other words, they seek a firm basis for trust in the ultimate meaningfulness of life in view of their own death.

In order to help secular people understand their experience better, he turned to theological ideas about humanity's fallenness expressed in secular philosophical terminology. The source of human alienation and anxiety lies in estrangement from our true essence. The story of Adam and Eve's fall into sin in Genesis 3 is a mythological depiction of this universal human condition. According to Tillich, there was never a time when humans lived in paradise and literally walked and talked with God. Rather, this is a way of expressing an ideal state of life in which human beings would be in perfect harmony with themselves and their environment. They would be in a state of dreaming innocence—blissfully ignorant of failure, pain, loss, and death.

This condition does not describe the actual existence of humans. Rather, they experience life as a tension between their essence (being what they really are supposed to be) and their actual existence. To Tillich, this was the real meaning of the fall: that all humans experience this inner conflict and are estranged from their own being. This illustrates how he used a biblical symbol, the fall, to speak to modern men and women about an existential condition that cannot be adequately explained or solved by secular thought.

How did Tillich represent the gospel, then? In terms of the question to which it is the answer—Tillich gave it a secular form. He tried to show that the only solution to the plight of estrangement would be belief in a power that could reunite human existence and essence by creating a new being beyond the inner split that causes anxiety and despair. Drawing on a long history of philosophical language, Tillich called the negative forces in human existence *non-being* or the *threat of non-being*. The solution to this threat, he suggested, is the realization of a power of being to overcome the threat of non-being. Where such a power is fully manifested and realized in a human life, a new being would be revealed. This new being would heal the conflicts and reunite essence and existence. Its example would offer hope and courage to the rest of humanity.

The new being would be "salvation" in its original sense of wholeness, unity, completeness. According to Tillich, the new being has appeared in human history in the man Jesus Christ. His life was free of the estrangement that leads to alienation, anxiety, and despair. He was at one with the ground of his own being, and therefore with his own human essence. This is the real "good news" for modern, secular men and women. A power of being overcomes the threat of non-being. Jesus Christ offers the power of hope and courage to conquer despair.

What about God in Tillich's updated, secularized version of the gospel? There has been much debate about his concept of God, because he radically reinterpreted God as the "Power of Being," the "Ground of Being," and even "Being Itself." He believed that traditional ideas of God are simply unbelievable for modern, educated men and women. Modern people cannot accept a supernatural, person-like God who exists in heaven and occasionally interferes in nature and history. Yet, his alternative seems to many Christians to be vague and impersonal—a kind of force or depth-dimension in life, rather than the personal Father revealed by Jesus.

Some have even suspected that Tillich was an atheist—a charge he almost invited by saying that "God does not exist." He apparently meant that the anthropomorphic (human-like) God of some belief-systems does not exist, but a God beyond that God does exist. Tillich's "God beyond God" seems to be a divine Power, an infinite Being that is the true, inner source of meaning in life, but not a supernatural, personal heavenly Father. It is something like the Soul of the Universe, and union with it is humanity's ultimate escape from alienation and despair.

Besides revising the classical Christian doctrines of God, humanity, sin, and salvation in terms of secular philosophy, Tillich also rejected all supernaturalistic ideas, such as Jesus' pre-existence, the virgin birth, a bodily resurrection, and the second coming. To him these were all symbols that express the significance of Jesus as the new being—the model of the ideal unity of humanity with Being Itself.

Tillich accomplished one of the finest accommodations of the gospel to contemporary culture which the Christian world has ever seen. To many, it is hardly recognizable, so overlaid is it with the language and thought-forms of secular philosophy. Yet many of his concepts have become parts of the common stock of religious language among cultured intellectuals: *Ground of Being, new being, ultimate concern, estrangement*. These witness to his enduring influence.

The average Christian in the church pew may never hear Tillich's name, yet still may be influenced by his ideas. This would be most likely in the more liberal churches where his accommodationist approach to relating the gospel to secular culture has had a tremendous impact on ministers, theologians, and denominational leaders. Liberal Christians of all denominations often find his idea of God, for instance, much more acceptable in the modern, scientific world than the older, classical theism that presents God as wholly other than this world, existing in eternality and self-sufficiency.

Reaction against secular culture

When scholars and pundits look back over the twentieth century to identify the most influential politician, business leader, scientist, and writer, one name will stand out as the only clear choice for most influential theologian: Karl Barth (1886–1968). Only a few Christian thinkers belong in the same category of influence, among them Augustine, Aquinas, Luther, and Calvin. *Time* honored him with a cover story in 1965. During the centennial of his birth in 1986 dozens of scholarly meetings were held throughout the Western world to continue the task of interpreting his thought. Very few met in honor of Tillich, who was born in the same year. Tillich's influence seems to be on the wane in the last years of the twentieth century. Numerous volumes have been written exploring

Karl Barth (1886–1968)

Barth's theological contribution, however, and more continue to appear every year. Scholars continue to collect, edit, and publish his life's correspondence. All this attention is given to a man who embodied the second Christian response to secular culture: *reaction against it*.

Like Tillich, Barth was the son of a pastor. His father was a minister and theological teacher of the Reformed Church of Switzerland. The younger Barth decided to become a theologian at the time of his confirmation and went on to study with some of the leading liberal theologians of turn-of-the-century Europe. He mostly accepted the early accommodationist approach to secular culture and looked upon Christianity as humanity's search for God through a critical, historical faith. After his university studies in Germany, Barth became pastor of the village church in Safenwil, Switzerland. He struggled mightily to preach his liberal theology to his working-class congregation, but he found it was largely irrelevant to their lives. Deep disillusionment with liberal theology set in when Barth read a declaration of support for the German Kaiser's militaristic war policy at the beginning of World War I and saw that almost all of his liberal theological teachers had signed it.

During his thirteen years of pastoral work in Safenwil, Barth underwent a gradual but marked transformation. He became convinced that Christians must stop allowing secular culture to determine how they think about God and must rediscover supernatural, divine revelation as the one and only truth about God. Instead of "man's search for God," he began to seek truth in God's Word to humanity. This Word of God is not identical with Scripture, according to Barth. Instead, it is identical with Jesus Christ, who was and is God's full self-revelation. Scripture and the preaching of the church *become* God's Word in the event of Jesus Christ becoming real and active in people's lives. For Barth, religious and philosophical ideas about God are generally contradicted by God's Word. It is the latter that must be obeyed by Christians in mind as well as in heart.

In 1919 Barth published a book entitled *Der Römerbrief* (*The Epistle to the Romans*) containing these and other radical ideas. Like Augustine, Luther, and Wesley, he believed he had found the truth for his time in Paul's letter to the church of Rome. One historian commented that *Der Römerbrief* fell like a bombshell on the playground of the theologians. Barth's strong affirmation of God's wholly otherness and of humans' inability to find God through reason and experience radically challenged the liberal tendency to identify God with the highest and best of humanity. Whereas liberal Christian thought tended to depict humans as basically good and capable of infinite perfection, Barth showed that Paul pictured humans as incapable of anything good apart from God's grace. With this book Barth set himself against secular culture's influence in Christian thought and declared theology independent of secular thought in general.

In 1923 Barth moved to Germany to teach theology and, like Tillich, soon fell into conflict with the Nazi movement and German Christians who supported it. He considered the German churches' support of Nazism an extreme idolatry of accommodating the gospel to secular culture. Barth was forced out of Germany in 1935 because of his role in an anti-Nazi denomination that declared only Jesus Christ, and not Hitler, to be God's Messiah. He spent the rest of his life teaching theology at the university in his hometown of Basel, Switzerland. Before his death he published a thirteen-volume systematic theology entitled *Church Dogmatics*.[3]

Barth's way of answering the question "What is humanity?" typifies the reactionary approach to secular culture. Instead of looking to philosophy, psychology, sociology, or other secular disciplines among the human sciences, he looked to Jesus Christ and asked, "What is revealed about humanity in Jesus?" Barth believed that one cannot discover true humanity anywhere but in Christ. Of course, all kinds of interesting information about human nature and existence can be provided by the human sciences. However, they simply cannot tell what *really* needs to be said about humanity. They cannot discover humanity's true being. That is because, Barth said, the greatest illusion humans have is that they can disillusion themselves. In other words, sin has so deeply affected the human mind that people cannot know themselves as they really are. In Jesus Christ God has revealed the truth about humankind, as well as about himself. Faith in Christ, which is possible only through an event of God's grace, is the sole foundation of true understanding.

According to Barth, Jesus Christ reveals that to be truly human is to be in relation to God. There is no such thing as godless humanity, although there is the reality of sinful rebellion against God. Even in the midst of this rebellion, Barth said, humans remain before God—encompassed and fully determined by God's sovereign will. Furthermore, humans are revealed in Jesus Christ as creatures who are called by God and able by his grace to respond. Most importantly for Barth, humans are part of a particular history—the history of God's primal decision to create and redeem humanity through Jesus Christ. Clearly, Barth's view of humanity was God- and Christ-centered. According to him, it is impossible to have a secular understanding of humanity, for that would be a misunderstanding. Humans come to know themselves truly only when they realize their proper place in God's plan and listen to and obey the Word of God to them.

Finally, Barth saw humanity as related, not only to God, but also to other human beings. Jesus Christ discloses that true humanity is always fellow-humanity, or humanity lived in community. This is the image of God referred to in Genesis 2:18–25 and elsewhere. It is epitomized in the man-woman relationship, which symbolizes the interdependence of all humans. Apart from Jesus Christ, Barth believed, humans do not know that they are created for each other and that true fulfillment of their humanity comes only in and through living wholly for others.

Barth's view of humanity broke radically with all modern secular or religious attempts to understand human nature and existence by beginning with natural knowledge. He dealt with the "acids of modernity," such as skepticism and naturalism, by neutralizing them. They have no validity in Christian thinking about God or about humanity. The task of the faithful Christian is not to meet secular thought halfway by beginning with its questions and trying to fit divine revelation answers to them. Rather, the Christian's task is to refuse to take secularity too seriously and to take God's revelation in Jesus Christ absolutely seriously. To Barth this revelation's truth has nothing to do with the historicity of the documents or the Person and life of Jesus Christ. These become real as the Spirit applies them to the heart.

Barth has contributed a great deal to the arsenals of those modern Christians who would combat secular culture rather than accommodate it. Like Tillich, he left a legacy of popular phrases and concepts that are most often heard among those who take a reactionary stance toward secularity: God as Wholly Other, Jesus as the Man for Others, Humanity as totally determined by God's grace. Christians who have never heard Barth's name are indebted to him for his powerful resistance to the cultural subversion of Christian faith against secularity in the modern world.

Mutual transformation of Christianity and culture

Reinhold Niebuhr (1892–1971) was an American-born, Protestant theologian who represented the third major approach to relating Christianity to secular culture: *mutual transformation*. That does not mean that he allowed secular culture to have equal weight with divine revelation in his theology. However, he sought to relate the two in a positive way and was always concerned to show the relevancy of the gospel to the modern situation, as well as how to show how the modern situation determines the shape of the gospel message.

Niebuhr also was a minister's son. His father was a pastor of the Evangelical Synod of North America, a denomination of mostly German Reformed immigrants that later merged with other bodies to form the United Church of Christ. Choosing to follow in his father's footsteps, young Niebuhr studied theology and intended to pursue a career in the ministry. At Yale Divinity School he showed early signs of outstanding scholarly potential, but chose to enter the pastorate instead of going on to earn a doctor's degree in theol-

Reinhold Niebuhr (1892–1971)

ogy. In 1915, at the age of twenty-three, Niebuhr became pastor of Bethel Evangelical Church in Detroit. During his thirteen-year tenure there he built a reputation as a radical social activist, speaking out frequently and vociferously against the rich and powerful industrialists who called themselves Christians but showed no compassion for their poor employees or for smaller businesses among their competitors. He became disillusioned with both accommodationist and reactionary approaches to theology and social ethics. The former he considered too sentimental and naïve in its view of humanity. The latter he considered too concerned with orthodox doctrine to be relevant to modern needs and problems.

In 1932 Niebuhr joined the faculty of Union Theological Seminary in New York City. Until his retirement in 1960 he was one of America's most respected and influential theologians. He trained a multitude of adoring students who called him "Reinie" and often packed the living room of his apartment for informal evening discussions. He traveled widely throughout Europe and America, speaking at hundreds of universities, seminaries, churches, civic clubs, and conferences. He founded two journals and wrote over a dozen books and hundreds of editorials, commentaries, and articles. Niebuhr served as an advisor to the U.S. State Department. His picture appeared on the cover of *Time* in 1948. Martin Luther King, Jr., and President Jimmy Carter publicly acknowledged their indebtedness to Niebuhr's theological and ethical ideas. Only two other American theologians rank near Niebuhr in influence: Jonathan Edwards and Walter Rauschenbusch. In many ways he represents a blending of these two, emphasizing with Edwards the sinfulness of humanity and the sovereignty of God, and with Rauschenbusch the social and ethical dimensions of the gospel.

Niebuhr's entire career was centered around his concern to bring together the Word and the world. His ultimate commitment was to the biblical message, although he saw the Bible as neither supernaturally inspired nor infallible. Like Barth, he considered the Bible to be a human book through which God speaks. Niebuhr had little or no interest in the details of the Bible. His commitment was to the fundamental worldview communicated through the Bible's symbols and stories. His secondary commitment was to the concrete, historic situation of the modern world. He believed passionately that the biblical message helps people to understand themselves and life in the world better than any other view of reality. In fact, for Niebuhr the truth of the biblical message is shown in its illuminating power—that is, in its ability to make sense of the widest possible range of human experiences and situations.

More than any other major contemporary Christian thinker, Niebuhr believed that the proper point of discussion between secular culture and Christianity lies in the study of humankind. In 1939 he was invited to deliver the world's most prestigious theological lecture series, the Gifford Lectures in Scotland. The subject he chose was, "The Nature and Destiny of Man." These lectures were later published in a two-volume work by that title that has become a classic in modern theology. In these lectures Niebuhr hardly seems more positive toward secular culture than does Barth. He surveys all the major Western views of humanity since the Renaissance and finds that they have tended toward two opposite extremes—a romantic idealism that overestimates the freedom and rational power of humanity, and a pessimistic naturalism that reduces humanity to a machine-like product of nature.

Much of *The Nature and Destiny of Man* is concerned with exposing the inadequacies of these philosophies and their hybrids. Both, for instance, destroy the essential dignity and freedom of the individual and reduce sin and evil to necessary results of natural causes. Niebuhr writes about the "Easy Conscience of Modern Man" and argues that secular versions of human nature have worked together, in spite of their differences, to excuse humans from responsibility for evil. Humans are either totally conditioned by natural causes (naturalism) or they are so rational that sin and evil are only the results of ignorance that will inevitably be overcome through education and social engineering (romanticism). Niebuhr concludes that modern humans are so sure of their essential goodness because they are so wrong about their status. They do not recognize that they have a freedom of spirit that transcends natural causes and they also have reason, which makes them responsible for evil in the world.

Against secular philosophies of human nature, which lead inevitably to humanity's easy conscience, Niebuhr proposed a paradoxical combination of transcending freedom (the image of God) and creatureliness. That is, humans are not simply animals who act out of conditioning and instinct. Nor can they be elevated to pure freedom without limits. They have *finite freedom*, which sets them apart from both animals and God. Niebuhr also defended the Christian doctrines of the fall and original sin as the best explanations of the actual condition of humanity in the world. Clearly Niebuhr was highly critical of secular culture, but he was not so reactionary in his stance toward it as was Barth. He maintained a tension between the gospel and its view of humanity, on the one hand, and secular views on the other hand. He found a glimmer of truth in the most anti-Christian philosophies and was quick to acknowledge the genuine contributions of secular thinkers. He presented a strong critique of Marxism as a view of humanity that cannot account for the spiritual dimension of the human person. However, he cautioned that this error must not blind Christians to Marx's positive contribution, discovery of the role economic interests play in humans' use of reason. In this Marx reinforced the Christian concept of depravity—that all human faculties and powers are corrupted by sinful selfishness. Niebuhr saw valuable insights in many other secularists as well. He was most critical of them when he believed they contradicted the basic biblical truths of a humanity created in God's image and yet sinfully fallen.

Niebuhr demonstrated his mutual transformationist approach in his application of Christian truth to social problems. In fact, he is much better known for his social ethics than for his theological writings. He believed two principles should guide Christian actions in relation to world problems: love and justice. First, Jesus' teaching about loving one's enemies is an ideal—an impossible ideal in certain situations. Real love, as Jesus taught and lived it, never resists evil and always turns the other cheek. Yet the efforts of some Christians to base social and even international relations on Jesus' love ethic are hopelessly naïve. Should Christians love Hitler and the Nazis who commit genocide against the Jews and enslave Europe? Should America love the Soviet Union and let it carry out its aim of dominating the world? Should oppressed workers love their corporation's capitalist owners and never strike for higher pay while their children go without shoes and health care? Niebuhr answered that selfless, passive love may be a possibility in small-scale relationships, but it cannot be the basis of large-scale social relationships.

Second, in society at large the closest approximation of the ideal of love is justice—a kind of rough-and-tumble working-out of rights that often involves conflict and coercion. According to Niebuhr, the duty of every Christian is to work for justice in society, even though that is a less perfect norm than love. Many Christians active in the civil rights and anti-war movements of the 1960s were influenced by Niebuhr's view and appealed to it to justify their confrontational tactics.

In many ways Niebuhr walked a fine line between modern, secular culture and traditional Christian orthodoxy. He refused to choose exclusively for one or the other, although his primary commitment clearly was to the gospel and the biblical worldview. His influence is seen in the fact that most thinking Christians in the Western world today take some form of Niebuhr's approach. They are eager to relate their faith in some positive way to secular knowledge without losing the distinctiveness of that faith. Niebuhr's influence is also reflected in the emphasis on justice in both Roman Catholic and Protestant social ethics. The average lay Christian may never know who Reinhold Niebuhr was, but he or she will nevertheless be touched in some way by his creative contribution to the ongoing search for the right way to be "in the world but not of it."

Tillich, Barth, Niebuhr, and Old First Church

Fred Johnson listened carefully to the new pastor. During his forty years as deacon and head usher at Old First Church in downtown Capital City he had sat under the ministries of three pastors, including this fresh-faced, eager newcomer. As minds tend to do during Sunday morning sermons, his wandered back to Rev. Dr. Van Dyke, who came to this venerable pulpit the same year Fred joined. Dr. Van Dyke wore robes as he led worship—a symbol of his scholarly training and interest in liturgy that had shocked the congregation at first. Fred smiled slightly as he remembered how the little tempest-in-a-teapot over robes had been drowned out by the fuss made when Dr. Van Dyke preached that modern people have trouble accepting miracles and the supernatural and need new answers instead of old theological clichés. One of his first sermons was "Man's Search for Meaning." He had talked about how even people who call themselves atheists because they cannot believe in a man upstairs have an ultimate concern that points them toward a power greater than themselves. Dr. Van Dyke called that power the "Ground of Being" and didn't mention "God" once in that whole sermon.

What a commotion! About a third of the congregation had fled to some church out in the suburbs that folks called "fundamentalist." Several folks from the college nearby joined, however. They said they were attracted to a church where the preacher talked their language.

Fred continued to daydream as the new pastor began to wind up on his second point. He remembered the convulsions the congregation went through around 1965 when some so-called Christian theologians announced that God was dead. Some folks in the church sort of blamed Dr. Van Dyke and his friends for some of that and determined to find a preacher who knew what the gospel was all about. About that time, Dr. Van Dyke graciously resigned to take up a position at the Council of Churches.

Pastor Will Thompson took up the duties of senior minister. Fred's face took on a slightly wistful look as he remembered those years of Pastor Will's preaching. His first sermon was, "The Word of God Versus the Word of Man." He said that the church needs to stop following after every fad, fancy, and whimsy of secular culture and, listening carefully to God's Word, speak prophetically to the world around it. He pounded the pulpit a little when he said, "It is not our thoughts about God that matter, but God's thoughts about us!"

Unlike Dr. Van Dyke, Pastor Will hardly ever quoted Freud or Einstein. Almost every sermon was about how the world needs to recover a sense of God's almighty presence and humanity's sinfulness. "God is in heaven and you are on the earth! And don't ever forget it!" was one of his favorite cryptic phrases. Fred shook his head slightly and furrowed his forehead as he remembered the many good folks who left to find other churches because Pastor Will was "just throwing the gospel at people's heads like a rock—Take it or leave it!" They had preferred Dr. Van Dyke's cautious, reasonable approach to Christianity.

What would this new pastor be like, Fred wondered? His mind had been wandering for about two whole points of the sermon now, so he thought he'd better listen more carefully. Rev. Andrew Carpenter was just saying that if the church of Christ is going to survive in the modern world it had better listen to the voices of people outside the church and learn how to meet their needs—spiritual, physical, and intellectual. However, he warned, it must not lose itself in the world by becoming overly committed to society's agenda for the improvement of humanity. The church must tell the world that it is sinful and cannot save itself through education and social programs alone. On the other hand, the church had better realize its own sinfulness and get down off its high horse and work alongside all kinds of folks to defeat oppression and suffering.

Fred couldn't remember the sermon title. He picked up a worship folder and found it: "The Word of God for Every Human Need." The warm sun was streaming in through the stained glass windows of the beautiful old sanctuary. Fred closed his eyes and leaned back a little.

"I wonder who'll leave this time?" he thought to himself.

Suggested readings

Grenz, Stanley J., and Roger E. Olson. *20th-Century Theology: God and the Word in a Transitional Age*. Downers Grove, Ill.: InterVarsity, 1992.

Hordern, William. *Layman's Guide to Protestant Theology*, rev. ed. New York: Macmillan, 1968.

LeFevre, Perry. *Understandings of Man*. Philadelphia: Westminster, 1966.

Olson, Roger E. *The Story of Christian Theology: Twenty Centuries of Tradition and Reform*. Downers Grove, Ill.: InterVarsity, 1999.

Stevenson, Leslie. *Seven Theories of Human Nature*, 2d ed. New York: Oxford University Press, 1987.

15

Twentieth-Century Europe: The Church in Decline

To World War II

While nineteenth- and twentieth-century European Protestants became increasingly liberal, the Roman Catholic Church continued on its profoundly conservative course well into the twentieth century. Politically, the Roman Church faced dramatic changes as it lost virtually all of its temporal power, along with control of the Papal States in central Italy. The popes had alienated Italian nationalists by resisting all attempts to unify Italy. As a result the nationalists drove Pope Pius IX (1792–1878) out of Rome in 1848. He appealed to France and Austria, who put him back in the Vatican Palace in Rome, further alienating the Italians. Politically dependent on the French and Austrians, the Church looked on helplessly as the Italian nationalists took the Papal States during a war against Austria in 1859, and captured Rome itself from the Church in 1870. When Rome fell the popes retreated to the Vatican Palace, which the Italians permitted them to keep, remaining in self-imposed imprisonment until 1929. They continued to press their claims to the Papal States, accusing the Italian government of usurpation, but to no avail.

Partly to compensate for the loss of his temporal power, Pius IX began to assert his spiritual power and authority over the Church. He began his campaign to control the Church by announcing the dogma of the Immaculate Conception of the Virgin Mary. According to this doctrine, the Virgin Mary, because God had chosen her to bear his son, was entirely free from sin, including original sin. Although this had been the subject of discussion for centuries, Catholic theologians had never been able to come to agreement on the issue. Pius decided simply to decree the dogma, using it as a test case to determine the extent of his power over the church. For the first time ever, a pope had promulgated a dogma without referring to a general council of the church. When he encountered little opposition, he was ready to move on to the next step, which did involve calling a general council.

Vatican Council I met in 1870 to consider the issues of papal primacy and papal infallibility. The doctrine of papal primacy means that the pope functions as the sole head of the Church and is its authoritative voice. The doctrine of papal infallibility means that the pope, when he speaks authoritatively or *ex cathedra*, can make no errors (see box 15.1). In meekly following Pius IX's lead, Vatican I decided that the authority of the pope superseded their own as a general council. The popes since

Pius IX saw the papacy through years of great tension and change. Seen as a political liberal who could heal tensions between the Papal State and Italy, he drastically changed his position after a revolution forced him to flee Rome in 1848. He had seen the pope's political power virtually disappear by 1869–1870 when Vatican Council I defined papal infallibility. He issued the *Syllabus of Errors* in 1864 to condemn religious liberalism and modern rationalism.

Pius IX, however, have used their power to speak infallibly only once. In 1950 Pope Pius XII (1876–1958) declared, in the doctrine of the Assumption of Mary, that Mary had not died a bodily death, but had been taken directly up to heaven at the end of her earthly life.

The strong claims made for the pope's power at Vatican I caused hardly a ripple outside of the Roman Catholic Church. Few non-Catholics cared how powerful the pope might claim to be in spiritual matters, since the church no longer had any political power. Spiritual matters were held to be the private business of the Church, to be decided as it saw fit.

Pius's successor, Leo XIII (1810–1903), continued to press the Church's claim to the Papal States and refused to allow Italian Catholics to recognize the validity of the state of Italy by participating in Italian national elections. As a result, Italian Catholics had virtually no influence in shaping the nation of Italy or Italian political decisions until after World War II. When World War I broke out, however, the forces of nationalism proved much stronger than religious ties, for both Catholics and Protestants.

15.1. Vatican I: Papal Infallibility

Hence we teach and declare that by the appointment of our Lord the Roman Church possesses a superiority of ordinary power over all other Churches, and that this power of jurisdiction of the Roman Pontiff, which is truly episcopal, is immediate; to which all, of whatever rite and dignity, both pastors and faithful, both individually and collectively, are bound, by their duty of hierarchical subordination and true obedience, to submit, not only in matters which belong to faith and morals, but also in those that appertain to the discipline and government of the Church throughout the world, so that the Church of Christ may be one flock under one supreme pastor through the preservation of unity both of communion and of profession of the same faith with the Roman Pontiff. This is the teaching of Catholic truth, from which no one can deviate without loss of faith and of salvation. . . .

Therefore faithfully adhering to the tradition received from the beginning of the Christian faith, for the glory of God our Saviour, the exaltation of the Catholic Religion, and the salvation of Christian people, the Sacred Council approving, We teach and define that it is a dogma divinely revealed: that the Roman Pontiff, when he speaks ex cathedra, that is, when in discharge of the office of Pastor and Doctor of all Christians, by virtue of his supreme Apostolic authority he defines a doctrine regarding faith or morals to be held by the Universal Church, by the divine assistance promised to him in blessed Peter, is possessed of that infallibility with which the divine Redeemer wills that His Church should be endowed for defining doctrine regarding faith or morals.

"*Pastor aeternus,*" trans. by H. E. Maning, in Philip Schaff, *Creeds of Christendom* (New York: Harper and Bros., 1931), 270–71.

Protestant leaders during the first decade of the twentieth century looked at the international political arena and saw signs that the kingdom of God was about to begin. They saw the process of international arbitration and international cooperation as leading to a new age of peace and prosperity in which the nations of the earth would turn their attention and scientific skill from building weapons to eradicating the ills of society.

World War I caught these Protestants, as well as the Roman Catholics, unprepared. They simply joined the spontaneous surge of nationalism that swept Europe in 1914, and as a result played little role in the conflict. World War I was, in fact, a curiously non-religious war, with the churches seeing little role for themselves apart from leading the cheers from the home-front sidelines. Certainly allied chaplains dutifully prayed on Sundays, well behind the lines, and German belt buckles bore the legend "*Gott mit uns*" ("God is on our side"), but songs like "The Bells of Hell Go Ting-a-ling-a-ling for You but Not for Me" were a more characteristic manifestation of religion in the trenches. Neither the established

Protestant nor the Catholic churches had much to offer either the soldiers or the nations between 1914 and 1918, though groups like the Salvation Army did serve at the front lines.

The First World War combined technology and democracy to devastating effect. Nineteenth-century optimists believed that science and technology were instruments of progress. World War I showed scientists devising ever more effective and efficient methods of killing. At the same time, World War I brought far more ordinary people into the conflict than had any previous war. Millions of young volunteers and draftees from all nations and every social class manned the trenches and learned the horrors of gas warfare and mechanized mass destruction first hand. These young men tended toward cynicism and disillusionment. Ernest Hemingway's character Lieutenant Henry describes his feelings: "I had seen nothing sacred, and the things that were [supposed to be] glorious had no glory and the sacrifices were like the stockyards in Chicago. . . . Abstract words such as glory, honor, courage were obscene."[1] The churches, so tied as they had been to their role as home-front cheerleaders, apparently had little to say to many of these veterans.

The churches did not survive the war unchanged, however. In academic theology, the chastened liberalism known as *dialectic theology* or *neoorthodoxy*, pioneered by Karl Barth, grew out of his war experiences. The pre-war Barth was a classic liberal, but in 1916 he lost his faith in the innate goodness of human beings and the inevitability of progress. He decided that theology had to start over with the text of the Bible, though he used the tools the liberals had given him to understand that text. Despite his liberal tools, he did not reach liberal conclusions. In *Der Römerbrief*, Barth argued that God was not present in the wonders of creation, but was entirely transcendent; he also argued, partly on the basis of his war experience, that human beings were entirely sinful and that social progress had no hope of ever bringing about God's kingdom. Only when Christ broke through time and history in person to bring the final judgment would the new heaven and the new earth begin.

For most Christians the dominant public force in the years between World War I and World War II was the rise of fascism in Italy, Germany, and Spain. In 1929 Pius XII reached an agreement with Mussolini, the Italian fascist dictator. Mussolini recognized Vatican City as a sovereign state, while the church finally gave up its claims to the Papal States. In 1933 the Vatican signed a concordat with the German Third Reich, after which the popes remained silent on European political events. The Spanish fascist General Francisco Franco (1892–1975), who came to power in the Spanish Civil War (1936–39), strongly supported the Catholic Church, as well as the army and business interests. The church, in turn, opposed socialism far more vigorously than fascism, partly because the Roman Catholic Church embodied the authoritarian ideals that fascism espoused. During World War II Pius XII remained silent on the Nazi atrocities against the Jews, though he protested Nazi harassment of Polish Catholics, since he felt he had to defend the honor of the Church. Since the Church and pope were involved in some behind-the-scenes efforts to rescue European Jews, Pius has both been despised for political cowardice and praised for pragmatic courage. The full story may never be known.

In 1933 Hitler combined all German Protestants into one *German Evangelical Church*, a church that enthusiastically supported the National Socialist (Nazi) program. For many Germans the rise of fascist Nazism marked a return to lost German Christian values. Pious Germans remembered Germany as the home of the great medieval Gothic cathedrals, the Reformation, and pietism, but believed that this once great Christian nation had fallen away from its first love. These Christians believed that German Christianity had become liberal and decadent, following secular thinkers such as Freud, Darwin, and Marx rather than the teachings of the Bible. As a result, they thought, God was sending his judgment on Germany in the form of inflation, economic chaos, and the depression of the 1930s.

Hitler agreed with this assessment and called Germany back to a historic German Christian ethic, which he interpreted as a strong, warlike, manly Christianity rooted in the German soil. Many German theologians fell into line with what became known as the nazification of the church and interpreted the Bible according to Nazi doctrine, using techniques of biblical criticism they learned from nineteenth-century liberal theologians. They stressed military virtues such as loyalty and obedience and glossed over biblical teachings on meekness and peace.

The "German Christians" in the German Evangelical Church revived the nineteenth-century belief in human perfectibility but applied the doctrine to the perfectibility of an Aryan race with a divine mission to civilize the world and establish the millennial kingdom under Hitler in Germany, using political and military means. The Germans also viewed themselves as strictly New Testament Christians, teaching that Jesus rejected Old Testament Judaism and stressing that the Jews had killed Christ. They had, according to the German Evangelical Church, willingly drawn God's curse upon their heads when they said "Let his blood be on us and on our children" (Matt. 27:25). Many sincerely believed that Jews had dominated the German press and economy before World War II, and that this Jewish domination had been part of God's judgment for Germany's unfaithfulness.

Yet if German Christians were Nazis for understandable reasons, it was not for excusable reasons. A sizable minority refused to follow the lead of the theologians. Led by mostly neoorthodox theologians, both Lutheran and Reformed pastors and teachers gathered at Barmen, Germany, in 1934 for a "witnessing synod." Delegates to that synod courageously approved and individually signed the *Barmen Declaration* (see box 15.2).

The Barmen Declaration became the foundation for the *Confessing Church*, which opposed Hitler's policies in the name of the gospel. Leading pastors in the Confessing Church were all drafted and sent to the front lines, and the theologians, along with all other German university professors, were required to sign a statement of unconditional loyalty toHitler and the Third

Adolf Hitler

15.2. Barmen Declaration

Jesus Christ, as he is testified to us in the Holy Scripture, is the one Word of God, whom we are to hear, whom we are to trust and obey in life and in death.

We repudiate the false teaching that the church can and must recognize yet other happenings and powers, images and truths as divine revelation alongside this one Word of God, as a source of her preaching.

We repudiate the false teaching that the state can and should expand beyond its special responsibility to become the single and total order of human life and also thereby fulfil the commission of the church.

We repudiate the false teaching that the church can and should expand beyond its special responsibility to take on the characteristics, functions and dignities of the state and thereby become itself an organ of the state.

We repudiate the false teaching that the church, in human self-esteem, can put the word and work of the Lord in the service of some wishes, purposes, and plans or other, chosen according to desire.

"The Theological Declaration of Barmen," in J. Gordon Melton, ed., *The Encyclopedia of American Religions: Religious Creeds,* 1st ed. (Detroit: Gale, 1988), 249–51.

Reich. Karl Barth refused to sign and fled to Switzerland, where he taught at the University of Basel for the remainder of his career.

One signer of the Barmen Declaration and perhaps the best-known Confessing Christian aside from Barth, Dietrich Bonhoeffer, (1906–1945) was living in safety as chaplain to a German Lutheran congregation in London, England. In 1935 the Confessing Church asked him to return to Germany and begin an underground seminary at Finkenwalde in Pomerania. Although his English friends tried desperately to persuade him to remain in England, he felt God's call to witness in Nazi Germany. The Nazis revoked his right to teach and preach in 1937 and closed the seminary, but Bonhoeffer continued to meet with students until the war broke out in

Dietrich Bonhoeffer

1939. He again was in safety in America, on a speaking tour, when news broke of the war; he became convinced that it was wrong for him to flee the difficulties of the Christian life in Germany for the ease of American Christianity. He immediately returned.

In Germany, Bonhoeffer faced direct persecution. He had already been forbidden from living in Berlin in 1938; in 1940 the Gestapo closed down the remnants of his seminary, and he was ordered not to speak in public or publish any of his writings. As the war went on Bonhoeffer became increasingly active in the anti-Nazi underground, rejecting his earlier pacifism as an easy answer in difficult times. He served as a mediator between the underground and the English government and even became involved in a plot to assassinate Hitler, feeling that, though murder is wrong, Hitler was a greater evil, and he had no choice.

In April of 1943 Bonhoeffer was arrested and sent to Flossenbürg Prison. He served his fellow-prisoners as chaplain and earned the respect of inmates and guards. As the American army moved in on Berlin and defeat was inevitable, the Third Reich decided that it needed to eliminate its worst enemies before they were freed by the advancing forces. Bonhoeffer was chosen as one of these and, after a hasty night court-martial, he was condemned to death and hanged on April 9, 1945, only a few days before the prison was liberated by the Americans.

15.3. Bonhoeffer

Cheap grace is the deadly enemy of our church. We are fighting for costly grace.

Cheap grace means grace as a doctrine, a principle, a system. It means forgiveness of sins proclaimed as a general truth, the love of God taught as the Christian "conception" of God. An intellectual assent to that idea is held to be of itself sufficient to secure remission of sins . . . no contrition is required. . . .

Costly grace is the gospel which must be sought again and again, the gift which must be asked for, the door at which a man must knock.

Such grace is costly because it calls us to follow, and it is grace because it calls us to follow Jesus Christ. It is costly because it costs a man his life, and it is grace because it gives a man the only true life. . . . Above all it is costly because it cost God the life of his Son. . . . Above all it is grace because God did not reckon his Son too dear a price to pay for our life, but delivered him up for us. Costly grace is the Incarnation of God.

Dietrich Bonhoeffer, *The Cost of Discipleship* (New York: Collier, 1959), 45, 47.

In England and among the other allies, most churches supported the war effort whole-heartedly. As in World War I this was partly out of patriotic motives, but in World War II there was more feeling of involvement in a righteous and necessary endeavor. People genuinely believed that Hitler was evil, and the war justified. For most English Christians World War II was no less than a war between the powers of light and the powers of darkness and evil. This was reinforced as more and more German bombs fell on London. As William Temple, the archbishop of Canterbury, put it, "The trouble with the Nazis is not that they do not practise what they preach; it is that they do preach what they practise. Their standards are perverted; their right is our wrong."[2]

Roman Catholics

After World War II the Roman Catholic church remained authoritarian, conservative, and stridently anticommunist. The papacy spent its energy protecting the church and working to increase its freedom and power. That policy changed dramatically in 1958 when John XXIII (1881–1963) came to the papal throne. At age 77 John knew he would have but a short time in the pontificate, so he set about the huge task of restoring communication between the church and the twentieth-century world with great vigor and determination. To the surprise and consternation of the church hierarchy, he immediately called an ecumenical council. Many Catholics thought that the time for councils had passed when the pope was declared infallible at Vatican I. John

XXIII did not believe that the pope should rule as an absolute monarch, but insisted on asking his "brother bishops" for advice instead of issuing commands. He was convinced that the church needed to be updated and believed that this could only happen in consultation with the bishops and the whole church sitting in a general council.

Vatican Council II (1962–65) was the only council ever called (unless one counts the first Acts 15 council) that did not condemn anyone or anything. Rather the leaders met with a completely positive agenda. When it opened in 1962 only 46 percent of its delegates came from Western Europe, Canada, or the United States, while 42 percent came from Latin America, Asia, and Africa. The delegates to Vatican II outran the vision of those who had prepared preliminary proposals, and most proposals were returned to their committees for drastic revision. Pope John XXIII did not live to see the fruits of Vatican II. His successor, Paul VI (1897–1978), though personally more conservative than John, allowed Vatican II to continue its work, and supported the direction the Council was taking.

Vatican II began at the center of Roman Catholic church life, the liturgy, declaring that: "as long as the essential unity of the Roman rite is preserved, in the revision of liturgical books, steps shall be taken for proper variations and adaptations according to the needs of various groups, regions, and peoples, particularly in mission territories."[3] Instead of the traditional Latin Mass, Roman Catholics began to worship in their own languages, and the weekly rhythms of the church began to change dramatically.

Vatican II proclaimed religious freedom and toleration—even for non-Catholics in Roman Catholic countries. Protestants were now called "separated brethren," not damned heretics. Along with this openness to non-Catholics, Vatican II declared the church's concern for, and solidarity with, the world's poor and the non-Western church. This new emphasis quickly provided a place for the Theology of Liberation, a Marxist-Christian synthesis growing out of the experiences of Third-World Catholic theologians.

After Vatican II the Roman Catholic church retrenched, especially after 1978 under the leadership of the Polish John Paul II (1920–), the first non-Italian pope since the time of the Reformation. While personally outgoing and sincerely concerned for the poor and disadvantaged, John Paul's theology is rooted in the medieval Catholic tradition, and his commitment to such traditionally Catholic teachings as adoration of the Virgin, a celibate male priesthood, and total opposition to any form of artificial birth control, reveals a theologically conservative pope.

John Paul II (1920–) was the son of a Polish soldier and grew up in poverty and completed his studies in Cracow during World War II. A member of the preparatory commission for Vatican Council II, he was elevated to cardinal in 1967 and immediately became a popular public speaker and conciliar representative in Europe and North America.

15.4. Pope John Paul II

Chosen pope in 1978, the Polish Karol Cardinal Wojtyla (1920–), became the first non-Italian pope since the sixteenth century. John Paul's pontificate has been marked by personal openness and warmth, strong social concern, and a deep-seated commitment to traditional Roman Catholic doctrine and teaching.

John Paul II deliberately set out to create the image of the pope as shepherd of the world Catholic community, not as a majestic leader at the head of the Catholic hierarchy. To that end he has traveled frequently, visiting his parishioners as a messenger of God's Word. Papal visits have not always been apolitical. A visit to his Polish homeland in 1982 proved a major impetus for Polish nationalism, while visits to Latin America and the United States have been marked by John Paul's attempts to calm the radicals in the church.

377

Eastern Christians

Orthodox Christians in the Soviet Union during the twentieth century experienced wrenching changes in the circumstances of their church and their personal lives as believers. The bookends of this period are the Bolshevik Revolution of 1917 and the demise of communism and dismemberment of Catherine the Great's empire after 1989.

The communist movement and its ideals spread deeply through the Russian populace after 1917. Marx was an atheist, but he had a more benign view of religion than the one for which he is often credited. He wrote: "Religion is the sigh of the oppressed creature, the heart of a heartless world, the spirit of soulless stagnation. It is the opium of the people."[4] But Lenin, the architect of the Bolshevik Revolution, was less gentle: "Every religious idea, every idea of God, even flirting with the idea of God, is unutterable vileness."[5]

Lenin and his successors built Soviet society around, among other things, opposition to religion. The Soviet period charts a history of alternating waves of persecution and relative toleration for Christians and other religious peoples. The first Soviet constitution of 1918 permitted "freedom of religious and antireligious propaganda." By 1929, with Stalin in power and the iron hand of tyranny pounding down on the Russian and other Soviet peoples, the constitution was amended to read "freedom of religious worship and antireligious propaganda." Henceforward, only atheists could spread their faith; Christians and other religious people could worship, but they were forbidden to evangelize. World War II brought hardships and the need to pull together, and religions were allowed to make a modest comeback. That was followed by a crackdown under Khrushchev in the 1960s, another period of partial toleration in the Brezhnev era, and confusion in the 1980s.

Atheism was promoted throughout the Soviet Union. Communist ideology stated that, with the coming of the Soviet state, religion would naturally wither away. But government people were happy to help the withering process along. Older Christians were allowed to attend services, but religious classes and public rituals were forbidden. Plainclothes police would come to churches and take down names, and sometimes forbid entrance to young worshipers. If one's name appeared on a list of church-goers, one was likely to feel the pain at school or on the job, where promotions usually went to the properly irreligious. School curricula espoused a frank atheism that ridiculed Christianity as witchcraft and superstitious tomfoolery. The government took over church buildings and publishing houses, and printed only minuscule numbers of Bibles.

Through this time, Orthodox Christians survived as a church with both underground and above-ground manifestations. National church leaders found themselves ever more circumscribed by government decrees—a situation they had known under such earlier rulers as Peter the Great, but one that galled, nonetheless. At least Peter had not been openly anti-Christian, even if he had pushed the church around to suit his own political purposes. Monks who spoke out against the communist government found themselves restricted or sent off to prison camps. Religious groups that lacked a historic identification with the Russian people, such as Pentecostals, Baptists, and Seventh-Day Adventists, usually drew harsher penalties than did Orthodox Christians. But despite common persecution, the various types of Christians did not pull together (nor, for that matter, did Jews or Muslims).

The Russian Orthodox Church usually found national leaders who could perform the delicate balancing act between an antagonistic government and their community of believers. But the public expression of Orthodox faith inevitably became timid, attenuated, and compromised. Father Dmitri Dudko, an outspoken activist of the 1970s and 1980s, described the situation in caustic terms: "Believers avoid priests. Priests run from believers or betray the interests of believers. . . . They are afraid of each other." The Orthodox Church, he said, had two aspects: "Outwardly, splendor. Inwardly, emasculation."[6]

Yet millions of Soviet citizens remained Christians. Even some Communist Party officials baptized their children. As the Soviet experiment ground to a halt in the 1970s and 1980s, an increasing number of people became involved in underground—and then in aboveground—Christianity. It was something of an anti-government political statement, as well as a yearning after spiritual things.

When communism unraveled in Russia after 1989, the Orthodox Church emerged from its dormant state. As the Union of Soviet Socialist Republics fell apart into smaller, ethnically-based national units, orthodoxy became a rallying point for Russian nationalism. At the same time, Muslims, American organizations, and others rushed in from abroad to evangelize. The political, economic, and cultural situations of Russia and its former dominions were so uncertain that few even attempted to make any predictions about the future of Christianity in the former Soviet lands.

Protestants after World War II

The story of European Protestantism after World War II is primarily one of steady decline and secularization. In Germany, England, and Scandinavia—the traditionally Protestant nations—church attendance slipped steadily until less than 10 percent of the population had significant contact with any organized religious body.

Theologians in the mainline churches reacted to the decline by seeking an accommodation with modern secular culture. Following the lead of Rudolf Bultmann (1884–1976), they tried to demythologize the Christian religion, seeking an ethical core of the gospel, beneath layers of mysticism and supernatural stories. The original ethical teachings of Christ, they believed, remained relevant, while miracles and superstitions did not.

Other Protestants tried to blend the insights of Marx and his revisionist followers. The neo-Marxist Ernst Bloch approved of early Christianity, seeing it as a protest movement based on the hope for a better future. Led by Jürgen Moltmann (1926–), these Protestant theologians interpreted Christianity as a religion of hope for a better world and a better life, a protest against injustice and hopelessness in society.

The evangelical minority tried to serve as salt and light, witnessing to what had become a post-Christian European culture. In France the *Eglise Reformee,* formed by the merger of two Reformed churches with Methodists and Congregationalists, focused its energies on evangelizing heavily industrialized cities. Meanwhile, Dutch evangelicals developed an influential broadcasting operation. In England, an evangelical revival within the Church of England spawned an active network of interconnected congregations. Evangelicals were training a disproportionate share of new pastors and as a result were beginning to take over parts of the church hierarchy.

European evangelicals also came together across denominational lines to talk and learn. In 1966 the Berlin Conference on Evangelism, addressed by Billy Graham, discussed the relationship between evangelical theology

15.5. Lausanne Covenant

The development of strategies for world evangelization calls for imaginative pioneering methods. Under God, the result will be the rise of churches deeply rooted in Christ and closely related to their culture. Culture must always be tested and judged by Scripture. Because man is God's creature, some of his culture is rich in beauty and goodness. Because he is fallen, all of it is tainted with sin and some of it is demonic. The Gospel does not presuppose the superiority of any culture to another, but evaluates all cultures according to its own criteria of truth and righteousness and insists on moral absolutes in every culture. Missions have all too frequently exported with the Gospel an alien culture, and churches have sometimes been in bondage to culture rather than to Scripture. Christ's evangelists must humbly seek to empty themselves of all but their personal authenticity in order to become the servants of others, and churches must seek to transform and enrich culture, all for the glory of God.

John R. Stott, *The Lausanne Covenant: An Exposition and Commentary,* Lausanne Occasional Papers, no. 3 (Minneapolis: World Wide Publications, 1975), 25.

and the practice of evangelism in Europe. This led to another conference in Amsterdam in 1971. In 1974 evangelists and missionaries from all over the world met at Lausanne, Switzerland; one-quarter of them were Europeans.

Pandenominational movements

Perhaps the dominant institution in mainline European Christianity after World War II was the *World Council of Churches* (WCC), which tried to breathe unity into Christendom and provide a common voice in a post-Christian world. The WCC grew out of concern among the international missionary community that they were not presenting a united front as they tried to convert non-Christians. Concerned missionaries came together in conferences, notably the *Edinburgh World Missions Conference* in 1910, which established the Faith and Order Movement. That movement and the Life and Work Committee of the World Alliance for Promoting International Friendship led directly to the WCC. Two world wars postponed the formation, but the WCC finally was born in a merger of the Faith and Order Movement and the Life and Work Committee at a constituting assembly in Amsterdam (1948). The *Amsterdam Assembly*, faced by the Cold War, called on its churches, Western and Eastern, to reject both communism and radical capitalism and to search for other alternatives.

From that beginning, the WCC met in Evanston, Illinois, in 1954 and New Delhi, India, in 1961. The New Delhi Assembly symbolized the beginning of the WCC's emphasis on the need to embrace the non-Western world. After 1961, the WCC came to be dominated by representatives of the newer churches of Africa, Asia, and Latin America. Its concerns were increasingly shaped by the Latin American theologians of liberation. As a result, European institutional Christianity came to be characterized by a global perspective and solidarity with the world's poor and oppressed.

These concerns for liberation reflect some dramatic theological changes in the thinking of mainline European churches. By the 1970s faith itself had come to mean something quite different than it did to nineteenth-century Christians, a change that reflected earlier shifts within formal theology. Just as Friedrich Schleiermacher and the liberal theologians who followed him replaced God-centered theology with a focus on human religious experience, now succeeding generations of Europeans applied the new theological focus to the entire span of Christian thought and practice.

Perhaps the most significant element in this transformation was a new understanding of salvation. While traditionally salvation frequently meant a personal relationship with Jesus leading to eternal bliss in heaven, the WCC and those influenced by its teachings began to see salvation as the process of creating true human beings by removing dehumanizing economic or racial oppression, ethnic bias, and sexist stereotypes. People became liberated, truly human, and saved through political, social, and economic change.

During the 1970s, as the WCC began to see salvation as social and political, rather than personal, they also came to see Christianity as less exclusive and its claims as less unique. Robert McAfee Brown, the keynote speaker at the 1975 Assembly in Nairobi, Kenya, argued that "We can learn from [Jews, Hindus, Marxists, and Humanists] rather than assuming that they must learn exclusively from us." European mainline Christians consequently stopped engaging in evangelism and started focusing exclusively on issues of justice and solidarity with the poor. Since those concerns were hardly unique to Christianity, those outside the faith who watched these Christians apparently felt no particular need to become Christians or join the church in order to participate, and church membership continued to decline.

A combination of the World Council of Churches and Vatican Council II in the Roman Catholic church led to a strong desire for institutional reunification. Anglicans, Lutherans, and Roman Catholics began serious ecumenical dialogue aimed at organic reunion in the late 1960s under the *Council on Church Union* (COCU). These discussions focused around the issues that had historically divided the churches. Anglicans and Roman Catholics centered their discussions on the Eucharist, the meaning and function of ordained ministry, and the nature and exercise of authority in the church. Although the dialogues reported progress, and the WCC supplemented these bilateral discussions with its multi-lateral report on baptism, Eucharist, and ministry, the churches remained a long distance from actual union.

Suggested readings

Bonhoeffer, Dietrich. *The Cost of Discipleship*. New York: Macmillan, 1963.

Cochrane, Arthur C. *The Church's Confession under Hitler*, 2d ed. Pittsburgh: Pickwick, 1977.

"C. S. Lewis,"*Christian History*, 4.3 (issue 7, 1985).

"Dietrich Bonhoeffer," *Christian History*, 10.4 (issue 32, 1991).

Ellis, Jane. *The Russian Orthodox Church: A Contemporary History*. Bloomington, Ind.: Indiana University Press, 1986.

Hastings, Adrian, *A History of English Christianity, 1920–1990*. London: SCM Press, 1991.

Huntemann, Georg. *The Other Bonhoeffer: An Evangelical Reassessment of Dietrich Bonhoeffer*. Grand Rapids: Baker, 1993.

16

Twentieth-Century America

The cultural setting

To understand how Christianity has been lived in America in the twentieth century one must start with the social setting in which Christians found themselves at its beginning.

Reaction against industrialism

The dominant fact of life in 1900 was industry. The United States had been undergoing an industrial revolution for several decades by 1900, and its social effects were all too apparent. Along with increased production and a rising standard of living for some came massive social dislocations for many. Factories drew people to cities. In 1800, 90 percent of the people were farming; by 1920 more than half lived in cities. Cities drew people from across the seas: Nearly 9 million immigrants came to the United States between 1900 and 1910, three-quarters of them came from Italy, Poland, Greece, and other southern and eastern European countries. Unlike earlier immigrants, many were Catholics and Jews, most were from the lower class, and almost none spoke English. America's cities became teeming cauldrons, mixing many peoples, languages, and ways of living. The rise of industry also increased the gap between rich and poor and made it more difficult for the poorest citizens to escape poverty.

The American people reacted in several different ways to these developments. Christians were prominent in each of the major movements of reaction, although none can be called a specifically

Christian endeavor. Farmers and miners of the South and West joined together in the *populist movement* late in the nineteenth century. This was a political movement designed to revive the declining fortunes of rural people through a complicated program involving government ownership of some businesses, taxing the incomes of rich people, inflationary fiscal policies to reduce farmers' debts, and other measures. Many populists were Protestants, and the most prominent populist, William Jennings Bryan, was also the most famous of a new group of Christians who were called *fundamentalists*.

Bryan was also a major figure in the *progressive movement*, a much more broadly based, mainly urban attempt to deal with the problems brought on by industrialism. Progressivism joined labor unions, forward-looking businesspeople, suffragettes, middle-class moralists, educators, and politicians in an attempt to make American society more fair, more equal, more homogeneous, and more efficient. The movement pushed in several directions, often contradictory, but it held the main stage of American politics for nearly twenty years. Many Christians were among the progressives, and the *social gospel* movement can be understood as a religious expression of progressivism. Many progressives shared the ideals of the nineteenth-century reformers, including prohibition and women's right to vote. And under progressive leadership these reforms were added to the U.S. Constitution. But progressivism was not centered around Christianity in the manner of nineteenth-century reform movements. To the left of progressives and populists stood *socialists*, a small but noisy group that advocated dismantling capitalism. There were Christians here, too, drawn by socialism's promises of justice and equality, although their numbers and impact were slight.

Nineteenth-century Christians had often hoped that the kingdom could be established on earth by the passage of proper laws to reform society. One of these laws was prohibition, an attempt by Protestants to gain control of America's morals. Attributing society's ills to strong drink, these people capped several decades of grassroots activity and agitation by passing the Eighteenth Amendment to the U.S. Constitution in 1919, outlawing "the manufacture, sale, or transportation of intoxicating liquor." Evangelist Billy Sunday predicted that prohibition would "turn our prisons into factories and our jails into . . . corncribs." Although drunkenness decreased and alcohol-related hospital admissions plummeted, prohibition ultimately failed because of its unpopularity. Millions of people wanted to drink and many were willing to defy the law to do so. Widespread evasion of the prohibition law contributed to the rise of organized crime. Among Christian liberals there was

William Jennings Bryan (1860–1925) campaigned vigorously for both the Eighteenth (prohibition) and Nineteenth (women's suffrage) amendments to the U.S. Constitution. He actually wrote more about religious and moral subjects than about politics. (Billy Graham Center)

16.1. The Great Commoner

William Jennings Bryan (1860–1925), lawyer, orator, newspaper editor, and politician, was the most famous fundamentalist of the early twentieth century. He embodied a commitment to liberal politics and conservative theology that has since all but vanished from the American scene.

Born and educated in Illinois, Bryan moved to Nebraska and entered politics in 1887. He served in the U.S. Congress and ran unsuccessfully for the Senate on a platform of agrarian populism, demanding more democracy and economic relief for Western farmers. His oratorical skills, opposition to imperialism, and commitment to the common people earned him the Democratic presidential nomination in 1896, 1900, and 1908; he was unsuccessful each time. He made the transition from populism to progressivism and served as secretary of state under Woodrow Wilson.

Bryan's decision to quit the Cabinet, over what he felt was Wilson's lack of evenhandedness between Britain and Germany in World War I, illustrates his essentially moral approach to public life. Despite his opposition to America joining that war, he loyally supported his country once war was declared.

In the 1920s he became more involved in religious activities. He served as moderator of the Methodist church and guest prosecutor in the infamous Scopes evolution trial of 1925, shortly before his death.

By 1875, when this *Temperance Crusade Almanac* was published, the movement had become a ubiquitous social movement within the church. The title of this heroic engraving is "Spiking the Guns." (Billy Graham Center)

continuing disillusionment with the ideals of the nineteenth-century reformers. The Eighteenth Amendment was repealed in 1933.

The same group that hoped prohibition would create a near-paradise helped to pass the Nineteenth Amendment, which allowed women to vote in federal elections. These progressives assumed that the corruption in American politics would be eliminated if politicians were sober and not under the influence of the liquor lobby, and if the morally superior qualities associated with womanhood were at work to elevate the quality of elected officials. In the 1920 election, when they first exercised their franchise, women voted overwhelmingly for Warren G. Harding—whose past dealings and presidential administration epitomized government corruption. Another of the dreams of nineteenth-century reformers was dashed.

American nativism

A right-wing reaction to the new social situation was a fear of foreigners and foreign ideologies. Americans whose ancestors had come earlier and from Northwest Europe looked with dismay on large numbers of newcomers who were unlike them. In the *Red Scare* of the 1920s thousands of radicals were assaulted, arrested, deprived of their civil rights, deported, and even killed. This xenophobia outwardly resulted from reaction to the Bolsheviks who had seized power in Russia and to radicals in general, but it also arose from a fear of the people with German and East European names who frequently spoke for the left. *Nativism*, the attack on recent immigrants, was an old American tradition, but it flared anew during and after World War I. By 1924, nativists had succeeded in passing a federal law that drastically cut the flow of immigrants from South and East Europe and eliminated Asian immigration entirely. Protestant Christians were among the most prominent exponents of the anti-radical and anti-immigrant movements of the late 1910s and early 1920s.

Perhaps the most blatant example of right-wing reaction was the renaissance of the Ku Klux Klan in the 1920s. In the 1860s and 1870s this hate organization fought a successful guerilla war to kill the North-dominated Reconstruction of the South. Part of their agenda had been to ensure white domination of a segregated Southern culture. Reborn in 1915 under the leadership of Atlanta evangelist William J. Simmons, the Klan achieved national prominence and respectability, even in some areas of the North, in the early 1920s. Its platform of "Christian Americanism" meant the rule of native, white Protestants and the elimination or subjugation of other peoples.

One of the groups attacked by nativists was the Roman Catholic community. Advocates of the nineteenth-century vision of a Protestant America identified Catholics with immigrants from Ireland and Eastern Europe and regarded their religion as a subversive foreign ideology. Catholic immigrants worshiped in ethnic parishes that spoke the languages and preserved the customs of their European homelands. Partly to still Protestant criticism, late nineteenth- and twentieth-century leaders such as James Gibbons (1834–1921), Isaac Hecker (1819–1888), and John Ireland (1838–1918) tried to "Americanize" Catholicism. Archbishop George Mundelein, for instance, stopped organizing ethnic parishes in Chicago and insisted that English be the only language used in parochial schools. But immigrant Catholics, especially those from French Canada and Southern and Eastern Europe, objected to giving up their ancestral distinctives. They accused the Americanizers of compromising historic Catholicism and persuaded Pope Leo XIII to chastise them.

16.2. Americanizing the Immigrant

Catholic liberals such as James Cardinal Gibbons (1834–1921) and Archbishop John Ireland (1838–1918) tried to bend Catholic practice to help their immigrant flocks fit into American society. Their sentiments on this score are apparent in these words by Ireland:

We should live in our age, know it, be in touch with it. . . . We should be in it and of it, if we would have its ear. . . . For the same reason, there is needed a thorough sympathy with the country. The Church of America must be, of course, as Catholic as even in Jerusalem or Rome; but as far as her garments assume color from the local atmosphere, she must be American. Let no one dare to paint her brow with a foreign taint or pin to her mantle foreign linings. *

Many immigrant Catholics took offense at this attack on their cultural heritage. But more effective opposition came from conservative bishops, who persuaded the pope that the Americanizers meant to remold Catholic doctrine in the image of the modern age. They convinced him to dismiss many of the Americanizers from church posts and to denounce them as "enemies of the Cross of Christ."

*Mark A. Noll, et al., eds., *Eerdmans' Handbook to Christianity in America* (Grand Rapids: Eerdmans, 1983), 386.

The intellectual setting

The hallmark of the nineteenth-century Protestant consensus had been the preaching of the full gospel: the dual necessities of individual salvation from sin by the blood of Jesus Christ and of corporate dedication to pursuing social righteousness. As the nineteenth century turned to the twentieth, that consensus fell apart, and Christians divided the gospel in two.

Liberalism

The first to move were people who came to be called *theological liberals* or *modernists*. Their movement began as an attempt by Protestant intellectuals to defend Christianity against the doubts of Charles Darwin's followers and against biblical higher criticism. They chose to deemphasize the literal, historical accuracy of some biblical passages that made claims of God's supernatural intervention. Instead, they stressed what they regarded as higher, more abstract truths. They spoke of God revealing himself in historical processes and of true religion changing to meet changing human circumstances. They insisted that the key test of the value of Christianity lay, not in jot-and-tittle adherence to some set of old writings or creeds, but in Christianity's ability to produce righteousness and happiness in people's lives. With such concerns paramount, and with some uneasiness about the literal claims of Scripture, it is no wonder that many modernists chose to emphasize the outward, social demands of Christianity.

16.3. Modernist Manifesto

Shailer Mathews (1863–1941), a theologian and dean of the University of Chicago Divinity School, was one of the most outspoken modernists. The following is his 1924 statement of beliefs, personal and tentative, yet one with which many other liberals would have agreed:

I believe in God, immanent in the forces and processes of nature, revealed in Jesus Christ and human history as Love.

I believe in Jesus Christ, who through his teaching, life, death and resurrection, revealed God as Savior.

I believe in the Holy Spirit, the God of love experienced in human life.

I believe in the Bible, when interpreted historically, as the product and the trustworthy record of the progressive revelation of God through a developing religious experience.

I believe that humanity without God is incapable of full moral life and liable to suffering because of its sin and weakness.

I believe in prayer as a means of gaining help from God in every need and in every intelligent effort to establish and give justice in human relations.

I believe in freely forgiving those who trespass against me, and in good will rather than acquisitiveness, coercion, and war as the divinely established law of human relations.

I believe in the need and the reality of God's forgiveness of sins, that is, the transformation of human lives by fellowship with God from subjection to outworn goods to the practice of the love exemplified in Jesus Christ.

I believe in the practicability of the teaching of Jesus in social life.

I believe in the continuance of individual personality beyond death; and that the future life will be one of growth and joy in proportion to its fellowship with God and its moral likeness to Jesus Christ.

I believe in the church as the community of those who in different conditions and ages loyally further the religion of Jesus Christ.

I believe that all things work together for good to those who love God and in their lives express the sacrificial good will of Jesus Christ.

I believe in the ultimate triumph of love and justice because I believe in the God revealed in Jesus Christ.

Such affirmations are more than the acceptance of biblical records, an-

cient facts or the successive doctrinal patterns of the Christian church. They are the substance of a faith that will move mountains. Under their control no man can deliberately seek to injure his neighbor or distrust his God. They are moral motive and direction for social action.

The final test of such generic Christianity is the ability of the Christian movement to meet human needs. And of this we have no doubt. Whoever does the will of God will know

that the gospel of and about Jesus Christ is not the dream of a noble though impractical victim of circumstance, but the revelation of the good will of the God of nature, the Father of our spirits, the Savior of His world. And through that knowledge he will gain the fruit of the Spirit— love, joy, peace, long-suffering, kindness, goodness, faithfulness, meekness, self-control.*

*Shailer Mathews, The Faith of Modernism (New York: Macmillan, 1926), 179–82.

Fundamentalism

As Protestant liberals walked off in one direction with half the gospel, conservatives walked off in the other direction with the other half. They are sometimes called *fundamentalists*, named for a series of twelve paperbacks, published between 1909 and 1915 and called *The Fundamentals*, in which their five Christian "fundamentals" were expounded: (1) the inerrancy of Scripture, (2) the virgin birth of Christ, (3) the substitutionary atonement, (4) the resurrection of Christ, and (5) the second coming of Christ.

The term *fundamentalist* was coined in 1920 to refer to the dispensationalist premillennial wing of the conservative denominations, those whose theology was characterized by both *The Fundamentals* and the *Scofield Reference Bible* notes. Quickly the name was applied nondiscriminately to all conservative Christians, sometimes in derision. Many embraced identification as fundamentalists; others did not consider themselves part of the movement. Fundamentalists also have been called *evangelicals*, after their warm desire to share their faith with others, although this name, too, technically refers to a separate movement that is not always aligned with fundamentalism.

Nevertheless, the overriding distinctive of fundamentalism was a conservative adherence to traditional Protestant doctrines as to the personal nature of God, the accuracy and authority of the Bible, the necessity of individual salvation, and the existence of all those supernatural things that made liberals so uncomfortable. Unfortunately their continuing battles with liberals over those points so obsessed the theological conservatives that most abandoned the nineteenth-century commitment to working out the gospel in society by serving humankind. Social reform and individual acts of charity were identified with the liberal social gospel agenda. Also, improving society seemed relatively unimportant and might even distract from what conservatives saw as the greater needs for individual salvation and the very survival of biblical faith.

Opponents caricatured fundamentalists as redneck ignoramuses, and there were always ample examples to give some credence to such a misperception. But, in fact, the conservative intellectual tradition was often quite distinguished. Its Reformed or Calvinist expression centered first around Princeton Theological Seminary, before a change in administration in the mid-1910s took that school in a modernist direction. Later it was centered around Westminster Theological Seminary, Dallas Seminary, Moody Bible Institute, and a squadron of colleges, such as Wheaton and Calvin. The theological faculties of such schools were often marked by first-rate technical skill, if not always by breadth of vision or flexibility of approach. Still, surveys showed that evangelical Christians had, on average, rather less education than liberal Protestants.

These conservatives belied their name in that they seemed (at least to most people outside the group) to make major issues where none had existed, and to serve up some startling theological innovations.

The doctrine of inerrancy in some form had always been in the church, in that most Christians had believed the Bible to be true. Nothing quite like the concept of inerrancy had ever been an issue, though, until the attacks of the higher critics had made conservatives feel compelled to defend every syllable of Scripture as Godbreathed and inviolable. An exceeding amount of energy and rhetoric was expended on this one matter at the expense of other issues, and the doctrine became a litmus test of the faith. Most inerrantists have specified that it is the original writings by the authors (*autographs*) that are inerrant, but one rather extreme Protestant view stated that the King James Version of the English Bible is totally free from error. Some Roman Catholics made similar claims about the Vulgate and the English translations based upon it. From the late 1800s through the 1920s, all the major denominations had gone through heresy trials over this or related issues, and the debate remained active through the century.

A more striking departure was *dispensationalism*. Where most strands of modernism were optimistic about human culture, dispensationalism was decidedly pessimistic. Where modernism used an interpretation of history to understand the Bible, dispensationalists used a theme they saw being taught in the Bible (literally interpreted) to understand history. Dispensationalists saw human history as a series of eras or *dispensations* between humans and God. Dispensational theologians have disagreed about the number of these stages, seeing anywhere between three and ten. The most frequently accepted number is seven. Each dispensation has differed in character from the others, and in each God interacted

Influenced by dispensationalism and millennial movements, a number of charts have been been prepared through the twentieth century in anticipation of Christ's return, the tribulation, and other "end-time" events.

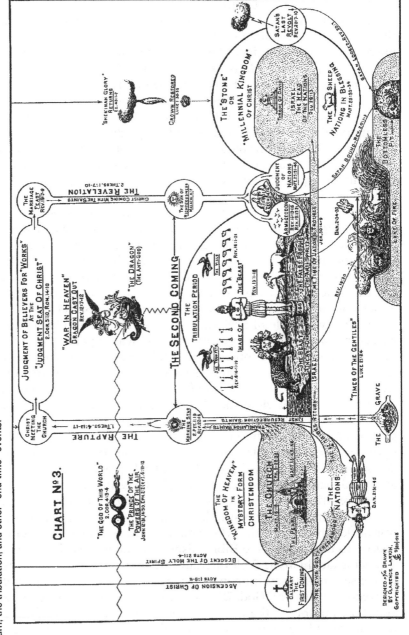

differently with the world and his people. Closely aligned with dispensationalism, the doctrine of *premillenialism* held that history would culminate, probably soon, in worldwide war and suffering, but that true Christians would be spared. Then Christ would return to establish a literal thousand-year reign on earth. By seeing the signs of what now is taking place in history, this view taught that Christians can understand how close it is to the final dramatic scenes and they should live accordingly. These signs were understood in the light of prophecies of Daniel, Matthew 24, the Epistles of Thessalonians, Revelation, and other Scriptures.

Pentecostal historian Grant Wacker suggests the source of dispensationalism's appeal by asking, "How does a man order his life when he really believes that the world is tottering on the precipice of the end of time? How does a woman act when she really believes that scripture is a giant cryptogram, which, when rightly decoded, can foretell the future with pinpoint accuracy?"[1]

In a time when science and psychology had cast doubt on older understandings of human nature and the cosmos, dispensationalism offered the comforting sense of having tapped into complex and mysterious certainties, the blueprint by which God was directing the universe.

Liberals and conservatives clashed over many issues. Perhaps the most bitter, unresolvable confrontation was the evolution controversy. Darwin's theory cast doubt on the first two chapters of Genesis, and by implication the entire underlying concept of direct creation of the universe by God. Conservatives were determined to defend the Genesis account, either as a literal series of twenty-four-hour days or as an outline for God's work over six eons of time. The 1925 trial of John Scopes, who was charged with having taught the theory of evolution in a Tennessee public school, attracted national attention. It was billed as a battle of the heavyweight public defenders of the two positions. On one side, technically defending Scopes but more truly arguing for acceptance of evolution in the classroom, was liberal attorney Clarence Darrow. Opposing him was the fundamentalist politician William Jennings Bryan. After a sideshow-like spectacle, Scopes was convicted but Bryan and the conservatives were widely ridiculed as witless ideologues flailing against scientific "fact." The battle was refought thereafter in many forums, without the creationists ever gaining much respect from the public at large. It eventually became difficult or impossible to teach creation or cast doubts on claims of evolutionary science in a public school classroom.

After the Scopes debacle, conservatives retreated to lick their wounds. Liberalism held the center stage of American Protestantism for more than a generation. Although millions of Christians held to the old verities, they were without many effective leaders. Virtually all mainline churches were affected theologically, and conservative wings of major denominations began to split away or retrench into an opposing faction to the majority. But contrary to liberal expectations, evangelical Christianity did not die; in fact, it built new institutions during its period out of the limelight and re-emerged a potent force in in the 1970s.

There was also a liberal-conservative controversy among Catholics, but it was over the question of how to balance independent thought with the authority of the church. Papal power had strengthened throughout the nineteenth century and with it the capacity of the church hierarchy to compel individuals and parishes to conform. This resulted, not only from Vatican I's introduction of papal infallibility in 1870 (see p. 370) but also from an ever-tighter bureaucratic structure. Turn-of-the-century Catholic liberals, including John Ireland and James Gibbons, called for a flexible Catholicism that was relevant to the problems of the age and inclusive of diverse thought. They called for a socially concerned Catholicism that echoed the agenda of secular progressives. Many seminaries and intellectuals supported Catholic modernism, but they were slapped down when Pope Leo XIII condemned "Americanism" in an 1899 letter to the American bishops. A final blow came in 1907 with a papal attack on

16.4. "Acres of Diamonds"

I say that you ought to get rich, and it is your duty to get rich. How many of my pious brethren say to me, "Do you, a Christian minister, spend your time going up and down the country, advising young people to get rich, to get money?" "Yes, of course I do." They say, "Isn't that awful! Why don't you preach the gospel instead of preaching about man's making money?" "Because to make money honestly is to preach the gospel."

Money is power, and you ought to be reasonably ambitious to have it. You ought because you can do more good with it than you could without it. Money printed your Bible, money builds your churches, money sends your missionaries, and money pays your preachers, and you would not have many of them, either, if you did not pay them. I am always willing that my church should raise my salary, because the church that pays the largest salary always raises it the easiest. You never knew an exception to it in your life. The man who gets the largest salary can do the most good with the power that is furnished to him. Of course he can if his spirit be right to use it for what it is given to him.

I say, then, you ought to have money. If you can honestly attain unto riches . . . , it is your Christian and godly duty to do so.

R. H. Conwell, *Acres of Diamonds* (New York: Harper, 1915), 18, 205, quoted in Edwin S. Gaustad, *A Documentary History of Religion in America*, Vol. 2, *Since 1865* (Grand Rapids: Eerdmans, 1983), 252.

modernist elements within the church. Thereafter, conservative, traditional, hierarchical Catholicism controlled the church for two-thirds of a century.

Success theology

The intellectual setting of twentieth-century American Christian experience was framed by more than just fundamentalism/evangelicalism and liberalism/modernism controversies, however. Another theme—*success theology*—broadly influenced Christians of every theological persuasion. It was an old idea that God blesses Christians in material ways, but it was given new attractiveness, even urgency, by Russell H. Conwell around the turn of the century as he toured the country with his prosperity motivational lecture, "Acres of Diamonds."

As the United States became the richest nation in world history, millions found in such crass materialism just the kind of encounter with God they wanted. They read Bruce Barton and learned that if Jesus had come to earth in the 1920s he would have worked in advertising. They learned the "power of positive thinking" from Norman Vincent Peale in the 1950s and experienced the "hour of power" with Robert Schuller in the 1980s. They made friends and money and declared that they had a ministry while selling Amway soap. Meanwhile, such Christians frequently ignored the more demanding aspects of traditional Christianity, such as personal holiness and interpersonal righteousness

Connecting with the Spirit

Revivalism

Schuller and Peale were among the many heirs of that most powerful tradition in American Christianity: revivalism. From the Pilgrims to late twentieth-century TV evangelists, Christian history in America can be viewed as a long succession of revival movements, interrupted only briefly by periods of relative spiritual deadness. In the twentieth century the pace quickened; evangelical enthusiasm seems always to have been active somewhere.

The revivals of Charles Grandison Finney and other nineteenth-century evangelists often drew newly dedicated Christians out of their individual concerns and into movements for social reform. In the twentieth century that was less often the case. When the preacher called a person to conversion, that person gained new spiritual dedication from an encounter with Jesus, but seldom did it lead to social reform. Personal piety was the order of the day, as many—dispensationalists especially—abandoned nineteenth-century optimism for an apocalyptic vision of the future and retreated into private concerns.

The progenitor of twentieth-century revivalism was Dwight L. Moody (1837–1899). Unlike George Whitefield or Charles Finney, Moody was not a powerful speaker. But he put together a highly efficient organization of publicists and support staff, and his earnest, businesslike pleas brought thousands of people back to Christ. He was fond of saying, "I look upon this world as a wrecked vessel. God has given me a lifeboat and said to me, 'Moody, save all you can.' " With his musical sidekick, Ira Sankey, Moody ministered to hundreds of thousands of people throughout America and England. His legacy included Moody Bible Institute in Chicago, which was a fountainhead of missionaries and other Christian workers throughout the twentieth century.

Next in the line of evangelical stars was Billy Sunday (1862–1935). A crude, combative, enthusiastic, and outspoken former major league ballplayer, Presbyterian Sunday attracted converts with a pugnacious, anti-intellectual style. He was proud to announce "I don't know any more about theology than a jack-rabbit knows about ping-pong, but I'm on my way to glory."

The outstanding revivalist preacher of the second half of the twentieth century is Billy Graham (1918–). He rocketed to national fame at a 1949 tent revival in Los Angeles, publicized by the Hearst newspaper chain because of Graham's anti-communism. By the end of the 1950s Graham was the best-known and best-loved American Christian, and he continues to hold those honors into the 1990s. One of his biographers claims, probably correctly, that "Billy Graham has been beheld personally by more people than any other human in history." He held huge rallies in every corner of the world and reached millions more through radio and TV. He is a personal acquaintance of many world leaders, including every U.S. president after Truman. Through his crusades and a vast supporting network, including subsidiary evangelists, books, and magazines, Graham's simple appeals to people to give their lives to Christ persuades millions.

Holiness and Pentecostalism

The most dynamic spiritual movement in modern world Christianity began in a warehouse in a poor section of Los Angeles in the spring of 1906. The *Azusa Street Revival* marked the beginning of *Pentecostalism*, a movement that by the 1980s claimed 30 million Americans and more than 100 million Christians worldwide. The roots of Pentecostalism lay in the nineteenth-century Holiness movement. All the revival preachers talked about salvation from sin, but the Methodists and other followers of John Wesley talked about going beyond salvation to becoming gradually "perfected." They did not think they would ever achieve perfection on this earth, but they were certain that God wanted them to try and that he would empower them to make progress.

As part of his work in the New York revival of 1876, Dwight L. Moody (1837–1899) lectured on evangelism to three thousand at the New York Hippodrome. (*Frank Leslie's Illustrated Newspaper*, April 15, 1876; copy Billy Graham Center)

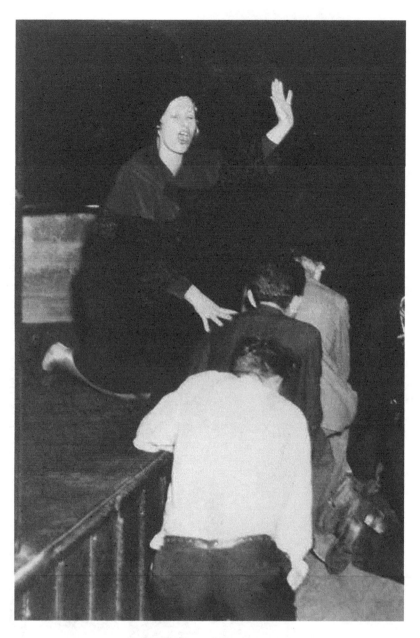

Aimee Semple McPherson (1890–1944) went to China with her husband, Robert Semple, in 1908. She returned with their child, Robert, after her husband's death. She subsequently married and divorced Harold McPherson. She pioneered in radio evangelism and became a popular faith healer in the 1920s and 1930s. The International Church of the Foursquare Gospel was organized as an outgrowth of her ministry in 1927. (Billy Graham Center)

16.5. Aimee Semple McPherson

Aimee Semple McPherson (1890–1944) carried out an itinerant evangelistic mission in the 1910s and 1920s, preaching a Pentecostal message called the *Foursquare Gospel*: Jesus as (1) Savior, (2) Healer, (3) Baptizer, and (4) Coming King.

She used startling costuming and special effects to dramatize her message. On one occasion she reportedly emerged suddenly, with clouds of dry ice and stark lighting, from a coffin placed at the front of the lecture hall, to preach on the Resurrection. Working out of Los Angeles, she appropriated some show business techniques and pioneered evangelistic radio on the West Coast. Her followers founded the International Church of the Foursquare Gospel. Her personal life was notorious. She was twice-divorced and apparently faked a kidnapping in order to have a tryst with her business manager.

Yet her dynamic and exciting pulpit manner won her long-lasting loyalty and firmly established the role of women as evangelists in the Pentecostal tradition.

The father of William "Billy" Sunday (1862–1935) died in the Civil War without ever seeing his child, and the children spent part of their childhood in an orphanage. Because of his skill as a runner and ball player he was signed in 1883 to play for the Chicago Whitestockings. After conversion, Sunday quit baseball to work full-time for the YMCA and began holding revival meetings in 1898. An estimated 1 million answered his invitations to accept Christ. (Billy Graham Center)

399

8 Great Days Of
REVIVAL

with Students of Wheaton College

Choruses!

Instrumental

Numbers!

Dynamic

Preaching!

Solos!

BILLY GRAHAM

Billy Graham, A Young Southern Evangelist With A Burning Message You Will Never Forget

Al Smith, Nationally-known Composer, Song Leader, Radio Artist!

Lloyd Fesmire, Pianist, Trombonist, Formerly With Percy Crawford's Famous Brass Quartet!

APRIL 13 = 20

The Church With The Sign "JESUS SAVES"

MOLINE, MICH.

Tune in Mel Trotter's Morning Mission Broadcast, Tuesday Thursday, 7 7:30 A.M.

Great YOUTH RALLY, Sunday, April 20, at 3 P. M.

The pastor of a small Baptist church in Western Springs, Illinois, William "Billy" Franklin Graham, Jr., resigned in 1945 to become a full-time evangelist for the Youth for Christ organization, conducting revivals like this one in Moline, Michigan, in the United States and Britain. He served as president of Northwestern Schools in Minneapolis from 1947 to 1951, resigning after his 1949 Los Angeles crusade catapulted him to prominence. (Billy Graham Center)

16.6. Oral Roberts

The career of Oral Roberts (1918–), TV evangelist and college president, paralleled that of Billy Graham in some ways. Roberts, ordained in the Pentecostal Holiness Church, held tent revivals emphasizing divine healing and the spiritual gift of tongues after World War II. He also used sophisticated mass mailing techniques and began television broadcasts in 1954.

As television audiences grew more sophisticated, Roberts changed his broadcast focus from healing to featuring celebrity guests and choreographed singing groups. At about the same time he switched from Pentecostal Holiness to the United Methodist denomination. Roberts founded Oral Roberts University, which opened in 1965 and was partially supported through his TV ministry. The university and other ambitious projects led to financial difficulties in the 1980s. Roberts resorted to unusual fund-raising appeals. He once implied that God might "call him home" unless sufficient funds came in by a certain date. This earned him ridicule in both secular and Christian press.

Holiness Christians—including some Methodists and people from the Reformed tradition as well—believed each person to be in one of three stages: unconverted, converted, or entirely sanctified. Entire sanctification came at a moment of second blessing (some time after conversion), when the believer was "baptized in the Holy Spirit." Usually he or she "spoke in tongues," that is, was overcome by ecstatic speech directed by the Holy Spirit as were the disciples on Pentecost in Acts 2. The Holiness movement produced a bewildering array of churches and sects in the late nineteenth century. This profusion multiplied when Pentecostalism appeared, adding dispensationalism's certainty of being near the end times to the other Holiness distinctives.

The worshipers on Azusa Street rent the night with shrieks and claimed all the spiritual gifts listed in 1 Corinthians 12 and 14. Quickly their enthusiasm spread to Christians in other parts of the country. In a decade, Pentecostal Christianity had been planted, without any apparent human strategy, on every continent. Pentecostals preached power to the powerless. The first believers in Los Angeles were lower-class blacks. Soon they were joined by poor southeastern farmers, white and black. Pentecostalism flourished wherever dispossessed people heard its message. The power it promised was the power of God's Holy Spirit. Not only theatrical tongues, but also prophecy and physical healings testified to God's power on loan to human beings. Most of the spectacular faith healers of the twentieth century, from Kathryn Kuhlmann to Oral Roberts, were Pentecostals.

Like Christians in many other times and places, these snake handlers believe the Bible calls them to routinely do the extraordinary and even dangerous as a test of their faith. They apply literally the statements of Mark 16:18 that Christians will be able in the last days to pick up snakes and drink poison as a sign. (Billy Graham Center)

In time, social mobility brought some Pentecostals into the middle class. Also, the Pentecostal experience spread beyond the bounds of strictly Pentecostal denominations, such as the Assemblies of God and the Church of God in Christ. In the 1960s "charismatic renewal"— essentially the practice of the Pentecostal or charismatic gifts among members of mainline denominations—began within Episcopal congregations in Los Angeles and Seattle, then spread to Roman Catholic, Lutheran, Baptist, and Presbyterian churches. Eventually every major tradition had at least some members, and even entire congregations, participating to some degree. The movement particularly affected how worship, prayer, liturgy, and music were conducted.

Mysticism

Another strand that emphasized direct contact with the Holy Spirit was the mystical tradition. It, too, took on new life in the mid-twentieth century. For Americans much of this influence came through the wide distribution of inexpensive paperbacks by mystics from a variety of traditions. Henri Nouwen, a Jesuit psychologist, communicated the development of an inner life in simple, accessible, but highly sophisticated writing. Richard Foster embodied the eclectic nature of

16.7. Thomas Merton and the Inward Search

Unless we discover this deep self, which is hidden with Christ in God, we will never really know ourselves as persons. Nor will we know God. For it is by the door of this deep self that we enter into the spiritual knowledge of God. (And indeed, if we seek our true selves it is not in order to contemplate ourselves but to pass beyond ourselves and find Him. . . .)*

But the pleasures of the interior life are so great and so pure; they so far transcend the crude joys of sense and of this world, that they exercise a terrible attraction upon the soul that meets them along its road to God. The thought of these pleasures, the memory of them and the hope of their recapture move a man to the very depths of his spirit and almost turn him inside out with the vehemence of great desire. He will do the wildest things if he believes that it will bring back two minutes of the joy he has once tasted in what seemed to be a vision of God. He will go to the ends of the earth to hear some unutterable word that once left him suspended between time and eternity. He will kill himself to hear some echo of that sweet voice.**

*John J. Higgins, *Merton's Theology of Prayer* (Spencer, Mass.: Cistercian, 1971), 26.

**Michael Mott, *The Seven Mountains of Thomas Merton* (Boston: Houghton Mifflin, 1984), 239.

twentieth-century mysticism. He was an evangelical Quaker who taught Baptists, Methodists, and Presbyterians how to use the spiritual disciplines of medieval Roman Catholic and Russian Orthodox monks. Thomas Merton (1915–1968), a Trappist monk, connected the monastic tradition of mysticism with social witness and non-Christian mystical traditions, especially Buddhist contemplation.

Politics and social action

The social gospel

While some American Christians were practicing the inward discipline of mysticism, others were practicing the outward discipline of social action. Many of those were proponents of, or heirs to, the tradition of the social gospel. The social activists met head-on the problems of the new industrial order.

Throughout the nineteenth century, evangelical Protestants had been at the forefront of many reform movements. From antislavery to women's rights, they and their allies had sought to make America a better, more just place. At century's end, they began systematically to criticize the base industrial structure that seemed to be at the root of much societal injustice. Pastors, such as Washington Gladden, and theologians, such as Walter Rauschenbusch, together with countless parishioners, fought for an eight-hour day, a six-day work week, and an end to child labor. This program did not differ much from that of secular progressives: a gentle critique of the structures of industrial capitalism, a call for somewhat more governmental regulation of the economy, and welfare aid for the poor.

Some opponents have charged that the social gospel was merely a sociological outgrowth of liberal theology, but this was not the case. Evangelicals, as well as liberals, subscribed to the social gospel—the Salvation Army may be seen as a social gospel organization—although with time most theological conservatives drifted away and left social Christianity largely in the hands of their liberal rivals.

16.8. The Social Creed of the Churches

In 1908 a coalition of American theological conservatives and liberals formed the Federal Council of Churches of Christ. This was one of the first expressions of the ecumenical movement that rose to prominence after World War II. Along with a desire for Christian unity, the Federal Council stressed missionary activity and the social gospel. The last theme is evident in the Council's "Social Creed of the Churches" (1908):

We deem it the duty of all Christian people to concern themselves directly with certain practical industrial problems. To us it seems that the churches must stand—

For equal rights and complete justice for all men in all stations of life.

For the right of all men to the opportunity of self-maintenance, a right ever to be wisely and strongly safeguarded against encroachments of every kind. For the right of workers to some protection against the hardships often resulting from the swift crises of industrial change.

For the principle of conciliation and arbitration in industrial dissensions.

For the protection of the worker from dangerous machinery, occupational disease, injuries and mortality.

For the abolition of child labor.

For such regulation of the conditions of toil for women as shall safeguard the physical and moral health of the community.

For the suppression of the "sweating system."

For the gradual and reasonable reduction of the hours of labor to the lowest practical point, and for that degree of leisure for all which is a condition of the highest human life.

For a release from employment one day in seven.

For a living wage as a minimum in every industry, and for the highest wage that industry can afford.

For the most equitable division of the products of industry that can ultimately be devised.

For suitable provision for the old age of the workers and for those incapacitated by injury.

For the abatement of poverty.*

*Mark A. Noll, et al., eds., *Eerdmans' Handbook to Christianity in America* (Grand Rapids: Eerdmans, 1983), 314.

The social implications of the gospel were also worked out among Roman Catholics. American Catholics had always practiced good works. But until after Vatican Council II most saw such works as personal acts of charity. Their primary concern was for personal piety and pursuit of the devotional life—prayer, saying the rosary, observing holy days, and similar personal elements of worship. Only a minority of liberal Catholics had concluded that social justice was also required by their faith and their situation in industrial America. Many of these were active in the labor movement, particularly a late nineteenth-century quasi-secret society called the Knights of Labor. Since most Catholics (far more than Protestants in percentage) were members of the immigrant working class, it was logical for them to embrace the cause of labor.

Their movement gained momentum from an 1891 papal encyclical, *Rerum Novarum*, which spelled out an approved program of reform for the industrial order. It condemned socialism and upheld private property, but it affirmed the right of workers to organize and condemned excessive capitalism and individualism. It called on the state to protect the rights of common people. *Rerum Novarum* led a significant minority of Catholics to adopt the social reform ideas of middle-class progressivism. In 1919 the *Bishops' Program of Social Reconstruction* called for minimum-wage and minimum working-age laws; public housing; old-age, health, and unemployment insurance; guarantee of the workers' right to organize; and close government regulation of public utilities and monopolies. But such people were a minority; most Catholics remained among the most conservative of Americans and tended to oppose progressive legislation.

It took the Great Depression to shake Catholics (and some Protestants) out of their conservative lethargy. Some of them began to follow an influential newspaper, *The Catholic Worker*, and its radical leader, Dorothy Day (1897–1981). Idealists who flocked to the Catholic Worker movement took voluntary oaths of poverty and set about serving others. Politically, most were socialists and firm pacifists, but they were also devout in their faith. Historian Jay Dolan described the Catholic Worker people thus:

> The Catholic Worker put no hope in the modern state; it put faith in the community of the sacred; the spiritual was more central to life than the material, peace was better than war, love in action was superior to love in dreams; the ideal of Christian perfection far surpassed the minimalism of the natural-law tradition; personalism outranked pragmatism; and in the end, the primacy of love would redeem history.[2]

These ideals affected many Catholics in the years before the Cold War.

Dorothy Day (1897–1981) worked as a reporter on various socialist publications and was active in the U.S. Socialist and Communist parties before joining the Roman Catholic church in 1927. With Peter Maurin she founded the *Catholic Worker* in 1933 to publicize church social programs and promote social help causes. She also opened a center for the homeless in New York City. (Marquette University Archives)

16.9. What *The Catholic Worker* Believes

The Catholic Worker believes in the gentle personalism of traditional Catholicism. *The Catholic Worker* believes in the personal obligation of looking after the needs of our brother. *The Catholic Worker* believes daily practice of the Works of Mercy. *The Catholic Worker* believes in Houses of Hospitality for the immediate relief of those who are in need. *The Catholic Worker* believes in the establishment of Farming Communes where each one works according to his ability and gets according to his need. *The Catholic Worker* believes in creating a new society within the shell of the old with the philosophy of the new which is not a new philosophy but a very old philosophy a philosophy so old that it looks like new.

Jay P. Dolan, *The American Catholic Experience* (Garden City, N.Y.: Doubleday, 1985), 410.

The progressive Christian tradition continued after World War II. One manifestation of the social side of Christianity was in the civil rights movement of the 1950s and 1960s. African-Americans had continued to suffer inequality and indignity after slavery ended in 1865. Hemmed in by segregation and a host of discriminatory laws and folkways, they had no chance at social or economic mobility. But in the mid-1950s, building on a half-century of work by the National Association for the Advancement of Colored People (NAACP) and other groups, southern blacks began to lay claim to an equal place in American society. The first leaders of this movement were nearly all evangelical ministers. From the Montgomery bus boycott to the Memphis garbage workers' strike, black ministers, such as Martin Luther King, Jr. (1929–1968), and Ralph David Abernathy (1926–), led blacks and a few sympathetic whites on a trail of bold assertion of their rights as citizens.

In the latter 1960s, the civil rights movement was overtaken by Black Power, a more militant and immediatist movement that lacked the core of Christian values and leadership of its predecessor. Some black theologians joined this new movement and promoted a distinctive black theology, which was related to the theology of liberation interpretation of Scripture and a soft-core Marxist analysis of social life.

One modern heir to the Roman Catholic social gospel tradition was John F. Kennedy (1917–1963). America's first Catholic president, Kennedy symbolized the emergence of Roman Catholics into the American mainstream. An activist president and a compassionate man, Kennedy's was a voice of hope to the have-nots of American society and a call to responsibility on the part of the more fortunate. Kennedy read *The Other America* by *Catholic Worker* disciple Michael Harrington, a book that caused many Americans to see poverty in their midst for the first time. Thereupon Kennedy initiated much of the legislation that would result in what his successor Lyndon Johnson (1908–1973) called *The Great Society*, a massive government attempt to end poverty and improve the quality of life for ordinary people.

16.10. Martin Luther King, Jr.

No American is more revered than Martin Luther King, Jr. (1929–1968). Born into a ministerial family in Atlanta, King attended all-black Morehouse College before taking B.D. and Ph.D. degrees at predominantly-white northern institutions. He returned to a pastorate in the South in 1954, a year before he was swept into leadership of a black boycott of the segregated bus system in Montgomery, Alabama.

For thirteen years thereafter, King led the civil rights movement, including people from all theological backgrounds, to challenge the racist laws and practices of the segregationist South. He combined spellbinding oratory and physical courage with a demanding philosophy of non-violence and a compelling vision of the future, the latter poignantly expressed in his "I Have a Dream" speech, delivered in 1963 on the mall in Washington, D.C.:

I have a dream that one day this nation will rise up and live out the true meaning of its creed: "We hold these truths to be self-evident—that all men are created equal." I have a dream that one day on the red hills of Georgia the sons of former slaves and the sons of former slave owners will be able to sit down together at the table of brotherhood. I have a dream that one day even the state of Mississippi, a desert state sweltering with the heat of injustice and oppression, will be transformed into an oasis of freedom and justice. I have a dream that my four little children will one day live in a nation where they will not be judged by the color of their skin but by the content of their character.

The work of King's Southern Christian Leadership Conference (SCLC) and thousands of supporters resulted in the gradual desegregation of public places and greater access to decent housing and education. Substantial gains for blacks and other minorities were built upon the Civil Rights Act of 1964, and the Voting Rights Act of 1965, passed largely as a result of the efforts of King and the civil rights campaign. Such accomplishments earned King international acclaim, including the Nobel Peace Prize in 1964.

Increasingly, King turned his attention to improving the lot of northern blacks and poor whites, and to ethical opposition to the U.S. war against Vietnam. Before much progress could be made on those fronts, however, King was assassinated in 1968. His death touched off racial rioting across the country and mourning by supporters of human rights, black and white.

The honors to King and his legacy have included designation of a U.S. national holiday in his memory.

The evangelical strain of the social gospel is evident in the career of Jimmy Carter (1924–). A self-described "born-again-Baptist-Sunday-school-teacher-deacon," Carter in 1976 became the first evangelical Protestant elected President since Garfield. His was, perhaps, the last presidency to follow the traditions of progressivism and the New Deal. His successors turned away from social justice toward other concerns. Carter as President consciously continued to pursue a social justice program that had first arisen from sources as disparate as Gladden, King, Kennedy, and Day. He made human rights and Third World development central to his foreign policy. While succeeding presidents dismantled most of what he had built, Carter as a private citizen continued a wide range of social service projects, from building homes for poor people with his own hands to raising money for people with physical handicaps.

Right-wing politics

If the social gospel was often labeled a left-wing voice in American public life, others were given the right-wing label for their political conservatism. Both labels were usually simplistic. Church members were associated with ideals and causes all along the spectrum. On the "right" this tended to extend from the genteel, upper-crust conservativism of wealthy members in mainline churches to the rabid reactionism of the Ku Klux Klan and similar self-proclaimed protectors of "white Christian Americanism."

Leaders of conservative movements were diverse. The careers of three of the more well known among them—Charles Coughlin, Gerald L. K. Smith, and Jerry Falwell—tell something of the history of the general political right Christian movement.

Father Charles Coughlin

One of the most influential political figures of the 1930s was a Canadian-born parish priest, Charles Coughlin (1891–1979). In 1926 Coughlin began to air sermons over the radio from his Shrine of the Little Flower outside Detroit. At first Coughlin used his mellifluous voice to attract a huge following with fairly standard sermons. But as the Depression deepened after 1930 he increasingly directed strident attacks against anyone whose great wealth was, in his view, destroying the ordinary people of America. A Coughlin biographer describes the impact of his messages on the weekly schedules of his listeners:

> In Brockton, Massachusetts, referees halted schoolboy football games shortly before three o'clock on Sunday afternoons so that parents, coaches, and players could get to a radio in time to hear Father Coughlin. When the sermons were over, the games resumed. In churches around the country, pastors rescheduled Sunday services so they would not conflict with the radio discourses. In urban neighborhoods throughout the East and Midwest—not only Irish communities, but German, Italian, Polish; not only Catholic areas, but Protestant and, for a time, even Jewish—many residents long remembered the familiar experience of walking down streets lined with row houses, triple-deckers, or apartment buildings and hearing out of every window the voice of Father Coughlin blaring from the radio. You could walk for blocks, they recalled, and never miss a word.[3]

Father Coughlin's initial support for Franklin Roosevelt and the New Deal turned to vitriolic opposition as he perceived Roosevelt to waffle on taking dramatic steps to aid lower-middle-class people. For a time, in 1934 and 1935, it appeared Coughlin and other dissidents, such as Louisiana senator Huey Long, might mount a forceful challenge to the New Deal. But their third party bid fizzled when Long was assassinated in 1935.

Coughlin never advocated structural changes in the American economy after the fashion of left-wing Christians. Rather, he called for a return to an idealized past era when small-scale capitalism, run by good Christian people, had been the basis for a more just society. Frustrated by dwindling public support and his failure to overthrow President Roosevelt, Coughlin turned more controversial. He opposed

American involvement in World War II, praised Adolf Hitler and Benito Mussolini, and launched frenzied attacks against what he saw as an international Jewish-Communist conspiracy. In 1940 he was driven from the air by public outrage and by censure from the Catholic hierarchy. He served out his days as a parish priest.

Gerald L. K. Smith

Gerald L. K. Smith (1898–1976) began where Coughlin left off. This charismatic speaker, a Disciples of Christ minister, began his political career as an advance man and organizer for Huey Long (then the Louisiana governor). Coughlin's themes of populism and sometimes frenzied anti-Semitism also ran through Smith's career. After World War II, Smith organized the Christian Nationalist Crusade, a political movement complete with uniformed youth auxiliary that resembled, too closely for the comfort of many, the Hitler Youth movement. It was based on the idea that Christian character was the basis for any real Americanism. Critics have charged that Coughlin, Long, and Smith represented a domestic American fascism.

Jerry Falwell

Jerry Falwell (1933–) is different from these mass media political preachers in that he did not challenge the assumptions of modern democracy. At the same time, he associated Americanism and evangelical values with one another and asserted the right of religious conservatives to speak out on political issues. Most of the time his advocacy group, the Moral Majority, supported a return to what many people regarded as traditional values. In the 1980s they provided solid support for some candidates, mostly Republican. Sensitive to charges that he was politicizing the Christian faith, in 1989 Falwell dissolved the Moral Majority, asserting that its agenda had been largely achieved. Falwell retained his radio and television programs and often spoke on political and social issues. Nevertheless, he stressed evangelism and Christian higher education as founder and president of Liberty University.

Falwell is sometimes credited with bringing right-wing Christians into national politics as supporters of Ronald Reagan in the elections of 1980 and 1984. But religious conservatives had been active in every election of the century. It can be argued that they were particularly decisive in the victories of Warren Harding in 1920 and Calvin Coolidge in 1924, and in the defeat of Catholic Al Smith in 1928. In each of these cases, conservatives struck a blow for homogeneity and material prosperity, and against the leveling impulses of the social gospel.

411

War and peace

One issue that stayed near the top of the political agenda throughout the century was the question of war and peace. Throughout, Christians were on both sides of this issue.

During World War I pugnacious evangelist Billy Sunday insisted that God wanted Christians to fight for America, while William Jennings Bryan and Harry Emerson Fosdick opposed the war on the ground of conscience. Most American Christians, however, were swept away by the world-saving rhetoric of President Woodrow Wilson. They found themselves embarrassed when, after the war, the world did not become as safe for democracy as they had expected. For the next two decades most Christians inclined toward pacifism, concluding that wars did not solve much. That consensus was battered by the bombs at Pearl Harbor in 1941. Most American Christians believed World War II fit Augustine's definition of a "just" war. Theologian Reinhold Niebuhr and some others found the holocaust in Europe so awful that they deemed it a positive duty of Christians to join the fight against the Axis alliance. Few, besides members of traditional peace churches (Quakers, for example) and the Jehovah's Witnesses, refused to participate in the war. Even those who did refuse to serve based their protest on individual conscience against all taking of life, not opposition to this particular war as a policy matter. Some of them served time in jail for refusing to accept being drafted.

War changed forever in August 1945 when the United States dropped atomic bombs on two Japanese cities. The nuclear nightmare born at Hiroshima and Nagasaki seemed so horrible to many Christians that they tried to get politicians to renounce war once and for all time. Even mainline churches became peace churches, at least with respect to nuclear weapons. Other Christians, however, soon became caught up in the passions of the Cold War with the Soviet bloc countries and supported the preparation of more and bigger weapons of mass destruction.

The war between the United States and Vietnam, lasting from 1954 to 1975, divided Christians once again. At first the war was small and marginal to Americans' consciousness. But by 1965 more than half a million American troops were in the field, and in the next decade more bombs were dropped on one small country than on all the countries that fought World War II combined. The vague aims, mismanagement, and dubious legality of the war effort made Vietnam an increasingly unpopular cause among all Americans, Christians included. Some, including Clergy and Laymen Concerned about Vietnam, took a leading role in opposition to the war.

After the bitter end of the Vietnam conflict many Americans turned away from that humiliation with an increasingly bellicose stance toward the rest of the world. Evangelicals and some Catholics were prominent among the supporters of an aggressive posture toward the U.S.S.R., as well as military adventures in Grenada, El Salvador, Nicaragua, Panama, and Kuwait in the 1980s and 1990s. Other Catholics and social liberal Protestants were active in opposing those military involvements.

Institutional changes

The ecumenical movement

If American Christians were ambivalent about wars among nations they cheerfully made war among themselves. The nineteenth century witnessed the split of several major denominations into Northern and Southern bodies over slavery. In the century after the Civil War, Baptists were rent into hundreds of groups such as General Baptists, Regular Baptists, Fundamental Baptists, Independent Baptists, Japanese Baptists, and Swedish Baptists. No other major tradition has quite the Baptists' seeming enthusiasm for schism, but none except Roman Catholics remained essentially whole. Some new denominations were born out of angry personal acrimony, others out of theological controversy, still others when revival touched some Christians and not their fellows. The proliferation of denominations is one of the most striking features of American Christianity, and one of the most puzzling to those from outside the North American churches. In addition to such conflicts, there was also the general mutual accusations and mistrust between Protestants as a whole and Roman Catholics. American Christianity, it seemed, was largely about conflict.

Yet in the middle of the twentieth century a counter-trend appeared. *Ecumenism*, the uniting of Christians across denominational lines, had been brewing a long time. The nineteenth century had seen the formation of Bible societies, the American Sunday School Union, antislavery associations, and other parachurch organizations that brought Christians together in pursuit of particular goals. Internationally, Christians had been coming together in such organizations as the Alliance of Reformed Churches (founded 1875), the Baptist World Alliance (1905), and the YMCA (1844). Many Protestant groups came together in a confederation in 1908 to found the *Federal Council of Churches of Christ* in pursuit of missions and the social gospel.

Facing the rising threat of totalitarianism and secularism in the 1930s, European Christians laid plans for a *World Council of Churches*, which took final form after the war. Soon a *National Council of Churches* brought together the American constituency of the World Council.

The National and World Councils operated mainly on behalf of mainline Protestant churches of modernist theological persuasion, although there was some communication with the Catholic hierarchy and, occasionally, evangelicals. The World Council harnessed the money and energies of Christians to aid refugees, organize international theological discussions, expand missionary efforts, and publicize abuses of human rights. The National Council became active in the 1960s in support of the civil rights movement and of migrant farmworkers, and in opposition to the war in Vietnam.

Many conservative groups stayed out of the ecumenical councils, on the grounds that their theology was impure, that their social action aims were inappropriate, or that such bodies threatened the autonomy of denominations and individual congregations. Some even claimed that the World Council (with the United Nations) was part of the Antichrist's plot to create one world government. Yet conservatives formed ecumenical organizations of their own, such as the *National Association of Evangelicals* (1942).

Another expression of the ecumenical impulse came in the form of denominational mergers. More than two dozen such mergers occurred in the first three quarters of the twentieth century. One of the most spectacular united six million Lutherans from three traditions into one church in the 1980s. Such mergers could cause almost as many dislocations for Christians as schisms. Denominational employees lost

16.11. Campus Crusade for Christ

Founded in 1951 at UCLA by Bill Bright, Campus Crusade for Christ is dedicated to evangelizing and nurturing the faith of college students, although its international ministries now extend beyond colleges and universities. One of its tools for witnessing is a pamphlet, designed to be shared by a Christian with an unbeliever, called "The Four Spiritual Laws." The presentation is built around the concepts:

1) God loves you and offers a wonderful plan for your life.

2) Man is sinful and separated from God. Thus he cannot know and experience God's love and plan for his life.

3) Jesus Christ is God's only provision for man's sin. Through him you can know and experience God's love and plan for your life.

4) We must individually receive Jesus Christ as savior and lord; then we can know and experience God's love and plan for our lives.

Though its widest appeal has been to what might be called the "keen teens"—"cheerleaders and jocks" from white, upper-middle-class backgrounds, Campus Crusade also has pioneered techniques for discipleship through cell-group Bible studies, sports personalities, and other role model spokespersons.

jobs as staffs were consolidated and headquarters moved. New theological controversies arose and some individuals and congregations left the merged denominations. But, by and large, denominational mergers erased minor barriers and brought like-minded believers into fellowship with one another.

Another aspect of ecumenism was the explosion of parachurch organizations after World War II. Some were older international organizations, such as the InterVarsity Christian Fellowship, which caught new life in America in the 1950s. Others, for example Young Life, Youth for Christ, and Campus Crusade for Christ, were homegrown agencies geared to youth. Some were ethnic, such as the North American Congress of Chinese Evangelicals. Some fit specific occupations—the Christian Booksellers Association. Some dealt with specific aspects of living—the marriage encounter movement. Old nondenominational missions took new life: the China Inland Mission became the Overseas Missionary Fellowship. New groups such as The Evangelical Alliance Mission (TEAM) formed. All these and many more organizations bespoke a change in the experience of the average believer. Where once a Christian identified with a denomination and received all nurture through the local church, after 1950 many became involved in Christian experiences that took place without reference to the church in which they worshiped on Sunday.

Changes in worship and leadership

For many, worship itself changed. Under the influence of the 1960s counterculture and the charismatic renewal, formal church services became informal and more participation oriented. Where before all was robes, vestments, organ music, and I-talk-you-listen preaching, even high church Episcopalian congregations sprouted guitars, blue jeans, and sharing times. After Vatican II Roman Catholic churches gave up the Latin liturgy for worship that communicated in language the believers could understand. Worship services moved into homes and onto streets. Baptisms went down by the lake. Democracy and declining formality in worship lent new freshness for some believers (but alienated others).

Interestingly, there was a simultaneous movement among some of the old informal groups toward more formality. Evangelicals discovered meaning in liturgy and serenity in litanies. A new appreciation for esthetics brought colorful banners and art hangings into many sanctuaries for the first time. All this contributed to a blurring of at least some distinctions between American Protestants and Roman Catholics. Each gradually began to notice and selectively appropriate the riches of the other, a process that brought worship renewal to both. Another influence was the charismatic renewal movement in many mainline Protestant and Catholic churches in the 1960s and 1970s. Both experienced some expression of tongues, healing, and prophecy in worship and body life. Slowly the old ritual was giving way, but new forms had not yet been decided upon. Variety and creativity were the order of the day.

Several changes in leadership overtook the church as well. The pastorate was the first profession to serve colonial North America and was the focus of the earliest colleges. But the ministerial concept underwent significant changes in the twentieth century. With the rise of a trained, specialized managerial class in business after the 1920s, priests and ministers began to adopt managerial models for their own work, reflecting what they saw in the more successful members of their congregations. By midcentury business values had so suffused American culture that many pastors often saw themselves as administrators of ecclesiastical enterprises. They attended time management seminars and hung flow charts in their offices.

A related development was the professionalization of the evangelical clergy. At one time in the nineteenth century it had been a badge of pride among Baptist or Methodist clergy that they had little or no education. But in the twentieth century even the most fundamentalist clergy tended to seek higher degrees and professional training certificates at a profusion of new seminaries and Bible institutes.

The democratic and inclusivist impulses extended beyond worship to leadership issues. In response to the revived feminist movement of the later 1900s in the larger society, women began to take on roles of spiritual leadership in respectable churches they had not known since the times of Deborah and Phoebe. In mainline Protestant churches, women became deacons and ministers and seminary professors, although not without occasional controversy. The Catholic Church was in a frequent state of crisis over demands of women for a greater role and the Vatican's intransigent response. Meanwhile the number of women taking holy orders plummeted. A severe shortage of nuns developed.

Among conservative Protestants, the trend was often the opposite of that for the mainline churches. At the turn of the century many evangelical groups perceived the field white unto harvest and wanted to send out all the workers they could find, without regard for education or gender. Many denominations trained, ordained, or employed women in ministerial roles. As fundamentalism lost its optimism and retreated in the 1920s, while simultaneously professionalizing its clergy, women were systematically pushed out of public ministry and limited to helper roles. As mainline churches threw open their ministries, conservative minorities who pulled away from them especially identified feminism with antibiblical theology. Where in 1920 female graduates of Moody Bible

"Home mass" Eucharist celebrations conducted by Roman Catholic women serving in the role of priests sometimes violated church law but came to symbolize a movement throughout Protestant and Roman Catholic churches toward acceptance of women in all aspects of ministry. (Image Bank)

16.12. Feminist Theology

Rosemary Radford Ruether, one of the most prominent speakers for feminist Christianity, wrote in a spiritual autobiography in 1982:

The teachings of Timothy about women keeping silence now appear, not as the uniform practice of the New Testament church, but as a reaction against the widespread participation of women in leadership, teaching, and ministry in first generation Christianity. The participation of women in the early church was not an irregular accident, but rather the expression of an alternative world-view. Women were seen equally as the image of God. The equality of women and men at the original creation was understood as restored through Christ. The gifts of the Spirit of the messianic advent were understood (in fulfillment of the prophet Joel) and poured out on the "menservants" and "maidservants" of the Lord alike (Acts 2:17–21). Baptism overcomes the sinful divisions that divide men from women, Jew from Greek, slave from free, and makes us one in Christ (Gal. 3:28). The inclusion of women in early Christianity expressed a theology in direct contradiction to the theology of patriarchal subordination of women. In this way the New Testament must be read, not as a consensus about women's place, but

417

> rather as a conflict of understandings of male-female relations in the church.
>
> This alternative theology of equality—of women as equal in the image of God, as restored to equality in Christ and as commissioned to preach and minister by the Spirit—did not just disappear with the reassertion of patriarchal norms in I Timothy; it can be seen surfacing again and again in different periods of Christian history. . . .
>
> Feminists engaged in recovering alternative histories for women in religion recognize that they are not just supplementing the present male tradition. They are, implicitly, attempting to construct a new norm for the interpretation of the tradition. The male justification of women's subordination in Scripture and tradition is no longer regarded as normative for the gospel. Rather, it is judged as a failure to apply the gospel norms of equality in creation and redemption authentically. This is judged a failure in much the same way that political corruption of the church, the persecution of Jews, heretics, or witches, and the acceptance of slavery have been so judged.
>
> Rosemary Radford Reuther, *Disputed Questions: On Being a Christian* (Nashville: Abingdon, 1982), 123–25.

Institute served in pulpits across the country, by 1970 the school refused to condone the ordination of women. The renewed feminist movement after midcentury had a much slower impact on evangelical Protestants.

Christian schools

In the beginning, all the schools in America were Christian—they were taught by Christians to Christians, often for the purpose of enabling believers to read the Bible, and they assumed a Christian worldview. Early institutions of higher education, such as Harvard and Yale, were founded specifically to train ministers. Only later did most educational institutions broaden their focus to train people for a variety of vocations. However, even public schools kept a good deal of Protestant content as late as the early twentieth century.

Catholics worried about their children losing the distinctives of their faith in public schools, so they founded hundreds and then thousands of Catholic schools and colleges. In the nineteenth century the building of schools was integral to the American Catholic Church. Public schools remained resolutely Protestant, and Catholic education expanded in self-defense. Late in the nineteenth century the Protestant character of public education faded into a more neutral secularity, but Catholic schools did not diminish. Immigrants seized on the parochial school as a vehicle to pass on religion, language, and culture. With Catholic elementary and secondary schools in abundance (Los Angeles had more than eighty in 1960), it was easy to maintain enrollment for hundreds of Catholic colleges as well—from Seattle University and Loyola Marymount on the West Coast to Boston College and Fordham in the East.

By the late twentieth century, many secular values had crept into public education. Gone were Bible stories, daily prayer, and a religious understanding of holidays. Curricula became religiously neutral, even vehemently secular. Partly this was the result of a legal onslaught from organized atheism, but mainly it reflected the secularizing tendencies of society at large. Some Protestants, fundamentalists particularly, found this intolerable. They launched loud campaigns to bring back religious education in the public schools. Those attempts almost always failed, and many fled to schools of their own.

Protestant church-related schools were not totally new. Some Reformed denominations, many Lutherans, Episcopalians, Anabaptists, and others had long maintained schools of their own. Suddenly, however, in the last quarter of the twentieth century a deluge of new day schools and academies were unleashed. Frequently these schools ran on almost no money, with underpaid and underqualified staff and poor facilities. Meanwhile, better-established Catholic schools gained Protestant students with their reputation for strict discipline and solid basic education. Another increasingly popular option among Protestants and some Catholics—whose institutions were closing by the 1980s due to fewer available teachers and higher costs—was the home school movement. Curricula were developed especially with parent-taught home schools in mind.

The twentieth century saw an evolution in sectarian higher education as well. The majority of colleges and universities had denominational origins, but few had retained their religious character. Yet new schools have continually been born to serve churches. In the seventeenth century Yale was founded by Puritans who believed Harvard had gone soft on its spiritual commitments. Similarly, in the late twentieth century, Bob Jones and Liberty universities were founded by those who feared Biola and Wheaton were losing their zeal. Some fringe Bible institutes were attached to traditionally anti-intellectual groups. Some had two-year programs that avoided "secular" subjects, such as chemistry and literature. Most, however, looked for a balanced program stressing a Christian worldview, and some schools that did not start out with strong academic goals soon moved toward them in search of academic respectability and accreditation.

If Protestant colleges were constantly ebbing toward a more non-sectarian outlook, the same was even more true of the major Catholic

16.13. Many Voices

The mid-twentieth century witnessed the publication of more new translations of the Bible in English than in all previous centuries combined. The King James Version gave way before a host of new Bibles written in more-or-less twentieth-century vernacular. Beginning with the Revised Standard Version in 1952 and continuing down to the New Revised Standard Version in 1990, nine major translations of the Scriptures appeared in the English-speaking world.

Partly, this was a democratization of Christianity, putting Scripture in the hands of lay people in a form they could easily understand. Partly it reflected a pop scholasticism; Christians now had arcane points of translation over which to argue. Those of all traditions and theological persuasions took part in this trend. Where in 1890 a Christian household would typically have one copy of the King James translation of the Bible, by 1970 there might be half a dozen Bibles, all different, competing for the family's attention. Some new versions of the Bible were:

The Good News Bible, Today's English Version, by the American Bible Society, 1966–76.

The Jerusalem Bible, for Roman Catholics, primarily in the United Kingdom, through Darton, Longman, and Todd, 1966.

The Living Bible, by Kenneth Taylor through Tyndale House, 1971.

The New American Bible (Confraternity), by the Catholic Biblical Association, 1966–70.

The New American Standard Bible, Lockman Foundation, 1960.

The New English Bible, by the British and Foreign Bible Society through Oxford University Press and Cambridge University Press, 1961–70.

The New International Version, by the International Bible Society, 1973–78.

The New King James Version, Thomas Nelson, 1979–82.

The New Revised Standard Version, by the International Council of Religious Education, 1990.

The Reader's Digest Bible, Reader's Digest Publishers, 1982.

The Revised Standard Version, by the Division of Christian Education, National Council of the Churches of Christ in the U.S.A., 1946–52.

schools. Where Notre Dame and Loyola were primarily religious schools at the beginning of the century, they are now mainly universities that happen to have a lot of priests on the faculty.

The electronic church

If the nineteenth century brought the industrial revolution to Europe and North America, the twentieth century brought the electronic revolution. Radio and television transformed life, including religious life. Religious radio began in 1921 when station KDKA in Pittsburgh started broadcasting programs from a local Episcopal church. Denominations and congregations continued to produce radio and, after

World War II, television shows. But quickly the main thrust went to independent entrepreneurs. Evangelists hit the airwaves in the 1920s and were a mainstay ever after. Politics, especially "conservative" views, was a popular product from Charles Coughlin to Jerry Falwell.

Among those who wanted to reach a larger market share, television put a premium on entertainment, especially appealing personalities and spectacular visuals. In the 1950s Catholic bishop Fulton Sheen and Baptist Billy Graham filled the bill with their warm, inspiring personalities. Later Pat Robertson and Robert Schuller projected more glitter but primarily used a similar projection of warm friendliness. But the masters of the airwaves were media-studied showmen, most from the charismatic and Pentecostal traditions. Oral Roberts began with a conventional approach of airing excerpts from his preaching and healing services. His expertise and production studios increased until his specials competed with any secular variety entertainment. When Jimmy Swaggart took to the air he opted for an blend of frenetic preaching and energetic musicianship. Televangelistic ministries expanded until, by 1980, nearly one-half of the American public watched religious TV each week, millions more than went to church. One effect was increased privatization of religion, a drawing away of people from the communities of their local congregations. The typical religious experience of many a believer came to revolve around listening to the preacher's warm reassurance on Sunday morning TV and then mailing in the weekly check.

Vatican II in America

The most important dates and places in twentieth-century Christian history are Los Angeles in 1906 and Rome in 1962 through 1965. The former heralded the Azusa Street birth of Pentecostalism. The latter marked Vatican Council II. The long-term impact of Vatican II may prove greater on the Third World, but it was substantial in the United States as well. Whereas Third World Catholics found in Vatican II a voice for the poor and oppressed (see p. 376), middle-class American Catholics found in it a voice for the individual. In the two decades following, hundreds of changes took place within American Catholic churches in the direction of openness and individual empowerment.

Most prominent at first was liturgical renewal. The altar was turned around so that the priest faced the people. He spoke in English rather than Latin, and people frequently spoke back in dialogue with him before God. The previously Protestant idea of the priesthood of all believers invaded Catholic doctrine to the point that the Mass was sometimes led by laymen and laywomen in their homes, with priests present as equal members of the parish. There were new emphases on the Bible and on spiritual gifts in some sectors, so that Catholics began to hold Bible studies like evangelicals and speak in tongues like Pentecostals. The new

16.14. "Declaration of Religious Freedom"

The part of Vatican Council II that meant most to many Christians was its statement on religious freedom, which read in part:

This Vatican Synod declares that the human person has a right to religious freedom. This freedom means that all men are to be immune from coercion on the part of individuals or of social groups and of any human power, in such wise that in matters religious no one is to be forced to act in a manner contrary to his own beliefs. Nor is anyone to be restrained from acting in accordance with his own beliefs, whether privately or publicly, whether alone or in association with others, within due limits.

The Synod further declares that the right to religious freedom has its foundation in the very dignity of the human person, as this dignity is known through the revealed Word of God and by reason itself. This right of the human person to religious freedom is to be recognized in the constitutional law whereby society is governed. Thus it is to become a civil right. *

"Religious Freedom" (Washington: National Catholic Welfare Conference, 1965), reprinted in Edwin S. Gaustad, *A Documentary History of Religion in America*, Vol. 2, *Since 1865* (Grand Rapids: Eerdmans, 1983), 476.

era brought Catholics a new sense of sin—more personal, less legalistic, but also less vivid. Where before worshipers would frequently enter the confessional to recite their sins, now they might interact face-to-face with a priest-counselor in a "reconciliation room"—or not confess at all.

One document with far-reaching impact was the Council's Declaration of Religious Freedom, which implied freedom of individual dissent from the church hierarchy. The stage was set for releasing new and long-smoldering conflicts between parishioner and priest, priest and bishop, bishop and pope. Some hard-core traditionalist priests used their new freedom to rebel against changes in worship and tried to stick with the Latin Mass; they were censured for their pains. More American Catholics went the opposite way, for example, daring to question church stands on birth control and abortion. Many, influenced by their national culture, came to believe that choices in these areas should be left up to the individual conscience. The pope particularly insisted on adhering to the traditional Catholic ban on all forms of birth control, a decision reaffirmed in the encyclical *"Humanae Vitae"* in 1968. Theologian Charles E. Curran of Catholic University was harassed for two decades and finally banned from teaching on account of his insistence on the individualist view. Some people left the Catholic Church over such issues. More stayed and simply defied the pope—a development unprecedented in Catholic history.

In the period of new openness, the status of clergy declined, as did the number of people taking vows. A startling number of priests and nuns left their religious vocations for lives as laypeople.

Vatican II also affected American Catholics by calling them to examine the structures of power in society and to side with the poor and oppressed. This fruit was much riper in Latin America than in the United

16.15. Economic Justice for All

A fruit of Vatican Council II was a new willingness among Roman Catholic leaders to speak out on controversial issues, from nuclear weapons to the economy. On the latter subject, the U.S. National Conference of Catholic Bishops published a pastoral letter in 1986 that echoed the social gospel and included the following themes:

Every economic decision and institution must be judged in light of whether it protects or undermines the dignity of the human person. . . . We judge any economic system by what it does for and to people and by how it permits all to participate in it. The economy should serve people, not the other way around. Human dignity can be realized and protected only in community. . . .

The obligation to "love our neighbor" had an individual dimension, but it also required a broader social commitment to the common good. . . .

All people have a right to participate in the economic life of society. Basic justice demands that people be assured a minimum level of participation in the economy. It is wrong for a person or group to be excluded unfairly or to be unable to participate or contribute *to the economy. For example, people who are both able and willing, but cannot get a job are deprived of the participation that is so vital to human development. . . .*

All members of society have a special obligation to the poor and vulnerable. From the scriptures and church teaching, we learn that the justice of a society is tested by the treatment of the poor. The justice that was the sign of God's covenant with Israel was measured by how the poor and unprotected—the widow, the orphan, and the stranger—were treated. . . . As followers of Christ, we are challenged to make a fundamental "option for the poor"—to speak for the voiceless, to defend the defenseless, to assess life styles, policies, and social institutions in terms of their impact on the poor. This option for the poor does not mean pitting one group against another, but rather, strengthening the whole community by assisting those who are most vulnerable. As Christians, we are called to respond to the needs of all our brothers and sisters, but those with the greatest needs require the greatest response.

Human rights are the minimum for life in community. In Catholic teaching, human rights include not only civil and political rights but also

economic rights. As Pope John XXIII declared, "all people have a right to life, food, clothing, shelter, rest, medical care, education, and employment." This means that when people are without a chance to earn a living, and must go hungry and homeless they are being denied basic rights. Society must ensure that these rights are protected. In this way, we will ensure that the minimum conditions of economic justice are met for all our sisters and brothers.

Society as a whole, acting through public and private institutions, has the moral responsibility to enhance human dignity and protect human rights. . . .

Our pastoral letter spells out some specific applications of Catholic moral principles. We call for a new national commitment to full employment. We say it is a social and moral scandal that one of every seven Americans is poor, and we call for concerted efforts to eradicate poverty. The fulfillment of the basic needs of the poor is of the highest priority. We urge all economic policies be evaluated in light of their impact on the life and stability of the family. We support measures to halt the loss of family farms and to resist the growing concentration in the ownership of agricultural resources. We specify ways in which the United States can do far more to relieve the plight of poor nations and assist in their development. We also reaffirm church teaching on the rights of workers, collective bargaining, private property, solidarity, and equal opportunity.*

*Economic Justice for All: Pastoral Letter on Catholic Social Teaching and the U.S. Economy (Washington: U.S. Catholic Conference Office of Publishing and Promotion Service, 1986), ix–xi.

States, but it did shape the activities of some North American Catholics as well. Further, social action of this sort was one way that Catholics began to reach out and draw in non-Catholics.

Conclusion

Nearing the end of the twentieth century, American Christians had seen their world fragment under a host of forces. Industry, immigration, the end of Protestant consensus, two world wars, the nuclear nightmare, the rise and sharp decline of the United States from the pinnacle of world power, and rapidly changing lifestyles all were profoundly unsettling.

The world of twentieth-century American Christians was one of flux and change, and the future seemed uncertain indeed.

Suggested readings

General

Ahlstrom, Sydney E. *A Religious History of the American People*. New Haven, Conn.: Yale University Press, 1972.

Gaustad, Edwin S., ed. *A Documentary History of Religion in America since 1865*. Grand Rapids: Eerdmans, 1983.

Marsden, George M. *Religion and American Culture*. New York: Harcourt Brace Jovanovich, 1990.

Noll, Mark A., et al, eds. *Eerdmans' Handbook to Christianity in America*. Grand Rapids: Eerdmans, 1983.

Black Christians

Lincoln, C. Eric, and Lawrence H. Mamiya. *The Black Church in the African-American Experience*. Durham, N.C.: Duke University Press, 1990.

Catholicism

Dolan, Jay P. *The American Catholic Experience: A History from Colonial Times to the Present*. Garden City, N.Y.: Doubleday, 1985.

Liberalism

Cross, Robert D. *The Emergence of Liberal Catholicism in America*. Chicago: Quadrangle, 1968.

Hutchison, William R. *The Modernist Impulse in American Protestantism*. Cambridge, Mass.: Harvard University Press, 1976.

Evangelicalism

Flake, Carol. *Redemptorama: Culture, Politics, and the New Evangelicalism*. Garden City, N.Y.: Doubleday, 1984.

Marsden, George M. *Fundamentalism and American Culture: The Shaping of Twentieth-Century Evangelicalism*. New York: Oxford University Press, 1980.

Weber, Timothy P. *Living in the Shadow of the Second Coming: American Premillenialism, 1875–1982*. Chicago: University of Chicago Press, 1987.

Political Christianity

Handy, Robert T., ed. *The Social Gospel in America, 1870–1920: Gladden, Ely, and Rauschenbusch*. New York: Oxford University Press, 1966.

Jorstad, Erling. *The Politics of Moralism: The New Christian Right in American Life*. Minneapolis: Augsburg, 1981.

Ribuffo, Leo. *The Old Christian Right: The Protestant Far Right from the Great Depression to the Cold War*. Philadelphia: Temple University Press, 1983.

17

Around the World Since World War II

The world since World War II

The most significant trend after World War II was the success of Third World nationalism. From the Philippines in 1945 to Namibia in 1990, nearly 100 nations achieved independence from colonial powers. Independence brought a host of opportunities and problems, from political stability and economic vitality in Singapore to poverty and incessant civil war in the horn of Africa.

Another major trend was global interconnectedness. Television satellites spread images and markets. Multinational corporations proliferated and expanded their economic power. Coca-Cola became a mainstay of the diet of Hong Kong, even as Europeans bought Japanese cars and American computer chips were manufactured in the Philippines. Interconnectedness meant, among other things, that some nations in Africa and Asia fell prey to the extractive, neocolonial relationships experienced by Latin America since an earlier era. But Third World nations often fought back to assert their independence, both politically and economically.

Population skyrocketed in many areas. While Europe and North America showed only modest growth, the population of China leaped from 470 million in 1900 to more than 1.1 billion in the mid-1980s. Nigeria grew from 16 million to 72 million between 1900 and 1980 and is projected to double in size again (to 135 million) by 2000. India had 230 million people in 1900 and 700 million in 1980. Brazil had 18 million in 1900 and is expected to have more than 200 million by 2000. Kenya had only 3 million inhabitants in 1900 but expects a tenfold increase by 2000.

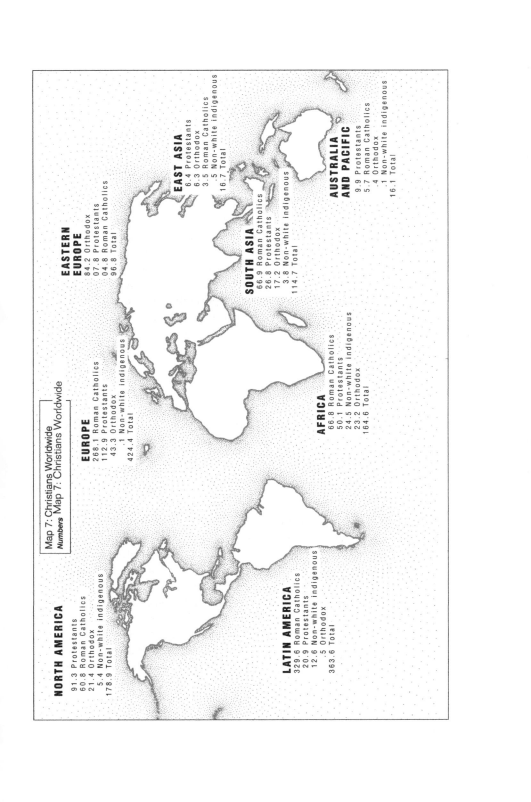

Map 7: Christians Worldwide
Numbers Map 7: Christians Worldwide

NORTH AMERICA

91.3 Protestants
60.8 Roman Catholics
21.4 Orthodox
5.4 Non-white indigenous
178.9 Total

EUROPE

268.1 Roman Catholics
112.9 Protestants
43.3 Orthodox
.1 Non-white indigenous
424.4 Total

EASTERN EUROPE

84.2 Orthodox
07.8 Protestants
04.8 Roman Catholics
96.8 Total

EAST ASIA

6.4 Protestants
6.3 Orthodox
3.5 Roman Catholics
.5 Non-white indigenous
16.7 Total

SOUTH ASIA

66.9 Roman Catholics
26.8 Protestants
17.2 Orthodox
3.8 Non-white indigenous
114.7 Total

AFRICA

66.8 Roman Catholics
50.1 Protestants
24.5 Non-white indigenous
23.2 Orthodox
164.6 Total

AUSTRALIA AND PACIFIC

9.9 Protestants
5.7 Roman Catholics
.4 Orthodox
.1 Non-white indigenous
16.1 Total

LATIN AMERICA

329.6 Roman Catholics
20.9 Protestants
12.6 Non-white indigenous
.5 Orthodox
363.6 Total

General population growth was accompanied by expansion of the church. The best estimates were that the Christian population would be nearly three times as large in the year 2000 as in 1900—about the same rate of growth as the world's population as a whole. But growth was much greater in some places than in others. Very few Christians were added to the population of Europe, while the projections were that the church of Asia would be multiplied by more than ten in the twentieth century and the church in Africa by more than forty. Part of this related to expansion in the general populations of Asia and Africa over that of Europe and North America. But much of it was due to the fact that Christianity claimed an ever-larger percentage of the Third World. In Africa, for instance, nearly 50 percent of the population is expected to be Christians by 2000, and the percentage is much higher in many other countries. All this adds up to a dramatic shift in the center of gravity of Christendom. In 1900, 85 percent of the world's Christians lived in Europe or North America. In 2000, 60 percent will live in Asia, Africa, or Latin America. At this writing, the church of Christ is already more than half black and brown and yellow.

Latin America

South America was long the continent with the largest percentage of Christians—94 percent in 1985. In the postwar era Latin Americans emerged as a major force within the Catholic Church and in world Christianity. There have been many trends in Latin American Christianity since World War II, but the two most prominent are the rise of liberation theology and the explosion of Pentecostalism.

Liberation theology

In the middle of the twentieth century nearly all of Latin America found itself in poverty and exploitation. Not only were Latin American economies subservient to the economy of the United States, but within most countries the majority of the people were poor. Land and political and economic power were held by entrenched oligarchies. As late as the 1980s the top 20 percent of the Latin American population received 66 percent of the income, while the bottom 20 percent received just 3 percent of the income. Nicaragua was an even more extreme case. In the 1970s the family of dictator Anastasio Somoza owned one-seventh of Nicaragua's land area and had a personal fortune in the hundreds of millions of dollars, while 200,000 peasants owned no land at all, and the median annual income was less than $900 a person. Democracy in such places was almost nonexistent, illiteracy was widespread, and life spans were short.

Roman Catholicism dominated church life, and the Catholic hierarchy had long supported the oligarchies. But the ground was being laid for change. A series of papal encyclicals, from *On the Conditions of the Working Classes* (1891) by Pope Leo XIII, to Pope Paul VI's *On the Progress of Peoples* (1967), gradually and tentatively encouraged the church to heed the sufferings of the poor and oppressed. There was little response at first from the Latin American hierarchy to calls for social conscience. But Catholic Action, a lay movement whose Latin American branch was begun in 1929, encouraged Catholics to support labor unions, peasant cooperatives, and calls for democracy. Christian Democratic political parties sought justice and prosperity through encouraging "development"—large-scale economic projects tied to the international market economy. Unfortunately, by the 1960s it had become clear that such development schemes had little to offer the Latin American poor. Although they helped raise a nation's productivity and total wealth, all the gains went into the coffers of the already rich.

When Vatican Council II had completed its work in 1965 (see p. 376), many Latin Americans were prepared to heed its call for greater popular participation and reorganized church structures. Bishops from all over Latin America convened the second *Latin American Episcopal Council* (CELAM) at Medellin, Colombia, in 1968. From that meeting emerged a program, formulated by such young theologians as Gustavo Gutiérrez and embraced by a majority of the bishops, that came to be called *liberation theology*.

Central to liberation theology was a "preferential option for the poor and oppressed." This did not mean charitable condescension *to* such people, but an understanding that God calls Christians to active involvement *with* people who suffer. This identification with the oppressed charts the course of the church, with the ultimate goal of achieving liberation for individuals and their larger society. "Liberation" was defined as freedom from oppressive social, economic, and political conditions, as well as emancipation from sin and acceptance of new life in Christ. A key to liberation theology was the concept of *praxis*. Theology was not to be the product of mere contemplation; it was to spring up naturally from the strivings of human existence. One did not *write* theology or *think* theology; one *did* theology. Finally, liberation theology stressed the sin of oppressive structures and power relationships in society more than the sins of individuals. This was based upon a particular strategy for interpreting Scripture. Biblical stories were read as mythological symbols for the struggle of justice and personal liberation. Central to the thinking of these theologians was the liberation of Israel from Egypt.

This formulation spread quickly through the universities and seminaries of Latin America and gained wide popularity. It connected with what already was happening in the lives of Latin Americans. During the 1960s, in Brazil especially, small, close-knit groups of Christians in slums and poor country towns had been meeting in *base ecclesial communities* (CEBs). Almost like house churches, here the predominantly poor Catholics read the Bible, prayed, sang, and talked about the difficulties they faced. Out of such communities came spiritual revival, and also critical social analysis and plans for action that meshed with aims of liberation theology. CEBs held evangelistic meetings and also built schools and clinics. Some began to call for land reform and fundamental social changes. In places like Nicaragua, base community Christians and liberation theologians took active parts in pursuing popular revolution. Years later the groups remained strong. By the mid-1980s more than a quarter of a million communities encompassed hundreds of millions of Christians.

All this activity did not go unopposed. The 1970s were a decade of increasing repression and military rule throughout Latin America. More than 1500 active Catholic clergy and laypeople were arrested, tortured, exiled, or killed between the Medellin gathering and the third CELAM conference at Puebla, Mexico, in 1979. That conference was presided over by a conservative bishop. Cardinal Josef Ratzinger, a powerful papal counselor, railed against liberation theology and called its advocates to the dock, while Pope John Paul II responded ambiguously. Although the bishops reaffirmed their Medellin positions, they did not extend them.

Liberation theology had plenty of critics. Some said it was more theological and less practical than it pretended—anything so popular in the universities could hardly be genuinely popular with the peasants. It was said that liberation theology's advocates exaggerated and idealized the role of the CEBs. Yet there really were a lot of base communities, and they were made up mainly of poor people.

There was also the opposite criticism—that liberation theologians were not theologians at all but sociologists in disguise. But liberation theologians in no way resembled rigorous social scientists; they merely were willing (as traditional theologians were not) to employ the ideas of social structural analysis to the problems of theology.

Some dismissed the liberation theologians as Marxists and not Christians at all. At least one, José Porfirio Miranda, did embrace Marxism, and several advocated varieties of soft-core socialism (as earlier theologians had endorsed capitalism or mercantilism or feudalism). But most liberation theologians asserted that God is not on the side of any one economic system, although they did insist on fundamental social changes in favor of the poor.

This led to a fourth complaint, that liberation theologians deemphasized individual evangelism in their stress on social liberation. That criticism had validity—there was a great deal of talk of "liberation" in the movement, and little mention of "salvation." But such a leading liberation theologian as the Peruvian priest Gutiérrez was passionately committed to evangelism and prayer, even as he called for social change, though his definitions of salvation and conversion could be somewhat vague, and his interpretations of Scripture could be unusual. He redefined conversion as a radical transformation of our relationship to both God and to the needs of the poor and despised. "To be converted," he wrote, "is to commit oneself to the process of liberation of the poor and oppressed. . . ."

It is not surprising that North American evangelicals, many of whom appreciated much of what Gutiérrez and other liberation theologians were doing and saying, had difficulty knowing what to make of this movement theologically. At least part of what was perceived as imbalance was a product of the Latin American situation. In a continent that was already over 90 percent Roman Catholic, the salvation story was widely known and accepted. What was most relevant to Latin Americans was for the church to address glaring poverty and social injustice.

17.1. Prophet, Martyr, Revolutionary

The lives of three priests—Oscar Romero, Camilo Torres, and Helder Cámara—show different ways that outstanding Latin American Christians responded to the crises in their countries.

The martyr, Oscar Romero (1917–1980), was at the time of his death the archbishop of San Salvador. He served under a series of repressive governments in El Salvador. Through the 1970s, as government abuses of human rights mounted and right-wing death squads roamed at will, Romero began to speak out against the violence, corruption, and suffering of poor peasants and workers. He was a leader of CELAM's calls for liberation and fundamental social change throughout the region. He explained his actions this way in February 1980:

I am a shepherd who, with his people, has begun to learn a beautiful and difficult truth: our Christian faith requires that we submerge ourselves in this world.

The course taken by the church has always had political repercussions. The problem is how to direct that influence so that it will be in accordance with the faith.

The world that the church must serve is the world of the poor, and the poor are the ones who decide what it means for the church to really live in the world. . . .

My life has been threatened many times. I have to confess that, as a Christian, I don't believe in death without resurrection. If they kill me, I will rise again in the Salvadoran people. I'm not boasting, or saying this out of pride, but rather as humbly as I can.

As a shepherd, I am obliged by divine law to give my life for those I love, for the entire Salvadoran people, including those Salvadorans who threaten to assassinate me. If they should go so far as to carry out their threats, I want you to know that I now offer my blood to God for justice and the resurrection of El Salvador.

Martyrdom is a grace of God that I do not feel worthy of. But if God accepts the sacrifice of my life, my hope is that my blood will be like a seed of liberty and a sign that our hopes will soon become a reality.

One month after writing this statement Romero was assassinated while saying Mass.[*]

Camilo Torres (1929–1965), the revolutionary, was a French-trained priest, sociologist, and critic of both church and government in his native Colombia. He worked with university students, workers, and peasants, organizing cooperatives, schools, and job training centers. He wrote and spoke tirelessly against government corruption and abuses. Torres' activities earned condemnation from his conservative superiors in the church, until finally in 1965 he left the priesthood. He joined the army of peasant guerrillas that was fighting to overthrow Colombia's government. Four months later he died in the ambush of a government patrol. He left behind a strident gospel message:

I took off my cassock to be more truly a priest.

The duty of every Catholic is to be a revolutionary,

The duty of every revolutionary is to make the revolution.

The Catholic who is not a revolutionary is living in mortal sin.[**]

Helder Cámara (1909–), the prophet, is a more placid, Ghandiesque figure. This tiny man had perhaps more effect than any other on the ministry of the church in Latin America from the 1950s on. Born to poverty in a family of thirteen children, Cámara became a priest at age twenty-two, Brazil's state secretary of education at twenty-five, and ultimately an archbishop. But most of his life was spent in ministry among the desperately poor of Brazil's urban slums, and in writing and speaking against poverty and oppression.

Cámara organized the National Conference of Bishops of Brazil in 1952 and, as its general secretary, called the church to push for social change. His Movement for Grassroots Education initiated the concept of base ecclesial communities. He brought education to hundreds of thousands of illiterate Brazilians and showed that poor people could think analytically about their social situations. Despite being banned from public communication by the military government that took power in 1964, Cámara was a major force at Vatican II, Medellin, and Puebla.

At least once an assassin was hired to kill him, but the killer was so disarmed by Cámara's gentle and unimposing spirit, that he went away with his task unfinished. Despite Cámara's fame as a writer and poet, and his deep involvement in the struggle for social change in Latin America, he regarded his task in life as primarily a ministry of prayer and spiritual leadership.

[*]Placido Erdozain, *Archbishop Romero* (Maryknoll, N.Y.: Orbis, 1981), 73–75.

[**]John Gerassi, *Revolutionary Priest* (New York: Random House, 1971), 1.

Oscar Arnulfo Romero y Galdames (1917–1980) was ordained in 1942 and served as general secretary of the Central American Bishops Conference. Romero became outspoken about violence and political repression of the poor after he was appointed archbishop in 1977. (Orbis Press)

At the close of Vatican Council II Helder Cámara (1909–) led a group of Third World bishops in a pastoral letter calling for church involvement in the plight of the poor. Cámara's development work at the Medellín CELAM II meeting helped establish liberation theology.

Pentecostal power

Latin American Pentecostals came at the problem of human liberation from another angle, and with just as startling success. Pentecostalism was born in the United States in 1906 (see p. 396) but grew much more rapidly in the Third World than in its country of origin. Including the more recent charismatics (devotees of Pentecostal-style ideas who stayed in mainline churches), there were more than 100 million Pentecostals and similar believers worldwide by the 1980s.

Theologically, Pentecostals resembled evangelicals. They were devoted to orthodox Protestant pietism without the modifications wrought by modern liberal scholarship. In fact, most were perceived to take an anti-intellectual stance. They stressed personal righteousness and continuing use of the charismatic gifts of healing, prophecy, and speaking in tongues.

Pentecostalism hit Latin America like an incendiary bomb. In 1909 the Methodist Episcopal Church in Valparaiso, Chile, was rocked by the flames of revival. Desiring to become like the first-century church, people sought and received gifts of healing and ecstatic speech. Soon the movement spread to Brazil and other parts of South America.

Pentecostalism's appeal, like that of liberation theology, was mainly to the poor. Like liberation theology, Pentecostalism promised liberation, but liberation for the individual rather than change of the social structure. Pentecostalism met the needs of powerless people for power and connectedness without politicizing them. They were in intimate contact with the mighty God who gives fantastic gifts. Pentecostal theology also gave a sense of community to the alienated, urban poor— not the intimacy of CEBs, but an overwhelming feeling of belonging that came with mass meetings involving thousands of believers. Because Pentecostalism valued enthusiasm over education and social status, it gave access to spiritual prominence to even the poorest and most unlettered. Because Pentecostal worship was very free-form, it could be adapted to fit almost any culture.

In Latin America, Pentecostals quickly became the second largest Christian group, after Catholics. Two of the three largest churches in the world in the 1980s were Latin American Pentecostal congregations: Jotabece Church in Santiago, Chile, with 80,000 members and Congregacao Crista in Sao Paolo, Brazil, with 61,000. The world's largest church, Korea's Full Gospel Central Church in Seoul, with 410,000 members, is also Pentecostal. Indigenous Pentecostals constituted the fastest-growing segment of the church in China and Africa as well. It must be stressed that the Pentecostal volcano was not the product of missionary effort. It was an indigenous movement almost everywhere, an outpouring of the Holy Spirit giving power to people.

Africa

African Christianity after World War II was characterized by six themes:

1. a renewed encounter with Islam;
2. explosive numerical growth;
3. continued flowering of independent, indigenous churches;
4. controversy over the question of the preservation of African culture;
5. involvement in the struggles for independence of many African nations;
6. controversy over the future of missions.

The question of the future of missions will be taken up below. The Islamic encounter plagued Christians in many parts of Africa, Asia, and the Middle East, especially after the rise of fundamentalist Muslim nationalism in the 1970s. By the early 1990s Sudanese

Christians and Muslims had endured a quarter century of intermittent ethnic and religious warfare. In Egypt the ancient Coptic Church steadily lost members to Islam and emigration, to the point that in the mid-1980s it numbered no more than one-fifth of the country's 30 million people.

Yet, if most of North Africa was Muslim, nearly all of the continent south of the Sahara was overwhelmingly Christian. In 1980, 63 percent of Ghana's people were professing Christians, compared to 49 percent in Nigeria, 72 percent in Zambia, 79 percent in South Africa, and 95 percent in Zaire. Throughout Africa the church was growing at a rate of nearly 4 percent each year, far ahead of the population explosion.

The independent churches described in chapter 13 (pp. 314–18) continued to grow. In Uganda, indigenous churches grew from 2.2 million to 3.5 million members between 1970 and 1980. In South Africa the jump was from 4.3 million to 6.2 million over the same decade; in Zaire from 3.5 million to 4.8 million; in Nigeria from 5 million to 7.7 million; and in Kenya from 1.6 million to 2.8 million members of African independent churches.

One example of a developing independent church occurred among the Luo of western Kenya. Anglican and Catholic missionaries late in the nineteenth century succeeded in converting the majority of Luo to Christianity. But by the 1910s, splinter groups began to form, basing their call for separation from whites on revelations received by prophets. The missionary churches tried unsuccessfully to keep the East African revival of the 1920s and 1930s away from the Luo. Missionaries earned popular resentment for their restrictions. The pace of Luo reactions against the missionary churches picked up in the 1950s, paralleling the rise of political nationalism. In 1952 a Luo woman, Mariam Ragot, claimed she received a vision that called on her to denounce the Catholic Church and the white race and to lead her people out of missionary domination. A separatist church, the Religion of Mary, organized around Ragot, just one of some fifty splinter groups that formed in the next two decades. Several hundred thousand adherents left missionary churches for indigenous churches. Theologies and practices varied. Some nearly resembled Catholicism, others Protestantism, others the East African religions, still others resembled projections of the personalities of charismatic leaders. Some split with the missionary churches over such issues as polygamy and female circumcision. Others objected to theological and moral laxity in the mission churches. By the time of Kenya's independence in 1963 the Luo people supported a bewildering array of growing independent churches, alongside established European denominations.

Festo Kivengere (1920–1988) was active in a ground-breaking movement to address Third World economic needs through the church. Under his leadership in the Episcopal Church and the nondenominational African Enterprise, resources were made available for those in Kenya, Uganda, and Tanzania. (Billy Graham Center)

17.2. Festo Kivengere

One feature of the independent churches was the growth of African organizations engaged in evangelistic and development work, either alone or in partnership with Christians from other parts of the world.

The career of Uganda's Festo Kivengere (1920–1988) reflects that trend, as well as the dangers of unstable political situations in the late colonial and early national periods.

Educated at a missionary college, Kivengere taught school from 1940 to 1962 and worked part-time as an evangelist. He became a Christian in 1941. Ultimately he acquired a theological education and ordination in the Anglican church. He became bishop of the diocese of Kigezi in 1972, shortly after Idi Amin seized power and began an eight-year reign of terror.

Kivengere was among a group of prominent clergy who protested Amin's abuses of human rights. The government retaliated in 1977 by arresting and killing Kivengere's superior, Archbishop Janani Luwum. Kivengere and his wife Mera fled the country and remained in exile until Amin was forced out in 1979.

Kivengere was the primary international spokesman for African Enterprise, an organization of African Christians that supported both evangelism and development work. By "development" they meant providing the means for people to become self-sufficient over the long term. African Enterprise channeled funds from outside Africa to relief, education, rural economic development, and medical enterprises run by East Africans and sought ways to facilitate communication and reconciliation in South Africa. In his capacities as bishop and spokesman for African Enterprise, Kivengere traveled throughout the world to foster awareness of the suffering of East Africans, and create an international, multiracial network to address these material needs.

The relationship of Christianity to African cultures occupied many African theologians and lay Christians. Their concerns were similar to those of the early generations of Christians in Europe and Latin America and of Asian Christians throughout history:

To what extent are received Christian ideas, rituals, and habitual concerns pure and timeless expressions of true Christianity?

To what extent are they merely the preoccupations of the particular people from whom one first learned about Christ?

To what extent may Africans alter the Christianity they received from Europe without betraying the essence of the faith?

These difficult questions go well beyond whether the church should allow polygamy. Such theologians as John S. Mbiti of Kenya and Aylward Shorter of Uganda have debated these matters at length, between each other and with others in the world theological community. Despite the extreme diversity of African cultures, African Christians do exhibit a certain commonality as compared to Europeans in such matters as their greater emphasis on community, the close relationship between the living and the dead, and their refusal to divide the sacred from the secular. Such perspectives as these informed the church leaders' gropings toward a distinctive African theology.

The involvement of some Christians in African nations' independence movements was highlighted in chapter 13 (pp. 318–20). Nearly all the nations of Africa achieved independence from colonial rule after 1950, and many leaders of independence movements, such as Kenneth Kaunda of Zambia and Julius Nyerere of Tanzania (see pp. 319–20), were committed Christians. Despite their best efforts and those of other national leaders, independence did not solve Africa's problems. Economic underdevelopment, exploding birthrates, interference from outside countries, warfare, mismanagement, and tribal divisions plagued much of the continent.

17.3. Three South African Calvinists

Andries Treurnicht, Beyers Naude, and Allan Boesak symbolize three movements that pulled apart the Dutch Reformed Church (DRC) after World War II.

Treurnicht (1921–) was the Boer past that would not die. Born of a farming family, Treurnicht became a DRC minister, newspaper editor, and speaker for the advancement of apartheid and white rule. In the early 1970s he became a member of Parliament and chairman of the Broederbond, the Afrikaner secret society that controlled much of South Africa's government. He held several cabinet posts for the ruling National Party and used them to push the pace of "separate development"— i.e., complete segregation of the black majority into tiny, barren, impoverished "homelands" where whites would not have to be troubled by them.

In 1982, however, the National Party began to make grudging, cosmetic reforms in apartheid, such as allowing Asians and people of mixed race (but not blacks) to elect representatives to essentially powerless parliaments of their own. Treurnicht and other arch-conservatives could not abide even this token in the direction of equality. They bolted and formed the Conservative Party, of which Treurnicht was chosen leader. The Conservative Party and the Afrikaner right steadily gained power as die-hard guardians of apartheid.

Naude (1915–) was an Afrikaner whose conscience would not resist the evidence of his senses. Raised

to privilege, Naude was a key member of the Broederbond. He was a minister and high elected official of the DRC. But in the 1950s and early 1960s the realities of racial oppression began to intrude on his consciousness. Black complaints against the white church alarmed him, and he was shocked when police killed sixty-nine black people at Sharpeville in 1960.

Naude became involved in attempts by an ecumenical group of South African church leaders to seek peace between the races, but they were rebuffed by the DRC and the government. They formed the Christian Institute in 1963, with Naude as director. Over the next several years the Institute gradually moved away from advocating discussion of moderate, white-controlled reform to calling for drastic changes in the power structure. By the time of the Soweto demonstrations of 1976, Naude and the Christian Institute were in full support of black aspirations. In 1977 the government outlawed the Christian Institute, sentenced Naude to prison for refusal to cooperate with a government inquiry, and banned him from public speaking or writing. In 1982 he became a member of the NGK in Africa, the black sister church of the DRC.

Allan Boesak (1945–) was also a minister of the DRC (its mixed-race affiliate) and perhaps a symbol of South Africa's future. He was a member of the mixed-race minority, active in the Christian Institute, and head of the United Democratic Front, an umbrella organization including many groups fighting apartheid. In 1982 Boesak was elected president of the World Alliance of Reformed Churches, and was instrumental in that body's censure of the DRC that condemned apartheid as a heresy, an elaborate theological justification for sin.

Like Treurnicht and Naude, Boesak was a Calvinist, but he believed his Calvinism called him to dramatically oppose the Afrikaner government. He regarded the struggle against apartheid as a struggle for the integrity of the gospel. Boesak was among theologians who advocated black liberation in Africa. He wrote widely on black theology, including the life and work of Martin Luther King, Jr., in the United States. He was arrested repeatedly for his activism.

Among the last countries to undergo independence struggles were the nations of southern Africa. Angola and Mozambique shed Portuguese imperialism in 1975. Zimbabwe (formerly Rhodesia) and South Africa (plus Namibia, which was dominated by South Africa) suffered a peculiar difficulty: They achieved early independence from Europe (Rhodesia in 1965, South Africa in 1910), yet power was retained by white minorities, descendants of the colonists. Black majorities remained in subjection. In both cases the whites erected complex legal and theological structures to reinforce their rule, at the same time exploiting tribal divisions to keep the blacks from uniting. After thirteen years of civil war, blacks in Zimbabwe finally succeeded in achieving majority rule in 1978.

The white population of South Africa, however, was larger, more powerful, more unified, and more fanatically entrenched (see pp. 313–14). Despite political and economic pressures from outside the country and the moral weight of black church leaders and some white Christians (see boxes 17.3, 17.4), and despite the growing disaffection of the white population, Afrikaners clung tenaciously to power until the 1990s. They were buttressed by the Dutch Reformed Church, which insisted that God had chosen the Boers as a special people to conquer, civilize, and keep South Africa. H. G. Stokr wrote in 1941:

> God willed the diversity of peoples. Thus far He has preserved the identity of our People. Such preservation was not for naught, for God allows nothing to happen for naught. He might have allowed our people to be bastardized with the native tribes as happened with other Europeans. He did not allow it. He might have allowed us to be anglicized, like for example, the Dutch in America. . . . He did not allow that either. He maintained the identity of our People. He has a future task for us, a calling laid away.[1]

Only in the 1990s, after great bloodshed and political turmoil, did the Afrikaner government begin to dismantle apartheid laws and relinquish its power to the black majority, and the future still seemed murky.

17.4. Desmond Tutu

Anglican Bishop Tutu (1931–), winner of the Nobel Peace Prize in 1984 and general secretary of the South African Council of Churches, became an international symbol of black resistance to apartheid. A man of prayer and a peacemaker among antagonistic factions, Tutu spoke out boldly for an understanding of Christianity that held the liberation of South Africans, black and white, at center stage:

I count Black Theology in the category of liberation theologies. I would hope that my White fellow Christian theologians would recognise the bona fides of Black and therefore liberation theology, since I don't want us to break fellowship or cease our dialogue. I desire this earnestly. But I want to say this with great deliberation and circumspection. I will not wait for White approbation before I engage in Black or liberation theology, nor will I desist from being so engaged while I try to convince my White fellow Christian about the validity of Black or liberation theology, for I believe that the Black or liberation theology exponent is engaged in too serious an enterprise to afford that kind of luxury. He is engaged in gut-level issues, in issues of life and death. This sounds melodramatic, but, you see, in the face of an oppressive White racism, it is not a merely academic issue for my Black people when they ask, "God, on whose side are you?" "God, are you Black or White?" "Is it possible to be Black and Christian at the same time?" These are urgent questions, and I must apply whatever theological sensitivity and ability I
have trying to provide some answers to them under the Gospel. Indeed I will subject my efforts to the criticism of fellow Christians and will attempt to pay heed to their strictures; but I will not be held back because they withhold their approval. For one thing, it is an evangelical task that is laid on me to ensure that the Black consciousness movement should succeed, and I will not be deterred by governmental disapproval or action. Because, for me, it is a crucial matter that Black consciousness succeeds as a theological and evangelical factor because I believe fervently that no reconciliation is possible in South Africa, except reconciliation between real persons. Black consciousness merely seeks to awaken the Black person to a realisation of his worth as a child of God, with the privileges and responsibilities that are the concomitants of that exalted status. . . .*

We are involved in the black liberation struggle because we are also deeply concerned for white liberation. The white man will never be free until the black man is wholly free, because the white man invests enormous resources to try to gain a fragile security and peace, resources that should have been used more creatively elsewhere. The white man must suffer too because he is bedevilled by anxiety and fear and God wants to set him free for our service of one another in a more just and open society in South Africa.*

*John W. DeGruchy, *The Church Struggle in South Africa*, 2d ed. (Grand Rapids: Eerdmans, 1986), 160, 186.

Asia

If one looks at the church in Asia from the point of view of Western missions, then the history of the last few decades of the 1900s was dismal indeed. Missionaries had become unpopular almost everywhere, and illegal in many places. In the Muslim countries—Afghanistan, Pakistan, Malaysia, Bangladesh, and Indonesia—foreign missionaries were unwelcome and domestic Christians were threatened by Islamic fundamentalism. China and India, the world's two largest countries, were secular states closed to any further foreign missionaries. Closed, too, were Burma, Nepal, North Korea, Kampuchea, and Vietnam. Japan and Taiwan, despite extensive missionary work over several generations, seemed predominantly secularist and resistant to the gospel. Only in South Korea and the Philippines were there large percentages of Christians. In all, only 5 percent of the population of Asia was Christian in 1985.

Yet such a Western-centered view misses most of what was happening among Asian Christians. The fact that a country is closed to foreign missionaries does not mean it is closed to the gospel, as the experience of church growth in China showed. Given the vast size and rapid growth of Asia's total population, it was theorized, even with only small percentages of the population of most nations being Christian, the center of gravity of world Christianity could shift to Asia by the mid twenty-first century.

In the second half of the twentieth century, Christians in Asia faced national revolutions that were often based in Islam, Marxism, and secularism, ideas hostile to Christianity. In Asia, unlike Africa, few Christians stood near the center of postwar independence movements. Christians had to endure persecution and ethnic strife. But in most parts of Asia their numbers grew and their churches were strengthened.

Rising Islam

Malaysia and Indonesia provide contrasting examples of countries deeply involved in the worldwide Islamic revolution. Malaysia was an increasingly Muslim-dominated state. Islam was the official religion and the king was pledged to defend it. Half of Malaysia's 7 million people were Muslims. Only six percent were Christians, and after independence in 1957, missionaries were increasingly unwelcome. There was very little dialogue between Christians and Muslims. Religion got mixed up with race relations, in that most of the Malay majority were Muslims, while Christianity was identified with the Chinese minority (although only a small percentage of Chinese Malaysians were Christians), and with tribal peoples. Hostility between the groups, together with a government ban on proselytizing Muslims, meant that the Malay majority counted almost no Christians among its numbers.

The situation in nearby Indonesia was rather different. Indonesia was the world's most populous Muslim country, with a total population of over 150 million in 1980, 70 million of them Muslims. It felt the pressures of Islamic enthusiasm in the postwar decades. But shortly after winning independence from the Dutch, the Indonesian government adopted a policy of *pancasila*, or equality, among its five major religions: Islam, Buddhism, Hinduism, Protestantism, and Roman Catholicism. Missionary activity was continuous, but the church's most dramatic growth spurt came, apparently, as a result of government action. In 1965 the government, in an attempt to foster Islam and combat communism, required all citizens formally to adopt a religion. In the next two decades 2.5 million nominal Muslims converted to Christianity. As of 1980, 17 million Indonesians (11 percent) were Christians. Perhaps 3 million of these were adherents of independent Indonesian churches, which broke off from the missionary churches for reasons similar to independent church people in Africa. Indonesia in recent years has begun sending missionaries to other parts of Asia.

The secular state

In 1947 India, the crown jewel of the British Empire, won its freedom. Among the principles on which it was founded was a commitment to maintaining a secular state. This meant that the government committed itself not only to neutrality but to attempting to keep any religious community from victimizing others. It could hardly have been otherwise, for India was then in the midst of a fratricidal conflict between the Muslim and Hindu branches of its independence movement. The Hindu-Muslim conflict did not recede, but was overtaken in the 1970s and 1980s by another religious battle, this time between Sikh separatists and the Hindu majority. This conflict cost countless lives, including that of Prime Minister Indira Gandhi. In such a conflict-laden religious situation a radical government commitment to neutrality would seem essential. Generally, Christians steered clear of conflicts and pursued pietistic ends within their religious communities. Still, the secular commitment put a limit on the number of missionaries who could come from outside, in that church-connected non-Indians found it increasingly difficult to obtain visas.

Roughly 4 percent of the Indian population was Christian—27 million people—in 1980. But these Christians were nearly all concentrated in a few very low castes. Christianity continued to be identified with lower-caste people and was therefore unattractive to most Indians. On the other hand, since most converts, as former outcastes, had no place in the Indian system, they saw very little that was good in that system. Instead of making Christianity incarnate in Indian culture, they tended to throw off their background and rapidly take on British morés once they became Christians. In the last third of the twentieth century the church grew rapidly, from 19 million in 1970 to a projected 50 million in 2000.

Agnes Gonxha Bejaxhiu (1910–1997) of Albania arrived in Calcutta under the Irish Loreto Sisters Roman Catholic missions organization in 1929 and took life vows as Teresa in 1937. A geography teacher, in 1948 she began work toward organizing a new congregation, the Missionaries of Charity, to reach the "poorest of the poor." Mother Teresa received the Templeton Prize in 1973 and the Nobel Peace Prize in 1979. (Billy Graham Center)

17.5. Mother Teresa

Born Agnes Gonxha Bejaxhiu in Yugoslavia in 1910, Mother Teresa began her novitiate at eighteen and was sent to India. She taught school in Calcutta for nineteen years, walking the streets and witnessing the incredible misery of millions of poor, sick, and starving people. On September 10, 1946, on a train to Darjeeling, Mother Teresa heard God calling her to leave the cloister and serve the poor.

Two years later she received permission from Rome, laid aside her habit, donned a white sari with a blue border and a cross at the shoulder, and took up residence in a Calcutta slum. She started a school for poor children. In time she was joined by many other women in a new order, the Congregation of the Missionaries of Charity. Mother Teresa and her coworkers worked tirelessly throughout India and at several other points of the Third World, helping the poor, the sick, the homeless, the illiterate, and the helpless. She received many international honors, including the 1979 Nobel Peace Prize, to recognize her work of mercy. She worked on into her eighth decade, despite criticism from some that she was not addressing the fundamental social structural causes of people's suffering, only ameliorating the effects. While she made no pretense of seeking major social changes, no one could deny the worth she invested in the dignity of individuals to whom she ministered:

The poor must know that we love them, that they are wanted. They themselves have nothing to give but love. We are concerned with how to get this message of love and compassion across. We are trying to bring peace to the world through our work. . . .

People today are hungry for love, for understanding love which is much greater and which is the only answer to loneliness and great poverty. That is why we are able to go to countries like England and America and Australia where there is no hunger for bread. But there, people are suffering from terrible loneliness, terrible despair, terrible hatred, feeling unwanted, feeling helpless, feeling hopeless. They have forgotten how to smile, they have forgotten the beauty of the human touch. They are forgetting what is human love. They need someone who will understand and respect them. [*]

[*]Desmond Doig, *Mother Teresa* (New York: Harper and Row, 1976), 159.

Flourishing under socialism

The communist revolution of 1949 looked like the end for the church in China. The government was being taken over by avowed atheists who said they believed all religions would inevitably wither on the vine before the hot blast of scientific socialism. By 1951, virtually all the foreign missionaries had been ordered out of the country. Chinese Christians found themselves in a position similar to that of Mexican Christians after *their* independence movement—despised, circumscribed, and identified with hated colonial powers.

In the next few decades, some groups of Christians openly opposed the new government. Others went underground and worshiped in secret. But others, especially those connected to large, urban churches that had no way to hide and many people to protect, found ways to accommodate the new regime. Many of these last were patriots who recognized that Western imperialism had crippled their country and were proud that China was at last standing up for itself.

Protestants who were willing to work with the new situation formed the *Three-Self Patriotic Movement*, a loose confederation designed to protect Christian people and preserve Christian witness. The "three selves" were self-propagation, self-government, and self-support, an old missionary slogan describing the goal of building an independent national church in China without missionary dependency. Similarly inclined Roman Catholics formed the *Catholic Patriotic Association*, although this meant they had to cut ties with foreign Catholics, even with the Vatican.

For a time, these organizations of open believers succeeded in buffering the church against the wrenching struggles that accompanied the reorganization of Chinese society under socialism. But they began to lose ground in the anti-rightist campaign of 1957–58, when anyone religious or intellectual or tied to the West came in for heavy criticism. Some church leaders found themselves jailed or sent to labor camps. Persecution came again during the Cultural Revolution (1966-76), when Christians all over China, and especially leaders of the Catholic Patriotic Association and the Three-Self Movement, lost their jobs, were publicly humiliated, and went to prison. Churches were turned into factories and people worshiped in hiding, if at all.

But after 1978 a new era dawned in China, during which the government turned away from classical Marxist ideology and sought simply to make China strong. It recognized that religious people, like others, could make important contributions. After that time, a new constitution was written that guaranteed religious freedom with few limits. Churches reopened, and new ones were built. By 1987, there were over 4000 open churches affiliated with the Three-Self Movement, and tens of thousands of home churches and unaffiliated meeting points. And they were full. Where there had been less than 1 million Christians in China in 1949, even the most conservative estimates found 6 to 7 million in 1987; some guesses ranged as high as 50 million. There was an especially vigorous expansion of Christianity in rural parts of certain provinces, where revival movements spread explosively. These were often indigenous Pentecostal movements, with lots of healing and prophesying, and with little connection to either the established churches or the missionary past.

China's Christians, such as this congregation at Tianjin, had been mostly missionary led and were relatively unprepared organizationally for the Communist takeover of their country. However, dedicated evangelists like Wang Mingdao, shown with his family, withstood persecution, and the church grew explosively. (Billy Graham Center)

Through this baptism by fire, late twentieth-century Chinese Christians succeeded in doing something that none of their predecessors had done in twelve centuries—convince their fellow citizens that Christianity had become Chinese. Some people who suffered greatly during the Cultural Revolution had a hard time forgiving those who had suffered less, much as fourth-century Christians in North Africa who had remained true to Christ during persecution had difficulty accepting fellowship with priests who had apostasized. There were also theological and stylistic differences—for instance between charismatic village healers and high-church Shanghai bishops. Yet the Chinese church in the 1980s and 1990s was remarkably strong and unified, despite such differences.

Christianity and capitalism

Few nations in the postwar world were as full of Christian culture as was South Korea, and few were as full of capitalism. It has already been remarked (pp. 333–34) that the Presbyterian stand against Japanese colonialism opened the way for a Christian growth impossible in countries where Europeans and Americans were both the missionaries and the colonial aggressors. Christians constituted 20 percent of the South Korean population in 1970 and 30 percent in 1980. They are projected to reach 50 percent by the year 2000.

Before the Korean civil war (which was attended by much of the rest of the world) most Christians lived in the North. But thousands fled south with the establishment of the communist government. They reformed their churches, found jobs, and began building toward Korea's recent economic miracle. For many Korean Christians, Christian faith, education at one of Korea's several Christian universities, and upward mobility went together in a litany akin to American success theology. Most Christians kept their heads down and their hands out of the political struggles among a succession of anti-communist dictators and students and others who demanded democracy. Pentecostal sects flourished (sometimes even within the Presbyterian Church), as did some clearly heretical offshoots (see box 17.6).

The range of Korean Christendom can be seen in two of the country's largest churches. Yongnak Presbyterian Church was founded in Seoul by Han Kyong-jik, a North Korean minister who fled Russian occupation and persecution of Christian leaders in 1945. It was a conservative church, emphasizing the sin of individuals, the need for personal redemption through God's grace, and careful Bible teaching. Yongnak had 60,000 members in 1986, twenty-two ordained pastors, twenty-three lay ministers, seven choirs, and a growth rate of 10 percent a year.

17.6. Sun Myung Moon

Sun Myung Moon (1920–) began a ministerial career rather like those of Han Kyong-jik and David (formerly Paul) Yonggi Cho in the 1940s, but Moon's career quickly took on a character quite outside Christian orthodoxy.

Born to a farming family in northwest Korea, Moon and his family became Presbyterians when he was ten. At fifteen and sixteen, Moon had visions. The first, like that of the Buddha centuries earlier, impressed on Moon the terrible suffering of human beings. He determined to help relieve that suffering. A year later Jesus visited Moon to tell him he was appointed to finish the work of salvation that Jesus had begun.

After high school and a stint at a Japanese engineering college, Moon returned to Korea in 1944 and began to preach. Soon he had won the enmity of the communist zone's rulers. Like many Christian leaders in the north, Moon was jailed, first in 1946 and again in 1948. But the Presbyterian Church disputed his Christian credentials; it excommunicated him in 1948 for placing himself in the role of latter-day messiah.

Moon took refuge in South Korea in 1950 and three years later officially founded the Holy Spirit Association for the Unification of World Christianity. In 1957 he expounded upon his understanding of the universe in the *Divine Principle*, which was later translated into many languages and distributed worldwide. In the 1960s God told Moon to transfer his base of operations to the United States. He obeyed in 1971 with the first of a series of evangelistic tours.

It was in America that Moon met the broadest and most favorable response. Thousands of American young people flocked to Unification Church meetings, houses, and camps, attracted by the insistent personal evangelism of Moon's followers. Seeking to become a mainstream church, the Unification Church bought scores of businesses, founded a highly-regarded conservative newspaper in Washington, D.C., and sponsored academic conferences and publications.

Despite such reaching after respectability, Moon's church came under frequent attack from governments and irate parents. Some parents hired detectives and "deprogrammers" to wrest their children from the grasp of what they regarded as a brainwashing cult. Moon and some of his followers were indicted by the South Korean government on draft-dodging and morals charges and by the U.S. government for tax fraud. The American indictment brought support from unlikely quarters. Mainstream American religious groups, including fundamentalists who regarded Moon as a heretic, opposed the federal charges as an infringement of the separation of church and state.

Over the years of his ministry, the complaints against Moon moderated. Where in the 1950s in Korea he was accused of requiring female church members to have intercourse with him in secret initiation rites, by the 1980s in the United States he had entered the relatively respectable realm of accused tax cheats. Still, the Unification Church's theology placed it beyond the pale of Christian orthodoxy. Christians found little evidence of devotion to Jesus, fidelity to the Bible, or respect for church tradition. In their place was the figure of Moon as divine savior.

Central Full Gospel Church on Yoido Island was a much flashier affair. David (formerly Paul) Yonggi Cho started conducting faith healing and revival meetings in the late 1950s, shortly after his conversion by an itinerant healer. By the mid-1980s, the church he founded had more than 400,000 members. Cho and the lay leaders of his church's many cells were aggressive evangelists, fervent South Korean nationalists, and celebrants of the material blessings they thanked God for bestowing on them as believers. Some observers complained that Cho's ministry amounted to little more than latter-day shamanism, but to materially-oriented members of Korea's rapidly growing middle class he offered a satisfying faith.

Small numbers of Koreans were also involved in the calls for political democracy, among them proponents of a variety of liberation theology called *Minjung Theology*, but they were clearly a minority voice among Korean Christians.

17.7. Cardinal Sin

Jaime Cardinal Sin (1928–) exercised a carefully limited but crucial role in the Philippines' 1986 democratic revolution.

Ferdinand Marcos had been popularly elected, but transformed his country's democracy into fourteen years of military rule, plunder, and human rights abuses. The conservative Catholic hierarchy had supported Marcos, but in the early 1980s Sin, archbishop of Manila, began to question Marcos' policies.

When Corazon Aquino mounted an election campaign against Marcos in 1986, the church, under Sin's leadership, provided critical organizational and communications help and the workers to get out the vote. During the election Marcos forces killed or intimidated thousands of Aquino supporters, stuffed some ballot boxes, and blatantly destroyed others. In response, Sin and the other bishops called Marcos to account:

The people have spoken. Or tried to. Despite the obstacles thrown in the way of their speaking freely, we *the bishops believe that what they attempted to say is clear enough. In our considered judgment, the polls were unparalleled in the fraudulence of their conduct.*

In an overwhelmingly Catholic country, that was all that was needed to push Marcos over the brink. The people of Manila and most of the army rose peacefully against Marcos, again with Sin's tacit blessing. Marcos fled to exile in the United States, and democratic political institutions began to be restored. The nation's manifest economic and military problems would take longer to solve.

This was no church-sponsored social revolution. Although Aquino proclaimed "People Power," she and her advisors were all from the same tiny clique of wealthy Filipinos who had run the country since independence, and they produced no major social or economic changes. Because of Jaime Sin's grace, spirituality, intellect, and diplomatic skill, he was frequently mentioned by Vatican observers as a potential candidate to become the first Third World pope.

Time (February 24, 1986), 31.

Jaime Cardinal Sin (1928–) became a mediating influence between the Roman church and its more radical priests when he cautiously involved the Philippines' large Roman Catholic population in the movement for political and social reform. Seeing himself as primarily a spiritual leader, Cardinal Sin called Christians to political involvement as a response of Christian love.

Whither missions?

Protestants did not do much about missions until the nineteenth century. Prior to that time, evangelism was left mainly to the Catholic and Orthodox branches of the faith. But, as the predominantly Protestant nations of northwest Europe and North America began to stretch their economic power, the missionary enterprise went with them. We have seen the effects of missions on various parts of Latin America, Africa, and Asia, and witnessed the lives of such people as Livingstone, Carey, and Taylor.

There was a great increase in American missionary activity after World War II. In that war Americans had, for the first time, acted with power around the globe, and many became keenly interested in other parts of the world. The upsurge of postwar missionary activity has been compared to the spread of American multinational corporations in the business sphere and of multinational military pacts such as the North Atlantic Treaty Organization (NATO) and South East Asia Treaty Organization (SEATO) in the political sphere. New denominations, such as the Baptist General Conference, got involved in missions for the first time. But there were new organizations as well, which were unfettered by denominational ties— New Tribes Mission and SEND International among the most successful. In an era when many of the older denominations—Presbyterians and Methodists, for instance—were beginning to turn control over to local Christians, most new denominations and parachurch organizations maintained the pith helmet mentality for another generation.

By the 1970s and 1980s most of the old notions about missions had begun to break down. At the Lausanne Conference on World Evangelization in 1974, two American factions debated whether the proper core of the gospel was preaching the message of salvation or establishing justice and ending human suffering. It took a small and largely neglected contingent of Third World delegates to remind their would-be American mentors that the gospel was about both those things. Despite the legacy of the Enlightenment, life is not separable into the spiritual and the secular, and salvation and justice are part of the same thing—equally imperatives of Scripture.

At the same time, some Third World Christians began to call for a moratorium on missions. In Africa, particularly, some Christians had come to believe that the age of Western missions had passed. That is, their continent was overwhelmingly Christian already. African Christians were in a good place to complete the evangelization of their own people, and Western missionaries had not shown much sensitivity for the delicate task of making Christianity incarnate in African culture. Yet the missionaries remained, still dominating relations with the African church, and some showed no signs of ever letting go.

Frustration with this situation led some African Christian leaders, such as John Gatu, head of the Presbyterian Church of East Africa, to call for the missionaries to go home, "because the missionaries regard Africans as ecclesiastical children."[2] Others, such as Pius Wakatama of Zimbabwe, were less strident, but still called on Western Christians to be less romantic in their notions about bringing light to darkest Africa. He also asked them to be more selective in their missionary ventures, coordinating them with the work of national Christians. Some had not the patience of either of these men and left the European-connected churches entirely, going instead to independent churches.

While some missions groups (and supporting American church people) tried to maintain the "great white father" self-image, most field missionaries began to look on themselves as co-workers with Third World Christians. Sometimes of necessity, their attitudes and activities began to take on a political cast. At the height of the American controversy over the question of Biblical inerrancy, an evangelical audience questioned a furloughed missionary as to his views. His reply was completely orthodox: he regarded the Bible as God-breathed in all its particulars. Observing the audience's satisfied sigh, he continued: "And I don't think it matters very much. Where I have been living, in Africa and Southeast Asia, the important theological issues are, 'Am I going to have enough to eat today?' and 'Is my government going to kill me tomorrow?' When we have solved these basic theological problems we can get on to the luxury items." His answer reflected a growing understanding that Third World Christians had important agendas and insights of their own to which the First World church would have to attend.

17.8. A Gentle Call for Reformation of Missionary Minds

Isabelo Magalit, general secretary of InterVarsity Christian Fellowship for the Philippines, exhorted several thousand American students to become missionaries at Urbana, Ill., in 1979. But he warned them to revise their vision of the missionary task:

When will Western, particularly North American, mission agencies wake up to the fact that their missionaries are simply not welcome in many parts of the world?

. . . Is the day of the Western missionary coming to an end? . . . No, definitely no. World evangelism is the responsibility of the whole church, no less of the older churches of Europe and America than of the younger churches of Asia, Africa, and Latin America. And no more the responsibility of the one group than of the other. . . .

The time has certainly come for Western-based missions to give more careful consideration to the kind of missionaries they send. . . .

You must face up to the significance of your distinction—especially you who are Americans—that you come from the world's mightiest nation, which has implications for the missionary enterprise launched from your shores. . . .

Your presence and your influence, your interests and your policies, your opinions and your goods—for example, Coke and Superman—are so ubiquitous around the globe that your missionaries cannot help being visible, easily identified as American.

You can affirm that identity unequivocally, without apology, sincerely believing that it stands for what is best in the world. . . . Or, you can repudiate it in a valiant effort to make sharp the difference between American culture and the eternal gospel. . . .

There is a third way. What we are asking of you is to affirm what is positive in your being American and to be sensitive to what is negative. . . .

We live in a world of incredible human needs. Hundreds of millions of people are poor and hungry, homeless and illiterate, battered by illness and die young. . . . Please do not send to us missionaries who insist on a dichotomy between evangelism and social concern. Missionaries who teach that evangelism is our main or even sole concern. Missionaries who say that ministry to the temporal needs of people will also be done, but only as we have time, and as our limited resources allow.

Such missionaries make it difficult for us to defend the gospel against the Marxist charge that Christians promise a pie in the sky for the by and by, [and] that Christians who have links with the West are but tools of Western imperialism, perhaps innocent, but helping to perpetuate the pockets of privilege, leaving the wretched of the earth to remain wretched!

We must not simply react to Marxist criticism, even though I realize that for many of you Marxism is a theoretical question, while for us the Communist system is a live and attractive option. if it can feed the hungry millions, why not, why not? But we are not simply reacting to Marxist criticism. Rather, we must come to realize that, unless our love is demonstrated in practical terms of helping to meet the need for daily bread, our gospel of love will eventually sound hollow and unconvincing. . . .

My North American brothers and sisters in Christ: Can we ever be partners? Partners. Why do you keep saying that you have a master plan for fulfilling the Great Commission and you want us to join you in carrying out your plans? Why can't you come to us and say: "I have come in obedience to the Great Commission. How can you and I fulfill it together?" Partnership means a fellowship of equals.

In addition to shifting perspective, the missionary movement began to shift personnel. For centuries nearly all missionaries traveling outside their home regions were Europeans or North Americans. Some Africans, Latin Americans, and Pacific Islanders did missionary work outside their own countries, but seldom outside their own continents. This began to change with the growing involvement of Third World churches in cross-cultural missions in the second half of the twentieth century. By the 1980s, over a thousand Korean missionaries were serving in other parts of the world, including Europe and North America.

This shift toward more Third World missionaries fit the developing First World missionary strategies of the 1970s and 1980s. It became increasingly clear to such scholars and promoters as American Ralph Winter that more than 90 percent of evangelical Protestant missionary activity, for example, was directed at reviving nominal Christians or converting members of the Catholic and Orthodox churches. This was a least partly because such people were easy for First World missionaries to reach. What was needed, according to this line of thinking, was to help Chinese Christians to evangelize other Chinese, and Arab Christians to evangelize other Arabs, and so on among every people.

Suggested readings

General

Anderson, Gerald H., and Thomas F. Stransky, eds. *Mission Trends No. 3: Third World Theologies*. New York: Paulist, 1976.

Barrett, David B., ed. *World Christian Encyclopedia*. Nairobi: Oxford University Press, 1982.

Keeley, Robin, et al., eds. *Christianity in Today's World*. Grand Rapids: Eerdmans, 1985.

Wakatama, Pius. *Independence for the Third World Church: An African's Perspective on Missionary Work*. Downers Grove, Ill.: InterVarsity, 1976.

Latin America

Berryman, Phillip. *Liberation Theology*. New York: Pantheon, 1987.

Cleary, Edward L. *Crisis and Change: The Church in Latin America Today*. Maryknoll, N.Y.: Orbis, 1985.

Ferm, Deane W. *Third World Liberation Theologies: An Introductory Survey*. Maryknoll, N.Y.: Orbis, 1986.

Gutiérrez, Gustavo. *A Theology of Liberation*, trans. by C. Inda, Sr., and J. Eagleson. Maryknoll, N.Y.: Orbis, 1973.

Lernoux, Penny. *Cry of the People: The Struggle for Human Rights in Latin America—The Catholic Church in Conflict with U.S. Policy*, rev. ed. New York: Penguin, 1982.

Martin, David. *Tongues of Fire: The Explosion of Protestantism in Latin America*. Oxford: Basil Blackwell, 1990.

Palmer, Donald C. *Explosion of People Evangelism*. Chicago: Moody, 1974.

Africa

Boesak, Allan. *Farewell to Innocence: A Socio-Ethical Study on Black Theology and Black Power*. Maryknoll, N.Y.: Orbis, 1977.

DeGruchy, John W. *The Church Struggle in South Africa*, 2d ed. Grand Rapids: Eerdmans, 1986.

Hastings, Adrian A. *A History of African Christianity, 1950–1975*. Cambridge: Cambridge University Press, 1979.

Hope, Marjorie, and James Young. *The South African Churches in a Revolutionary Situation*. Maryknoll, N.Y.: Orbis, 1981.

Sanneh, Lamin. *West African Christianity: The Religious Impact*. Maryknoll, N.Y.: Orbis, 1983.

Tutu, Desmond. *Hope and Suffering*. Grand Rapids: Eerdmans, 1984.

Asia

Adeney, David. *China: The Church's Long March*. Ventura, Calif.: Regal, 1985.

Clark, Donald N. *Christianity in Modern Korea*. Lanham, Md.: University Press, 1986.

Covell, Ralph. *Confucius, the Buddha, and Christ: A History of the Gospel in Chinese*. Maryknoll, N.Y.: Orbis, 1986.

Koyama, Kosuke. *Waterbuffalo Theology*. Maryknoll, N.Y.: Orbis, 1974.

McGavran, Donald A. *Ethnic Realities and the Church: Lessons from India*. Pasadena, Calif.: William Carey, 1979.

Phillips, James M. *From the Rising of the Sun: Christians and Society in Contemporary Japan*. Maryknoll, N.Y.: Orbis, 1981.

Song, Choan-Seng. *Third-Eye Theology: Theology in Formation in Asian Settings*. Maryknoll, N.Y.: Orbis, 1979.

Wickeri, Philip L. *Seeking the Common Ground: Protestant Christianity, the Three-Self Movement, and China's United Front*. Maryknoll, N.Y.: Orbis, 1989.

Expansion of Christianity in Millions of People

Time period:	100	300	500	800	1000	1500	1650	1800	1900	2000
Africa										
Population	17.2	18.4	20.0	25.0	33.0	46.0	58.0	70.0	107.9	813.4
Christians	0.4	6.0	8.0	8.0	5.0	1.3	3.0	1.0	9.9	393.3
% Christians	2.3	32.6	40.0	32.0	15.2	2.8	5.2	1.4	9.2	48.4
South Asia										
Population	62.7	71.0	79.5	97.0	113.1	145.7	198.4	251.0	413.4	2268.6
Christians	0.3	6.5	21.2	23.0	14.8	3.0	5.0	8.0	16.9	192.3
% Christians	0.5	9.2	26.7	23.7	12.1	2.1	2.5	3.2	4.1	8.5
East Asia										
Population	59.6	59.9	54.9	56.5	73.5	131.6	170.6	366.1	532.7	1373.2
Christians	0.0	0.0	0.0	0.3	2.0	0.2	0.4	0.3	2.2	32.3
% Christians	0.0	0.0	0.0	0.5	2.7	0.2	0.2	0.1	0.4	2.4
Oceania										
Population	1.0	1.1	1.2	1.4	1.5	2.0	2.5	2.5	6.2	32.7
Christians	0.0	0.0	0.0	0.0	0.0	0.0	0.1	0.1	4.8	27.7
% Christians	0.0	0.0	0.0	0.0	0.0	0.0	4.0	4.0	77.6	84.8
Latin America										
Population	4.6	5.5	6.4	7.6	8.5	13.0	10.9	17.5	65.2	619.9
Christians	0.0	0.0	0.0	0.0	0.0	0.2	6.5	14.9	62.0	571.2
% Christians	0.0	0.0	0.0	0.0	0.0	1.5	60.0	85.0	95.1	92.1
North America										
Population	0.3	0.4	0.5	0.5	0.5	1.0	1.1	6.5	81.6	296.2
Christians	0.0	0.0	0.0	0.0	0.0	0.0	0.1	5.8	78.8	253.6
% Christians	0.0	0.0	0.0	0.0	0.0	0.0	9.1	89.2	96.6	85.6
Europe										
Population	31.8	30.7	25.5	25.5	32.0	69.0	88.0	144.0	287.3	539.8
Christians	0.3	7.3	14.0	17.9	28.2	67.8	86.9	142.1	278.4	431.4
% Christians	0.9	23.7	55.0	70.0	88.1	98.2	98.8	98.7	96.9	80 0
Russia										
Population	4.3	5.0	5.5	6.4	7.1	17.0	23.0	45.0	125.7	315.0
Christians	0.0	0.1	0.2	0.3	0.4	8.5	15.0	36.0	105.0	118.1
% Christians	0.0	1.0	3.0	4.7	5.4	50.0	65.0	80 .0	83.6	37.3
World										
Population	181.5	192.0	193.4	219.9	269.2	425.3	552.2	902.6	1619.9	6259.6
Christians	1.0	19.9	43.4	49.5	50.4	81.0	116.9	208.2	558.1	2019.9
% Christians	0.6	10.4	22.4	22.5	18.7	19.0	21.2	23.1	34.4	32.3

Source: David B. Barrett, ed., *World Christian Encyclopedia* (Nairobi: Oxford University Press, 1982), 796.

Appendix B

Christian Population of Major Traditions
on Each Continent, 1985

	Orthodox	Protestant	Roman Catholic	Non-Roman Catholic	Third World Indigenous	Marginal Protestant
Africa	25,762,353	56,160,635	77,559,168	694,544	29,148,347	1,755,084
South Asia	4,050,476	31,274,677	76,343,764	52,350	20,346,442	404,685
East Asia	47,299	7,432,639	3,696,949	1,300	7,863,484	291,423
Oceania	458,816	9,644,842	6,352,762	12,136	113,077	336,398
Latin America	566,906	22,756,669	369,454,862	172,679	14,949,030	1,673,211
North America	5,578,973	84,675,508	61,533,080	702,086	22,260,529	9,101,912
Europe	44,379,711	108,658,113	272,224,061	1,965,715	116,018	2,193,401
Former USSR	88,803,986	8,409,491	4,940,000	0	0	14,500

Source: David B. Barrett, ed., *World Christian Encyclopedia* (Nairobi: Oxford University Press, 1982), 791.

Notes

Chapter 1

1. Jacob Neusner, *From Testament to Torah: An Introduction to Judaism in Its Formative Age* (Englewood Cliffs, N.J.: Prentice Hall, 1988), 29.

Chapter 2

1. B. Keil, ed., *Panagyric to Rome* (Berlin, 1898), *Oratio* 26.100, cited in W. H. C. Frend, *The Rise of Christianity* (Philadelphia, 1984), 165.

2. Ignatius "To the Smyrnaeans." See *The Apostolic Fathers*, 2d ed., trans. by J. B. Lightfoot and J. R. Harmer; edited and revised by Michael W. Holmes (Grand Rapids: Baker, 1989), 112–13.

3. Tertullian quoted (sarcastically) the enemies of Christians thus: "But even such acts of great love set a stain on us in the eyes of some people. 'Look.' they say, 'how they love each other' (for they hate each other). 'See, how ready they are to die for one another' (for they would sooner kill each other)." Apology 39, 40.

4. *Acts of Paul,* in Edgar Hennecke, ed., *New Testament Apocrypha*, trans. by A. J. B. Higgins, ed. by W. Schneemelcher (Philadelphia: Westminster, 1963), 2.389.

5. Some of these 1500 were widows and orphans supported by the fellowship. Eusebius *History of the Church* 6.43.

Chapter 3

1. Computing the number of years of Christian ascendancy is somewhat subjective. That given here refers roughly from the Galerian persecution (c. 305) to the reign of Constantius II over both the eastern and western Empire (350).

2. Sermon 43; commentary on John 29.6.

Chapter 5

1. N. H. Baynes, *Byzantine Studies* (London, 1955), 52.

2. St. John of Damascus, *On Icons*, 1.16, quoted in Timothy Ware, *The Orthodox Church*, rev. ed. (Harmondsworth, U.K.: Penguin, 1969), 41.

3. Nicholas Zernov, *The Russians and Their Church* (London, 1945), 107–8.

4. Ware, *Orthodox Church*, 51.

5. S. Runciman, *The Eastern Schism* (Oxford, 1955), quoted in Ware, *Orthodox Church*, 58.

6. *Christian History*, 7.2, (issue 18): 10–11.

7. Ibid., 11.

8. Ware, *Orthodox Church*, 113.

9. Henri Troyat, *Daily Life in Russia* (London: George Allen and Unwin, 1961), 66.

10. Ibid., 76.

11. Ibid., 77.

Chapter 6

1. Peter Falk, *The Growth of the Church in Africa* (Grand Rapids: Zondervan, 1979), 46.

2. Aziz S. Atiya, *A History of Eastern Christianity* (London: Methuen, 1968), 127–28.

Chapter 7

1. William Langland, *Piers the Plowman*, trans. by J. F. Goodridge (New York: Penguin, 1959).

2. Chaucer, *Canterbury Tales*, trans. by D. Wright (New York: Random House, 1965), 5–6.

3. James B. Ross and Mary M. McLaughlin, eds., *Portable Renaissance Reader* (New York: Penguin, 1958), 14.

4. John P. Dolan, ed., *The Essential Erasmus* (New York: NAL/Dutton, 1964), 130.

5. Ibid., 149.

6. Ibid.

7. Ibid., 130.

Chapter 8

1. Translated from the Weimar edition of *D. Martin Luthers Werke*; quoted in Hans J. Hillerbrand, ed., *The Reformation: A Narrative History Related by Contemporary Observers and Participants* (New York: Harper and Row, 1964), 27.

2. Roland H. Bainton, *Here I Stand: A Life of Martin Luther* (Nashville: Abingdon-Cokesbury, 1955).

3. *Table Talk.*

4. "The Twelve Articles of the Peasants," third article. Translation cited in Hillerbrand, *The Reformation*, 390.

5. Tim Dowley, *Eerdmans' Handbook to the History of Christianity* (Grand Rapids: Eerdmans, 1977), 400.

6. William R. Estep, *Renaissance and Reformation* (Grand Rapids: Eerdmans, 1986), 186.

7. Dowley, *Eerdmans' Handbook*, 402.

8. John Calvin, *Commentary on the Book of Psalms*.

9. Reformation theology scholar Richard Muller believes that presbyterian polity was the major factor in England, at least partly a factor in Switzerland, and relatively unimportant in Germany and the Rhineland.

Chapter 9

1. Leland Ryken, *Worldly Saints* (Grand Rapids: Zondervan, 1986), 1.

Chapter 10

1. H. G. Koenigsberger, *Early Modern Europe, 1500–1789* (White Plains, N.Y.: Longman, 1987), 252.

2. John Wesley, *The Journal of John Wesley*, quoted in *Christian History*, 2.1 (1983): 32.

Chapter 11

1. Mark Noll, et al., eds., *Eerdmans' Handbook to Christianity in America* (Grand Rapids: Eerdmans, 1983), 137.

2. Ibid., 142.

3. Charles Mabee, "Thomas Jefferson's Anti-Clerical Bible," *Historical Magazine of the Protestant Episcopal Church*, 48 (December 1979): 473–81.

4. Whitney R. Cross, *The Burned-Over District* (1950; repr. ed., Ithaca, N.Y.: Cornell University Press, 1982), 173–208.

5. Timothy L. Smith, *Revivalism and Social Reform* (1957; repr. ed., Baltimore: Johns Hopkins University Press, 1980), 228ff.

Chapter 12

1. Albert Raboteau, *Slave Religion* (New York: Oxford University Press, 1978), 214.

2. Ibid., 248.

3. Ibid., 249.

4. Timothy L. Smith, *Revivalism and Social Reform* (Baltimore: Johns Hopkins University Press, 1980), 226–27.

5. Among those who take this view are Immanuel Wallerstein (*The Modern World System* [New York: Academic, 1974]) and L. S. Stavrianos (*Global Rift: The Third World Comes of Age* [New York: Morrow, 1981]).

Chapter 13

1. Ram Desai, ed., *Christianity in Africa As Seen by the Africans* (Denver: Alan Swallow, 1962), frontispiece.

2. John W. DeGruchy, *The Church Struggle in South Africa*, 2d ed. (Grand Rapids: Eerdmans, 1986), 19.

3. Desai, *Christianity in Africa*, 16.

4. Erasto Muga, *African Response to Western Christian Religion* (Nairobi: East African Literature Bureau, 1975), 194.

5. Stephen Neill, *The Story of the Christian Church in India and Pakistan* (Grand Rapids: Eerdmans, 1970), 121.

6. Jessie Lutz, ed., *Christian Missions in China* (Lexington, Mass.: Heath, 1965), 54.

7. Dun J. Li, *Modern China* (New York: Scribner's, 1978), 41–45.

Chapter 14

1. Chicago: University of Chicago Press, 1967.

2. Paul Tillich, *Ultimate Concern: Tillich in Dialogue*, D. M. Brown, ed. (New York: Harper, 1965), 88.

3. Authorized English translation by G. T. Thomson (New York: Scribner's, 1955–), *Church Dogmatics: A Selection*, trans. and ed. by G. W. Bromiley (New York: Harper and Row, 1962).

Chapter 15

1. Ernest Hemingway, *A Farewell to Arms* (New York: Scribners, 1929).

2. William Temple, *The Hope of a New World* (New York: Macmillan, 1940), 11.

3. W. Abbot, *The Documents of Vatican II* (Chicago: Follet, 1966), 151.

4. Karl Marx and Friedrich Engels, *Works* (Moscow: Marx-Engels-Lenin Institute, 1938–48), 1.385.

5. V. I. Lenin, *Works*, 4th ed. (Moscow: Marx-Engels-Lenin Institute, 1941–50): 1.89–90.

6. Dmitri Dudko, *Our Hope*, trans. by P. D. Garrett (Crestwood, N.Y.: St. Vladimir's Seminary Press, 1977), 181–82.

Chapter 16

1. Grant Wacker, review of Timothy P. Weber, *Living in the Shadow of the Second Coming* (Chicago: University of Chicago Press, 1987), in *Church History*, 49(1979): 96.

2. Jay P. Dolan, *The American Catholic Experience* (Garden City, N.Y.: Doubleday, 1985), 411.

3. Alan Brinkley, *Voices of Protest* (New York: Knopf, 1982), 83.

Chapter 17

1. T. Dunbar Moodie, *The Rise of Afrikanerdom* (Berkeley, Calif.: University of California Press, 1975), 67.

2. Pius Wakatama, *Independence for the Third World Church: An African's Perspective on Missionary Work* (Downers Grove, Ill.: InterVarsity, 1976), 10.

Index

Paul R. Spickard (Ph.D., University of California at Berkeley) is professor of history at the University of California, Santa Barbara. His specialty is twentieth-century American social and cultural history. **Kevin M. Cragg** (Ph.D., University of Michigan) is professor of history at Bethel College where he teaches ancient and medieval European history. The two of them have also co-edited a volume titled *World History by the World's Historians*.